THE ILLUSTRATED ENCYCLOPEDIA OF
PROPELLER AIRLINERS

THE ILLUSTRATED ENCYCLOPEDIA OF
PROPELLER AIRLINERS

Editor-in-chief BILL GUNSTON

Exeter Books

NEW YORK

in association with Phoebus

Contents

Introduction

For the first 30 years of commercial aviation, from 1920 to 1950, all airliners had propellers. Over the next ten years, to 1960, jet airliners slowly and hesitantly penetrated the extremely conservative and ultra-cautious airline industry. But by 1960 the airlines had become so polarized around the jet that efficient and successful turboprop airliners, such as the Electra and Vanguard, lost their builders a lot of money because the customers thought them obsolete. Then, again very gradually, airline managements began to realize that those who said turboprops were efficient and burned less fuel were telling the truth. As oil prices soared, so the propeller began to make a come-back. Therefore, though mainly an account of past history, this volume ends with a buoyant industry that cannot build turboprop airliners fast enough.

Included in this book are early airliners, among which are those that carried the world's very first fare-paying passengers, and the first small sack of air-mail letters, long before World War I. After that great war, aircraft were not only more capable but also more reliable; but travel by air was still not far removed from science fiction, and something totally outside the lives of all ordinary people. Those few who did buy airline tickets were advised to wear a stout leather coat, gloves and if possible goggles and a hat well tied-on. In a space that often resembled a small box they bumped and lurched at about the same speed as an express train – with hardly the slightest concession to comfort, and in noise of unbelievable intensity – until they either reached their destination, or landed to enquire the way, or landed in a precipitate and often disastrous manner because of engine failure.

Gradually new and more reliable civil engines such as the Bristol Jupiter and Wright Whirlwind put the struggling air transport industry on a slightly less shaky foundation. Though occasionally designers got carried away by their enthusiasm and made aircraft that were too large and failed to sell – examples were the Fokker F.32 and Dornier Do X – the size and capability of airliners grew in step with the traffic.

The 1930s saw a never-to-be-repeated transformation from fabric-covered biplanes to stressed-skin mono-planes, equipped with retractable landing gear, flaps, variable-pitch propellers and many other new features. A few of the famous aircraft in that section, notably the immortal DC-3, were still important in the 1940s, which traces the introduction of pressurization, new navigation aids and many other advances, as well as a doubling in engine power from 1000 to 2000 hp and, at the end of that decade, still more powerful engines such as the 3250 to 3500-hp Pratt & Whitney Wasp Major and Wright Turbo-Compound, the latter being an established piston engine to which were added three turbines driven by the hot exhaust gas.

These ultimate piston engines were immense mechanical accomplishments, but they could not survive in the face of competition from jets and turboprops. The first commercial turboprop, and quite a crude engine at that (its compressor was a scaled-up Griffon piston-engine supercharger), was the Rolls-Royce Dart. This was first run in 1945, and after prolonged development and power-growth entered airline service with the outstanding Viscount in 1953. It is an extraordinary fact that in 1980 not only are hundreds of Dart-powered aircraft still in service but engines almost indistinguishable from the 1953 model are in large-scale production, and selling briskly to new as well as to existing customers. But that does not mean technical development is dormant.

Today competition in the turboprop market is intense. Rocketing oil prices have thrust propellers back into favour with the airlines; their doldrums in the 1960s and 1970s were due entirely to fashion, which thought the jet easier to sell to the travelling public. Today most large airline constructors have studies for turboprops, including large long-haul passenger and freight aircraft for a market where the jet today has more than 99%. Back in the 1960s airlines were often embarrassed at turboprop equipment and tried by various means to convey the impression they operated jets. Today the picture has changed. In 1979–80 the number of completely new jet airliners launched was zero; the number of completely new turboprops four.

Bill Gunston

Contributors: Dennis Baldry,
Chris Chant, John Stroud

Color illustrations: John
Batchelor, Terry Hadler
Line illustrations: Terry
Allen Designs Ltd, Ray
Hutchins, Martin Woodford,
research by Arthur Bowbeer
Color realization: Helena
Zakrzewska-Rucinska
Cutaways: © Pilot Press Ltd
Three-view drawings: © Pilot
Press Ltd, © Phoebus
Publishing Company

First published in USA 1980
by Exeter Books
Distributed by Bookthrift, Inc
New York, New York

Phototypeset by
Tradespools Limited,
Frome, Somerset, England

Printed in Great Britain by
Redwood Burn Limited,
Trowbridge, Wiltshire

ISBN 0–89673–078–6

Humber-Sommer

FIRST FLIGHT 1910

THE place in aviation history of the otherwise unimportant Humber-Sommer biplane is assured by the fact that it was an aircraft of this type which undertook the world's first carriage of mail by an aircraft. This event was part of the Universal Postal Exhibition held in Allahabad in India during February 1911. During the exposition, the French pilot Henri Pecquet, on February 18, flew across the Jumna river from Allahabad to Naini Junction, in all some 8 km (5 miles) with 6500 letters. This bizarre and isolated journey is generally accepted by philatelists as the world's first aerial post and some actual examples of the postmark still exist. Four days later, a 'regular' service for the duration of the exhibition was opened by Pecquet and Captain Walter G Windham, the aircraft that they used again being the Humber-Sommer biplane.

Though a number of aircraft types were produced by Humber before World War I, none of them was designed by the company, whose principal interests lay in the motor industry. The first machine produced by Humber, in 1910, was the Humber-Blériot Monoplane, a copy of the Blériot XI, followed by the Humber-Le Blon Monoplane and the Humber-Lovelace Monoplanes, two in number. The fifth aircraft produced by Humber was the British version of the biplane designed by the French pioneer Roger Sommer, and derived essentially from the Farman III biplane of 1909. This was itself a reworking of the classic Voisin biplane, though the concept of inherent lateral stability had been abandoned in favour of positive control by ailerons. Humber appear to have hedged their bet to a certain extent, for the Humber-Sommer was fitted with sloping side-screens between the upper and lower wingtips, outboard of the ailerons, in a fashion similar to the side-screens favoured by the Voisin brothers, Gabriel and Charles.

The Farman III is one of the classic aircraft of all time, and, with the Blériot XI, was the most popular European aircraft in the period from 1909 to 1911, appearing in a number of forms. Sommer's interest in the type stemmed from 1909, when he flew the second Farman III at the great aviation meeting held at Rheims under the auspices of the champagne industry. During the aviation rally, Sommer's best performance, in about ten flights, was a distance of 60 km (37 miles).

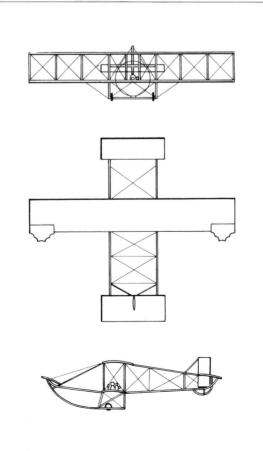

Top: The frail aircraft that pioneered the world's airmail service
Above: The Humber-Sommer ready for take-off. Flying at this time was a hazardous exercise normally restricted to short 'hops'

Humber-Sommer

Type: utility aircraft
Maker: Humber Ltd
Span: 13.92 m (45 ft 8 in)
Length: 12.19 m (40 ft)
Height: not available
Wing area: 47 m² (506 sq ft)
Weight: not available
Powerplant: one 50-hp Humber 4-cylinder water-cooled inline engine
Performance: maximum speed approx 56 km/h (35 mph) at sea level; range not available
Payload: 91 kg (200 lb); seat for 1 passenger
Crew: 1
Production: not available

Benoist Type XIV
FIRST FLIGHT 1913

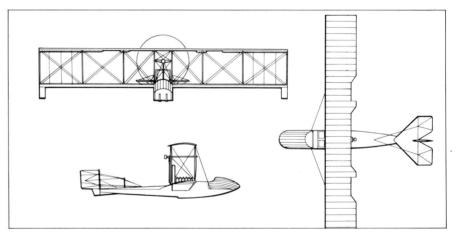

Above: The Benoist Type XIV flying boat. Its modest cockpit accommodated one passenger who paid a surcharge if they weighed more then 91 kg (200 lb)
Left: The start of the world's first airline at St Petersburg, Florida, in January 1914

THE world's first airline to operate a scheduled service with heavier-than-air aircraft was the St Petersburg-Tampa Airboat Line, which had been formed on December 4, 1913 by Paul E Fansler. It was promised an operating subsidy by St Petersburg in Florida on December 13, and signed a contract with Thomas Benoist for the operation of the airline on December 17, 1913, ten years to the day after the Wright brothers made the world's first flight in a powered fully controllable heavier-than-air craft.

The whole operation was the brainchild of Fansler and Benoist. Benoist had made himself an extremely rich man in the automobile business, and was now somewhat obsessive in his belief that aircraft could become valuable instruments of civil transport. To this end he had set himself up as a manufacturer of aircraft in St Louis, Missouri; and in the St Petersburg to Tampa route he found an ideal opportunity for an airline. St Petersburg, a growing town, was separated from the nearest shopping centre by a 2-hour boat trip, 12-hour rail journey, or day-long car trip over very poor roads.

The aircraft used for the service, which operated over a route of 29 km (18 miles) and cost $5 per single trip, was the Benoist Type XIV flying boat, a conventional pusher aircraft of slim and attractive lines based on the Curtiss formula. The first scheduled flight was made on January 1, 1914, the passenger being A C Pheil and the pilot Tony Jannus. The service consisted of two round trips per day, and the overall profitability of the service was soon no longer in doubt. Though the company

had negotiated a subsidy of $50 per day during January and $25 per day during February and March, in January the airline was able to repay the city the sum of $360, and operated at a profit during February and March. Indeed, so great was the demand for the service that late in January a larger Benoist flying boat was put into service, piloted by Roger Jannus.

The airline's contract with the city of St Petersburg ended on March 31, 1914, by which time 1204 passengers had been carried, and the service had lost only eight days to weather and mechanical problems. The airline continued independently during April, but with the end of the tourist season and the growing fears of war with Mexico demand declined and the service was ended.

Type XIV

Type: transport flying boat
Maker: Benoist Aircraft Co
Span: 10.97 m (36 ft)
Length: 7.92 m (26 ft)
Height: not available
Wing area: not available
Weight: maximum 637 kg (1404 lb); empty not available
Powerplant: one 75-hp Roberts 4-cylinder inline water-cooled engine
Performance: cruising speed 72 km/h (45 mph) at sea level; range 80 km (50 miles)
Payload: 100 kg (220 lb); seat for 1 passenger
Crew: 1
Production: approx 10

Bolshoi, Sikorsky

FIRST FLIGHT 1913

ALTHOUGH the name Sikorsky is generally associated with the development of the helicopter as a practical flying machine, Sikorsky is also notable as a great designer of flying boats, and also as the father of the world's first four-engined aircraft. The origins of this last title lay in Sikorsky's appointment as head of the Russo-Baltic Wagon Works' design department after he had produced a number of relatively successful biplanes for the Imperial Russian air service. In the early summer of 1912 Sikorsky was helped by G I Lavrov with the design of the *Bolshoi Baltiskii* or 'Great Baltic One'. This was a large twin-engined airliner featuring accommodation for seven passengers and crew in a fully enclosed cabin.

The aircraft, which had been nicknamed the 'Tramcar with Wings' by the builders, first flew in March 1913 on the power of a pair of 100-hp Argus inline piston engines, though trials immediately showed that the aircraft was hopelessly underpowered. With the facility of aircraft designers before World War I, Sikorsky merely added another pair of Argus engines on the trailing edges of the lower mainplanes in line with the first two engines, and driving pusher propellers. Flight trials with this Bolshoi Baltiskii Type B began on May 13, 1913 and soon revealed a marked improvement compared with the original model.

Further improvement was already on the way, however, with the building of another model, the *Russki Vityaz* or 'Russian Knight'. This definitive model was slightly larger than its predecessor, and was designed with bombing in mind. Span was increased by 0.5 m (19⅔ in) from 27.5 m (90 ft 2⅔ in), the four Argus inline engines were now located along the leading edges of the lower wings, driving tractor propellers, and maximum take-off weight had risen by 650 kg (1433 lb) from 3550 kg (7826 lb). The *Russki Vityaz* first flew on July 23, 1913 and on August 8, stayed in the air for 1 hour 54 min with eight people on board.

Yet greater things were afoot with the *Ilya Mouromets*, which was completed in 1913 and first flown on December 11 of that year. This aircraft spanned some 34.5 m (113 ft 2¼ in) and had a weight of 4800 kg (10 582 lb). Notable were auxiliary winglets behind the mainplanes, a railed promenade deck on the rear fuselage, a large cabin (with sofa, four armchairs and table), a wardrobe, a lavatory and cabin lighting and heating.

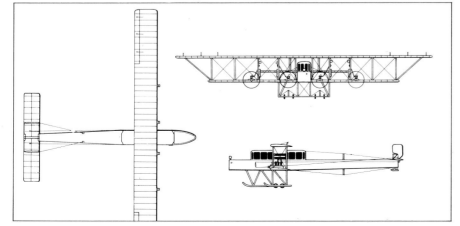

Russki Vityaz

Type: short-range transport
Maker: Russo-Baltic Wagon Works (RBVZ)
Span: 28 m (91 ft 10 in)
Length: 19 m (62 ft 4 in)
Height: approx 4 m (13 ft 1½ in)
Wing area: 120 m² (1292 sq ft)
Weight: maximum 4200 kg (9259 lb); empty not available
Powerplant: four 100-hp Argus 4-cylinder water-cooled inline engines
Performance: maximum speed approx 95 km/h (59 mph) at 1000 m (3280 ft); range 402 km (250 miles)

Payload: seats for up to 8 passengers
Crew: 2
Production: 1

Top: The *Russki Vityaz* or 'Russian Knight'
Above: The Bolshoi touches down. It had an observation platform in the front with a substantial well-lit cabin behind

CL-4S, Boeing

FIRST FLIGHT 1918

Left: William Boeing's C-700 (Model 5) after modification to CL-4S in 1918
Below: Boeing and Edward Hubbard, who flew the first mail service between Canada and the USA

THE Boeing CL-4S holds a unique place in the history of civil aviation as the aircraft used for the world's first International Contract Air Mail Service, in this instance between Seattle in the state of Washington, USA, and Victoria in the province of British Columbia, Canada, on March 3, 1919. Air mail was not new: since February 18, 1911 there had been at least 14 separate air services in eight countries; but the service flown on March 3, 1919 was the first formally constituted international service.

The CL-4S used by Edward Hubbard, with William Boeing as a passenger, was the sole CL-4S, which Boeing had built as a personal aircraft under the designation C-700 as the aircraft followed on from a batch of 50 Model C (or Model 5) floatplane primary trainers built for the US Navy with the serials C-650 to C-699. The C-700 was at first identical with the US Navy's Model Cs, but in December 1918 Boeing modified it to accommodate the new 100-hp Hall-Scott L-4 inline in place of the 100-hp Hall-Scott A-7A used in the navy aircraft. The aircraft was in no way distinguished, being a conventional machine by the standards of the day, though it did have the unusual feature of having no fixed tailplane, longitudinal stability being catered for by the relative angles of incidence of the wings, coupled with their heavy stagger. The elevators were quite small in area.

The flight by Hubbard and Boeing may with some justice be regarded as the first commercial air service in the USA after World War I, but though 60 letters were carried, the operation was in reality

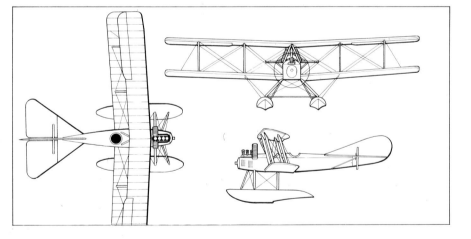

a survey flight for the definitive service, which began with a number of trials in July 1920 and became a regular operation only on October 15, 1920, thus giving Aeromarine Airways the distinction of being the first US operator to initiate a regular service after World War I. The service operated by Hubbard was part of the mail route to the Far East, Victoria being the terminus for the Japanese ship *Africa Maru*. The regular service was operated by a B-1 flying boat, which first flew on December 27, 1919.

As the CL-4S was operating in Canada, it had to carry a registration marking, and in the absence of US markings at that time, it was registered G-CADR, the G for Great Britain, and the C for Canada.

CL-4S

Type: floatplane transport
Maker: Boeing Airplane Co
Span: 13.36 m (43 ft 10 in)
Length: 8.23 m (27 ft)
Height: 3.84 m (12 ft 7 in)
Wing area: 45.99 m²
(495 sq ft)
Weight: maximum 1086 kg
(2395 lb); empty 861 kg
(1898 lb)
Powerplant: one 100-hp
Hall-Scott L-4 4-cylinder
inline water-cooled engine
Performance: maximum
speed 117.4 km/h (73 mph);
range 322 km (200 miles)
Payload: seat for 1 passenger
Production: 1

DH.4A, Airco

FIRST FLIGHT 1919

IN the immediate aftermath of World War I, the Allied powers conducted lengthy negotiations with Germany towards the eventual peace settlement embodied in the Treaty of Versailles of June 1919. At the express request of Bonar Law, therefore, a number of DH.4 bombers powered by Rolls-Royce Eagle VIII engines were converted to accommodate a minister and his secretary for high-speed travel between London and Paris.

To this end de Havilland produced the DH.4A. The two passengers were seated face-to-face in the rear fuselage in a cabin with sliding windows on each side. To ensure sufficient headroom, the cabin was provided with a fabric-covered wooden roof unit, which hinged with the right-hand side to allow the passengers in and out; this was faired into the tail by a new upper fuselage decking. As considerable extra weight was thus placed in the rear fuselage, the wings were re-rigged to restore the aircraft's centre of gravity, the upper wing being moved back 0.305 m (1 ft) in relation to the lower wing.

With the signing of the Treaty of Versailles, the Royal Air Force's requirement for such aircraft disappeared, the 12 survivors of the 13 DH.4As converted for No 2 (Communications) Squadron being sold to Handley Page in September 1919.

The success of these military examples had already prompted civil production, four new DH.4s being converted during July 1919 by Airco for the Aircraft Transport & Travel Company, the builder's airline subsidiary. Of these, one ditched in the English Channel on October 29, 1919, another crashed at Caterham on December 11, 1919, and the two others were scrapped in November 1920 when their operating costs became too great.

Handley Page also produced DH.4As, three from new aircraft, and the last by refurbishing an ex-RAF machine. Two of these were operated by Handley Page Transport, and the other two by the Belgian operator SNETA until they were burned in a hangar fire on September 27, 1921.

The last civil DH.4A was produced by the A V Roe company for Instone Air Line Ltd, receiving its certificate of airworthiness on February 19, 1920 as a DH.4 and as a DH.4A in February 1921. This was the last DH.4A to survive, being part of Imperial Airways' inventory when that company was formed in June 1924.

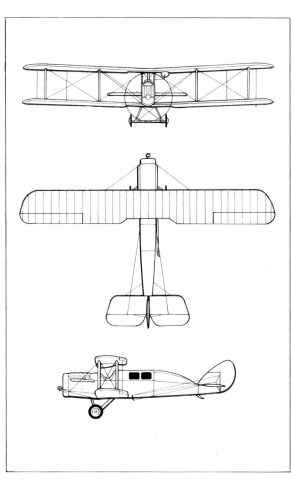

DH.4A

Type: short- and medium-range transport
Maker: Aircraft Manufacturing Co Ltd; Handley Page Ltd; A V Roe and Co Ltd
Span: 12.92 m (42 ft 4⅝ in)
Length: 9.3 m (30 ft 6 in)
Height: 3.35 m (11 ft)
Wing area: 40.32 m² (434 sq ft)
Weight: maximum 1687 kg (3720 lb); empty 1179 kg (2600 lb)
Powerplant: one 350-hp Rolls-Royce Eagle VIII water-cooled V-12 engine
Performance: maximum speed 195 km/h (121 mph); range 402 km (250 miles)
Payload: seats for 1 to 2 passengers
Crew: 1
Production: 13 (military), 8 (civil)

Below: The *City of York*, a DH.4A of Instone Air Line

Goliath, Farman

FIRST FLIGHT 1919

THE Farman Goliath series is of seminal importance in the history of air transport, but unlike other civil developments and conversions of wartime bombers, the Goliath family was produced in relatively large numbers. The origins of the type lay with the FF.60-BN.2 twin-engined, twin-seat night bomber.

Of typically blocky Farman appearance, the F.60 Goliath was apparently completed in the closing stages of 1918, and was notable for its distinctly humped rear fuselage, on later models faired smoothly into the tail unit. Accommodation for 12 passengers was provided in two fairly roomy cabins separated by the open cockpit for the two crew. Some 1.3 m (4 ft 4 in) wide, the rear passenger cabin held eight wicker seats, while the forward cabin was of the same width but held only four similar seats. The type's origins as a bomber may be discerned in the fact that the prototype had spanwise diagonal bracing members in the cabin, but these were deleted from production aircraft. Another distinguishing feature of early F.60s was the use of two 230-hp Salmson/Canton-Unné 9Z water-cooled radial piston engines, though these were later replaced by a pair of 260-hp Salmson 9Cm radials. Yet another distinguishing feature of early F.60s was the provision of overhanging balanced ailerons on all four wings; later replacement by plain ailerons reduced span from 28 m (91 ft 10 in) to 26.5 m (86 ft 11 in).

The F.60 was extensively tested during 1919, and examples of the type established several world

Above: A Farman Goliath in the striking colours of Air Union in the early 1920s. When the first aircraft were converted from bombers they had rather crude interior fittings but the cabins were fairly roomy
Below: A Goliath on a grass airfield during a maintenance check. Just visible is the open cockpit in which the crew sat

records. Perhaps the most notable of these were an altitude of 5100 m (16 732 ft) in 75 min with 25 passengers, and a non-stop flight of 2050 km (1274 miles) from Paris to Casablanca in 18 hours 23 min, with a crew of eight.

It was on March 29, 1920 that the Goliath entered service, the Compagnie des Grands Express Aériens inaugurating an irregular service from Le Bourget outside Paris to Croydon outside London. This service was soon supplemented by another flown with Goliaths, this time of the Compagnie des Messageries Aériennes. These two companies operated 12 and 15 (possibly 16) Goliaths respectively. Other notable operators were the Société Générale de Transports Aériens (Lignes Farman) with 18, used mainly on the route inaugurated on July 1, 1920 between Paris and Brussels, extended on May 17, 1921 to Amsterdam and later to Berlin; and the Belgian line SNETA and Czech operator CSA each had six, the Czech aircraft being licence-built by Avia and Letov with the exception of a single Farman-built aircraft. Some 15 Goliaths from Compagnies des Grands Express Aériens and des Messageries Aériennes were with Air Union on formation in 1923.

As was the case with many aircraft of the period, the basically exterior mounting of the engines greatly facilitated the substitution of many other powerplants, this often leading to the adoption of another designation. Examples of this in the case of the Goliath are the F.60*bis* with 300-hp Salmson 9Az radials, the F.61 with 300-hp Renault 12Fe inlines, and the F.63*bis* with 380-hp Gnome-Rhône

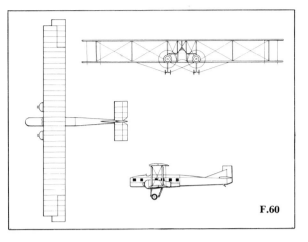

F.60

Jupiter 9A radials. Other engines known to have been fitted are Maybach Mb.IVb inlines, Lorraine-Dietrich inlines, Armstrong Siddeley Jaguar radials, and Walter-built Bristol Jupiter radials. Experimental and record-breaking models with four (two tandem) or three Salmson radials were built, and the final development of the type was powered by a pair of Gnome-Rhône-built Bristol Jupiter 9Akx radials. This was the F.169 of 1929. The last Goliath appears to have been withdrawn from airline service in 1933, and among the type's many 'firsts' is that of being involved in the first mid-air collision between two airliners, when F-GEAD of the Compagnie des Grands Express Aériens collided with the Daimler Airway's DH.18 G-EAWO over Poix on April 7, 1922.

F.63*bis*

Type: short-range transport
Maker: Société Henri et Maurice Farman
Span: 26.5 m (86 ft 10 in)
Length: 13.9 m (45 ft 7 in)
Height: approx 5.6 m (18 ft 4½ in)
Wing area: 161 m² (1733 sq ft)
Weight: maximum 5395 kg (11 894 lb); empty 3030 kg (6680 lb)
Powerplant: two 380-hp Gnome-Rhône Jupiter 9Aa 9-cylinder air-cooled radial engines
Performance: maximum speed 152 km/h (94 mph) at 2000 m (6562 ft); range 400 km (249 miles)
Payload: seats for up to 12 passengers
Crew: 2
Production: approx 60

Salon, Breguet

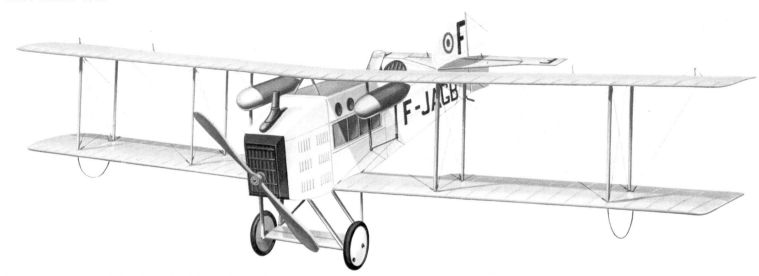

THE most prolific aircraft of French origin to emerge from World War I, the Breguet Bre.14 day bomber and reconnaissance aircraft, eventually ran to some 17 variants with production exceeding 5500. In common with many other military types, the Bre.14 found itself pressed into civil service during 1919, in this instance thanks to the pioneering air freight service inaugurated by the specially formed Compagnie des Messageries Aériennes. With the start of passenger services between Paris and London, CMA found itself in need of a comfortable passenger aircraft, preferably one which could be produced virtually on the spot. The result was the Bre.14T2 Salon.

Derived from a standard Bre.14, the Bre.14T2 had accommodation for two passengers in a some-

what cramped compartment located around the pilot's former cockpit. Just sufficient space for the passengers was provided by heightening the fuselage above the upper longerons. Light was provided by windows on each side of the compartment's upper sides, and by a third window area located at the forward end of the upper decking. A door was let into the right-hand side of the compartment, and the open pilot's cockpit was positioned just aft of the passenger cabin.

Of basically similar design was the Bre.18T Berline, also first produced in 1919. This was powered by the 450-hp Renault 12Ja V-12 in place of the Bre.14T2's 300-hp Renault unit, and had accommodation for four passengers. There was no demand for the type, however, and the concept was

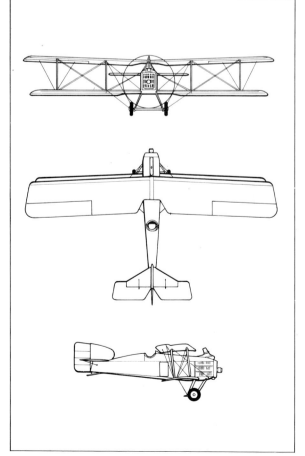

Bre.14T2

Type: short-range transport
Maker: Société Anonyme des Ateliers d'Aviation Louis Breguet
Span: 14.36 m (47 ft 1¼ in)
Length: 9 m (29 ft 6 in)
Height: 3.3 m (10 ft 10 in)
Wing area: 50 m² (538 sq ft)
Weight: maximum 1984 kg (4374 lb); empty 1328 kg (2928 lb)
Powerplant: one 300-hp Renault 12Fe water-cooled V-12 engine
Performance: cruising speed 125 km/h (78 mph) at 2000 m (6562 ft); range 460 m (286 miles)
Payload: seats for 2 passengers
Crew: 1
Production: minimum 135

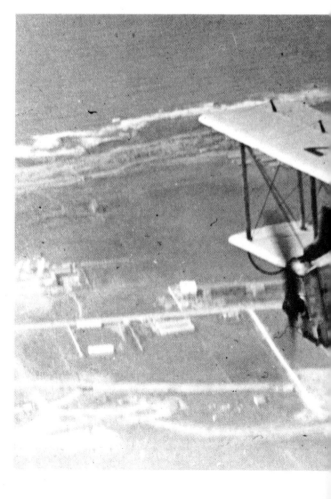

therefore developed into the revised Bre.14T2 with seating for three passengers, and the 300-hp Renault reinstated.

So successful were the Bre.14T2s that in 1921 an improved version appeared. This was the Bre.14T *bis*, basically an amalgamation of the Bre.14T and Bre.18T. It was distinguishable from its predecessors mainly by the different cabin windows: these now consisted of four rectangular windows on each side of the cabin, plus four circular windows on each side of the upper decking.

These civil variants of the Bre. 14 were capable of operations on a float undercarriage, such an aircraft having been displayed at the 1919 Paris Air Show. The main user of this sub-type was the Compagnie des Transports Aériens Guyanais, which had at least five float-equipped Bre.14T*bis* aircraft. These machines were carried on a large central float, with a smaller float under the tail and two stabilizing floats which were located under the lower wings at mid span.

Another variant of the Bre.14 adapted for civil use was the Bre.14 Torpédo, also known as the Breguet Latécoère and used in large numbers by the Lignes Aériennes Latécoère (Compagnie Générale d'Entreprises Aéronautiques) for the carriage of mail. The payload was carried in two streamlined pods under the inboard ends of the lower wings. These aircraft were converted wartime Bre.14A2s, and like the passenger conversions, these aircraft had a rear cockpit. The fuel tanks were removed from the fuselage to be replaced by twin streamlined tanks under the

inboard ends of the lower wings, to try to ensure that in the event of a crash, spilled fuel would not reach the passengers or freight. The removal of the fuel tanks was also designed to provide internal passenger space in cabin models.

The Belgian airline SNETA also used the Bre. 14, but its three aircraft were converted Bre.14A2s with 280-hp Fiat V-12 engines. Being heavier than their military counterparts, the aircraft consequently had a lower performance. It should be noted that apart from aircraft converted or produced specifically for airline and air-mail use, many other examples of this very adaptable aircraft were converted by their owners for a variety of civil tasks, raising the total of civil Bre. 14s to well past the 135 mark.

Left and above: One of the 25 Breguet 14T2 Salons of Compagnie des Messageries Aériennes (CMA) in 1920. The firm operated between Paris and Lille and later expanded to include Belgium, Holland and England
Below left: A Salon of Lignes Aériennes Latécoère which opened its service from Toulouse to Barcelona on Christmas day 1918. Their operations reached as far as Casablanca and Algeria

Vimy Commercial, Vickers

FIRST FLIGHT 1919

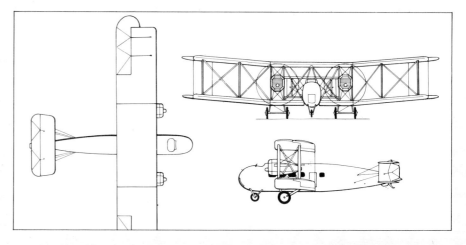

THE Vickers Vimy, immortalized as the aircraft in which Alcock and Brown made the first non-stop aerial crossing of the Atlantic on June 14, 1919, was designed as the FB.27 heavy bomber but was too late to see service in World War I. With the type's general qualities and load-carrying capabilities clearly evident, Vickers in November 1919 made the sensible decision to develop a civil variant of the bomber.

But whereas other manufacturers were largely content to produce interim airliners by minimal modification of current military aircraft, Vickers decided to undertake a more radical modification of the Vimy, replacing the slim, angular fuselage of the bomber with an oval-section monocoque passenger forebody faired into the box-section rear fuselage of the bomber. Apart from providing a roomy passenger compartment, the 'stressed-skin' plywood-covered fuselage was free of internal obstructions, adding to the comfort of the ten passengers seated in wicker or leather seats. Removal of the seats could also provide a freight capacity of 1134 kg (2500 lb).

Named the Vimy Commercial, the prototype appeared in February 1919, and first flew on April 13, 1919. Flight tests showed the aircraft to have a performance marginally superior to that of the bomber, except in range where the extra drag of the larger fuselage was a severe penalty. This meant that on the standard London to Paris route the Vimy Commercial had to land once to refuel. Nevertheless, trials were generally satisfactory, though the aircraft was lost at Tabora in Tanga-

nyika on February 27, while attempting the elusive London to Cape Town flight.

The range deficiency of the Vimy Commercial militated against the type's sales in Europe, but production was assured by an order for 40 of the type placed by the Chinese government in 1919. Finance at first proved difficult, but the aircraft of the Chinese order were eventually built between April 1920 and February 1921. Only three other Vimy Commercials were built: one each for Instone Air Line, Compagnie des Grands Express Aériens and the Russian air force. This last was delivered in September 1922, and was in fact a hybrid aircraft combining features of the Vimy Commercial and Vernon transport, and was powered by Napier Lion engines.

Vimy Commercial

Type: medium-range transport
Maker: Vickers Ltd
Span: 20.73 m (68 ft)
Length: 13 m (42 ft 8 in)
Height: 4.76 m (15 ft 7½ in)
Wing area: 123.56 m² (1330 sq ft)
Weight: maximum 5670 kg (12 500 lb); empty 3534 kg (7790 lb)
Powerplant: two 360-hp Rolls-Royce Eagle VIII water-cooled V-12 engines
Performance: maximum speed 158 km/h (98 mph) at sea level; range 724 km (450 miles)
Payload: 1134 kg (2500 lb); seats for up to 10 passengers
Crew: 2
Production: 44

Left: Lord Gorell and General Sir Frederick Sykes admiring *City of London*, a Vimy Commercial of Instone Air Line, while making an inspection of the working of the London Terminal Aerodrome at Croydon
Below: First flown in April 1919 this Vimy had a brief career, crashing at Tabora, Tanganyika in February 1920

O/7, Handley Page

FIRST FLIGHT 1919

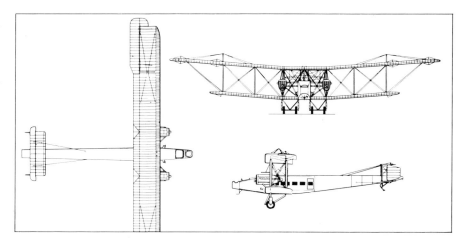

WITH the Defence of the Realm Act effectively preventing the immediate implementation of an Aircraft Transport & Travel plan for a civil service between London and Paris, in 1917 Frederick Handley Page set about producing at relative leisure civil conversions of the O/400, 16 of which he bought back brand new from the Ministry of Munitions. The use of the O/400 for 'civil' tasks had already been pioneered by the Royal Air Force's No 86 (Communications) Wing for freight and mail carriage. Of the 16 new aircraft bought by Handley Page, four were finished and the other 12 in the last stages of production.

The Act, however, did not preclude the civil carriage of newspapers, and the four completed O/400s were converted for this use. The 16-cell bomb bay was altered to a six-cell unit from which the newspaper packages could be parachuted to provincial cities. Provision was also made for seven passengers on extemporized seats forward and aft of the bomb bay, while another two passengers could be squeezed into the nose gunner's cockpit. Six other O/400s were sold as transport aircraft to the government of China.

With the implementation of the Air Navigation Act in February 1919, Handley Page established his company and revealed his proposed civil O/400, with seats for 16 passengers. The definitive O/700, as the type was designated at first, was basically similar to the O/400, but had the fuselage fuel tankage relocated to the rear of the engine nacelles, a rearranged fuselage interior with five inward-facing pairs of wicker seats, and accommo-dation for another two in the nose cockpit. There were seven windows on each side of the fuselage.

Later redesignated O/7, the civil O/400s totalled 11 built as new. Six of these were the aircraft sold to China, and the other five were operated by Handley Page. One of the Handley Page aircraft was used in South Africa until it crashed on February 23, 1920 and the other four were flown by Handley Page Indo-Burmese Transport Limited. One of these, intended for H H Sir Wahjie Bahadur, the Thakur Saheb of Morvi, was destroyed on the ground by a storm in October 1920, but the other three survived until withdrawn from service in July 1921. European operations were the preserve of conversions to O/7 standard not actually graced with the designation.

O/7

Type: long-range transport
Maker: Handley Page Ltd
Span: 30.48 m (100 ft)
Length: 19.16 m (62 ft 10¼ in)
Height: 6.7 m (22 ft)
Wing area: 153.1 m² (1648 sq ft)
Weight: maximum 5466 kg (12 050 lb); empty 3777 kg (8326 lb)
Powerplant: two 360-hp Rolls-Royce Eagle VIII water-cooled V-12 engines
Performance: maximum speed 156 km/h (97 mph) at sea level; range approx 966 km (600 miles)
Payload: seats for up to 14 passengers
Crew: 2
Production: 11 (plus conversions)

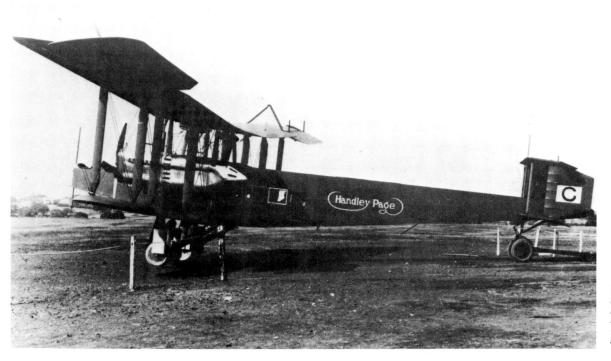

Left: A Handley Page O/7. Six of these aircraft were exported to China and four were operated by Handley Page Indo-Burmese Transport

O/10, Handley Page

FIRST FLIGHT 1920

O/10

Type: long-range transport
Maker: Handley Page Ltd
Span: 30.48 m (100 ft)
Length: 19.16 m (62 ft 10¼ in)
Height: 6.7 m (22 ft)
Wing area: 153.1 m² (1648 sq ft)
Weight: maximum 5466 kg (12 050 lb); empty 3777 kg (8326 lb)
Powerplant: two 360-hp Rolls-Royce Eagle VIII water-cooled V-12 engines
Performance: maximum speed 156 km/h (97 mph) at sea level; range approx 966 km (600 miles)
Payload: seats for up to 12 passengers
Crew: 2
Production: 10

THE success of the 11 original Handley Page O/7s persuaded Handley Page to produce another type of O/400 conversion, the O/11, which appeared in March 1920. The type was intended principally for the carriage of freight and mail, though provision was made to accommodate five passengers, three in a small cabin at the rear of the aircraft and the other two in the open position formerly occupied by the nose gunner.

The first three O/11s were used mainly for airmail carriage to Brussels and Amsterdam, but with the beginning of a fine summer in 1920, there was so great a demand for joyrides and genuine passenger traffic that Handley Page converted two of the O/11s to passenger standard as O/10s, with windows running the full length of the passenger cabin. The immediate success of the type, which could seat ten, prompted the swift conversion of another seven O/400s into O/10s.

Perhaps the most noteworthy of these aircraft was the O/11 which had been kept in reserve. This was the only civil conversion of an O/400 available to meet the Thakur Saheb of Morvi's requirement after the loss of his O/7 in October 1920, and Handley Page swiftly converted G-EASX into what the Handley Page employees called the 'Pink Elephant': the interior was finished to a high standard in pink silk, and the exterior of the aircraft was gloss painted in pink overall, the engine nacelles being finished in blue.

By the end of 1920 the fledgling British civil aviation was in financial difficulties as it ran on strictly commercial lines while French airlines were

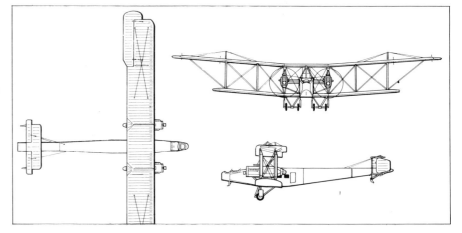

government subsidized and British commercial air traffic was temporarily halted in February 1921. But Handley Page had troubles of its own, largely because of the limitations of the O/400 type for civil aviation. The trouble lay with the generally increasing weight of the civil conversions, and the limited power of the water-cooled engines. Passenger capacity was cut first to eight, and then to five in an effort to ensure single-engined safety, and then later in 1921 it was again raised to eight after stringent checks and engine retuning had been carried out on the surviving aircraft. Nevertheless, when Imperial Airways was formed in March 1924, the reserve O/10 G-EATH was the only O/400 conversion still in 'flying' condition. It was scrapped in June 1925.

W.8, Handley Page

FIRST FLIGHT 1919

RIGHT from the beginning of its O/400 conversion programme, Handley Page had intended the type to be no more than an interim airliner pending the development of a machine with a custom-designed fuselage free of the tie-rods/tubular bracing of the military and civil O/400s. The result was the W/400, which flew in 'prototype' form as C9713 on August 22, 1919. The key features of the new aircraft were wings based on those of the V/1500 combined with elements of the O/400's, and a fuselage based on that of the O/400 but considerably revised to do away with internal bracing in the passenger area. The new fuselage thus had an unobstructed floor area of 6.71 m (22 ft) by 1.37 m (4 ft 6 in). This allowed a maximum seating capacity of 16 in two longitudinal rows separated by a central gangway.

C9713 was never intended as more than an aerodynamic prototype, and the definitive production model was to be the W/400, later redesignated W.8. Power for this was to have been provided by a pair of 400-hp Cosmos Jupiter radials, but the non-availability of these engines led the Air Ministry, which was on excellent terms with Handley Page and also interested in the Type W to meet its requirement for a Large Transport Aeroplane, to lend the company a pair of 450-hp Napier Lion inlines. The extra power allowed the chief designer, G R Volkert, to reduce span from 25.91 m (85 ft) to 22.86 m (75 ft).

The single W.8, registered G-EAPJ, first flew on December 2, 1919 and proved to have an impressive performance, establishing a British payload-to-altitude record on May 4, 1920 by carrying 1674 kg (3690 lb) to 4276 m (14 029 ft). The aircraft also impressed visually, with its glossy white exterior and eight circular windows on each side and an interior featuring a fitted carpet, cane seats, electric candelabra, a clock and a fitted lavatory. Despite the type's commercial potential, and the granting of a certificate of airworthiness on August 7, 1920, the W.8 could not be used in airline service as its engines were government property until the company finally bought a pair of the engines in the summer of 1921. By this time the maximum passenger capacity had been reduced to 12, but even so the government subsidy made the W.8 a viable commercial proposition from its first service on October 21, 1921 until it crashed at Poix on July 10, 1923.

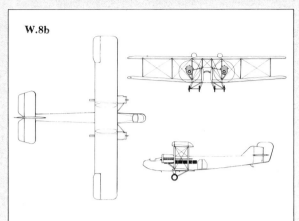

W.8b

Other engines had meanwhile been considered, leading to the proposal for a W.8a with two Bristol Jupiter radials. This came to nothing, but the W.8b with 350-hp Rolls-Royce Eagle VIII V-12s proved more successful, though performance was lowered by the less powerful engines. Three W.8b aircraft were ordered for Handley Page Transport in November 1921. These were similar to the W.8 apart from the different engines, rectangular instead of round windows, and the fuel tanks relocated to the upper wings from the engine nacelles. The first W.8b entered service on May 4, 1922 and apart from the three aircraft for Handley Page, another four W.8b aircraft were built for the Belgian airline SABENA, one by Handley Page and the others by SABCA.

W.8

Type: long-range transport
Maker: Handley Page Ltd; SABCA
Span: 22.86 m (75 ft)
Length: 18.36 m (60 ft 3 in)
Height: 5.64 m (18 ft 6 in)
Wing area: 135.26 m² (1456 sq ft)
Weight: maximum 5557 kg (12 250 lb); empty 3629 kg (8000 lb)
Powerplant: two 450-hp Napier Lion IB water-cooled W-12 engines
Performance: maximum speed 185 km/h (115 mph) at sea level; range 805 km (500 miles)
Payload: seats for up to 12 (later 14) passengers
Crew: 2
Production: 1

W.8b

Specification similar to W.8 except in following particulars:
Length: 18.31 m (60 ft 1 in)
Weight: maximum 5443 kg (12 000 lb); empty 3493 kg (7700 lb)
Powerplant: two 350-hp Rolls-Royce Eagle VIII V-12 engines
Performance: maximum speed 167 km/h (104 mph)
Production: 7

Above: G-EAPJ, the original W.8
Below: The Imperial Airways W.8b which was operated by Handley Page as *Prince Henry*

W.10, Handley Page

FIRST FLIGHT 1926

THE basic soundness and flexibility of the Handley Page O/400 is in no way better attested than in the fact that having stemmed from the O/100 bomber of 1915, it in turn produced a whole series of progeny: the civil O/400 conversions; the prolific W sub-series; and also military types such as the Hyderabad, Hinaidi and Clive. The key to the later developments was the W.8, for this aircraft led eventually to the W.10 airliner.

The W.10 was a contemporary of the W.9a, Imperial Airways having ordered the type in October 1925 just as the W.9a was beginning its flight trials. But whereas the W.9a was a competitor for the Armstrong Whitworth Argosy on the Cairo to Karachi route, the W.10 was intended as an improved W.8 for European operations, principally between London and Paris. As the airline needed four aircraft which had to be ordered no later than the end of March 1926, Handley Page had to mate the flying surfaces and rear fuselage of a Hyderabad with the forward fuselage of a W.8. Able to carry 14 passengers in two seven-seat longitudinal rows divided by a central aisle, the W.10 was powered by two 450-hp Napier Lion IIB W-12 engines. The first W.10 flew on February 10, 1926 and received its certificate of airworthiness on March 5, followed by the other two W.10s on March 9, and the third on March 13. All four aircraft were thus handed over to Imperial Airways on March 30, one day ahead of the contract date. The first aircraft entered service on May 4, 1926 and all four machines helped to run a transport service during the general strike of that year.

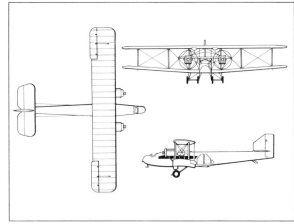

One of the W.10s crashed in the English Channel on October 26, 1926, but the other three aircraft were gainfully employed without further major problem until a second machine crashed, also in the English Channel on June 26, 1929. The fleet was restored to three again when the W.8f Hamilton was brought up to W.10 standard under the designation W.8g, with two Rolls-Royce F.XIIA inlines. After only one year in service, it crashed near Neufchatel on October 30, 1930.

The last two W.10s (in fact the first two built) soldiered on until 1934, when the first crashed at Aston Clinton on September 24, and the second was scrapped in Malta during the same year thus heralding the end of 16 years of civil aviation with the O/400 and its offspring.

W.10

Type: long-range transport
Maker: Handley Page Ltd
Span: 22.86 m (75 ft)
Length: 18.08 m (59 ft 4 in)
Height: 6.12 m (20 ft 1 in)
Wing area: 136.56 m² (1470 sq ft)
Weight: maximum 6251 kg (13 780 lb); empty 3674 kg (8100 lb)
Powerplant: two 450-hp Napier Lion IIB water-cooled W-12 engines
Performance: maximum speed 161 km/h (100 mph) at sea level; range 805 km (500 miles)
Payload: seats for up to 16 passengers
Crew: 2
Production: 4

Above: The first Handley Page W.10, which made its maiden flight at Cricklewood on February 10, 1926

Aeromarine F-5L

FIRST FLIGHT 1920

THE story of the F-5L used by Aeromarine Airways from 1920 is an interesting one. The aircraft were civil conversions of the F-5L patrol flying boats built in 1918 by Curtiss, Canadian Aeroplanes and the US Navy's Naval Aircraft Factory. But these F-5Ls were in turn merely Liberty-powered American-built versions of the Felixstowe F.5 developed in Great Britain.

Compared with the F.5, the F-5L had more powerful engines, wings of 25.4 mm (1 in) greater span, a loaded weight some 144 kg (318 lb) greater at 5897 kg (13 000 lb), and a wing area reduced from 130.9 m² (1409 sq ft) to 129.8 m² (1397 sq ft) by the fitting of parallel-sided rather than inversely tapered ailerons.

Aeromarine Airways had started by buying war-surplus Curtiss HS-2 flying boats, which it converted to six-passenger transports for sale and for use by the airline on its inaugural New York to Atlantic City, New Jersey flight in August 1919. This provided the company with the finance and experience to undertake a more drastic modification of the big F-5L boats, redesignated Type 75 by the airline. While the flying surfaces and lower hull remained untouched, the upper fuselage was heavily altered to provide accommodation for up to 14 passengers. The open pilot's cockpit was located in the top of a bulged upper decking between the engines, this decking providing a measure of headroom in the hull for the passenger cabins, one forward and the other aft of the cockpit.

During 1920 Aeromarine Airways bought Florida West Indies Airways and with an initial

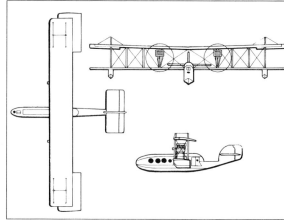

pair of F-5Ls, Aeromarine operated the Key West to Havana mail route with passengers as well as mail. Flights were also made between Miami and Nassau, both foreign termini being outside United States jurisdiction and therefore popular with customers wishing to evade the restrictions of prohibition.

In September 1921 Aeromarine expanded its operation to include a 'High Ball Express', with F-5Ls operating a route from New York to Havana via Atlantic City, Beaufort, Miami and Key West. As such traffic was at its highest during the winter, Aeromarine in 1922 decided to use its F-5Ls as commuter aircraft between Cleveland and Chicago. However, the airline finally went out of business in September 1923.

F-5L

Type: medium-range transport flying boat
Maker: Curtiss Aeroplane and Motor Co Inc
Span: 31.64 m (103 ft 9¼ in)
Length: 15.03 m (49 ft 3¾ in)
Height: 5.72 m (18 ft 9¼ in)
Wing area: 129.79 m² (1397 sq ft)
Weight: maximum 6169 kg (13 600 lb); empty 3955 kg (8720 lb)
Powerplant: two 400-hp Liberty 12A water-cooled V-12 engines
Performance: maximum speed 144.8 km/h (90 mph); range 1336 km (830 miles)
Payload: seats for up to 14 passengers
Crew: 2
Production: not available

Above: The F-5L *Santa Maria* arriving in New York with 12 passengers

E-4250, Zeppelin Staaken

FIRST FLIGHT 1920

ALTHOUGH it never entered airline service and was limited in production to a single example, the Staaken E-4250 (also known as the E.4/20) built by the Zeppelin concern at Staaken near Berlin has the distinction of being the first truly 'modern' airliner in the world. Designed largely by one of the world's great aeronautical pioneers, Dr Adolf Rohrbach (the 'father' of all-metal stressed-skin construction), the E-4250 was conceived as a 18-passenger airliner to operate on the route between Friedrichshafen and Berlin, and clearly owed much to the all-metal giant bombers being developed at Staaken during 1918.

Construction of the E-4250 began in May 1919, using advanced techniques: the fuselage was built up round formed duralumin profiles riveted together and covered with thin dural sheet. The wing was of thick section, clearly inspired by the Junkers design philosophy, built up round a massive box-spar, one-third of the wing chord in width and 1.5 m (4 ft 11 in) deep at the root, largely covered in sheet dural (varying in thickness from 4/25 in [4 mm] at the leading edge to 2/25 in [2 mm] at the trailing edge).

Located in the leading edges of the wings were the four 245-hp Maybach Mb.IVa inline engines, a mere two of which were to keep the aircraft in the air. The wing, again as a result of Junkers inspiration, was designed as a cantilever structure, but was provided as a safety measure with lift-bracing wires running up to the front and rear of the box-spar at two-thirds of the span from points on the lower edge of the fuselage just forward and aft of

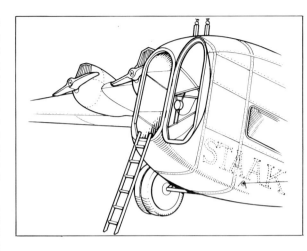

the wings. The tail surfaces were also metal cantilever structures. The undercarriage consisted on each side of a sturdy horizontal V hinged at its open end to the lower fuselage and supported at the outboard end, just beyond the twin mainwheels, by a shock-absorber strut running out and up into the wing spar.

The pilot's cockpit was located on top of the fuselage, and was at first open; later the fuselage in front of the cockpit was lowered and a glazed canopy was added. The passengers entered by means of a door in the extreme nose of the aircraft and were seated in pairs under the wings, with four oblong windows on each side. Aft of the passenger cabin were a washroom, lavatory, mail room, baggage compartment and radio room.

Left: The unusual passenger entrance in the nose of the Zeppelin Staaken. The passengers were seated in pairs with a small table between them. The aircraft also carried a radio room, lavatory, washroom and a hold for mail

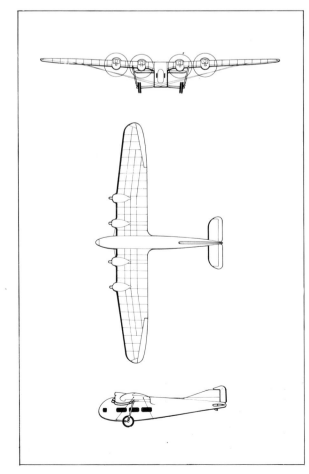

E-4250

Type: medium-range transport
Maker: Zeppelin-Werke GmbH
Span: 31 m (101 ft 8½ in)
Length: 16.5 m (54 ft 1⅔ in)
Height: 5.2 m (17 ft 0¾ in)
Wing area: 106 m² (1141 sq ft)
Weight: maximum 8500 kg (18 739 lb); empty 6072 kg (13 386 lb)
Powerplant: four 245-hp Maybach Mb.IVa 6-cylinder water-cooled inline engines
Performance: maximum speed 225 km/h (140 mph); range not available
Payload: seats for up to 18 passengers
Crew: probably 3
Production: 1

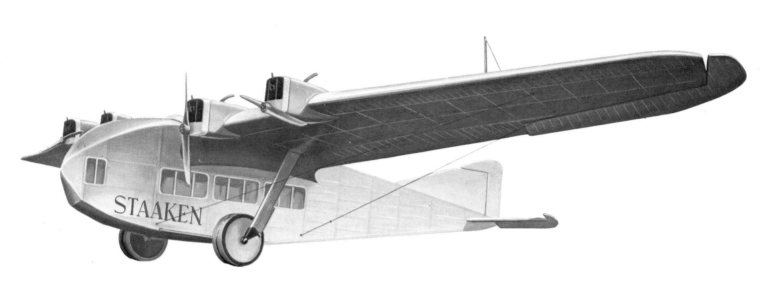

The E-4250 was completed on September 30, 1920 and its early flight trials showed it to have excellent performance, though flight could not be sustained on two engines alone as had been hoped. The construction and trials of the aircraft had been closely followed by members of the Inter-Allied Control Commission, and as a result of their report on the type's potential as a military aircraft, the E-4250 was scrapped on November 21, 1922, the commission having refused Zeppelin permission either to sell or to give away the machine.

The fate of the E-4250 makes an interesting contrast to that of the Junkers F13 which was developed at about the same time. Each project was supervised by the Inter-Allied Control Commission, but the F13 was deemed to have no

military potential and so construction was allowed. The Staaken however had been built by a firm that had produced bombers and the commission saw it as a possible prototype for an advanced bomber. While they were right to suspect the Germans of wishing to build military types, their decision to scrap the E-4250 held up aircraft design for nearly ten years.

The commission also realized that if Zeppelin had the jigs and skilled engineers for building a large aircraft these could be switched to the construction of bombers. There was also a suspicion that the decision was delayed so that the development and building costs would bankrupt the Zeppelin company who would be unable to recover the money through sales.

Above: The Staaken, named after the Berlin suburb in which it was constructed, was a very advanced design for 1919
Below: The curious front view of the E-4250. The pilot sat in a cockpit above the fuselage

F13, Junkers
FIRST FLIGHT 1919

THE Junkers F13 light transport was derived conceptually and structurally from the Junkers all-metal monoplane fighters of World War I, but has a unique place in the annals of civil aviation history as the world's first metal airliner. Also notable in the F13 was the provision of a semi-enclosed pilot's cockpit, the provision of seat belts as standard, and the fact that the type was a cantilever monoplane at a time when almost all its competitors were braced biplanes.

Key to the success of the F13 was the clean design of the aircraft, with its monoplane layout and absence of any bracing wires, and its immensely strong metal structure. The wing, for example, was based on nine tubular duralumin spars braced to form a metal girder and then covered with a corrugated dural skin. The fuselage, based on a number of metal frames, was also covered with corrugated dural. The structure proved ideally suited for airliners operating in all weathers, and was used on all Junkers transport aircraft up to the equally classic Ju 52/3m. The strength of the F13 is attested by the fact that the prototype, which first flew on June 25, 1919, was still used as a Berlin joyriding aircraft in 1939.

This prototype spanned 14.47 m (47 ft 5¾ in) and was powered by a 160-hp Mercedes D.IIIa inline, but production F13a aircraft, of which some 12 were built in 1919, spanned 17.75 m (58 ft 2¾ in) and were powered by the far more effective BMW IIIa inline. The F13 remained in production until 1932 and up to that date was produced in some 70 variants on wheel, ski and float undercarriages.

Powerplant installations were extremely varied: 265-hp Junkers L 2 inline in the F13ba, ca, da and fa; the 380-hp Junkers L 5 inline in the F13be, ce, de and fe; the improved L 5 in the F13dle, fle, ge, he and ke; the 250-hp BMW IV inline in the F13bi, ci, di and fi; and the 360-hp BMW Va in the F13co, fo and ko.

Among the many airline users of the F13 were the German Junkers Luftverkehr with about 60 and Deutsche Lufthansa with 72, Aerolot of Poland with 16, the Romanian LARES with 9, the Swedish AB Aerotransport with 6, and the Swiss Ad Astra Aero with 6. The importance of the F13 cannot be overestimated in opening up air transport in Europe and in many other parts of the world lacking any other means of 'modern' travel.

F13a

Type: medium-range transport
Maker: Junkers Flugzeugwerke AG
Span: 17.75 m (58 ft 2¾ in)
Length: 9.6 m (31 ft 6 in)
Height: 3.6 m (11 ft 10 in)
Wing area: 44 m² (473.6 sq ft)
Weight: maximum 1730 kg (3814 lb); empty 1150 kg (2535 lb)
Powerplant: one 185-hp BMW IIIa 6-cylinder water-cooled inline engine
Performance: maximum speed 177 km/h (110 mph); range approx 650 km (404 miles)
Payload: seats for up to 4 passengers
Crew: 2
Production: approx 350

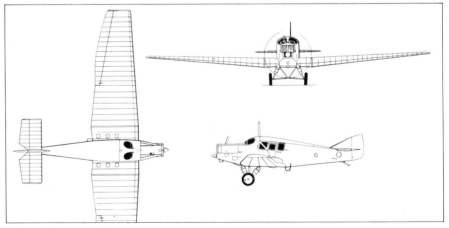

Top: A Junkers F13 of the Brazilian airline Syndicato Condor. This airline operated German aircraft exclusively. The F13 also flew with skis or a wheeled undercarriage
Left: An F13 in service with Eurasia, a subsidiary of Lufthansa. Because of the atrocious state of the airfields in the Far East, F13s had to use special balloon tyres

DH.16, de Havilland

FIRST FLIGHT 1919

THE Aircraft Manufacturing Company (Airco) was ideally placed for the swift development of civil aircraft after World War I not only because it manufactured the easily convertible de Havilland bomber types, but also because its transport and travel subsidiary could supply the manufacturer with detailed information about airline needs.

Experience with the DH.4A had shown it to carry too few passengers for economic operation, and so de Havilland turned his attentions to the DH.9A bomber as the basis for the DH.16. The earlier DH.9 had already been used as the basis of the DH.9 (Civil) and DH.9B civil conversions, but with the DH.16 a more comprehensive modification, of the later DH.9A, was undertaken.

The main modifications necessary were those concerned with the installation of the 320-hp Rolls-Royce Eagle VIII inline, and the widening of the rear fuselage to seat four passengers in two facing pairs. The extensively glazed cabin was similar in concept to the DH.4A's, with the right-hand side and roof hingeing to the left to allow passengers to board up a short ladder. However, when flight trials began in March 1919, the type immediately proved far superior to the DH.4A: despite a nominal drop of 30 hp, the DH.16 was faster than the earlier aircraft, and could carry four passengers instead of two, thereby more than halving seat-mile costs. It is worth noting that the DH.16 entered service with the Aircraft Transport & Travel Company in May 1920, one year after the receipt of its certificate of airworthiness, and thus beat the DH.4A into civil service by nearly three months.

Production was limited to nine aircraft before the line closed in June 1920, and only one of these machines was not sold to the Aircraft Transport & Travel Company, going instead to the Sociedad Rio Platense de Aviacion of Buenos Aires for its ferry flights across the River Plate to Montevideo. The other eight aircraft performed creditably, the type undertaking the Dutch carrier KLM's first scheduled flights from Amsterdam to Croydon.

The last three aircraft were powered by the 450-hp Napier Lion W-12, giving the aircraft an ample reserve of power. With the collapse of the Aircraft Transport & Travel Company in December 1920, its seven DH.16s were placed in storage: five were broken up in 1922, but the other two were taken over by de Havilland Aeroplane Hire Service. One of these crashed and the other was scrapped.

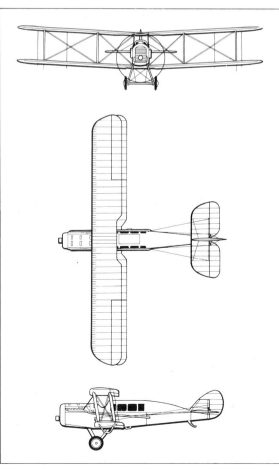

Top: The de Havilland DH.16 which operated with Air Transport & Travel and de Havilland Aircraft Co Ltd at Stag Lane. It crashed at Stanmore in January 1923
Above: Taking baggage aboard at Croydon airport in 1920

DH.16

Type: short- and medium-range transport
Maker: Aircraft Manufacturing Co Ltd
Span: 14.17 m (46 ft 5¾ in)
Length: 9.68 m (31 ft 9 in)
Height: 3.45 m (11 ft 4 in)
Wing area: 45.5 m² (490 sq ft)
Weight: maximum 2155 kg (4750 lb); empty 1431 kg (3155 lb)
Powerplant: one 450-hp Napier Lion water-cooled W-12 engine
Performance: maximum speed 218 km/h (136 mph); range 684 km (425 miles)
Payload: seats for up to 4 passengers
Crew: 1
Production: 9

DH.18, de Havilland

FIRST FLIGHT 1920

DESPITE the relative success of the DH.16, it was still felt by Airco that mere conversions of wartime bombers could be nothing more than an expedient pending the introduction of custom-designed civil transports. Design of a DH.16 successor to meet this requirement began in 1919, resulting in the neat DH.18.

The aircraft was a conventional biplane, with a deep fuselage filling the complete interplane gap. At the extreme nose was the 450-hp Napier Lion W-12 engine, mounted with its bearers, radiator and oil tank as an easily changed powerpack. Just aft of this was the passenger compartment with seating for eight passengers (two seated by the engine bulkhead facing aft, two by the aft bulkhead facing forward, and in the centre four single seats with the two right-hand seats facing forward and the other two aft). This passenger section was a sturdy structure of plywood, with a door on the left side, waterproofed to provide a measure of protection in the event of a crash landing in the sea, two escape hatches being provided in the roof of the compartment. The rest of the airframe was conventional.

The pilot sat in an open cockpit just aft of the passenger compartment, with the baggage hold under him. Provision was also made for the seats to be stripped out of the cabin for the carriage of 7.25 m³ (256 cu ft) or 998 kg (2200 lb) of freight. A particularly interesting feature of the design was the use of very long undercarriage legs, the object being to ensure a minimal landing distance, much drag being produced by the wings with their incidence angle of 17° with tail grounded.

The first DH.18 was built at the beginning of 1920, made its initial flight during February, and was delivered to the Aircraft Transport & Travel Company on March 5, beginning scheduled service from Croydon to Paris on April 8. It was wrecked in a crash landing on August 16, 1920.

The next two examples were the first aircraft finished by the new de Havilland Aircraft Company, and were designated DH.18As as they incorporated a number of improvements. They had been started by Airco, but the third DH.18A was a completely de Havilland product. The three DH.18As were bought for Instone Air Line by the Air Council, and delivered in March, April and May 1921 to operate the subsidized services to the continent. The second DH.18A crashed in May

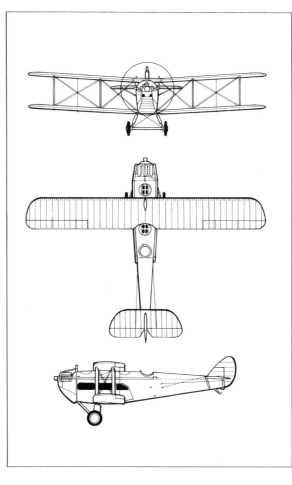

1921, and the first was withdrawn from service in November of the same year when its certificate of airworthiness expired. The Air Council therefore ordered two more aircraft, designated DH.18B because of their improvements (inertia engine starting, plywood covering for the rear fuselage and extra emergency exits) for Instone Air Line. These were delivered in December 1921 and January 1922, the first ditching in the North Sea on May 2, 1924 and the second being scrapped in 1923.

The DH.18A which had been withdrawn was used for experiments by the Royal Aircraft Establishment until November 10, 1927. The third DH.18A was lost in the world's first mid-air collision between airliners, hitting a Farman Goliath over Grandvilliers on April 7, 1922.

DH.18B

Type: short- and medium-range transport
Maker: Aircraft Manufacturing Co Ltd; de Havilland Aircraft Co Ltd
Span: 15.61 m (51 ft 2¾ in)
Length: 11.89 m (39 ft)
Height: 3.96 m (13 ft)
Wing area: 57.72 m² (621 sq ft)
Weight: maximum 3228 kg (7116 lb); empty 1955 kg (4310 lb)
Powerplant: one 450-hp Napier Lion water-cooled W-12 engine
Performance: maximum speed 205 km/h (128 mph); range 644 km (400 miles)
Payload: 998 kg (2200 lb); seats for up to 8 passengers
Crew: 2
Production: 6 (including DH.18 and DH.18A)

Left: The prototype DH.18 at Hounslow in September 1919. It was subsequently delivered to Air Transport & Travel Ltd at Croydon in March 1920, but crashed in August that year at Wallington, Surrey

DH.34, de Havilland

FIRST FLIGHT 1922

EARLY commercial operations by types such as the DH.18, showed that profitable airline operations would only be possible with aircraft that were faster and capable of carrying a greater payload per horsepower. After detailed discussions with two possible users and the Air Council, de Havilland embarked on the design of the DH.34, which was to be a development of the DH.32 concept with features of the DH.29.

The fuselage was based on that of the DH.29, with the pilot located between the engine and passengers to mitigate the effects of engine noise in the cabin. As with the DH.18, the 450-hp Napier Lion W-12 and its accessories were mounted as a detachable powerpack. The cabin and right door were designed to carry a replacement engine for use on remote airfields.

The type was launched with two orders from Daimler Hire and seven from the Air Council. The first DH.34 flew on March 26, 1922, was handed over to Daimler Hire on March 31, and flew its first service, from Croydon to Paris, on April 2. Instone Air Line leased several Air Council aircraft, and one of these also made the airline's inaugural flight, again to Paris, on the same day. Airline service soon confirmed the potential of the DH.34 as an immensely sturdy and serviceable aircraft. The type's commercial viability was confirmed by the two initial Daimler Hire DH.34s, which were privately owned and operated successfully on non-subsidized routes such as Manchester to Amsterdam via Croydon. The last of de Havilland's initial production batch of ten DH.34s had been ordered by the Russian airline Dobrolet, and was shipped to Russia in June 1922.

By contemporary standards the DH.34 had the high landing speed of 113 km/h (70 mph) and after a fatal crash involving one of the aircraft, de Havilland took the opportunity to fit larger wings (spanning an extra 0.91 m [3 ft]) to an aircraft they were rebuilding after a ditching. With these wings the aircraft became the DH.34B, with landing speed reduced to 101 km/h (63 mph).

In April 1924 the newly formed Imperial Airways took over seven DH.34s for use on its routes to Brussels and Amsterdam. Two of these aircraft were lost in accidents (including the original DH.34B), two were converted into DH.34Bs, and the surviving five aircraft were withdrawn from service in 1926 and scrapped.

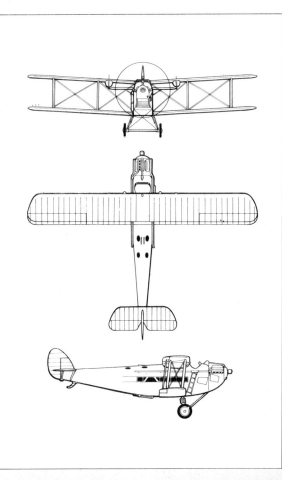

DH.34

Type: short-range transport
Maker: de Havilland Aircraft Co Ltd
Span: 15.65 m (51 ft 4 in)
Length: 11.89 m (39 ft)
Height: 3.66 m (12 ft)
Wing area: 54.81 m^2 (590 sq ft)
Weight: maximum 3266 kg (7200 lb); empty 2075 kg (4574 lb)
Powerplant: one 450-hp Napier Lion water-cooled W-12 engine
Performance: maximum speed 205 km/h (128 mph); range 587 km (365 miles)
Payload: seats for up to 9 passengers
Crew: 1
Production: 12

Below: A DH.34 under construction at Stag Lane aerodrome, Edgware
Bottom: The DH.34 which was delivered to Daimler Hire Ltd in 1924, was subsequently transferred to Imperial Airways in 1924 and scrapped in 1926

F.II, Fokker

FIRST FLIGHT 1919

IN the first 15 years after World War I, the two main European builders of transport aircraft were Junkers and Fokker: whereas the former concentrated on low-wing all-metal monoplanes, the latter concerned itself chiefly with high-wing monoplanes with wooden wings and steel-tube fuselages. Points in common were that both companies believed right from the outset in enclosed passenger accommodation and in the use of thick-section wings, which were high in drag, but provided good lift and were sufficiently strong to be built as cantilever structures.

Both companies also developed their aircraft from fighters of World War I, the Fokker line drawing heavily upon the design concepts pioneered by Reinhold Platz. It was this designer who was responsible for Fokker's first postwar civil design, the V.44 which was to have entered production as the F.I. To have been powered by a 185-hp BMW IIIa inline, the six-passenger V.44 resembled a scaled-up Fokker D.VIII parasol-wing fighter, but only the wing was complete when Fokker decided to forgo the type in favour of the V.45, which entered production as the F.II. The open cockpit for the passengers was replaced by an enclosed cabin, but otherwise the aircraft was closely similar to the abortive V.44.

The V.45 first flew in October 1919, and was of typical Platz design: the wing was made entirely of wood, tapering slightly in chord and greatly in thickness, covered in plywood and built as a single piece that was then bolted straight onto the flat upper surface of the fuselage, which was con-

structed of welded steel tube and covered with fabric. All the control surfaces were aerodynamically balanced, and there was no fixed fin. Accommodation for four passengers was provided in a cabin under the wing, with three windows on each side and a door on the left side. A fifth passenger could be seated next to the pilot.

The F.II was built in Germany at Schwerin and after the first example had received its German certificate of airworthiness in March 1920, it was flown to Holland for evaluation by the Dutch carrier KLM, which ordered two examples including the first aircraft. These aircraft entered service in September 1920. There followed several changes of ownership, but one aircraft survived until World War II. A third F.II was built for Deutsche Luft-

Above: A Fokker F.II at Tempelhof airport Berlin. Lufthansa had connections to 16 cities in Europe and even operated a night service
Below: A Fokker-Grulich F.II. Although it had a shorter range, it had a more powerful engine and could lift heavier payloads

Reederei, and at least another three examples were built for use in the German enclave in Poland, centred on Danzig. These early F.IIs had the BMW IIIa as standard, though a German example at one time had the 250-hp BMW IV inline.

After an interval of some six years, the F.II re-entered production in modified form as the Fokker-Grulich F.II, with many improvements and higher weights, powered at first by the 250-hp BMW IV, though some 14 were later re-engined with 320-hp BMW Va inlines under the designation F.IIb. At least 19 of this model were built, mainly for use by Deutsche Luft-Reederei, later passing through the hands of Deutscher Aero Lloyd before coming into the hands of Deutsche Lufthansa in 1926. By the summer of 1928 Deutsche Lufthansa was using its 19 F.IIs for passenger operations on 13 routes, these numbers declining to ten aircraft on four routes by 1934.

The Fokker-Grulich F.II was dimensionally identical with the Fokker F.II, but the extra power available from the later BMW inlines allowed greater weights. The maximum take-off weight was in the order of 2300 kg (5071 lb) and empty weight about 1650 kg (3638 lb), though on some aircraft these figures appear to have been lower. Range was considerably reduced, however, that of the Grulich-engineered aircraft being only 600 km (373 miles) with the BMW Va, compared with the 1200 km (746 miles) of the Fokker-built F.IIs.

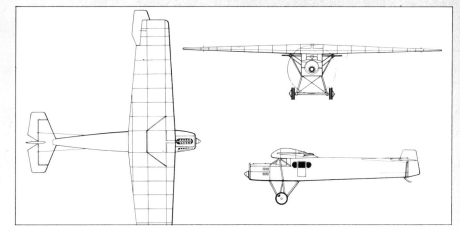

F.II

Type: long-range transport
Maker: Fokker Flugzeugwerke GmbH
Span: 16.1 m (52 ft 10 in)
Length: 11.65 m (38 ft 2¾ in)
Height: 3.2 m (10 ft 6 in)
Wing area: 42 m² (452 sq ft)
Weight: maximum 1900 kg (4188 lb); empty 1200 kg (2646 lb)

Powerplant: one 185-hp BMW IIIa 6-cylinder water-cooled inline engine
Performance: maximum speed 149 km/h (93 mph); at sea level; range 1200 km (746 miles)
Payload: 400 kg (881 lb); seats for up to 5 passengers
Crew: 1
Production: 30

Wal, Dornier

FIRST FLIGHT 1922

IN many respects the Dornier Do J Wal occupies the same place in the development of maritime civil aviation as does the Junkers F13 in that of land-based civil aviation. It proved itself immensely durable and versatile, was built in a number of models, and helped bring air transport to many hitherto inaccessible areas. In production from 1922 to 1936, the Wal appeared in more than 20 civil and military versions.

Evolved from the Dornier Gs I and Gs II flying boats, the Wal first flew on November 6, 1922 and was immediately impressive for its relatively large size and metal construction. The wing was built up of two steel spars with duralumin ribs, with no taper in chord or thickness, and was located above the hull by two N-struts. The two engines were located in tandem above the centre section. The hull was of two-step design, built of metal with an alloy skin, and featured (in place of stabilizing wingtip floats) a large sponson on each side of the fuselage, the wings being braced to the outer ends of these sponsons by parallel struts.

The construction in Germany of such an aircraft was prohibited by the Treaty of Versailles, but Dornier had already foreseen the problem and arranged for the production of the type in Italy by a Dornier subsidiary, Costruzioni Meccaniche Aeronautiche SA. The first CMASA-built Wal flew in 1923, and eventually some 150 of the type were built in Italy by CMASA and Piaggio.

The first operator of the Wal was Spain, which ordered six of the type for delivery in 1923. The most celebrated of these was an example named *Plus Ultra* and powered by two 450-hp Napier Lions: between January 22 and February 10, 1926, piloted by Commandante Ramon Franco, *Plus Ultra* covered some 10 072 km (6258 miles) between Palos de Moguer in Spain and Buenos Aires in Argentina in a flying time of 59 hours 35 min. Other notable Wal flights included Arctic exploration flights by Roald Amundsen.

Early passenger Wals carried up to 12 passengers: ten in a cabin in the bows, and another two in an open cockpit under the wing leading edge. Engines for the Wal were extremely varied, ranging from the 185-hp BMW III to the 750-hp Fiat A.24R via some 20 other types. Four wing spans were used, ranging from the original 22.5 m (73 ft 10 in) to the ultimate 27.2 m (89 ft 2¾ in), and maximum weight rose gradually from 4000 kg

(8818 lb) to 10 000 kg (22 046 lb). The first Wals to be built as series aircraft in Germany appeared in 1932, and were of the Do J II 8-ton Wal type, and were used mainly for airmail flights by Deutsche Lufthansa. The ultimate development of the type was the Do J II 10-ton Wal, or Wal 33 as it first flew on May 3, 1933. This version featured an enclosed cockpit.

Ultimate expression of the Wal concept was the Do R Super Wal, which first appeared in 1926. This was basically an enlarged Wal powered by two 700-hp or four 450-hp engines. Up to 19 passengers could be carried at a cruising speed of up to 195 km/h (121 mph) over a range of up to 1000 km (621 miles). Some 16 examples were built in Germany, and an unknown number in Spain.

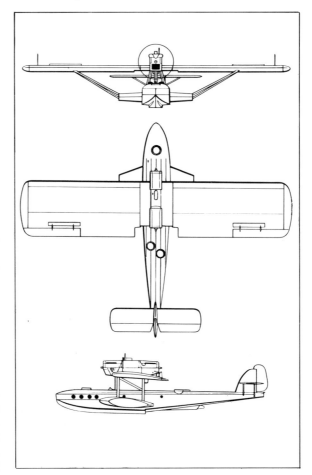

Top: The Dornier-built *Grönland Wal* of Deutsche Lufthansa in its 1933 livery. This aircraft was flown by von Gronau in an Atlantic crossing in August, 1930
Above: Recovery is made by using a trailing 'apron', onto which the aircraft is manoeuvred

Wal 33

Type: long-range transport flying boat
Maker: Dornier Werke GmbH; Costruzioni Meccaniche Aeronautiche SA (CMASA); Construcciones Aeronauticas SA (CASA); Aviolanda; Kawasaki; Piaggio
Span: 23.2 m (76 ft 1½ in)
Length: 18.2 m (59 ft 8½ in)
Height: 5.35 m (17 ft 6⅔ in)
Wing area: 96 m² (1033 sq ft)
Weight: maximum 8000 kg (17 637 lb); empty 5100 kg (11 243 lb)
Powerplant: two 600-hp BMW VI 12-cylinder water-cooled inline engines
Performance: cruising speed 193 km/h (120 mph); range 2200 km (1367 miles)
Payload: seats for up to 10 passengers
Crew: 2
Production: approx 300

Sea Eagle, Supermarine

FIRST FLIGHT 1923

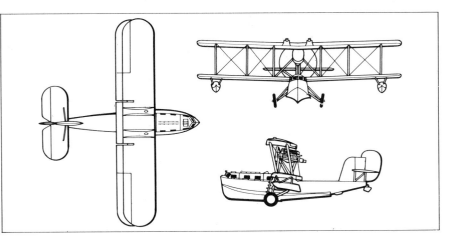

THE Supermarine Aviation Works Limited, as Pemberton-Billing Limited was renamed in 1916, had considerable experience with naval aircraft before the end of World War I. With the coming of peace and the end of lucrative military orders, Supermarine and most other aircraft manufacturers turned to civil aviation. Supermarine's first such venture was conversion to civil use of a number of A.D. Flying Boats, built by the company in its former guise, bought from the Air Ministry. Re-engined with more economical Beardmore inlines of 160 hp each, these aircraft, ten in all, became Supermarine Channel Is, and were the first civil flying boats to receive a British certificate of airworthiness, on July 23, 1919. The aircraft were used mainly for pleasure trips.

In 1923 Supermarine established a government-subsidized British Marine Air Navigation Company, and for this operator R J Mitchell, who had sprung to prominence as the designer of the Sea Lion flying boats which had won the 1919 and 1922 Schneider Trophy races, designed the neat Sea Eagle flying boat. Based on the Linton-Hope type of hull developed in World War I, the Sea Eagle was a compact biplane powered by a 350-hp Rolls-Royce Eagle IX located on two N-struts under the upper wing centre section and driving a four-blade pusher propeller. The hull provided excellent sea-keeping qualities, as well as ample room in the bows for a low enclosed cabin for the six passengers, who peered out through four windows on each side of the compartment and two windows in the front. As with the A.D. Flying Boat and

Channel, the wings were arranged to fold forward to allow the aircraft to be hangared: in this condition the Sea Eagle had a 'span' of 6.43 m (21 ft 1 in). Another notable feature of the boat was its amphibious capability, the wheels folding up under the lower wings for flying boat service.

Sea Eagle services from Woolston to the Channel Islands began in 1923, and were very popular. However, one aircraft crashed on May 21, 1924 and this left Imperial Airways, which had taken over the British Marine Air Navigation Company on April 1, 1924, with only two Sea Eagles. Another machine was lost when it was rammed in St Peter Port harbour by a steamer and sunk on January 10, 1927. The last Sea Eagle was finally withdrawn in 1929.

Sea Eagle

Type: transport amphibian
Maker: Supermarine Aviation Works Ltd
Span: 14.02 m (46 ft)
Length: 11.38 m (37 ft 4 in)
Height: (flying boat) 4.48 m (14 ft 8¼ in)
Wing area: approx 28.8 m² (310 sq ft)
Weight: maximum 2744 kg (6050 lb); empty 1791.6 kg (3950 lb)
Powerplant: one 350-hp Rolls-Royce Eagle IX water-cooled V-12 engine
Performance: maximum speed 150 km/h (93 mph) at sea level; range approx 483 km (300 miles)
Payload: seats for up to 6 passengers
Crew: 1
Production: 3

Left: The Sea Eagle which flew in the King's Cup Race of 1923

F.VII/3m, Fokker

FIRST FLIGHT 1925

THE tri-motor Fokker F.VIIs are amongst the most important transport aircraft of all time, and also featured in a number of classic long-distance flights. As with many other Fokker civil transports, the F.VIIa from which the first tri-motors evolved was itself derived closely from the original F.VII. Only five F.VIIs, each powered by a single 360-hp Rolls-Royce Eagle, were built before the much cleaner F.VIIa appeared in early 1925.

Powered in its prototype form by the 400-hp Packard Liberty 12 V-12, the F.VIIa had rounded wingtips, inset ailerons and a much more refined undercarriage. This last comprised, on each side, a steel-tube V the open end of which was hinged to the lower longeron, with the apex just inboard of the single wheel, supported by a telescopic leg running vertically up to the wing. Fokker built 37 single-engined F.VIIa aircraft for European sale, and an important feature of the type's sales success was the fact that a variety of engines could be fitted, as usual, the aircraft being stressed to accept powerplants ranging from 350 to 525 hp.

What was to transform the F.VIIa, however, was the addition of another pair of engines. The concept originated as a single aircraft intended for the Ford Reliability Trial of September 1925. This was intended to promote reliability in aircraft intended for airline use, and Anthony Fokker saw in it a golden opportunity to 'advertize' his F.VIIa by a conclusive success in the tour. An F.VIIa was accordingly modified to a tri-motor configuration

Below left: Loading cargo into the forward bay of an F.VII/3m at London in 1933
Right: The F.VII with its original single Rolls-Royce Eagle engine
Below right: An F.VIIa in service with Swissair in 1927. It had an improved undercarriage and could be fitted with different engines

F.VIIb/3m

1 Right wingtip tie down shackle
2 Right navigation light
3 Aileron cables
4 Aileron control horn
5 Right aileron
6 Plywood wing skinning
7 Fixed trailing edge construction
8 Rear spar
9 Wing ribs
10 Front spar
11 Leading-edge nose ribs
12 Right engine nacelle mounting struts
13 Engine instruments
14 Control cable duct to engine nacelle
15 Cooling air louvres
16 Right main undercarriage leg
17 Right engine
18 Three-bladed propeller
19 Exhaust collector ring
20 Wright J6 nine-cylinder radial engine
21 Engine accessories
22 Engine mounting struts
23 Fireproof bulkhead
24 Oil cooler
25 Centre engine oil tank
26 Oil tank filler cap
27 Cockpit floor level
28 Nose baggage compartment
29 Landing/taxiing lamp
30 Wind driven generator
31 Undercarriage strut mounting
32 Mail locker
33 Rudder pedal bar
34 Elevator control linkages
35 Instrument panel
36 Windscreen panels
37 Co-pilot's seat
38 Control column handwheel
39 Pilot's seat
40 Radio
41 Cockpit bulkhead
42 Wing spar/fuselage attachment
43 Fuel selector cocks
44 Aileron cable runs
45 Wing lifting lugs
46 Fuel tank filler cap
47 Fuel tanks
48 Fuel vent pipes
49 Right cabin window panel
50 Passenger seats
51 Rear spar/fuselage attachment
52 Overhead luggage racks
53 Cabin rear bulkhead
54 Cabin doorway
55 Toilet compartment
56 Water tank
57 Right baggage door
58 Entry door
59 Rear baggage compartment
60 Steel-tube upper longerons
61 Fuselage stringers
62 Control cable runs
63 Horizontal spacers
64 Right tailplane
65 Elevator horn balance
66 Right elevator
67 Tailfin construction
68 Rudder horn balance
69 Sternpost
70 Fabric-covered rudder construction
71 Tailplane bracing wire
72 Elevator control horn
73 Fabric-covered left elevator construction
74 Elevator horn balance
75 Tailplane construction
76 Rudder control horn
77 Tailplane bracing strut
78 Fuselage fabric covering
79 Tailplane trim adjustment
80 Tailskid
81 Elastic cord shock absorber
82 Vertical spacers
83 Diagonal wire bracing
84 Steel-tube bottom longeron
85 Welded fuselage construction
86 Rear spar girder construction
87 Step
88 Spar plywood facing
89 Trailing edge ribs
90 Left aileron construction
91 Aileron control horn
92 Wingtip tie down shackle
93 Wingtip stringer construction
94 Left navigation light
95 Leading edge construction
96 Pitot tube
97 Aileron cables
98 Plywood ribs
99 Front spar girder construction
100 Passenger cabin floor level
101 Engine nacelle floor struts
102 Nacelle attachment joints
103 Left engine instruments
104 Oil tank
105 Exhaust pipe
106 Oil cooler
107 Welded steel-tube nacelle construction
108 Left Wright J6 engine
109 Exhaust collector ring
110 Cooling air intake louvres
111 Main undercarriage leg strut
112 Elastic cord shock absorber
113 Mudguard
114 Undercarriage lower V-struts
115 Left mainwheel
116 Hydraulic brake
117 Tyre valve access
118 Wheel disc cover/tyre lacing

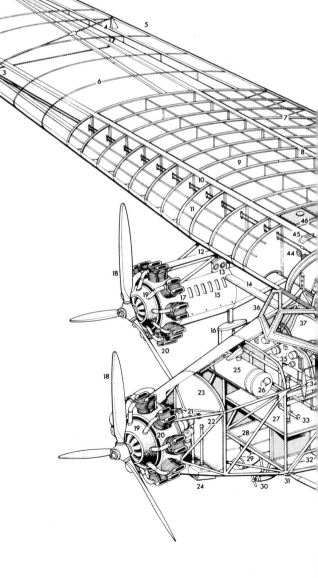

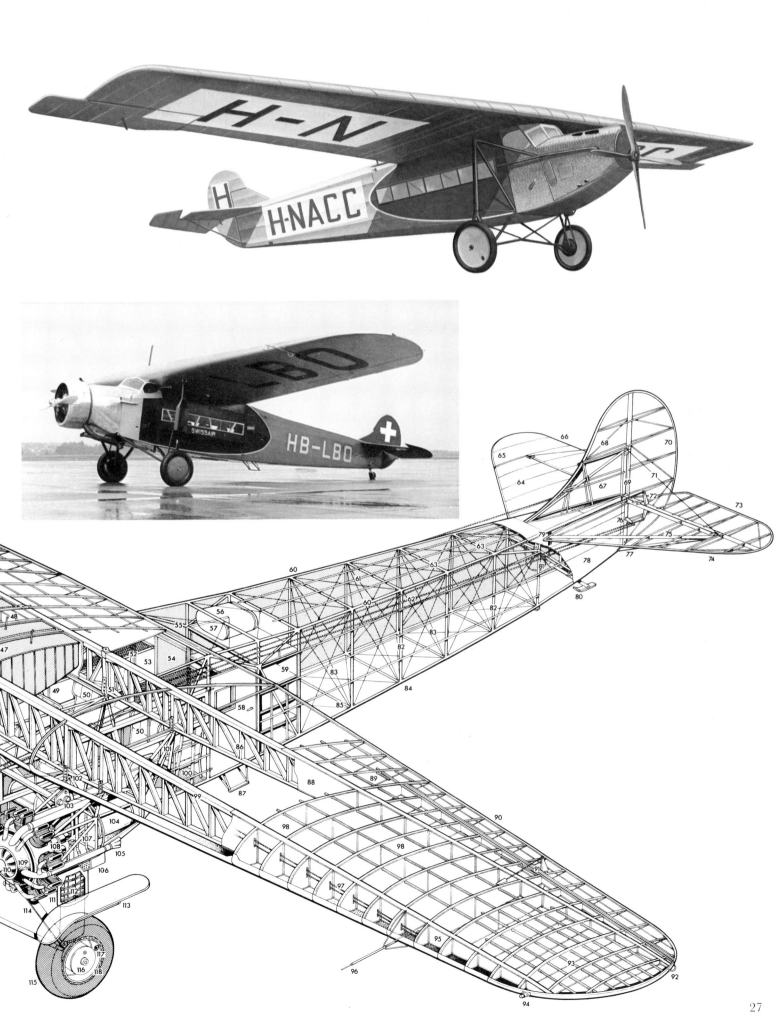

FOKKER

Left: The Fokker F.VIIa/3m flown by Commander Byrd in the Ford Reliability Tour. It was subsequently flown over the North Pole in 1926
Below: A Fokker F.X production line at the Atlantic Aircraft Corporation plant at Hasbrouck Heights, New Jersey. The F.X was the American equivalent of the F.VII/3m
Bottom: Anthony Fokker checks a Wright engine while the engine's designer David L Lawrence offers assistance

with three 200-hp Wright Whirlwind J4 radials.

Fokker had specified that the two outer engines were to be located in the wing leading edges, but for a variety of reasons Reinhold Platz opted to locate them on the vertical undercarriage members on simple steel-tube mountings. Completed in late August 1925, the Fokker F.VIIa/3m first flew on September 4, 1925. It was soon dismantled for shipping to the USA, where its performance in the Ford Reliability Contest was excellent. On May 9, 1926 the aircraft, equipped with a ski undercarriage, was reputedly flown over the North Pole by Floyd Bennett and Richard E Byrd. It is now in the Ford Museum.

Two F.VII aircraft were ordered for the 1926 Arctic expedition led by Sir Hubert Wilkins: one was a typical F.VIIa powered by a 450-hp Liberty, but the other was the precursor of the F.VIIb series. This had a larger wing, 21.71 m (71 ft 2¾ in) compared with 19.31 m (63 ft 4¼ in), and was powered by three 200-hp Wright Whirlwinds. The expedition failed, but the second aircraft was sold to Charles Kingsford Smith, in whose hands it was renamed *Southern Cross* to become possibly the most celebrated individual aircraft between the wars. On May 31, 1928, *Southern Cross* took off from Oakland in California and then flew to Brisbane in Australia, which was reached on June 9, after 83 hours 11 min in the air. The flight had covered 11 891 km (7389 miles) and had had only two stopping points, in Hawaii and Fiji.

Southern Cross was essentially a hybrid, with the fuselage of the F.VIIa and the wings of the American Fokker F.X. The position was regularized by the production F.VIIb/3m, which appeared in 1928. The pioneer of the series, apart from *Southern Cross*, was a big-wing F.VII/3m built in late 1927 for the Byrd Antarctic Expedition and named *Friendship*. The first four production F.VIIb/3m aircraft appeared in July and August 1928, to an order from KNILM, the Dutch carrier in the Netherlands East Indies. As with the F.VII, part of the type's success was attributable to the variety of engines which could be fitted and to the reliability of having three engines.

The type was widely built under licence in Belgium, Czechoslovakia, France, Great Britain (as the Avro Ten), Italy, Poland, and the USA (the basically similar Atlantic Aircraft and Fokker Aircraft F.X. and F.Xa).

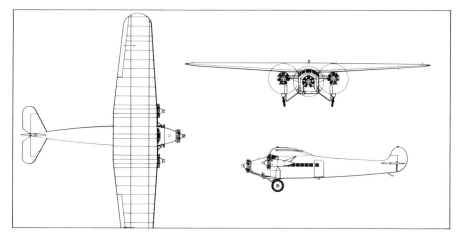

F.VIIb/3m

Type: medium-range transport
Maker: Fokker BV; SABCA; E Plage & T Laskiewicz; Avia; Officine Ferroviarie Meridionali; A V Roe and Co Ltd
Span: 21.71 m (71 ft 2¾ in)
Length: 14.5 m (47 ft 7 in)
Height: 3.9 m (12 ft 10 in)
Wing area: 67.6 m² (729 sq ft)
Weight: maximum 5300 kg (11 684 lb); empty 3100 kg (6834 lb)
Powerplant: three 300-hp Wright R-975 Whirlwind J6 9-cylinder air-cooled radial engines

Performance: maximum speed 207.5 km/h (129 mph); range 1200 km (746 miles)
Payload: 1080 kg (2381 lb); seats for up to 10 passengers
Crew: 2
Production: approx 145

F.III, Fokker

FIRST FLIGHT 1921

THE Fokker F.III was produced as a scaled-up version of the successful F.II, with all five passengers now accommodated in the cabin. This meant that fuselage width had to be increased by some 30 cm (11⅘ in), and the wings were also increased in span. However, the removal of the fifth passenger from the pilot's cockpit allowed the designer, Reinhold Platz, to adopt an unusual expedient of locating the pilot just to the right of the nose-mounted engine.

Design took place during 1920, and the prototype was built at Fokker's German factory at Schwerin. Powered by a 185-hp BMW IIIa, this aircraft first flew in April 1921 and soon revealed the performance advantages of this fully cantilever design (the F.II had featured a certain amount of wing bracing), though the structure otherwise followed the pattern established on the F.II.

The first airline to order the type was the Dutch carrier KLM, which received 12 F.IIIs powered by the 230-hp Siddeley Puma inline in 1921 and early 1922. The first scheduled service was flown on April 14, 1921 between Amsterdam and Croydon by two aircraft flying the route in opposite directions. Other notable aircraft of the first production batch were a Danzig-registered F.III of Deutsche Luft-Reederei, powered by a 350-hp BMW, and an F.III of the Hungarian airline Malert with a 230-hp Hiero IVH engine. Malert also had four F.IIIs with BMW IIIa engines, which flew the regular service between Budapest and Vienna, and Budapest and Graz, from 1923 to 1929 without a single accident.

The next model was powered by the 350-hp Rolls-Royce Eagle VIII, and had the pilot to the left of the engine. Some of these sub-models had their wings parasol-mounted, and about ten were delivered to the Russo-German operator Deruluft. The last F.IIIs built by Fokker left the factory in 1922. A wide variety of engines was fitted, including the 400-hp Gnome-Rhône Jupiter VI and 240-hp Gnome-Rhône Titan radials.

Subsequent production of the F.III followed the pattern established by the F.II, with Deutsche Luft-Reederei in 1923 beginning production of the modified Fokker-Grulich F.III. Most of these aircraft were powered by the 250-hp BMW IV, though examples re-engined with the 320-hp BMW Va were not uncommon, with the revised designation F.IIIc.

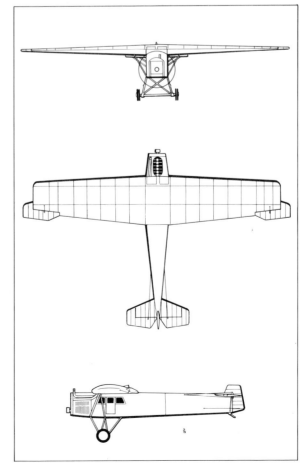

Top: A Dutch F.III powered by a Rolls-Royce Eagle engine with the pilot's position on the left

Above: A German F.III of Aero Lloyd landing at Hamburg. Note the stylized crane symbol on the fin, later retained by Lufthansa

F.IIIc

Type: short- and medium-range transport
Maker: Fokker Flugzeugwerke GmbH; NV Vliegtuigenfabrik Fokker; DLR
Span: 17.62 m (57 ft 9½ in)
Length: 11.07 m (36 ft 3¾ in)
Height: 3.66 m (12 ft)
Wing area: 39.1 m² (421 sq ft)
Weight: maximum 2300 kg (5070 lb); empty 1550 kg (3417 lb)
Powerplant: one 320-hp BMW Va V-12 water-cooled engine
Performance: cruising speed approx 150 km/h (93 mph); range 600 km (372 miles)
Payload: 450 kg (992 lb); seats for up to 5 passengers
Crew: 1
Production: approx 78

ANT-3, Tupolev

FIRST FLIGHT 1925

IN common with several other Russian aircraft of the 1920s, the Tupolev ANT-3 shows marked signs of Junkers influence – hardly surprising in view of the fact that from 1922 to 1927 Junkers had built aircraft, with the active support of the new Soviet government wishing to use the aircraft and to gain practical experience of modern design and construction, at the former Russo-Baltic Wagon Works at Fili just outside Moscow. With the end of Junkers' lease, the factory was assigned to Tupolev as Factory No 22.

By 1924, with series production of the de Havilland DH.9A bomber well on the way under the Russian designation R-1, the high command of the Soviet air force issued a specification for a more advanced light bomber and reconnaissance aircraft of all-metal construction. With development of his Junkers-inspired all-metal ANT-2 light transport out of the way, Tupolev was well placed to respond. During the year 1924 Tupolev's team, under the auspices of the Central Aerohydrodynamic Institute (TsAGI) in Moscow, designed the ANT-3 (or R-3 as it was designated by the military). The design was for a neat sesquiplane to be built of Kolchugalumin, an aluminium alloy developed by the Russians and claimed to be stronger than duralumin.

Completed during the late summer of 1925, the ANT-3 was at first powered by a 450-hp Lorraine-Dietrich V-12, but this first example was later re-engined with the Russian-built version of the 400-hp Liberty 12, the M-5. It was this engine which also powered the production variants.

Initial flight trials were undertaken during September and October 1925 by V N Phillipov, and then the ANT-3 was piloted successfully through its state trials by V M Gromov. These trials were completed in May 1926, and the ANT-3 immediately entered large-scale production, with the Soviet air force as the initial main customer.

The ANT-3 soon began to appear in the aviation news as a result of some excellent long-distance flights. The first of these, between August 31, and September 2, 1926, was flown by a special ANT-3 powered by a 450-hp Napier Lion W-12; crewed by M M Gromov and one Radzevich, RR-SOV flew the Moscow-Königsberg-Berlin-Paris-Rome-Vienna-Warsaw route. One year later another ANT-3, piloted by the great long-distance flier V P Chkalov with a man named Fufayev as his mechanic, flew RR-INT over a course of 22 000 km (13 671 miles) from Moscow to Tokyo and back in a flying time of 153 hours. Taking off on August 20, Chkalov ran into the most appalling weather on the outward leg of his journey, which thus took 11 days, but it says much of the ANT-3's capabilities that the flight was only slowed rather than halted.

This sturdiness evinced by the ANT-3 was of course essential in a military aircraft, but also played an important part in the ANT-3's civil career as a mailplane, where punctuality and a reliable service were of paramount importance. Also useful was the ANT-3's triangular-section fuselage, with the apex at the bottom, which gave the pilot a good field of vision downwards, useful for landing on airfields in remote areas.

Right: The ANT-3 powered by an M-5 engine, the Russian-built version of the Liberty 12. It was built from Kolchug – an aluminium alloy stronger than duralumin

Below: The pilot of an ANT-3 checks his parachute before take-off. This aircraft has a Napier-Lion W-12 engine

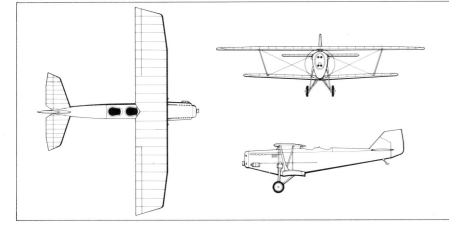

ANT-3

Type: mailplane
Maker: Tupolev Design Bureau
Span: 13.2 m (43 ft 3¾ in)
Length: 9.9 m (32 ft 5¾ in)
Height: 3.9 m (12 ft 9½ in)
Wing area: not available
Weight: maximum 2085 kg
(4596 lb); empty not available
Powerplant: one 400-hp M-5
water-cooled V-12 engine
Performance: maximum
speed 205 km/h (127 mph) at
sea level; range 700 km
(435 miles)
Payload: 300 kg (661 lb)
Crew: 2

Production: approx 80
(civil) and minimum 200
(military)

Jabiru, Farman

FIRST FLIGHT 1923

WHATEVER its other attributes, the Farman F.121 Jabiru must surely rank as one of the most ungainly aircraft ever built, thanks largely to its very low aspect-ratio wing set above a graceless fuselage, its angular tail surfaces, its obtrusive undercarriage and the location of its four engines as tandem pairs at the ends of the lower stub wings.

The origins of the F.121, also known as the F-3X, lay in the 1923 Grand Prix des Avions Transports, a competition designed to promote the development of safer civil transports. The F.121 was designed specifically for the competition, and carried off the first prize. Key to the F.121's safety was the use of a high-set wing of great area: this was of wooden construction and strut-braced, and a peculiarly massive unit. Spanning 19 m (62 ft 4 in), the wing had a root chord of no less than 6 m (19 ft 8¼ in) and a thickness of almost 76 cm (2 ft 6 in); the taper on both leading and trailing edges was curved, and most pronounced on the outboard third of the span; tip chord was 3 m (9 ft 10 in). The fuselage was similar to that of the Goliath, built of metal and wood, with a nose almost 3 m (9 ft 10 in) tall. In the nose was a cabin for two passengers, behind this a small compartment for a single occupant with the open cockpit for the two crew above it, and behind this the main cabin for six. Cooling for the two rear engines proved difficult, and only the installation of a pair of Lamblin radiators above each tandem set of engines allowed the F.121 into service during 1926.

These sustained cooling problems were probably the reason for the development in 1924 of two

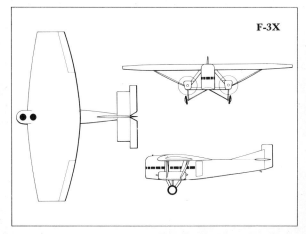

F-3X

variants: the F-4X with three 300-hp Salmson 9Az water-cooled radials (two on the stub wings and the third high on the nose) and the apparently undesignated model with two 400-hp Lorraine-Dietrich V-12s.

The Farman Line operated the first four F.121s, and this fleet was matched by that of Danish Air Lines (DDL), which ordered two from Farman and another two licence-built examples from Orlogsvaerftet.

From the F.121 type was developed the smaller F.170 Jabiru, which could carry up to eight passengers on the 500 hp of its single water-cooled Farman 12We. Production of this model totalled 13, while that of the marginally larger F.170*bis* for nine passengers reached four.

F.121 Jabiru

Type: medium-range transport
Maker: Avions H et M Farman; Orlogsvaerftet
Span: 19 m (62 ft 4 in)
Length: 13.68 m (44 ft 10½ in)
Height: not available
Wing area: 81 m² (872 sq ft)
Weight: maximum 5000 kg (11 023 lb); empty 3000 kg (6614 lb)
Powerplant: four 180-hp Hispano-Suiza 8Ac water-cooled V-8 engines
Performance: cruising speed 175 km/h (109 mph) at 2000 m (6562 ft); range 650 km (404 miles)
Payload: 880 kg (1940 lb); seats for up to 9 passengers
Crew: 1 to 2
Production: 9 (F-3X) and 4 (F-4X)

Below: A Farman Jabiru with three Gnome-Rhône Jupiter engines. It has French registration possibly for pre-export trials
Bottom: A four-engined Jabiru in service with the Danish airline DDL in the late 1920s

M.20, Messerschmitt

FIRST FLIGHT 1928

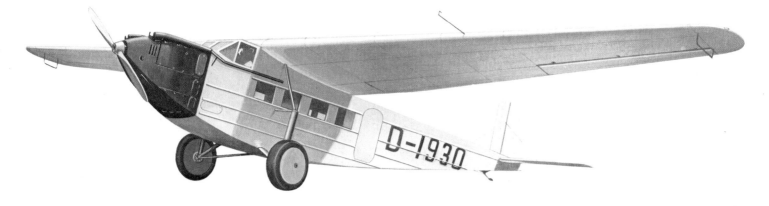

AN attractive aircraft apart from its angular engine cowling, the Messerschmitt M.20 was in basis a scaled-up development of the Messerschmitt M.18d, itself an eight-seat development of the basic three/four-seat M.18. The M.18 was designed in 1925, and in its prototype form, of which only a single example was built, was powered by the 80-hp Siemens und Halske Sh 11 radial. The production M.18a was built of wood and metal, rather than just wood.

The M.18d was the last model of the series with accommodation for éight passengers, an improved landing gear with a vertical shock absorber running up into the wing, and power provided by a variety of engines from the 150-hp Walter Mars to the 325-hp Wright Whirlwind radial. M.18d production reached at least eight.

The M.20 resembled the M.18d quite closely, but was chiefly of metal construction. Though the growth of the design is clear from the fact that span had increased from the M.18b's 15.6 m (51 ft 2¼ in) to the M.20's 25.5 m (83 ft 8 in), the most important factor in the scaling-up process was in power as the M.20 had a 500-hp BMW VIa V-12.

The first M.20 flew on February 26, 1928 and unfortunately crashed during this flight. Messerschmitt was hampered by financial problems and so the second aircraft did not fly until some five months later, when Deutsche Lufthansa were sufficiently impressed to order the whole production run of 13 aircraft.

The first two Lufthansa aircraft were described as M.20a aircraft, with raked-forward undercarriages and modified tail surfaces. The remaining 12 were operated under the designation M.20b, and had deeper fuselages, strut-braced tailplanes and rounded rather than square vertical tail surfaces.

The M.20 was introduced in 1929, initially on the routes from Stuttgart to Barcelona via Geneva and Marseilles, and from Basle to Amsterdam via Mannheim, Frankfurt, Köln and Essen. The type was also used as a freighter, and remained in scheduled service until 1937. Some of the aircraft were then used for seasonal operations between Germany's major cities and coastal resorts until the outbreak of World War II, and at the end of 1942 there were still an M.20a and an M.20b in Lufthansa service. The M.20b2, which appeared in 1932, was merely an M.20b re-engined with the 640-hp BMW VIu.

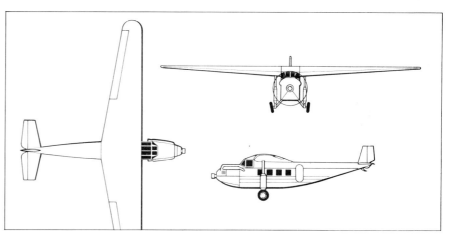

M.20b

Type: medium-range transport
Maker: Bayerische Flugzeugwerke GmbH
Span: 25.5 m (83 ft 8 in)
Length: 15.9 m (52 ft 2 in)
Height: 4.2 m (13 ft 9¼ in)
Wing area: 65 m² (700 sq ft)
Weight: maximum 5600 kg (10 141 lb); empty 2800 kg (6172 lb)
Powerplant: one 500-hp BMW VIa water-cooled V-12 engine
Performance: maximum speed 175 km/h (109 mph); range approx 1000 km (621 miles)
Payload: 1500 kg (3307 lb); seats for up to 10 passengers
Crew: 2
Production: 14

Top: A Lufthansa Messerschmitt M.20 with a 500-hp BMW VIa engine
Above left: The interior of an M.20 showing some of the ten seats
Left: The M.20b D-2005 *Odenwald*, one of 12 aircraft which operated with Lufthansa from 1929 to 1942. They were used on holiday routes in the mid 1930s

Komet, Dornier

FIRST FLIGHT 1921

THE Dornier Do C III Komet was the land-plane equivalent of the Cs II Delphin transport flying boat of 1920, and first flew in 1921. The conversion of the basic design to land-plane configuration entailed the removal of the planing hull, which allowed the engine to be located at the top of the upswept nose rather than in the ugly upward extension of the Delphin's nose. The undercarriage main unit consisted of a pair of single wheels carried on short stub legs projecting almost horizontally from the lower fuselage, thus keeping the lower fuselage within inches of the ground.

The passenger cabin was located in the deepest portion of the fuselage, under the strut-braced high-set monoplane wing, and contained two seats facing forward, and another pair facing aft. The pilot's cockpit, of the conventional open type, was normally located ahead of the wing, but at least one instance is known of its location behind the wing. The powerplant consisted of a single 185-hp BMW IIIa, though this engine's altitude performance was in contravention of the limitations placed on German aircraft, and was occasionally replaced by a 180-hp BMW III. One important feature of the Komet I was its very large wing which had a constant chord of 3 m (9 ft 10 in) representing one-third of the aircraft's overall length.

The Soviet Union bought one Komet and the Swiss operator Ad Astra Aero employed two such aircraft, but most of the limited production total, the number of which is uncertain, were used by Deutsche Luft-Reederei. When Deutsche Luft-Reederei became part of Deutscher Aero Lloyd in

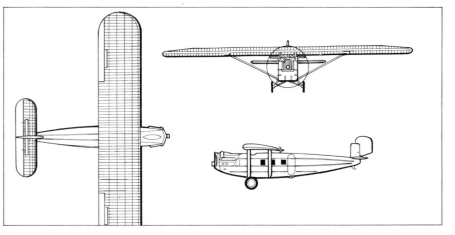

March 1924, the Komets passed to this new owner, and similarly to Deutsche Lufthansa in 1926.

Deutsche Lufthansa's two Komets were supplemented by a single Komet II. This variant first appeared in 1922, and was powered by the 250-hp BMW IV. A year later another type, with the same designation, appeared with the 260-hp Rolls-Royce Falcon. The Falcon-engined Komet II was used in Colombia, Spain, the Ukraine and the USSR. Deutsche Lufthansa's Komets were subsequently upgraded to Komet II standard, remaining in service until 1928 on scheduled services, and until 1930 for excursion and charter work. The Komet III first flew in December 1924 and, despite its name, was in fact the land-plane equivalent of the Delphin III flying boat.

Do C III Komet II

Type: short-range transport
Maker: Zeppelinwerk Dornier Lindau GmbH
Span: 17 m (55 ft 9¼ in)
Length: 10.3 m (33 ft 9½ in)
Height: not available
Wing area: 50 m² (538 sq ft)
Weight: maximum 2200 kg (4850 lb); empty 1500 kg (3307 lb)
Powerplant: one 250-hp BMW IV 6-cylinder inline water-cooled engine
Performance: cruising speed 135 km/h (84 mph) at sea level; range approx 500 km (311 miles)
Payload: seats for up to 4 passengers
Crew: 1
Production: not available

Top: The Komet III fitted with a four-blade propeller
Far left: A Komet I is readied for a flight from Berlin to London. At the time, this aircraft was described as being 'as luxurious as an American parlor car', an especially comfortable railway coach
Left: A Komet II about to touch down

Merkur, Dornier

FIRST FLIGHT 1925

IN December 1924 Dornier had flown its Komet III light transport as the land-plane equivalent of the Delphin III flying boat. With accommodation for six passengers, a crew of one or two, and the possibility of using any one of several engines (it was at first offered with the 360-hp Rolls-Royce Eagle IX, 400-hp Liberty 12, or 450-hp Napier Lion), it was immediately attractive to airlines. Like the earlier Komet and Komet II, it had a large wing without taper in thickness or chord, which ensured a low landing speed, and was immensely strong as its structure was of steel and duralumin. Several European airlines bought the Komet III, and the type was also built under licence in Japan by Kawasaki.

Then on February 10, 1925 Dornier flew the first Merkur: powered by the 600-hp BMW VI, and having a span of 19.6 m (64 ft 3½ in) compared with the Komet III's 19 m (62 ft 4 in), the Do B Merkur was virtually indistinguishable from the Komet III. The position was exacerbated when Komet IIIs were later re-engined first with the 450-hp BMW IV and later with the 600-hp BMW VI inlines and then redesignated Merkur.

The largest single user of the Komet III and Merkur was Deutsche Lufthansa, which had some 36 of the two types, with at least seven of them conversions of the Komet III into Merkur. Of the Deutsche Lufthansa aircraft, about 22 were used on the night service part of the Berlin to Moscow route, running between Berlin and Königsberg. Deruluft, the Russo-German operator, used at least nine of the type, all ex-Deutsche Lufthansa aircraft, in the Moscow area.

Perhaps the most significant single flight made by the type was one of some 100 air hours from Zürich to Cape Town between December 7, 1926 and February 21, 1927, by a Swiss Merkur. Flown by Walter Mittelholzer and carrying two passengers, the aircraft was fitted with twin floats for the flight. Float-equipped Merkurs were also popular in South America.

The two final versions of the design were the Do B Bal, with greater take-off weight, and the Do B Bal 2 up-engined model with the 640-hp BMW VIu. This latter had a maximum take-off weight of 4100 kg (9039 lb) and a cruising speed of 193 km/h (118 mph), thus trading increased payload against slightly reduced cruising speed compared with the basic Merkur.

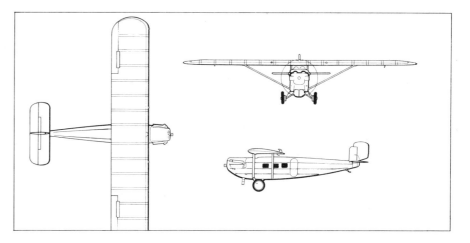

Do B Merkur

Type: medium-range transport
Maker: Dornier Werke GmbH; Kawasaki
Span: 19.6 m (64 ft 3½ in)
Length: 12.5 m (41 ft)
Height: not available
Wing area: 62 m² (667 sq ft)
Weight: maximum 3600 kg (7936 lb); empty 2100 kg (4629 lb)
Powerplant: one 600-hp BMW VI water-cooled V-12 engine
Performance: cruising speed 180 km/h (112 mph); range not available
Payload: seats for up to 6 passengers
Crew: 1 to 2
Production: 70

Above left: A float-equipped Merkur, almost indistinguishable from the Dornier Komet III
Left: An up-engined Merkur with a four-blade propeller
Below: A Merkur in the livery of Deruluft. This Russo-German airline began a Berlin-Königsberg-Riga-Moscow service using Merkurs in July 1927

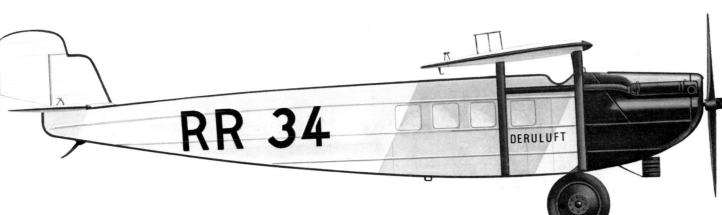

W34, Junkers

THE family relationship of the Junkers W33 and W34, both of which appeared in 1926, with the classic F13 of 1919 is attested by the fact that the two later aircraft were built on the F13 production line, using the same jigs. The span of all three aircraft was the same, at 17.75 m (58 ft 2¾ in).

The W33 and W34 were basically the same aircraft with the exception of the engines, the former being powered by the Junkers L 5 inline, rated at 310 hp; and the latter initially by the Gnome-Rhône Jupiter VI radial, rated at 420 hp. Later powerplants included the 540-hp Siemens Sh 20 (Jupiter) and the 600-hp BMW Hornet.

The first W33 was produced by modifying an F13, the type it was designed to supplement with a greater load-carrying capability, thanks mainly to the use of a more powerful engine. The fuselage was aerodynamically superior to that of the F13, being slightly longer and lacking the marked dorsal hump of the F13. Early models of both the W33 and W34 had an open cockpit and lacked any windows in the fuselage, but later models had a window in the fuselage, and examples intended for passenger operations had additional windows.

It was the W34 that was almost invariably used for passenger operations. Both types could carry six passengers, however, or an alternative load in the cabin, which had a volume of 4.8 m³ (169 cu ft).

Both models could be operated as ski-planes or twin-float seaplanes, the fitting of the floats adding some 30 cm (11⅘ in) to the 10.5 m (34 ft 5½ in) length of the W33, and 73 cm (2 ft 4¾ in) to the 10.27 m (33 ft 8¼ in) of the W34. Production of the W33 was in some 30 versions, while the W34 was produced in more than 70 variants.

Both types made some great flights. The W33 in particular is notable for a world endurance record of 52 hours 23 min on August 3–5, 1927 and the first non-stop crossing of the North Atlantic from east to west in 37 hours on April 12–13, 1928 between Baldonnel near Dublin in Ireland to Greenly Island off Labrador.

The W33 and W34 played a key part in consolidating the efforts of the F13 in opening up air transport in remote areas of the world, such as South America's less accessible regions. Production of the W34 ended in Germany during 1934 but over 900 served with the Luftwaffe and Luftdienst during World War II and the last operational W34 was retired in September 1962.

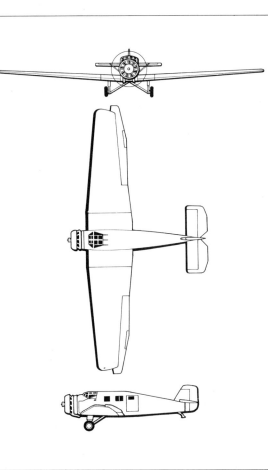

Top: A Junkers W34 floatplane. One such aircraft in Canada made its last flight in 1962 and because of this remarkable service period was placed in a museum
Above: One of the W34s operated by Lufthansa in the late 1930s

W34he

Type: medium-range transport
Maker: Junkers Flugzeugwerke AG
Span: 18.48 m (60 ft 7½ in)
Length: 10.27 m (33 ft 8¼ in)
Height: 3.58 m (11 ft 7 in)
Wing area: 44 m² (474 sq ft)
Weight: maximum 3200 kg (7055 lb); empty 1700 kg (3748 lb)
Powerplant: one 660-hp BMW 132A 9-cylinder air-cooled radial engine
Performance: cruising speed 233 km/h (145 mph); range 900 km (559 miles)
Payload: 4.8 m³ (169 cu ft); seats for 6 passengers
Crew: 2
Production: 1791 (W34)

S36, Junkers

FIRST FLIGHT 1927

THE Junkers S36 was produced ostensibly as a mailplane, but was merely a subterfuge for the development of the military aircraft which the 1919 Treaty of Versailles had forbidden Germany to build. The most difficult task faced by the German planners was the building of the flying hardware into which weapons, provided especially by the Soviet Union and Sweden among other countries, could later be added. The restrictions on Germany's aircraft production were lifted somewhat in 1926, and this helped the country to develop military aircraft at home and abroad, the latter by means of subsidiary companies closely controlled by the parent organizations in Germany.

It was this political and economic situation which led, therefore, to the development of the S36 'mailplane' (S standing for *Spezial* or special, in much the same way as other Junkers aircraft were designated by numbers prefixed by a letter, F standing for *Flugzeug* or aircraft, G for *Grossflugzeug* or large aircraft, and W for *Wasserflugzeug* or seaplane).

Designed in 1926, the S36 appeared in 1927, and it is hard to see how the charade of the type as a mailplane could have been entertained with any seriousness. With its three open cockpits along the upper surface of the typically Junkers fuselage, the S36 was clearly a military aircraft, the nose and dorsal cockpits obviously being unsuitable for any purpose other than as gunner's positions. After early flight trials the aircraft reappeared as the prototype K37 light bomber (K standing for *Kampfflugzeug* or combat aircraft). In this form the S36 had been updated with more extensive glazing and modified vertical tail surfaces. Another such aircraft was built by the Junkers subsidiary in Sweden, A B Flygindustri, and both machines were exhaustively tested in their military role at the Germany facility at Lipetsk in the Soviet Union. In 1933 the first K37 was handed over to the German air force as a bomber trainer, being revised for this role with an enclosed pilot's cockpit in an upper fuselage of more pronounced hump.

The Swedish-built model was sold to Japan, which produced an up-engined bomber variant in three forms: the Kawasaki Ki-1, the Mitsubishi Ki-2-I and the Mitsubishi Ki-2-II. Production in Japan reached 174 examples. Technically, the S36 is of interest as the first Junkers type with a retractable undercarriage.

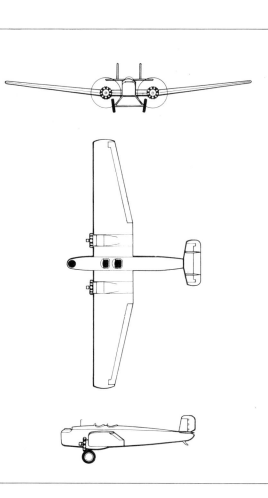

S36

Type: mailplane
Maker: Junkers Flugzeugwerke A G; A B Flygindustri
Span: 21.35 m (70 ft 0½ in)
Length: 11.45 m (37 ft 7 in)
Height: 4.5 m (14 ft 9 in)
Wing area: 54.25 m² (584 sq ft)
Weight: maximum 4300 kg (9480 lb); empty 2570 kg (5666 lb)
Powerplant: two 480-hp Bristol Jupiter 9-cylinder air-cooled radial engines
Performance: maximum speed 245 km/h (152 mph); range 950 km (590 miles)
Payload: 500 kg (1102 lb)
Crew: 2 to 6
Production: 2

Below: The Junkers S36 D-1252 which was eventually transferred to the Luftwaffe for bomber training in 1933 Bottom: The S36 as a mailplane. With its open cockpits and typical Junkers fuselage, it looks every inch a military aircraft

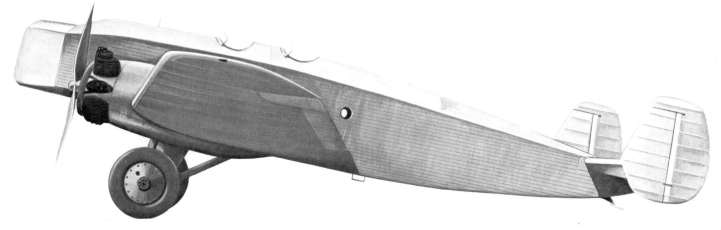

Argosy, Armstrong Whitworth

FIRST FLIGHT 1926

THE Argosy was the first civil aircraft designed by Armstrong Whitworth, and was produced in response to an Imperial Airways requirement for a multi-engined airliner. Formed in April 1924, Imperial Airways had inherited from its predecessor airlines a number of single-engined types with relatively poor safety records. This safety record, coupled with the need of the new airline to operate routes over inhospitable terrain, led Imperial Airways to revive a 1922 requirement for a 'Middle Eastern' airliner able to fly 805 km (500 miles) against a 48-km/h (30-mph) headwind. Issued in 1925, this requirement led to the Argosy, which Imperial Airways considered suitable for its European routes and so ordered two examples, a third being ordered by the Air Ministry.

As it appeared at the time of its first flight on March 16, 1926, the initial Argosy reflected the degree to which British airliner design had fallen behind that of European countries. The three 385-hp Armstrong Siddeley Jaguar III direct-drive radials were uncowled, the fuselage was a blocky structure of steel tube covered with fabric, the large biplane wings were, with the exception of the centre section, built of wood and covered with fabric, and the empennage consisted of biplane horizontal and triple vertical surfaces. The contrast with contemporaries such as the Junkers W33 and Fokker F.VIIa/3m is most revealing.

Nevertheless, Imperial Airways did not have to compete in economic terms with European airlines, and the Argosy was just what was needed, with its high safety factor and capacity for 20 passengers. The first three aircraft, later designated Argosy Mk Is, entered service in August and September 1926 and March 1927, and proved very popular. With passenger capacity reduced to 18, there was room for a bar at the rear of the cabin, to run which a steward was carried. The type's success is reflected in the fact that before the Argosy entered service, Imperial Airways had carried only 40% more passengers than its French rival on the prestige route between London and Paris, this figure rising to 100% after the type's introduction. Ton-mile costs were also only two-thirds of those of the Handley Page W/10 and two-fifths of those of de Havilland DH.34.

In 1928 Imperial Airways ordered another three Argosys, this figure soon being raised to four. The aircraft were delivered in May, June, July and August 1929, and were of the improved Argosy Mk II type, with more powerful Jaguar IVA geared engines in Townend ring cowlings, Handley Page leading-edge slats on the upper wings to improve low-speed handling, increased fuel capacity, maximum passenger capacity of 28, and servo-operated ailerons. The Townend rings were removed in service, but nonetheless the Argosy Mk II could operate at higher weights than its predecessor, and had 306 km (190 miles) more range making a total of 837 km (520 miles).

The Argosy Mk I aircraft were re-engined with Jaguar IVA radials, with the intention that they be used for Middle Eastern mail routes. Three Argosys crashed, and the others were scrapped in 1935 and 1936.

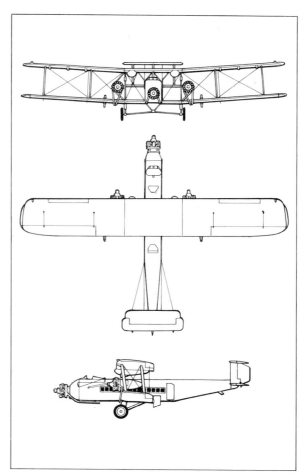

Argosy Mk II

Type: medium-range transport
Maker: Armstrong Whitworth Aircraft Ltd
Span: 27.53 m (90 ft 4 in)
Length: 20.42 m (67 ft)
Height: 6.1 m (20 ft)
Wing area: 174.01 m² (1873 sq ft)
Weight: maximum 8709 kg (19 200 lb); empty 5484 kg (12 090 lb)
Powerplant: three 410-hp Armstrong Siddeley Jaguar IVA 14-cylinder air-cooled radial engines
Performance: cruising speed 153 km/h (95 mph); range 837 km (520 miles)
Payload: 2268 kg (5000 lb); seats for up to 28 passengers
Crew: 2
Production: 4

DH.66 Hercules, de Havilland

FIRST FLIGHT 1926

THE de Havilland DH.66 Hercules was designed at about the same time as the Armstrong Whitworth Argosy, and displayed many similarities to the other machine in basic configuration, though the general impression left by the de Havilland aircraft was of a much lighter and more graceful design than that of the Armstrong Whitworth. The origins of the DH.66 lay in the Air Ministry's 1925 agreement to pay Imperial Airways a subsidy of £500 000 per year to take over the Royal Air Force's mail route from Cairo in Egypt to Karachi in India. Imperial Airways thus issued a requirement for a multi-engined aircraft suitable for this task of fortnightly freight, mail and passenger flights across inhospitable territory.

De Havilland's reply was the DH.66: a large biplane powered by three 420-hp Bristol Jupiter VI radials, with wings of wooden construction and a fuselage built of steel tube, containing two large plywood boxes. The forward of the two contained seats for seven passengers, the radio operator and his equipment, and stowage for 13.2 m³ (465 cu ft) of mail; the rear comprised 4.4 m³ (155 cu ft) of baggage volume. The design appeared eminently suitable, and five of the type were ordered, the first flying on September 30, 1926. The new aircraft was named Hercules, and in December 1926 it set off for Cairo where the eastbound service was inaugurated on January 12, 1927.

Up to 1929 the air-mail service operated only between Cairo and Basra at the head of the Persian Gulf, but in April of that year it was extended to Karachi, and to Jodhpur and Delhi later in 1929.

In 1928 West Australian Airways had been awarded the mail and passenger route between Perth and Adelaide. The airline not unnaturally selected the DH.66 as its prime aircraft, and ordered four modified examples with an enclosed pilot's cockpit, accommodation for 14 passengers and a reduced mail load. The first aircraft was ready in March 1929 and entered service in Australia on June 2, 1929.

West Australian Airways' fourth DH.66 was sold to Imperial Airways in July 1930 to help make up for operational attrition. Imperial Airways had already ordered two more DH.66s, but the combination of increased demand and the loss of two aircraft necessitated Imperial Airways' approach to West Australian Airways.

A third DH.66 was lost on April 19, 1931 near Kupang (formerly Koepang) on the island of Timor while on the first experimental mail flight linking Croydon with Melbourne (the mail was rescued and flown to its destination by Charles Kingsford Smith in his celebrated Fokker tri-motor *Southern Cross*). A second Australian aircraft was sold to Imperial Airways in 1931, the British airline being short of aircraft with the opening of its route to Cape Town from Croydon. The DH.66s soldiered on in British service until 1935, when another crashed. Two were then scrapped, and the other three sold to the South African air force. The two Australian DH.66s were sold to Stephens Aviation of New Guinea in 1936 to operate a ferry service between Lae and Wau. One crashed and the other was destroyed by the Japanese.

DH.66

Type: medium-range passenger and freight transport
Maker: de Havilland Aircraft Co Ltd
Span: 24.23 m (79 ft 6 in)
Length: 16.92 m (55 ft 6 in)
Height: 5.56 m (18 it 3 in)
Wing area: 143.72 m² (1547 sq ft)
Weight: maximum 7103 kg (15 660 lb); empty 4110 kg (9060 lb)
Powerplant: three 420-hp Bristol Jupiter VI 9-cylinder air-cooled radial engines
Performance: cruising speed 177 km/h (110 mph); range not available
Payload: 13.12 m³ (465 cu ft); seats for up to 14 passengers and reduced mail
Crew: 3
Production: 11

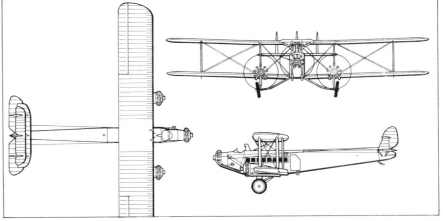

Top: The massive 5.56-m (18 ft 3-in) biplane tail unit of the DH.66 Hercules. The name Hercules was chosen in a competition run by *Meccano Magazine* in 1926 and was won by EF Hope-Jones of Eton College
Left: The DH.66 Hercules *City of Cairo* which crashed near Koepang, Timor on April 19, 1931

G31, Junkers
FIRST FLIGHT 1926

THE Junkers G31 appeared in 1926 as a larger and heavier counterpart to the G24 of 1925, itself a development of the G23 of 1924. Both of these tri-motors were of typical Junkers concept and construction, available as float seaplanes, and both of importance in the development of air transport during the 1920s and early 1930s.

Although basically similar to the G23 and G24, the G31 had twin vertical tail surfaces (later connected by an upper tailplane), and accommodation for 15 passengers in place of the nine carried in the two earlier aircraft. The first G31 retained an open cockpit, and power was provided by a trio of 310-hp Junkers L 5 inline engines. During 1927 these were replaced by 450-hp Gnome-Rhône (Bristol) Jupiter radials, and it was to be radials which powered the production G31s, either the Jupiter (usually licence-built by Siemens) or the Pratt & Whitney Hornet (usually licence-built by BMW) being used.

With extra fuselage length available, Junkers were able to provide compartmentalized seating. In the front cabin were five seats, three facing forward and the other two aft; in the centre cabin were six seats, with two facing pairs on the right side and two facing single seats to the left of the aisle and in the rear cabin were the entrance door on the left and two facing pairs of seats on the right. This basic seating plan could be converted to five sleeper berths, and another five berths could be lowered from the cabin walls for an upper tier.

European customers for the G31 were Deutsche Lufthansa, which operated nine, and Österreichische Luftverkehr with one. Deutsche Lufthansa operated the aircraft between 1928 and 1936; the first route was from Berlin to London.

The last three G31s were ordered by the Bulolo Gold Dredging company (two aircraft for use in New Guinea) and Guinea Airways. These aircraft were all specially modified for operations in the heavy freight role in New Guinea, a role they fulfilled most ably until World War II. As with the passenger G31s, these three aircraft were some 1 m (3 ft 3⅖ in) longer than the prototype, and had a cargo hold measuring 7.3 m (23 ft 11½ in) in length, 1.95 m (6 ft 4¾ in) in width and 1.75 m (5 ft 9 in) in height; loading was effected through a dorsal hatch 3.6 m (11 ft 9¾ in) in length and 1.52 m (5 ft) wide. The fact that this hatch had a domed cover added 300 mm (11⅘ in) to the height of the hold.

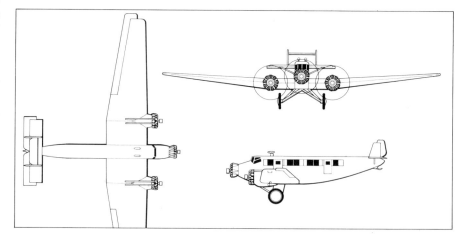

Above: A Junkers G31 ordered by the Bulolo Gold Dredging company in New Guinea. The aircraft could be loaded through a dorsal hatch
Left: Engine overhaul for a G31 at the Lufthansa maintenance centre at Berlin-Staaken airport
Bottom: The interior of a G31 showing seats and sleeping berths

G31fo

Type: medium-range transport
Maker: Junkers Flugzeugwerke AG
Span: 30.3 m (99 ft 5 in)
Length: 17.28 m (56 ft 8¼ in)
Height: not available
Wing area: 102 m² (1098 sq ft)
Weight: maximum 8500 kg (18 739 lb); empty 5000 kg (11 023 lb)
Powerplant: three 525-hp BMW Hornet 9-cylinder air-cooled radial engines
Performance: cruising speed 170 km/h (106 mph); range with a 1005-kg (2216-lb) payload 1000 km (621 miles)
Payload: 2500 kg (5511 lb); seats for up to 15 passengers
Crew: 3
Production: 13

Romar, Rohrbach

FIRST FLIGHT 1928

THE Rohrbach Romar (Rohrbach Marine) was developed in 1927 as a three-engined flying boat to give Deutsche Lufthansa a transatlantic capability. The main design parameters of the Romar, which succeeded the unsuccessful Rocco flying boat, were a payload of 1100 kg (2425 lb) to be carried over a range of 4000 km (2486 miles).

The first Romar flew on August 7, 1928, and displayed the extremely advanced design and construction philosophy typical of Rohrbach. The high-set wing was an all-metal cantilever structure based on a wide-chord box spar, the leading- and trailing-edge sections being bolted to this spar to make the whole wing watertight. Of considerable root depth, the wing had pronounced taper in both thickness and chord. The deep duralumin-covered fuselage had a single-step planing bottom of sharp V shape. In the fashion of contemporary flying boats, the Romar's three 500-hp BMW VI inline engines were located on pylons above the wing and drove pusher propellers. The central engine was placed farther forward than the two flanking units.

In the nose of the hull was the compartment for the navigator and radio operator; behind this was the enclosed pilot's cockpit and engineer's station; in the centre of the hull was the passenger accommodation, consisting of eight- and four-seat compartments separated by the lavatory.

The first two Romars were delivered to Deutsche Lufthansa in 1929, but were found to be unsuitable for open-ocean operations. They were therefore used for services in the Baltic, with their base at Travemünde. The two Romars were followed into service by the sole civil Romar II, which was powered by three 750-hp BMW VIuz V-12s: this allowed a maximum take-off weight some 1200 kg (2646 lb) greater than the Romars' 18 500 kg (40 785 lb), and improved cruising speed very marginally. The greatest improvements of the Romar II compared with the Romars, however, were an increase in passenger capacity from 12 to 16 (and at times to 20), and an increase in range of 2350 km (1460 miles). The generally poor type was withdrawn from airline service in 1933.

The fourth boat of the Romar type was a military version of the Romar II delivered to the French navy as part of Germany's war reparations.

The main significance of the Romar was its extremely advanced structure, similar to that of aircraft 15 years later.

Left: Military visitors examine a Rohrbach Romar at Tempelhof airfield Berlin
Bottom: The Romar in service with Lufthansa in 1929 at their Baltic base at Travemünde

Romar II

Type: long-range transport flying boat
Maker: Rohrbach-Metall-Flugzeugbau GmbH
Span: 36.9 m (121 ft 1 in)
Length: 22 m (72 ft 2 in)
Height: not available
Wing area: 170 m² (1830 sq ft)
Weight: maximum 19 700 kg (43 431 lb); empty 11 625 kg (25 628 lb)
Powerplant: three 750-hp BMW VIuz water-cooled V-12 engines
Performance: cruising speed 178 km/h (111 mph); range 4350 km (2700 miles)
Payload: 1080 kg (2380 lb); seats for up to 20 passengers
Crew: 4
Production: 2 (Romar), 1 (Romar II)

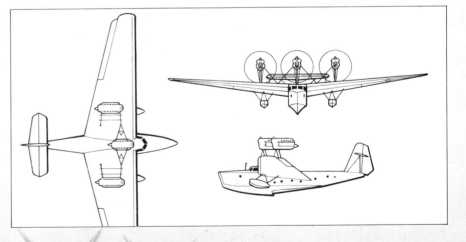

Tri-Motor, Ford

FIRST FLIGHT 1926

AMONG the classic airliners of the 1920s and early 1930s the great Ford Tri-Motors (Models 4-AT and 5-AT) must inevitably have an important place. The type served for more than 40 years as an effective transport, at first with the big US airlines and then with gradually more remote operators in less accessible parts of the world.

In August 1925 Stout Metal was bought by the Ford Motor Company. Stout accordingly set about developing a three-engined version of his 2-AT mailplane as the 3-AT. However, after a row, Stout's dismissal, and a drastic design revision there emerged for its first flight on June 11, 1926 the Ford 4-AT, at the time the largest civil aircraft produced in the United States. Powered by three 200-hp Wright Whirlwind J4 radials, the initial 4-AT set the pattern for later examples.

The initial 4-AT-A, of which 14 were built, was closely similar, with accommodation for two crew in the open cockpit, and up to eight passengers in an enclosed cabin. The type was an immediate success, entering service with the Ford Motor air service on August 2, 1926.

In 1927 there appeared the 4-AT-B with 220-hp Whirlwind J5 radials, accommodation for 12 passengers, span increased from 22.53 m (73 ft 11 in) to 22.56 m (74 ft), and increased operating weights. Production of the model reached 35, and the single 4-AT-C was identical with the exception that the nose engine was a 400-hp Pratt & Whitney Wasp. The three 4-AT-Ds were all different: one had three 200-hp Whirlwind J4s and features of the 5-AT-A's wing; the second had two 220-hp Whirlwind J5s and one 300-hp Whirlwind J6-9, enabling the type to carry 15 passengers; and the third had three 300-hp Whirlwind J6 radials. There followed 24 4-AT-Es, with three 300-hp Whirlwind J6s and detail improvements. The single 4-AT-F was almost identical.

Already in production was the 4-AT's main variant, the 5-AT: this had a wing spanning 23.72 m (77 ft 10 in), an enlarged cabin for 13 passengers, and power increased by the fitting of three 420-hp Pratt & Whitney Wasp radials. Only three of this type, the 5-AT-A, were built in 1928 before production switched in 1929 to the 5-AT-B with seating for 15 and three 420-hp Wasp C-1 or SC-1 radials (42 produced). This was followed by the 5-AT-C with seating for 17 (48 produced), and finally by the 5-AT-D with increased weights and three 450-hp Wasps (24 produced).

This covers only the main variants of the type, which was used with wheel, ski, or float undercarriages and fitted with a considerable variety of engines. They were used for purposes as diverse as passenger carrying, freighting, exploration, crop-spraying, fire-fighting, aerial tanker, advertising, and paratrooping. Later variants included the 6-AT-A, 7-AT-A, 9-AT, 11-AT, 12-A, 13-A and 14-A civil models, plus a number of military derivatives. The only other civil model produced in quantities of more than one was the 6-AT, of which four were produced with 300-hp Whirlwind J6 radials instead of the Wasps of the 5-AT-C from which the model was derived. Development ended in 1932; however examples are still in service in the United States and South America.

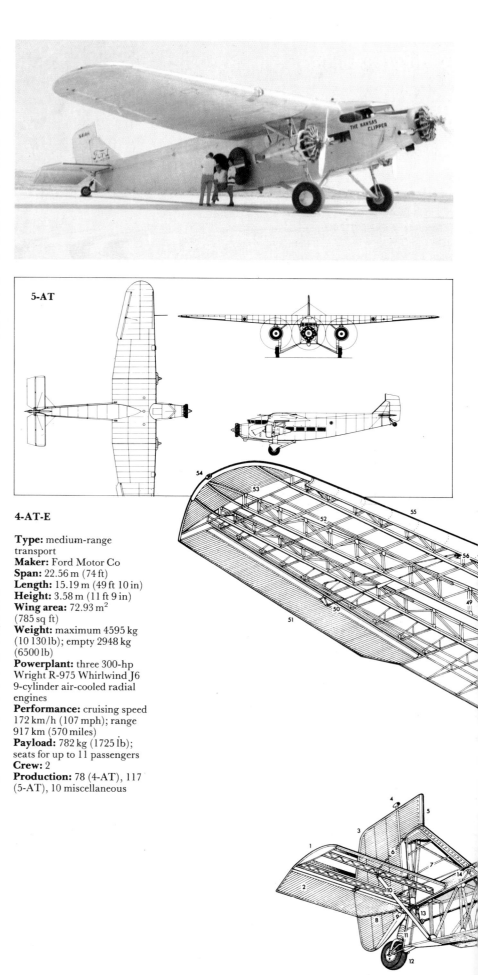

5-AT

4-AT-E

Type: medium-range transport
Maker: Ford Motor Co
Span: 22.56 m (74 ft)
Length: 15.19 m (49 ft 10 in)
Height: 3.58 m (11 ft 9 in)
Wing area: 72.93 m² (785 sq ft)
Weight: maximum 4595 kg (10 130 lb); empty 2948 kg (6500 lb)
Powerplant: three 300-hp Wright R-975 Whirlwind J6 9-cylinder air-cooled radial engines
Performance: cruising speed 172 km/h (107 mph); range 917 km (570 miles)
Payload: 782 kg (1725 lb); seats for up to 11 passengers
Crew: 2
Production: 78 (4-AT), 117 (5-AT), 10 miscellaneous

5-AT-D

1 Right tailplane
2 Right elevator
3 Rudder
4 Tail navigation light
5 Rudder horn balance
6 Tailplane bracing wire
7 Tailfin
8 Corrugated tailplane skins
9 Elevator hinge control
10 Tailplane bracing strut
11 Tailwheel shock absorber
12 Tailwheel
13 Tailplane incidence screw jack
14 Fin attachment
15 Rear fuselage construction
16 Left elevator
17 Left tailplane
18 Incidence control shaft
19 Fuselage top decking
20 Corrugated fuselage skins
21 Tail control cable pulleys
22 Flare dispenser
23 Wash basin

24 Step
25 Cabin door
26 Toilet compartment
27 Fire extinguisher
28 Rear cabin seating
29 Cabin roof luggage racks
30 Cabin windows
31 Fuselage strut bracing construction
32 Bottom longeron
33 Right mainwheel
34 Shock absorber leg strut
35 Right Pratt & Whitney Wasp engine
36 Two-bladed propeller
37 NACA cowling ring
38 Engine cooling air shutters
39 Engine mounting framework
40 Oil tank
41 Exhaust pipe
42 Engine cowling fairing
43 Engine pylon struts
44 Centre wing panel
45 Wing corrugated skins
46 Spar attachment joints
47 Drop-down mail and baggage lockers

48 Outer wing panel spars
49 Wing spar strut bracing
50 Aileron hinge control
51 Right aileron
52 Wing rib bracing
53 Wingtip construction
54 Right navigation light
55 Reinforced leading edge
56 Aileron cable pulley
57 Landing and taxi lamp
58 Corrugated leading-edge skin
59 Outer wing panel attachment rib
60 Fuel tanks
61 Cabin roof fairing
62 Fuselage main frame
63 Passenger seats
64 Right undercarriage swing axle
65 Cabin floor
66 Cabin heater duct fairing
67 Centre engine exhaust pipe
68 Air vents
69 Battery
70 External control cables
71 Co-pilot's seat
72 Cockpit side windows

73 Instrument panel
74 Control column hand-wheel
75 Cockpit roof windows
76 Sliding windscreen panel
77 Windscreen frame
78 Centre engine fairing air louvres
79 Oil tank
80 Centre engine mounting framework
81 Rudder pedals
82 Exhaust collector ring
83 Centre Pratt & Whitney Wasp radial engine
84 Engine cooling air shutters
85 Two-bladed propeller
86 Left Pratt & Whitney Wasp engine
87 NACA cowling ring
88 Engine pylon fairing
89 Left landing and taxi lamp
90 Reinforced leading edge
91 Instrument pitot head
92 Left wing tip
93 Left navigation light
94 Outer wing panel construction
95 Aileron hinge control

Above left: The preserved 5-AT-C Ford Tri-Motor *Kansas Clipper*
Above: One of the 11 Tri-Motors operated by TAT in the USA. The Tri-Motor was known affectionately as the 'Tin Lizzie' or 'Tin Goose'. It survived nearly 40 years of service and some very rough handling

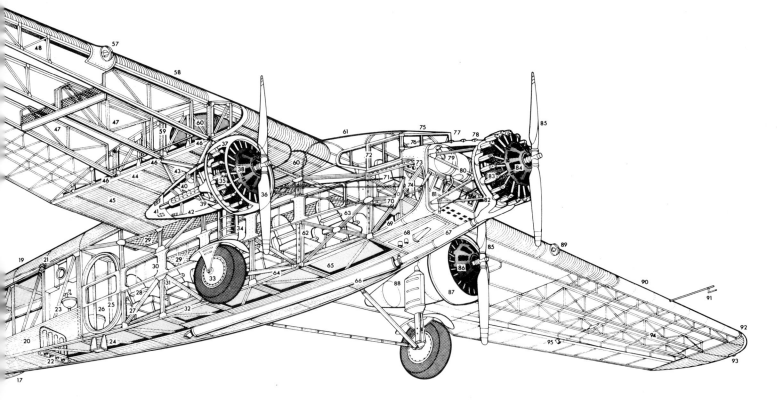

Vega, Lockheed
FIRST FLIGHT 1927

A NEAR contemporary of the Ford 4-AT Tri-Motor, the Lockheed Vega of 1927 was an entirely different aircraft with, at the same time, features markedly in advance or in arrears of the 4-AT. For whereas the Ford aircraft had the advanced features of a multi-engine powerplant and all-metal construction, the graceful Vega marked the limits of wooden design and single-engined performance, but was better streamlined than almost all contemporary aircraft.

It was produced in six months and for minimal cost; it first flew on July 4, 1927, and was bought as a racing aircraft. Despite its loss in a race from California to Hawaii, the type clearly met the requirements of smaller airlines: with four passengers and a pilot, the Vega Model 1 could reach 217 km/h (135 mph) on the 220 hp of its Wright Whirlwind J5. Some 28 Vega 1s were built, and it has been estimated that the seat-mile costs of the Vega and 4-AT were almost the same, despite the Vega's smaller capacity, thanks to its greater speed and economy.

The Vega entered airline service in September 1928, and was soon joined by the improved Vega Model 5, of which 35 were built and another seven converted from other models. The Vega Model 5 was dimensionally identical to its predecessor, but was powered by the 450-hp Pratt & Whitney Wasp B, giving a maximum speed of 266 km/h (165 mph) compared with the Ford 5-AT-C's 217 km/h (135 mph). Five Vega Model 5s were fitted as floatplanes, two were converted into six-seaters for Pan American, and nine were produced as Vega Model 5As for employment in the executive role.

Next to appear, paradoxically, was the Vega Model 2, a five-seater powered by the 300-hp Whirlwind J6. Five of this model were built, while a sixth was converted from a Vega Model 1. Only one Vega Model 2A, with accommodation for six passengers, was built. The most celebrated mark was the Vega Model 5B, however: with passenger seating for six and power provided by the 450-hp Wasp C, this model reached a production total of 29, while three landplane and two floatplane conversions from earlier models were made.

Six Vega Model 5Cs were built, and another 27 were converted to this standard. The only other variant was the Detroit Aircraft Corporation DL-1, which was a Vega with a duralumin fuselage.

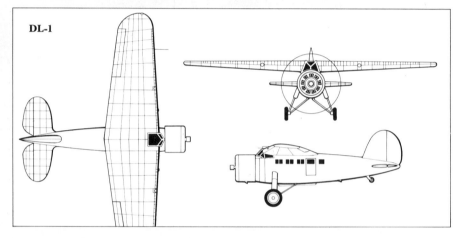

DL-1

Vega Model 5

Type: light transport
Maker: Lockheed Aircraft Corporation
Span: 12.5 m (41 ft)
Length: 8.38 m (27 ft 6 in)
Height: 3.73 m (12 ft 3 in)
Wing area: 25.55 m² (275 sq ft)
Weight: maximum 1829 kg (4033 lb); empty 1130 kg (2492 lb)
Powerplant: one 450-hp Pratt & Whitney Wasp B 9-cylinder air-cooled radial engine
Performance: maximum speed 266 km/h (165 mph); range approx 1127 km (700 miles)
Payload: seats for up to 4 passengers
Crew: 1
Production: 128 (all models)

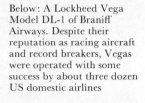

Express, Lockheed

FIRST FLIGHT 1928

Left: The Lockheed Air Express was primarily a mail carrier and was a similar aircraft to the Lockheed Vega

Air Express

Type: mail and passenger transport
Maker: Lockheed Aircraft Corporation
Span: 12.95 m (42 ft 6 in)
Length: 8.38 m (27 ft 6 in)
Height: 2.55 m (8 ft 4½ in)
Wing area: 20.25 m² (288 sq ft)
Weight: maximum 1984 kg (4375 lb); empty 1149 kg (2533 lb)
Powerplant: one 450-hp Pratt & Whitney R-1340 Wasp 9-cylinder air-cooled radial engine
Performance: maximum speed 269 km/h (167 mph); range not available
Payload: 454 kg (1000 lb); seats for up to 6 passengers
Crew: 1
Production: 8

ALTHOUGH it had not been designed as an airliner, the Lockheed Vega enjoyed a successful career in this capacity as a result of its performance and the fact that it was the right aircraft at the right time when the US airline business began to burgeon in the late 1920s. However, the passing of the Air Commerce Act in 1926 obviously presaged very considerable growth in the near future, and Lockheed set about preparing an aircraft to take advantage of this. The aircraft was the Air Express Model 3, based on the Vega designed by John K Northrop, but awarded a different Approved Type Certificate on November 1, 1929. Development of the Express began late in 1927, and was designed specifically to meet the requirements of Western Air Express on the air-mail route between Salt Lake City and Los Angeles. The same basic plywood monocoque fuselage and cantilever wing as used in the Vega were retained, but only with significant changes: the enclosed pilot's position forward of the wing was replaced by an open position just aft of the trailing edge, and the high-set wing of the Vega gave way to a parasol wing on short struts raising it just above the pilot's line of sight. The open cockpit was designed to appeal to the current air-mail pilots, and this in turn necessitated Northrop's adoption of a wing position some 45.7 cm (18 in) higher than before to ensure foward and downward visibility. Payload was accommodated in a cabin under the wing: up to 454 kg (1000 lb) of mail or six passengers, or a mixture of the two. Power for the new type was provided by a 410-hp Pratt &

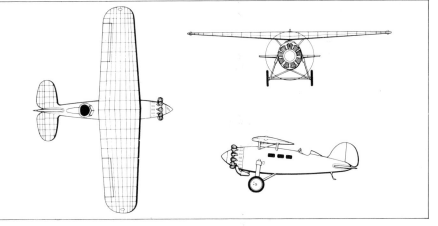

Whitney Wasp radial in a neat installation, the cylinders projecting through the sides of the well-faired nose.

The first Air Express was ready in the first part of 1928, and was extensively tested by the company and Western Air Express. Six other Air Expresses were built for airlines: two each for New York, Rio, & Buenos Aires Line (NYRBA) and Pan American Airways, and one each for American Airways and Texas Air Transport. The last Air Express was built as a 'special' for an attempt on the New York to Paris record by a woman, in this case Laura Ingalls. Delays during 1931 put Miss Ingalls out of the running for the record, but in 1934 she made a classic flight round South America in the Air Express.

Boeing 40

FIRST FLIGHT 1925

WITH its Model 40 of 1925, Boeing brought a new elegance and level of performance to biplane design for civil aircraft. The origins of the Boeing 40 lay with the US government Post Office Department which issued a specification in 1925 for an air-mail biplane to be powered by the 400-hp Liberty 12 V-12. The Model 40 first flew on July 7, 1925, but further development of the type was abandoned when the Post Office Department failed to order the Boeing 40 into production.

The whole airline situation in the US was altering, however, with the Contract Air Mail Act (Kelly Act) of 1925 and the Air Commerce Act of 1926: the first meant the transfer of the air-mail service from the POD to private operators, and the second formalized the legislative framework in which modern airlines could be established. The newly formed Boeing Air Transport had the right aircraft in the Model 40, which Clair Egtvedt developed into the remarkable Model 40A. Powered by the 420-hp Pratt & Whitney Wasp radial, the Model 40A could carry the same mail load as its competitors but with the additional advantage that two passengers could also be accommodated in the completely redesigned fuselage, now of steel-tube rather than of wooden construction. Able to take passenger fares into account, Boeing could thus make the lowest air-mail tender possible on the Chicago to San Francisco route and got the contract.

The first production Model 40A flew on May 20, 1927, and Boeing Air Transport began services with the type on July 1, 1927. Boeing Air Transport operated 24 of the 25 Model 40As built, the last going to Pratt & Whitney as an engine testbed. This led to the appearance of the Model 40B in early 1928: the 19 surviving Model 40As were converted to the new standard, with 525-hp Pratt & Whitney Hornet radial. The Model 40B had slightly higher weights and performance. Two of these aircraft were also modified to have tandem cockpits with dual controls.

The Boeing 40C appeared in the middle of 1928, differing from its predecessors in having seating for four passengers, and power provided by a 450-hp Wasp. Production totalled ten, nine going to Pacific Air Transport and the last to National Park Airways. The final production variant was the Model 40B-4 (the earlier Model 40B thereupon becoming the Model 40B-2) with seating for four passengers and powered by 525-hp Hornet.

Above: The novelty of air travel is reflected in the faces of the passengers about to take off in this Boeing 40
Below: A Boeing 40A carrying mail and four passengers on the San Francisco-Chicago run in 1930

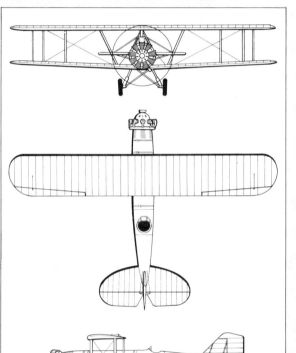

40A

Boeing 40B-4

Type: light transport and mailplane
Maker: Boeing Airplane Co
Span: 13.47 m (44 ft 2¼ in)
Length: 10.12 m (33 ft 2¼ in)
Height: 3.74 m (12 ft 3¼ in)
Wing area: 50.92 m² (547 sq ft)
Weight: maximum 2756 kg (6075 lb); empty 1688 kg (3722 lb)
Powerplant: one 525-hp Pratt & Whitney Hornet B 9-cylinder air-cooled radial engine
Performance: cruising speed 201 km/h (125 mph); range 861 km (535 miles)
Payload: 227 kg (500 lb); seats for up to 4 passengers
Crew: 1
Production: 1 (Model 40), 25 (Model 40A), 43 (Model 40B-4, including Canadian-built Model 40H-4s)

F.XI, Fokker

FIRST FLIGHT 1929

Left: A British-registered
Fokker Universal, part of the
Surrey Flying Services at
Croydon in 1932. G-EBUT
had a varied career including
operations in Africa and
Australia. A few Fokker
F.XIs were built in Europe,
but it was mostly famed as a
US-built transport under the
names Universal and Super
Universal

THE Fokker F.XI was developed in 1928 to meet the requirements of small airlines operating over short routes with a relatively low density of traffic. In essence the F.XI was a cross between two types produced by Fokker's American subsidiary, the Atlantic Aircraft Corporation: the Universal of 1925 and the Super Universal of 1927. The fuselage of the F.XI was typical of Fokker practice with its steel-tube construction and fabric covering, but the wings were very similar to those designed by Robert Noorduyn for the Universal, being built of wood in two halves, which were then bolted to the upper longeron and braced by parallel struts to the lower longeron.

The first F.XI was powered by the 240-hp Lorraine 7Aa radial, and could carry up to four passengers and a crew of one or two. This aircraft first flew in early 1929 and was handed over to the Swiss operator Alpar after the completion of its airworthiness test programme.

The only two other F.XIs built were ordered by the Hungarian airline Malert, and differed from the Alpar aircraft in most details other than dimensions. Accommodation was provided for six passengers with two crew with power provided by the 500-hp Gnome-Rhône Jupiter VI radial.

The Universal, designed by Noorduyn for Atlantic Aircraft just before it became Fokker Aircraft on September 16, 1925, was one of the classic transport aircraft of the era, and 45 were built in three variants, powered by the 200-hp Wright Whirlwind J4, 220-hp Whirlwind J5 and 330-hp Whirlwind J6. All carried a crew of one or two, plus up to

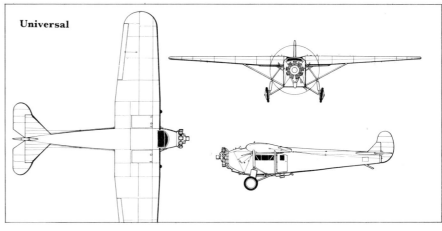

Universal

four passengers on individual staggered seats.

Production of the Universal ended in 1931, but by this time the Fokker Aircraft Corporation had introduced the Super Universal, which had first appeared at the end of 1927 as the Universal Special. This was essentially a scaled-up Universal, with an enclosed pilot's cockpit, span increased from 14.55 m (47 ft 9 in) to 15.44 m (50 ft 7¾ in), maximum take-off weight improved from the 1728 kg (3810 lb) of the J5-engined Universal to 2390 kg (5270 lb) of the Nakajima-built Super Universal powered by the 450-hp Bristol Jupiter radial. Passenger accommodation was raised to six by lengthening the cabin. Production of the Super Universal reached 123, including 29 built in Japan and 14 in Canada.

Super Universal

Type: short-range transport
Maker: Atlantic Aircraft Corporation; Nakajima Aircraft Co
Span: 15.44 m (50 ft 7¾ in)
Length: 11.15 m (36 ft 7 in)
Height: 29.9 m (9 ft 1 in)
Wing area: 34.37 m² (370 sq ft)
Weight: maximum 2390 kg (5270 lb); empty 1475 kg (3250 lb)
Powerplant: one 450-hp Nakajima-built Bristol Jupiter 9-cylinder radial engine
Performance: cruising speed 190 km/h (118 mph); range 1086 km (675 miles)
Payload: seats for up to 6 passengers
Crew: 1 to 2
Production: 123

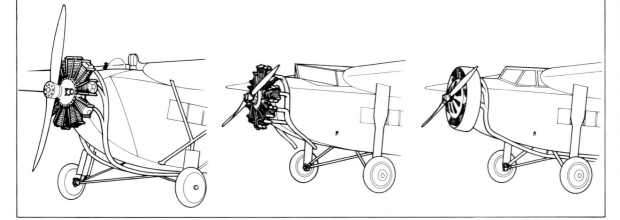

Left: Engine and cockpit arrangements on the US-built F.XIs. From the left is the Universal, with open cockpit, headrest and a Wright Whirlwind J6; a Super Universal with enclosed cockpit, reverse-slope windscreen, and a Pratt & Whitney Wasp; a Super Universal with a Wasp engine in a Townend ring and enclosed cockpit

Boeing 80
FIRST FLIGHT 1928

THE success of the Boeing 40 on the route between Chicago and San Francisco prompted Boeing Air Transport to reconsider the economics of its route. Whereas the Boeing 40 had been conceived as a mailplane able to carry passengers as a supplement, the growing demand for fast, comfortable air transport during the second half of the 1920s led Boeing to the conclusion that passengers should be the primary payload, with mail as a supplement. The Model 80, which made its initial flight in August 1928, was the result.

Construction was of mixed metal and alloy. The fuselage as far aft as the rear of the passenger cabin was of steel tubing, with aluminium tubing aft of this, while the wings were of duralumin. Seating was three abreast, with a pair of seats to the left of the aisle and a single seat to the right, in four rows. At the rear of the cabin was a 'jump seat' for the air stewardess, a feature introduced with the Boeing 80: the first such was Ellen Church, who made the first stewardess flight on May 15, 1930.

Production of the 80 was just four before it was superseded in production by the 80A, of which ten were built during 1929. The three 410-hp Pratt & Whitney Wasps were replaced by 525-hp Pratt & Whitney Hornets in low-drag NACA cowlings; the wings were revised, the vertical tail surfaces were modified, and passenger accommodation was increased to 18 carried at a cruising speed of 201 km/h (125 mph) in place of the 80's 185 km/h (115 mph). All ten 80As were redesignated 80A-1s after conversion to a mixed-capacity configuration, with seating for 12 passengers and space for 519 kg (1145 lb) of freight or mail. Auxiliary surfaces were also added to supplement the standard fin and rudder, and fuel capacity was reduced.

Production of the 80A was originally to have been 12, but the last two examples were modified on the production line into different models. The twelfth aircraft became the single 80B, in which the nose was recontoured to provide an open pilot's cockpit with good rearward vision, following pilot criticism of the enclosed cockpit of the 80 and 80A. Service familiarization convinced pilots of the benefits of the enclosed cockpit, and the 80B was reconverted to 80A standard. The eleventh 80A became the single Model 226, an executive aircraft for the Standard Oil Company: seating for six passengers was provided, together with a lavatory, stove, refrigerator and de luxe furnishings.

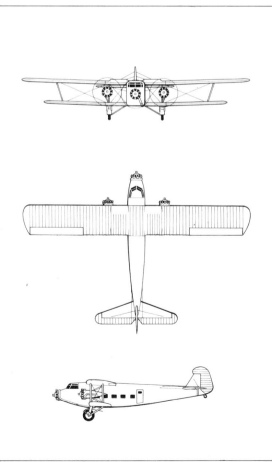

Top left: The Boeing 80A with its enclosed cockpit and early pattern engine cowlings
Top: The 80B with open cockpit which was high enough for the crew to see to the rear over the wing
Above: Loading fire-fighting equipment into a Boeing 80A at Spokane Airport in August 1935

Boeing 80A

Type: short- and medium-range transport
Maker: Boeing Airplane Co
Span: 24.38 m (80 ft)
Length: 17.22 m (56 ft 6 in)
Height: 4.65 m (15 ft 3 in)
Wing area: 113.34 m² (1220 sq ft)
Weight: maximum 7938 kg (17 500 lb); empty 4800 kg (10 582 lb)
Powerplant: three 525-hp Pratt & Whitney Hornet B 9-cylinder air-cooled radial engines
Performance: maximum speed 222 km/h (138 mph); range 740 km (460 miles)
Payload: 407 kg (898 lb); seats for up to 18 passengers
Crew: 2
Production: 10

K-4, Kalinin

FIRST FLIGHT 1928

Left: The prototype K-4 was reported to have been powered by a 300-hp BMW VI engine but a 240-hp engine was standard for the production models
Bottom: The K-5 was a scaled up version of the K-4 and was used by Dobrolet on its services within the USSR

K-4

A PROLIFIC designer of light transport aircraft in the time up to his arrest in 1938, Konstantin Alekseevich Kalinin was an early adherent of the elliptical wing planform and careful streamlining, and these features mark most of the 16 aircraft designed by Kalinin up to 1938. Designed as a feederliner for the Ukrainian operator Ukrvoz-dukhput and the national carrier Dobrolet, the K-4 appeared in 1928, and was reportedly powered in its prototype form by the 300-hp BMW VI V-12. The design capitalized on the best features of the earlier K-1, K-2 and K-3 light transports, which were strut-braced high-wing monoplanes with engines in the 170- to 240-hp range and able to accommodate three or four passengers.

Russian aircraft design at the time was fairly innovative, and the K-4 reflected this. The wings were of advanced elliptical planform and built of alloy with a light alloy covering; the fuselage, on the other hand, was of metal structure with metal skinning as far aft as the rear of the passenger compartment, with the tail section built of wood and covered with plywood and fabric. The pilot's cockpit, just under the wing leading edge, was open, but the extensively glazed passenger cabin for four to six travellers was enclosed.

In production form the passenger variant was normally powered by the 240-hp BMW IV inline, though some of the ambulance variants appear to have 290-hp M-6 V-8s (licence-built Hispano-Suizas) or 310-hp Junkers L 5 inlines.

Production of the K-4 was only on a limited scale compared with that of its successor, the somewhat larger K-5, of which about 260 seem to have been built between 1930 and 1934. Spanning 20.5 m (67 ft 3 in) compared with the K-4's 16.72 m (54 ft 10 in), the K-5 was essentially a scaled-up model of the earlier type, with a crew of two and accommodation for up to eight passengers. The prototype was powered by a 525-hp M-15 radial (licence-built Bristol Jupiter), and may have been re-engined with a Pratt & Whitney Hornet of the same power, but the engines favoured in production K-5s were the 500-hp M-17F or 480-hp M-22. Although an enclosed cockpit for the two crew was provided, the wings reverted to the otherwise obsolescent construction of wooden structure with fabric covering, though the planform of this and the tailplane were the ellipses seen in the K-4.

Type: short-range transport
Maker: K A Kalinin Design Bureau
Span: 16.72 m (54 ft 10 in)
Length: 11.35 m (37 ft 2¾ in)
Height: not available
Wing area: 40 m² (430½ sq ft)
Weight: maximum 2400 kg (5291 lb); empty 1400 kg (3086 lb)
Powerplant: one 240-hp BMW IV 6-cylinder water-cooled inline engine
Performance: cruising speed 160 km/h (99 mph); range not available
Payload: seats for up to 6 passengers
Crew: 1
Production: approx 22

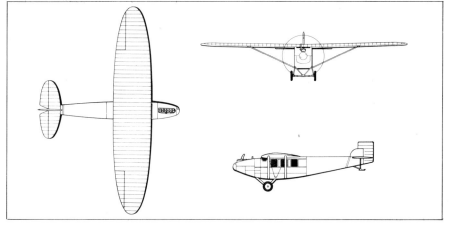

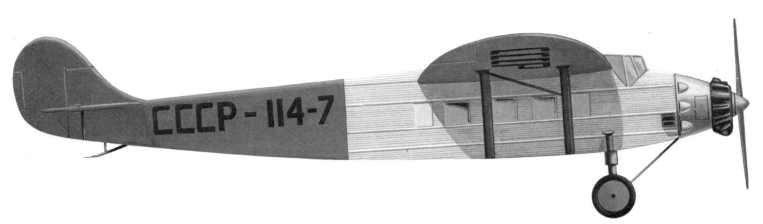

Calcutta, Short

FIRST FLIGHT 1928

ALTHOUGH the eventual establishment of major air routes linking Great Britain with Australia and South Africa had been conjectured before World War I, it was in 1917 that the Civil Air Transport Committee was established to consider the prospects for civil aviation after the end of the Great War. There followed a period of uncertainty as the government vacillated over the question of whether or not the government itself should become involved in civil aviation directly or by means of subsidies.

The issue was resolved first by paying subsidies to independent airlines, and then by the formation of Imperial Airways on April 1, 1924. The new state airline was faced with the need for rapid re-equipment for the routes it was to open to the south-east, towards India and Australasia, and to the south, towards South Africa. Clearly multi-engined types would be needed to ensure safety over inhospitable areas, and equally clearly there was a demand for flying boats to operate over water and areas with no airfields.

In 1926, therefore, the Air Council decided to order two civil flying boats on behalf of Imperial Airways. These were to be derived from the Short S.5 Singapore I military flying boat, and with the name Calcutta have three engines in place of the Singapore Is' two, but use the same general design and all-metal structure, with only the flying surfaces covered in fabric.

The basic design was closely akin to that of the Singapore I, though the wings were of slightly greater area, and the hull was both wider and deeper. The three engines were 480-hp Bristol Jupiter IX radials located in the interplane gap on steel struts and driving tractor propellers. Consideration of the need for operations away from base was reflected in the surfacing of the lower-wing centre section with duralumin sheet to provide a working space for mechanics, and the installation of a Bristol gas starter for all three engines in the rear of the central nacelle. When not needed in this capacity, the gas starter worked the bilge pump and provided electricity. The open cockpit for the pilots was in the bows, with the enclosed radio office just behind it. Passenger accommodation was provided for 15 (four rows of three, one row of two and a single seat aft) in a cabin of ample size: 5.18 m (17 ft) long, 1.98 m (6 ft 6 in) wide and 1.91 m (6 ft 3 in) high.

The first Calcutta was launched on February 13, 1928 and made its initial flight on the following day. It was handed over to Imperial Airways on August 9, 1928 and immediately started a series of proving flights. The second aircraft was handed over on September 21, and differed from the first Calcutta in having Handley Page automatic slats on the upper-wing leading edges. Cross-Channel flights on a regular basis were operated until February 1929, fully confirming the Calcutta's capabilities. Imperial Airways had accepted a third Calcutta on April 11, 1929, five days before Imperial Airways' first Calcutta flight on the primary route from Genoa to Alexandria on the service from Croydon (London) to Karachi (India). This third aircraft was unfortunately lost in a gale off Genoa during October 1929.

Two more Calcuttas were already under construction for Imperial Airways, however, and the sixth example of the type had been ordered by France. The Calcutta eventually entered production in France as the Breguet Bre.530 Saïgon, in an enlarged form of which two were built. One other Calcutta was built by Short for Breguet.

By 1932 the advent of larger boats allowed Imperial Airways to redeploy its Calcuttas to routes with less traffic, and the route between Khartoum and Kisumu in Africa became the type's main responsibility. One was lost off Alexandria in December 1935. During 1936 the three surviving aircraft became trainers, one being lost in January 1937, another scrapped in the same year, and the last scrapped in 1939.

Right: Short Calcutta *City of Alexandria* with early engines
Bottom: G-EBVG with Tiger VI engines at Rochester in 1935

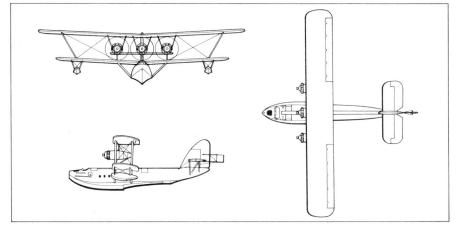

S.8 Calcutta

Type: medium-range transport flying boat
Maker: Short Brothers Ltd
Span: 28.35 m (93 ft)
Length: 20.12 m (66 ft)
Height: 7.18 m (23 ft 6¾ in)
Wing area: 169.55 m² (1825 sq ft)
Weight: maximum 10 206 kg (22 500 lb); empty 6280 kg (13 845 lb)
Powerplant: three 480-hp Bristol Jupiter IX 9-cylinder air-cooled radial engines
Performance: maximum speed 190 km/h (118 mph); range 1046 km (650 miles)
Payload: seats for up to 15 passengers
Crew: 4
Production: 7

F.XII, Fokker

FIRST FLIGHT 1931

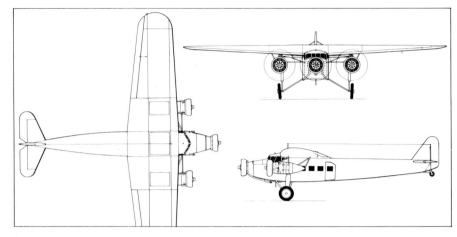

THOUGH it has strong ties with most of the Fokker airliner family of the 1920s and early 1930s, the closest relationship of the Fokker F.XII lies with the F.VIIb/3m. Designed during 1930, the F.XII was intended as a larger and slightly more advanced airliner than the F.VIIb/3m, but without the capacity of the 20-seat F.IX.

Produced to meet a requirement by KLM for a medium-capacity airliner the F.XII was powered by three of the well-proved 425-hp Pratt & Whitney Wasp C radials. The first example flew early in 1931, and set off for Batavia on a route-proving trial on March 5, 1931. This went well, and the F.XII entered scheduled service on the route on October 1, 1931. Fokker built 11 of the type: eight for KLM, two for KNILM (the Dutch East Indies operator) and one for the Swedish operator AB Aerotransport. This last was powered by 500-hp Pratt & Whitney Wasp T1D1 radials, and had accommodation for only 14 passengers compared with the Dutch machines' 16. This Swedish aircraft had Townend rings round the engines to reduce drag, and was originally provided with a spatted undercarriage. These two features were a spasmodic retrofit to the Dutch aircraft. The Swedish aircraft was finally destroyed in a hangar fire at the end of 1946.

The commercial attractions of the F.XII were instrumental in persuading the Danish airline DDL to acquire the type, in this instance a single example produced in only three months by Orlogsvaerftet. Powered by three 465-hp Bristol Jupiter VI radials and able to carry 16 passengers, it was delivered in May 1933. The type was successful, and DDL thus ordered an improved model, the F.XIIM. This was about 20 km/h (12 mph) faster than the Dutch-built F.XIIs. Both aircraft appear to have been scrapped in 1947.

The two F.XIIs operated by KNILM were probably destroyed in World War II. Of the seven F.XIIs used by KLM (the first aircraft having crashed in 1935), one was sold to Air Tropic in 1936 and then faded from the scene, and the remaining six aircraft were sold to British operators. Four were bought by Crilly Airways in 1936, and two by British Airways. Four were then sold to Spain, one crashed in November 1936, and the last was scrapped in 1940, when it had passed into the possession of BOAC.

F.XII

Type: long-range transport
Maker: Fokker BV; Orlogsvaerftet
Span: 23.02 m (75 ft 6¼ in)
Length: 17.8 m (58 ft 4¾ in)
Height: 4.73 m (15 ft 6 in)
Wing area: 83 m² (893 sq ft)
Weight: maximum 7750 kg (17 086 lb); empty 4350 kg (9590 lb)
Powerplant: three 425-hp Pratt & Whitney R-1340 Wasp C 9-cylinder air-cooled radial engines
Performance: cruising speed 205 km/h (127 mph); range 1300 km (808 miles)
Payload: 1620 kg (3571 lb); seats for up to 16 passengers
Crew: 2
Production: 13

Left: OY-DIG *Merkur*, a Fokker F.XII built by Orlogsvaerftet in Denmark in 1933. It operated on a Berlin–Copenhagen and Hamburg–Hanover run

Falcon, Curtiss
FIRST FLIGHT 1928

THE name Falcon was applied to a large number of Curtiss designs stemming from a US Air Service competition for an observation aircraft powered by the 400-hp Liberty 12 V-12 engine. The Curtiss model designed to meet this need appeared in 1924 as the Model 37 XO-1 prototype, from which descended a prolific series of attack, fighter, observation and trainer aircraft for the US air services, both military and naval.

These Falcons for the armed forces were produced in very considerable numbers, whereas the civil Falcons were produced in a comparable number of variants, but in strictly limited numbers only. A batch of 20 was started in 1928.

The first of these was the Conqueror Mailplane, a demonstration aircraft similar to the O-1B but with a 600-hp Curtiss V-1570 Conqueror V-12 engine. While on loan to Transcontinental Air Transport it crashed on August 21, 1928.

The Lindbergh Special was built for Charles A Lindbergh in June 1928, based on a standard A-3B but fitted with a Curtiss D-12D V-12, later changed to a Wright Cyclone radial. The D-12 Mailplane was similar to the Conqueror, but powered by the 435-hp Curtiss D-12D V-12.

The Conqueror Demonstrator was basically an O-1B with the cockpit area of an O-1G, and powered by a Prestone-cooled Conqueror. It was delivered in September 1928 and sold to an unidentified foreign customer.

The next model, the Liberty Mailplane (or Curtiss Falcon Cargo), was the most prolific of the civil Falcons, and 14 of the type were built for

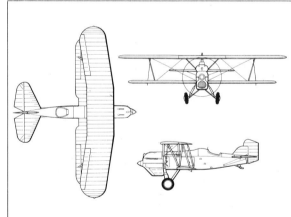

National Air Transport between November 1928 and June 1929. At least three of the type were used for rum-running during the prohibition era.

The Geared Conqueror Mailplane was produced in August 1929 by converting a Falcon Cargo to the more powerful 600-hp geared Conqueror.

The PAA Cyclone Falcon was the Lindbergh Special modified in October 1930 with the 575-hp Wright R-1820E Cyclone radial for use by Pan American Airways in South America.

The last civil Falcon variant was the 1934 Falcon II with the 745-hp Wright SR-1820F-53 Cyclone radial, a NACA low-drag engine cowling, a single-strut undercarriage and a glazed enclosure for both cockpits. The sole example was lost when its wings tore off in a dive on November 6, 1934.

Liberty Mailplane

Type: mailplane
Maker: Curtiss Aeroplane and Motor Co
Span: 11.58 m (38 ft)
Length: 8.38 m (27 ft 6 in)
Height: 3.32 m (10 ft 11 in)
Wing area: 32.6 m² (351 sq ft)
Weight: maximum 2318 kg (5110 lb); empty 1442 kg (3179 lb)
Powerplant: one 425-hp Liberty 12A water-cooled V-12 engine
Performance: maximum speed 235 km/h (146 mph); range 1172 km (728 miles)
Payload: 372 kg (820 lb) of mail
Crew: 1
Production: 14

Top: The Falcon mailplane fitted with floats. This example was bought by Columbia in 1928 and after evaluating the O-1B they bought 15

S-38, Sikorsky

FIRST FLIGHT 1928

IGOR Sikorsky is now remembered largely as the man responsible for the development of the helicopter as a practical means of flight, but during the 1920s and 1930s his company was concerned mainly with the development of flying boats as a safe method of passenger transport.

Sikorsky's first waterplane was the experimental S-34, on which were tested many of the features of the production S-36. This latter was an amphibian with seating for eight passengers and powered by two 220-hp Wright Whirlwind radials. In the event only five S-36s were produced, but one of these was used in scheduled service for a short time in December 1927 and onwards by Pan American Airways. The S-34 and S-36 nevertheless proved satisfactory aircraft inasmuch as they led directly to the S-38, whose success established the Sikorsky company as major manufacturers of flying boats.

The key to the early Sikorsky flying boats was the use of a short, elegantly contoured hull with a wooden (oak and ash) frame covered with duralumin: this had adequate planing properties with small drag penalties, and provided an adequate structural base for the sesquiplane wings with the twin air-cooled radials mounted slightly above the mid-gap position. The lower wing had the two stabilizing floats attached by short struts to their lower surfaces, while from the trailing edges of the upper wing stretched the twin booms holding the monoplane tailplane and twin vertical surfaces in the most effective position in the twin propeller slipstreams. The retractable mainwheels could be actuated separately, and this feature was of great

use for tight manoeuvring on the water, where the extra drag of a single extended wheel helped to reduce the aircraft's turning circle.

The first S-38 flew on June 25, 1928, and proved highly successful apart from a problem that was to beset the whole family: until the boat rose onto the planing step during take-off, clouds of spray were thrown up onto the windscreen, effectively blinding the pilot. The first production model, of which 11 were built, was the S-38A with two 410-hp Pratt & Whitney Wasp radials. The main users of the model were New York, Rio, & Buenos Aires Line (NYRBA), Pan American Airways for its Caribbean routes, and Western Air Express for its Pacific route to Santa Catalina island.

Next came the major production model, the S-

Above: A Sikorsky S-38 of Inter-Island Airways
Below: Although the S-38 looked unusual it was well-liked by its crew. The undercarriage could be used for manoeuvring on the water like a keel

38B of which some 75 were built. This featured 420-hp Wasp engines and greater fuel capacity. This model was available in five different interior layouts: for commercial operations with seating for ten, nine or eight passengers; and as 'air yachts' with seating for eight or six passengers. The ten-seater had two double bench seats at the front of the compartment, four wicker seats in the centre, and two single bench seats at the rear; the nine-seater had a triple bench seat across the front of the compartment, four armchairs in the centre and two single bench seats at the rear; the eight-seater had six armchairs and two single bench seats; the eight-seater air yacht had a four-place bench seat along the left side of the compartment, two armchairs and a folding table along the right side, and the two single bench seats at the rear; and the six-seater air yacht had two pairs of armchairs and folding tables, and the standard two single bench seats at the rear. All variants had provision for a lavatory in the extreme tail of the hull.

The final civil development of the S-38 was the S-38C, which was intended for shorter-haul operations: fuel tankage was reduced, and provision made for an extra pair of seats. The main operator of the S-38C was Inter-Island Airways, which had four on its routes linking the various Hawaiian islands; and at least three were operated by Colonial Western Airways. The largest user of the whole family was Pan American, which bought at least 30 for itself and its subsidiaries. The type was also widely used in South America, the Dutch East Indies and West Africa.

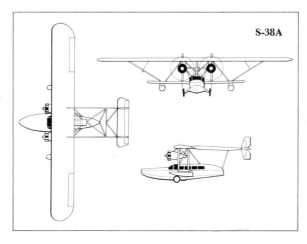

S-38A

S-38B

Type: medium-range transport flying boat
Maker: Sikorsky Manufacturing Corporation
Span: 21.84 m (71 ft 8 in)
Length: 12.27 m (40 ft 3 in)
Height: 4.22 m (13 ft 10 in)
Wing area: 66.89m² (720 sq ft)
Weight: maximum 4754 kg (10 480 lb); empty 2948 kg (6500 lb)
Powerplant: two 420-hp Pratt & Whitney R-1340 Wasp 9-cylinder air-cooled radial engines
Performance: cruising speed 177 km/h (110 mph) at sea level; range 958 km (595 miles)
Payload: 748 kg (1650 lb); seats for up to 10 passengers
Crew: 2
Production: 120

Left: The simple interior of the S-38 amphibian. The seating arrangement could be revised to almost any plan specified
Below: A Hawaiian Airlines S-38 delivering newspapers to the island

Kingbird, Curtiss

FIRST FLIGHT 1929

Kingbird D-2, Model 55

Type: light transport
Maker: Curtiss Aeroplane
and Motor Co
Span: 16.61 m (54 ft 6 in)
Length: 10.59 m (34 ft 9 in)
Height: 3.05 m (10 ft)
Wing area: 37.63 m²
(405 sq ft)
Weight: maximum 2774 kg
(6115 lb); empty 1759 kg
(3877 lb)
Powerplant: two 300-hp
Wright Whirlwind J6-9 9-
cylinder air-cooled radial
engines
Performance: maximum
speed 228.5 km/h (142 mph);
range 668 km (415 miles)
Payload: seats for up to 7
passengers
Crew: 1
Production: 16

THE Curtiss Model 55 Kingbird series of civil aircraft was developed in parallel with the single-engined Model 56 Thrush, and was basically a scaled-up and twin-engined version of the Thrush, with accommodation for eight passengers rather than the five of the single-engined aircraft, plus improved performance and safety from the use of two engines. The most interesting feature of the Kingbird design was the short fuselage nose and inboard location of the engines, with their propellers overlapping the nose. This feature of the Kingbird, the first of whose three prototypes took to the air for its initial flight in May 1929, was intended to minimize asymmetric-thrust problems in the event of an engine failing.

The first prototype was designated Kingbird C, and was initially powered by a pair of 185-hp Curtiss Challenger radial engines. It was converted into the Kingbird J-1 with 240-hp Wright Whirlwind J6-9 radials. It crashed in 1930.

There followed a pair of Kingbird D-1s, the second and third prototypes of the series, powered by 225-hp Wright Whirlwind J6-7s. The third prototype had been the Kingbird J-2 before becoming the D-1, but with no production of the D-1 type, it was converted into a D-2. The second prototype was developed into the Kingbird J-3.

The main production model was the Kingbird D-2, of which 14 were built as such, and two were converted from the D-1 prototypes (the second before its conversion into the J-3 mailplane). The 14 Kingbird D-2s built as such were used by Eastern Air Transport, which was largely owned

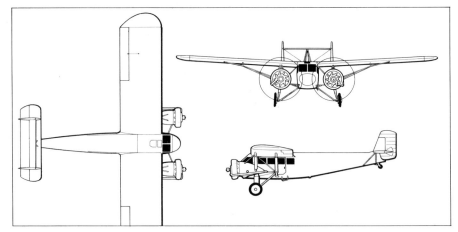

by the Curtiss-Wright Corporation. The company had operated with a miscellany of Ford and Fokker types during the first part of 1930 pending the delivery of the Curtiss types that were to form the definitive equipment of the operator: the Curtiss Condor and the Curtiss Kingbird D-2. Both types entered service on December 10, 1930.

The last civil Kingbird was the single Kingbird D-3, powered by a pair of Whirlwind J6-9s each rated at 330 hp. This model featured a reduction in passenger capacity to five to allow the carriage of up to 117 kg (259 lb) of mail or freight, increased fuel and a lavatory. This aircraft entered service in August 1931. Production of the series was ended by a sole Kingbird D-2 ordered for the US Marine Corps as the JC-1, later altered to RC-1.

Latécoère 28

FIRST FLIGHT 1929

LATÉCOÈRE had entered the aviation business in 1919 with the Lignes Aériennes Latécoère, one of the earliest French airlines and a specialist in the carriage of air mail.

By the mid 1920s Latécoère aircraft began to improve both in looks and performance with the appearance of the Latécoère 17, 25 and 26 series of parasol-wing monoplanes, of which 120 were built.

In 1929 Latécoère introduced the Model 28, a high-wing braced monoplane of commendable aerodynamic cleanliness and appealing lines. The design originated in Aéropostale's need for a modern aircraft with which to operate its joint mail and passenger services in France, and between France and West Africa. Two initial models were produced for competitive evaluation: the 28-0 with the 500-hp Renault 12Jb V-12, and the 28-1 with the 500-hp Hispano-Suiza 12Hbr V-12. In other respects the aircraft were alike, with two crew and accommodation for up to eight passengers.

Both models entered fairly widespread production, though it is difficult to assess exactly how many of each type as there was a certain amount of conversion from one to the other. Aéropostiale received 38 or more, three went to Aviacion Nacional Venezolana, two to Linea Aeropostal Venezolana and four to Aeroposta Argentina, making a total of at least 47 of the 28-0 and 28-1 variants. It is known that some 14 28-0s were converted to 28-1 standard.

Other known variants are the 28-3 mailplane with a twin-float undercarriage, greater wing area and power provided by a 600-hp Hispano-Suiza

12Lbr V-12; and the 28-5 powered by the 650-hp Hispano-Suiza 12Nb but otherwise identical with the 28-3. The designation 28-6 was given to the three Latécoère 28s supplied to Aviacion Nacional Venezolana.

The Laté 28 was used for several record-breaking flights. On May 12–13, 1930, for example, the celebrated pilot Jean Mermoz flew the 28-3 *Comte de la Vaulx* from St Louis in Senegal across the South Atlantic to Natal in Brazil, a flying time of 21 hours, as part of the first air-mail service from Toulouse to Rio de Janeiro. Also in 1930, Lieutenant de vaisseau Paris of the French navy flew a 28-5 named *La Frégate* to nine world records for speed, range and endurance with payloads of 500 kg (1102 lb), 1000 kg (2204 lb) and 2000 kg (4409 lb).

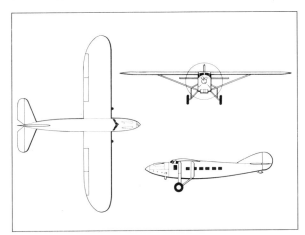

Bottom: A Latécoère 28 mail and passenger plane in service with Aéropostale in the early 1930s

Laté 28-3

Type: medium-range transport
Maker: Forges et Ateliers de Construction Latécoère
Span: 19.25 m (63 ft 1¼ in)
Length: 13.5 m (44 ft 3½ in)
Height: 5.4 m (17 ft 8 in)
Wing area: 58.2 m² (626 sq ft)
Weight: maximum 5017 kg (11 060 lb); empty 2637 kg (5814 lb)
Powerplant: one 600-hp Hispano-Suiza 12Lbr water-cooled V-12 engine
Performance: cruising speed 200 km/h (124 mph) at 3000 m (9842 ft); range 3200 km (1988 miles)
Payload: 299 kg (659 lb)
Crew: 3
Production: approx 50

ANT-9, Tupolev

FIRST FLIGHT 1929

NUMERICALLY the most important of Tupolev's designs up to the mid 1930s was the ANT-9 tri-motor transport, the first of which was completed on April 28, 1929. As with other Tupolev aircraft of the period, there were strong Junkers influences apparent in the design, which had an all-metal structure with corrugated skinning. Unlike Junkers aircraft, however, the ANT-9 was a high-wing monoplane, and made extensive use of the Russian-developed Kolchugalumin alloy. The divided main undercarriage members were reminiscent of Fokker practice, with steel-tube Vs hinged at their open ends to the lower fuselage, and supported at their outboard ends by telescopic legs running up to the centre section of the three-part wing structure.

The prototype ANT-9 was powered by three 230-hp Gnome-Rhône (Bristol) Titan radials, and was slightly smaller than production aircraft, with a span of 23.7 m (77 ft 9 in) but a length of 17 m (55 ft 9¼ in). This prototype was fitted out with the standard accommodation for two flight crew in an enclosed cockpit forward of the wing, seating for nine passengers in the centre fuselage, and in the rear fuselage a lavatory and baggage hold. The type returned a maximum speed of 209 km/h (130 mph) and had a range of 1000 km (621 miles). Between June 6 and 12, 1929 it made an exhibition tour in the USSR; then between July 10 and August 8, 1930, named *Krilya Sovetov* (Wings of the Soviets) for the occasion, it made a 9037-km (5615-mile) tour of western Europe.

The ANT-9 was produced in two forms, the first similar in size to the prototype but powered by three 300-hp M-26 radials, and the second with three 365-hp Wright Whirlwind J6 radials. This latter model spanned 23.85 m (78 ft 3 in) and was 16.65 m (54 ft 7½ in) long, and was at 205 km/h (127 mph) some 20 km/h (12 mph) faster than the model powered by the M-26, though range fell by 300 km (186 miles) from 1000 km (621 miles).

In 1932 there appeared the PS-9 variant, powered by a pair of licence-built BMW VI V-12s, named M-17 by the Russians. Despite the increase in weight from 6000 kg (13 228 lb) to 6200 kg (13 669 lb), the PS-9 had much superior performance due to the greater power available and the reduction in drag effected by the elimination of the third engine. All ANT-9s and PS-9s could operate from ski undercarriages in winter.

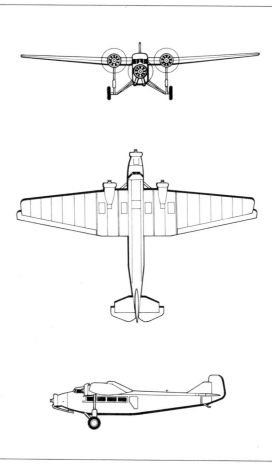

Top: An ANT-9 fitted with a ski undercarriage and powered by M-26 radials
Above: An ANT-9 with the name of the German airline Deruluft, in Russian script on the side of the fuselage. The aircraft in the background is a Junkers Ju 52/3m

ANT-9-M-17 (PS-9)

Type: medium-range transport
Maker: Tupolev Design Bureau
Span: 23.73 m (77 ft 10¼ in)
Length: 17 m (55 ft 9¼ in)
Height: 5.5 m (18 ft 0¾ in)
Wing area: 84 m² (904 sq ft)
Weight: maximum 6200 kg (13 669 lb); empty 4400 kg (9700 lb)
Powerplant: two 680-hp M-17 water-cooled V-12 engines
Performance: maximum speed 215 km/h (134 mph); range approx 1000 km (621 miles)
Payload: 810 kg (1786 lb); seats for up to 9 passengers
Crew: 2
Production: approx 70

Condor, Curtiss-Wright
FIRST FLIGHT 1929

IN the late 1920s and early 1930s, Curtiss produced two quite distinct Condor transports to meet the needs of airlines requiring higher-capacity aircraft for the longer routes which were beginning to attract an increasing proportion of the passenger trade.

The first airliner Condor was essentially a modification of the Curtiss B-2 Condor bomber, of which 12 were ordered by the US Army in 1928 and 1929. The design was released for civil use in 1928, and Curtiss immediately started to build six civil transports. The design of the first three aircraft, designated Model 53 Condor CO (Condor 18), was essentially that of the bomber, with the gunner's positions in the rear of the two engine nacelles faired over, and the fuselage modified for a flight crew of three in an enclosed cockpit, and stretched to seat 18 passengers three abreast in six rows. The second three were more extensively modified, with the fuselage shortened by 58.4 cm (23 in) to 16.94 m (55 ft 7 in), taller vertical tail surfaces, wider-span horizontal tail surfaces and revised engine nacelles.

All six aircraft remained unsold, despite the attraction of their high seating capacity, until January 1931 when they were bought by Eastern Air Transport, largely owned by the Curtiss-Wright Corporation. The six machines were retired from airline service in 1934 and four of them became the property of Clarence D Chamberlin, who used them for joyriding flights in the middle 1930s.

In 1932 Curtiss began to produce its T-32

Condor, so named for its payload of 1452 kg (3200 lb), but it was often known in service as the Condor II. Although this had certain similarities to the earlier Condor, it was in fact a totally new design produced to give the company a saleable transport as the airline business began to emerge from the worst effects of the depression. The chief designer was George A Page, who had also been responsible for the Condor CO. Compared with the Condor CO, the T-32 had a rounder fuselage, single horizontal and vertical tail surfaces, two neatly cowled 750-hp Wright SGR-1820-3 Cyclone radials, and a semi-retractable main undercarriage, the main units of which swung to the rear into the lower engine nacelles leaving only part of the wheels exposed to facilitate wheels-up landings.

Top: A Curtiss Model AT-32-A Condor of American Airways in 1934. It could be used as a 12-passenger sleeper or day transport
Above: The Condor Model 18 in Transcontinental Air Transport livery. TAT tested two Condors on its routes but eventually decided not to buy them

Despite the fact that far more advanced types, such as the Boeing 247 monoplane, were under development, Curtiss managed to secure orders for five Condor IIs, later raised to nine aircraft, from each of two airlines, American Airways and Eastern Air Transport. The first Condor II flew on January 30, 1933 and entered service with American Airways on May 5, 1933. Both its users appreciated that the type could not hope to compete with the monoplanes in terms of speed, and so they attempted to capitalize on the type's large interior volume by fitting their aircraft with special soundproofing and using them on night sleeper routes, in which speed was supposedly no virtue. Sleeper accommodation was 12. Apart from the 18 aircraft for Eastern Air Transport and American

Airways, Curtiss produced another three Condor IIs: two as YC-30s for the US Army, and the last with increased fuel tankage and a fixed undercarriage (intended mainly for floats or skis) to meet the requirements of the Byrd Antarctic Expedition of 1933.

In 1934 Curtiss took advantage of technical developments to introduce the AT-32, with variable-pitch propellers (compared with the T-32's ground-adjustable units), supercharged Wright SGR-1820F-2 or -3 Cyclones of 720 hp (in place of the earlier R-1820F of 720 hp), full NACA low-drag cowlings, and increased tankage. Eleven civil AT-32s were built in four variants: three AT-32As for American Airlines (ex-American Airways) for sleeper or day transport; three AT-32Bs for Ameri-

Right: The Condor II appeared during a change in engine cowling design. Its 720-hp Wright Cyclones were first installed with the Townend ring (left) and later with the long-chord cowlings which became the standard practice in the 1930s. Both installations featured a cabin-heating take-off from the engine exhaust
Below: An AT-32-C Condor 15-passenger day transport. The Swiss bought this aircraft and operated it on the Zurich-Berlin service for a few months before it crashed in 1934

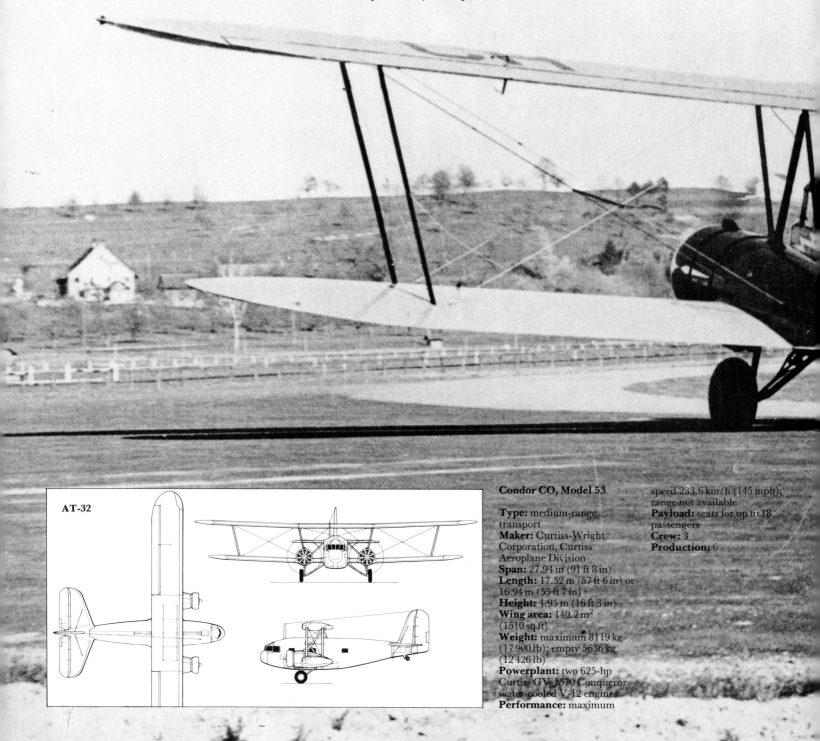

AT-32

Condor CO, Model 53

Type: medium-range transport
Maker: Curtiss-Wright Corporation, Curtiss Aeroplane Division
Span: 27.94 m (91 ft 8 in)
Length: 17.52 m (57 ft 6 in) or 16.94 m (55 ft 7 in)
Height: 4.95 m (16 ft 3 in)
Wing area: 140.2 m² (1510 sq ft)
Weight: maximum 8119 kg (17 900 lb); empty 5636 kg (12 426 lb)
Powerplant: two 625-hp Curtiss GV-1570 Conqueror water-cooled V-12 engines
Performance: maximum speed 233.6 km/h (145 mph); range not available
Payload: seats for up to 18 passengers
Crew: 3
Production: 6

can Airlines with improved engines; one AT-32C day transport (15 passengers) for Swissair; and four AT-32Ds with unsupercharged engines for American Airlines. It should be noted that ten T-32s were later brought up to AT-32 standard with the designation T-32C. Final US production was of two AT-32E 12-passenger VIP transports for the US Navy and Marine Corps under the designation R4C-1. Of the other 11 Condor IIs built, eight were BT-32 bombers for export, and the last three CT-32 heavy military freighters, also for export.

The Condor II was withdrawn from US scheduled service by 1936, but then enjoyed a long career in ever more remote parts of the world. The last Condor II was apparently operated by the Peruvian air force up to 1956.

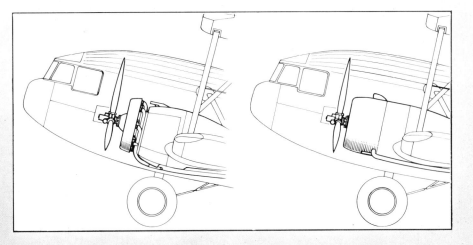

AT-32 Condor II

Type: medium- and long-range transport
Maker: Curtiss-Wright Corporation, Curtiss Aeroplane Division
Span: 24.99 m (82 ft)
Length: 14.8 m (48 ft 7 in)
Height: 4.97 m (16 ft 4 in)
Wing area: 112.22 m² (1208 sq ft)
Weight: maximum 7938 kg (17 500 lb); empty 5550 kg (12 235 lb)
Powerplant: two 720-hp Wright R-1820F Cyclone 9-cylinder air-cooled radial engines
Performance: maximum speed 305.7 km/h (190 mph); range 1152 km (716 miles)
Payload: 1452 kg (3200 lb); seats for up to 12 sleeper passengers
Crew: 2
Production: 30 (civil) and 13 (military)

G38, Junkers

FIRST FLIGHT 1929

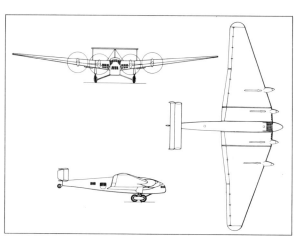

THE firm of Junkers began work on the G38 in 1928. This was essentially a large flying wing, accommodating the payload, fuel and engines, stabilized to the rear by fairly vestigial tail surfaces on a short fuselage. Wing span was 44 m (144 ft 4¼ in) chord 10 m (32 ft 9½ in) and thickness about 1.7 m (5 ft 7 in). In the wings proper were located the engines, fuel and seating for four passengers, while the section of the fuselage between the wings housed the other 26 passengers. The short fuselage of this all-metal aircraft terminated in biplane horizontal and triple vertical tail surfaces, and although the tandem-wheel main undercarriage units were at first spatted, the fairings were subsequently removed.

The G38 was also notable for its use of the important slotted ailerons (or 'double wing') characteristic of most Junkers aircraft for the next ten years, and first tested on the T29 trainer of 1925. The use of the combined flaps and ailerons kept the G38's landing speed down to a remarkable 78 km/h (48 mph).

Powered by two 400-hp Junkers L 8 inlines outboard and two 800-hp L 88 V-12s (coupled L 8s) inboard, the G38a first flew on November 6, 1929. Registered D-2000, this aircraft was handed over to Deutsche Lufthansa in June 1930 for route-proving trials. The G38a was never used for regular commercial services, which were left to the only other G38 built, the G38ce. This was handed over to Deutsche Lufthansa on September 1, 1931, and featured several modifications compared with the G38a. The slotted ailerons covered the entire

trailing edge, rather than the portion outboard of the engines; the fuselage was deeper, with accommodation rising to 34 thanks to the provision of a two-deck layout.

In the extreme nose were two seats and on each side of the centre section were three more seats, with windows let into the wing leading edges to provide a magnificent view. The G38a was later brought up to the same standard as the G38ce, these designations in fact being applied in 1932 when the first aircraft was re-engined with two 800-hp L 88 and two 800-hp L 88a engines, and the second with four L 88as. In 1934 the G38a was fitted with four 750-hp Junkers Jumo 204 diesel engines, and in 1935 the G38ce was fitted with the same powerplant.

G38

Type: long-range transport
Maker: Junkers Flugzeugwerke AG
Span: 44 m (144 ft 4¼ in)
Length: 23.2 m (76 ft 1¼ in)
Height: 7.2 m (23 ft 7½ in)
Wing area: 300 m² (3229 sq ft)
Weight: maximum 24 000 kg (52 910 lb); empty 14 880 kg (32 804 lb)
Powerplant: four 750-hp Junkers Jumo 204 6-cylinder water-cooled inline engines
Performance: cruising speed 208 km/h (129 mph); range 1900 km (1181 miles)
Payload: 3000 kg (6614 lb); seats for up to 34 passengers
Crew: 6
Production: 2

Far left: D-AZUR *Deutschland* which crashed at Dessau in 1936
Left: The spacious interior of a G38 which included its own smoking area
Below left: The cockpit and controls of the Junkers G38
Below: The G38 had seats in the wings which gave passengers a unique forward view in flight

F.XXXII, Fokker

FIRST FLIGHT 1929

DESIGNED by the American Fokker company, the F.XXXII marked a departure from earlier Fokker practice in not being numbered in consecutive sequence from the previous model (this would have made the type the F.XII, the previous model having been the F.XIA amphibian), but rather to indicate the seating capacity.

The F.XXXII was designed to the requirements of Western Air Express, part of General Aviation Corporation which had acquired a controlling interest in Fokker Aircraft in early 1929. The new owners wished to expand their airline interests, and so required a new type with a higher capacity than their current equipment.

Intended for operation as a day airliner with 32 passengers and as a night sleeper with 16 passengers in berths, the F.XXXII was the last US Fokker design, and showed that the company had failed to appreciate that by 1930 – in the United States, at least – the writing was on the wall for the type of aircraft traditionally produced by Fokker, with composite construction and relatively unsophisticated aerodynamics. Two features of the F.XXXII are of interest, however: the four engines which were located in two tandem pairs braced by a plethora of light struts but fixed mainly to the main landing gears; and the use of a layer of balsa wood in the construction of the fuselage to provide a means of soundproofing. The engine arrangement was one of the type's worst features, producing a large amount of drag, and making it all but impossible for the rear engine of each pair to be cooled adequately. The problem was never solved in the type's short service career, though Farman and others persisted with it. Drag was also a problem with the fixed landing gear. Various types of spat and trouser were tried, but Fokker did not retract the wheels into the nacelles as did Farman.

The F.XXXII nevertheless entered service with Western Air Express on April 1, 1930. By this time the order had been reduced to two. Passengers were pleased with the comfort of this new airliner, currently the world's largest civil transport, but were less pleased with the type's almost continual problems with overheating engines. The failure of the aircraft was confirmed when Universal Air Lines System's first F.XXXII crashed, and the company cancelled its order for another four of the type. The US Army tested one example as the YC-20 transport, but made no orders.

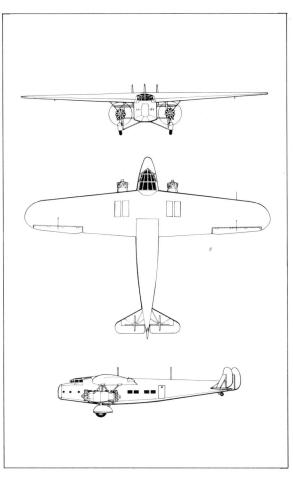

Top: A Western Air Express F.XXXII. The use of the number '32' in the aircraft designation was the result of a request from the airline who wanted to give customers an idea of the seating capacity of the aircraft. The most successful route operated was San Francisco–Los Angeles
Above: A Western Air Express F.XXXII being put to good use as a stage during the company's fourth birthday celebrations

F.XXXII

Type: large-capacity transport
Maker: Fokker Aircraft Corporation
Span: 30.18 m (99 ft)
Length: 21.29 m (69 ft 10 in)
Height: 5.03 m (16 ft 6 in)
Wing area: not available
Weight: maximum 11 000 kg (24 250 lb); empty 6441 kg (14 200 lb)
Powerplant: four 575-hp Pratt & Whitney R-1690 Hornet 9-cylinder air-cooled radial engines
Performance: cruising speed 225 km/h (140 mph); range 805 km (500 miles)
Payload: seats for up to 32 passengers
Crew: 2
Production: 10

Do X, Dornier

FIRST FLIGHT 1929

ONE of the most ambitious aircraft ever built, the Dornier Do X flying boat proved unsuited for its task, and was built in only two prototype forms. The aircraft was designed in 1926 to satisfy Dr Dornier's wish to scale up the proven Wal formula to the greatest possible size. The first Do X was built at the new Dornier works at Altenrhein in Switzerland, and when it appeared in 1929 it was the world's largest aircraft, and by far the heaviest and most powerful. The Do X first flew on July 25, 1929, and on October 21 of that year carried into the air a record-breaking number of people: 169, made up of 150 passengers, 10 crew and 9 stowaways.

Of typical Dornier design, the Do X was of modern all-metal construction, and consisted of a two-step hull, with stressed duralumin skin; a high-set monoplane wing of low aspect ratio, without taper in chord or thickness, covered with fabric except on the leading edge and the walkway under the engines. The tail surfaces were a complex affair with single vertical surfaces, sesquiplane horizontal surfaces and a number of auxiliary surfaces. Wing and tailplane were strut-braced, the wings to the large waterline sponsons by means of triple parallel struts. The elevators and ailerons were balanced by enormous 'park bench' auxiliary surfaces located above and forward of them.

Built up from the wing were six pylon struts, connected at their upper ends by an auxiliary wing. These push/pull nacelles could be entered from a tunnel inside the wing to allow the engineers access to the engines mounted in tandem pairs. The original powerplant comprised 12 Siemens-built Bristol Jupiter radials, each of 525 hp, driving four-blade propellers. This arrangement was not entirely successful, and though there was no trouble in practice Bristol never sanctioned the Jupiter's use as a tandem pusher. Dornier were dissatisfied with the poor ceiling of only 420 m (1378 ft). The Jupiters were accordingly replaced by even more powerful Curtiss V-1570 Conqueror V-12s, with frontal radiators. The auxiliary wing was removed and the nacelles supported on double-N struts. The effect of the change was to prove that the fault lay in the basic design with a short-span heavily loaded wing, ceiling rising by a mere 80 m (270 ft). The heavy engines reduced payload, making revenue service impossible.

Accommodation was spacious and luxurious, with several cabins, usually with 32 double seats and two singles, on the main deck of this three-deck aircraft. The lower deck contained fuel and stores, while the upper deck housed the enclosed cockpit, captain's cabin, navigation office, engine control room and the radio office.

On November 2, 1930 the Do X left Friedrichshafen for a transatlantic proving flight, but New York was reached only on August 27, 1931 after an eventful and inauspicious flight. Transferred to Deutsche Lufthansa, the Do X was almost immediately handed over to the German aviation research establishment DVL. It was destroyed in a Berlin museum by an air raid in World War II.

The only other Do Xs were two built for Italy, and powered by Fiat A.22Rs with streamlined nacelles and radiators in the pylons.

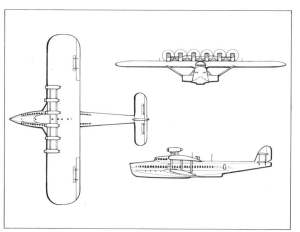

Do X

Type: long-range transport flying boat
Maker: AG für Dornier-Flugzeuge
Span: 48 m (157 ft 5¾ in)
Length: 40.05 m (131 ft 4¾ in)
Height: 9.6 m (31 ft 6 in) over propellers
Wing area: 450 m² (4844 sq ft)
Weight: maximum 48 000 kg (105 820 lb); empty 29 500 kg (65 036 lb); Jupiter 28 250 kg (62 280 lb); other engines 34 820 kg (76 764 lb)
Powerplant: twelve 525-hp Siemens Jupiter 9-cylinder radials, or 640-hp Curtiss Conqueror or 580-hp Fiat A.22R water-cooled V-12 piston engines
Performance: maximum speed 215.6 km/h (134 mph); range 2800 km (1740 miles)
Payload: Jupiter, 17 050 kg (37 588 lb); other engines 13 180 kg (29 056 lb); seats for 66 passengers
Crew: 6
Production: 3

Above left: The Do X against the Manhattan skyline during the proving flight in 1930
Left: The recreation and dining rooms of the Do X. The designers attempted to copy the luxury of ocean liners
Below: The Do X touches down

S.66, Savoia-Marchetti

FIRST FLIGHT 1932

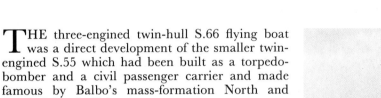

THE three-engined twin-hull S.66 flying boat was a direct development of the smaller twin-engined S.55 which had been built as a torpedo-bomber and a civil passenger carrier and made famous by Balbo's mass-formation North and South Atlantic flights.

The S.66 had a large thick-section tapered wooden wing mounted above two single-step wooden hulls. Booms running aft from the hulls carried the tailplane, one-piece elevator and the fins and rudders. The three Fiat engines were strut-mounted side-by-side above the wing and each drove a four-blade pusher propeller.

The cockpit, fully enclosed, was in the wing centre section and a tunnel gave the crew access to the hulls, each of which had seven or nine seats, some being double units.

The prototype, with 550-hp Fiat A.22R engines, first flew in 1932 and 24 examples were built, all with 750-hp engines. Aero Espresso Italiana and SA Navigazione Aerea (SANA) both used S.66s on their Mediterranean services, and their successor, Ala Littoria, employed at least 23.

The S.66s took over from S.55s on the Rome-Tunis route in April 1934; they also worked between Rome and Tripoli, and from April 1937 operated the Brindisi-Athens-Rhodes-Haifa services.

At various times the first S.66 was used by Italo Balbo and the second was assigned to Benito Mussolini. One Ala Littoria S.66 is known to have been lost between Cagliari and Rome at the cost of 20 lives, and others are believed to have been written off, but 16 were still in service early in 1939. In 1940 five passed to 613 squadron of the Regia Aeronautica, some remaining in service until at least 1943 as transports and for air-sea rescue.

Although Ala Littoria planned to replace the S.66s with more modern SM.87 three-engined seaplanes and Macchi C.100 flying boats, Savoia-Marchetti did produce the prototype of an improved S.66. This was the SM.77 with revised hulls and three 800-hp Alfa-Romeo 126 RC.10 air-cooled radial engines mounted in much cleaner nacelles, fitted with streamlined cowlings and driving three-blade tractor propellers.

It is believed that two were laid down but only one completed, in 1937, and that this was delivered to the Regia Aeronautica. Unfortunately the design was too outdated for airline operation.

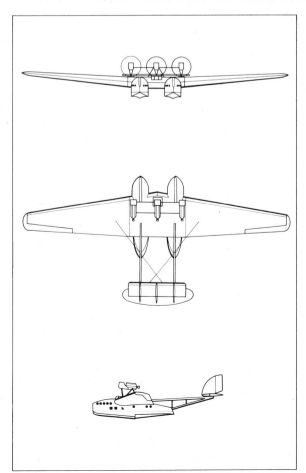

Top and above: The SM.66 which operated with Ala Littoria, SAM and Aero Espresso until remaining aircraft were pressed into service with the Italian Air Force in 1940

S.66

Type: passenger transport flying boat
Maker: Società Idrovolanti Alta Italia
Span: 33 m (108 ft 3¼ in)
Length: 16.63 m (54 ft 6¾ in)
Height: 4.93 m (16 ft 2 in)
Wing area: 126.7 m² (1364 sq ft)
Weight: maximum 11 500 kg (25 353 lb); empty 7960 kg (17 548 lb)
Powerplant: three 750-hp Fiat A.24R V-12 water-cooled engines
Performance: cruising speed 222 km/h (138 mph); range 1185 km (736 miles)
Payload: seats for up to 18 passengers
Crew: 3
Production: 24

Commodore, Consolidated

FIRST FLIGHT 1929

TOWARDS the end of February 1928 the United States Navy ordered a long-range patrol flying boat from Consolidated. This was the XPY-1 Admiral powered by two 425-hp Pratt & Whitney Wasp engines. The XPY-1 was not put into production, but it had been designed so that a commercial variant could easily be built and it was this civil boat that New York, Rio and Buenos Aires Line (NYRBA) ordered for the operation of its planned service between Miami and Brazil and the Argentine.

The civil type was the Consolidated 16 Commodore and the first example appears to have been completed in September 1929, its type certificate being awarded on November 20 that year.

The Commodore closely resembled the Admiral but had well-appointed passenger accommodation and was powered by 575-hp Pratt & Whitney Hornet engines. In layout the Commodore was a parasol monoplane with untapered wing mounted on struts above the hull. The engines were strut-mounted beneath the wing and a further system of struts carried the large stabilizing floats and the outer wings.

The hull appeared to be relatively shallow but was of sufficient volume to provide cabins 2.43 m (8 ft) wide and 1.52 m (5 ft) high. A superstructure on the rear of the hull carried the strut-braced tailplane, one-piece elevator and twin fins and rudders – the fins being strut-braced to the tailplane.

The entire structure of the Commodore was of metal. The wing leading edge was metal-skinned, as was the hull, but the remainder of the wing and the tail surfaces were fabric-covered. The engines were uncowled driving three-blade propellers.

Initially the pilots' cockpit, with side-by-side seats, was open but soon it was enclosed by a raised structure with large windows. Rudder pedals were provided for each pilot, and the control wheel could be swung over for use by either man. There were three passenger cabins with facing pairs of seats on each side in the two forward cabins and accommodation for four in the rear cabin, although a full load of 20 passengers could be carried only on short stages. Forward of the main cabins were a lavatory and a radio compartment.

NYRBA ordered a fleet of 14 Commodores, although only ten were delivered, and the type

Above and below: The Commodore's main operator, with ten aircraft, was the New York, Rio and Buenos Aires Line, which was founded in 1929 specifically to provide air service to major South American cities
Below right: Commodores under construction at the Consolidated Aircraft factory, then at Buffalo

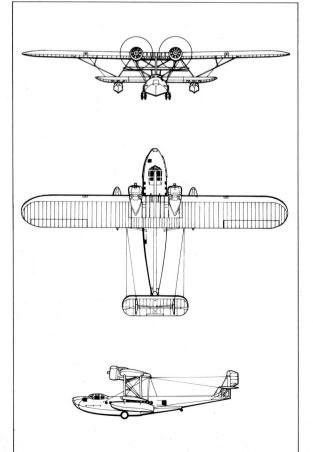

Commodore 16

Type: long-range transport flying boat
Maker: Consolidated Aircraft Corporation
Span: 30.48 m (100 ft)
Length: 20.73 m (68 ft)
Height: 4.77 m (15 ft 8 in)
Wing area: 103.1 m² (1110 sq ft)
Weight: maximum 7983 kg (17 600 lb); empty 4763 kg (10 500 lb)
Powerplant: two 575-hp Pratt & Whitney Hornet 9-cylinder air-cooled radial engines
Performance: cruising speed 173.8 km/h (108 mph); range 1609 km (1000 miles)
Payload: seats for up to 32 passengers
Crew: 3
Production: 14

entered service on February 18, 1930, with the first departure from Miami. The first four NYRBA flying boats were named *Buenos Aires*, *Rio de Janeiro*, *Havana* and *Cuba*. The last of this batch was reported to be a slightly modified Model 16-1 of which nine are believed to have been built, and the first Model 16 was converted to this standard with 30 to 32 seats and a lengthened hull.

The Commodores proved highly successful over the 14 484-km (9000-mile) route from Miami to Buenos Aires, which they covered in seven days, but in September 1930 Pan American Airways acquired the assets of NYRBA and took over the ten Commodores which had been delivered. The remaining four on order were delivered direct to Pan American. Two of the Pan American 'boats

were Commodore 16-2s, essentially like the 16-1s but with cowled engines.

One of the main features of the Commodore was its long range and when Pan American acquired the type it was able to operate non-stop services between Jamaica and the Panama Canal Zone.

During its brief existence NYRBA had set up a Brazilian subsidiary known as NYRBA do Brasil. In October 1930, after the Pan American takeover, this concern became Panair do Brasil, and when the Commodores were replaced by more modern aircraft at least six were transferred to Panair do Brasil for Brazilian operations.

Some Commodores are known to have been flying in 1935 and one served Pan American as a navigational trainer but their final fate is unknown.

S-40, Sikorsky

FIRST FLIGHT 1931

Left and below: The Sikorsky
S-40 operated on Pan
American Airways'
Caribbean routes. The
wheeled landing gear was for
beaching or possible forced
landings. PanAm later
adopted the larger
S-42 for longer routes

THROUGHOUT the 1920s Sikorsky designed
and built a series of flying boats and amphibians of rather antique concept, not unlike the NC-4
which had made the first transatlantic flight in
1919. The Sikorskys had moderately short hulls
and carried high tail units mounted on booms
attached to the main wing and strut-braced to the
rear of the hulls. The early designs were biplanes
but later struts replaced the lower wings.

Pan American Airways had already taken an S-
36, a few S-38s and a couple of S-41s. All were of
modest size, and Pan American required a bigger
aircraft with considerable range.

To meet these requirements Sikorsky built the
last of this series, the S-40 which appeared after the
S-41. Construction of the first hull began in 1930
and the aircraft was completed early in 1931, with
its type certificate being granted that October. In
the following month it left Miami on its first flight
to the Panama Canal Zone and proved its ability
by flying the 966-km (600-mile) overwater sector
from Kingston, Jamaica, to Panama, which was
then claimed as the longest sector on a scheduled
air service. From Panama, Consolidated Commodores completed the flight to Buenos Aires, thus
opening the entire route to the Argentine.

There were only three S-40s, *American Clipper*,
Caribbean Clipper and *Southern Clipper*, but they were
the first of a long line of aircraft to carry the Pan
American copyrighted *Clipper* title.

The S-40s had two-step metal hulls divided into
seven watertight compartments, and in a number
of separate cabins wider than Pullman railway

carriages had accommodation for 32 passengers.
The crew had an enclosed cockpit in the bow and
there were fore and aft entry hatches in the hull.

The fabric-covered wing (with metal-covered
leading edge) was strut-mounted above the hull
and the tailplane, twin fins and rudders were
carried on twin booms. Originally there were
retractable undercarriages but to save weight these
were removed. The four 575-hp Pratt & Whitney
Hornet engines were strut-mounted beneath the
wing driving two-blade metal propellers.

It is thought that all three S-40s remained in
service until 1939 and it is known that *Caribbean
Clipper* became a US Navy navigational trainer,
remaining in operation until 1944 and flying a total
of nearly 13 000 hours.

S-40

Type: passenger flying boat
Maker: Sikorsky Aviation
Corporation
Span: 34.75 m (114 ft)
Length: 23.37 m (76 ft 8 in)
Height: 7.26 m (23 ft 10 in)
Wing area: 161.6 m² (1740 sq
ft)
Weight: maximum 15 422 kg
(34 000 lb); empty 9526 kg
(21 000 lb)
Powerplant: four 575-hp
Pratt & Whitney Hornet 9-
cylinder air-cooled radial
engines
Performance: cruising speed
185 km/h (115 mph); range
1448 km (900 miles)
Payload: seats for 32
passengers
Crew: 3 to 4
Production: 3

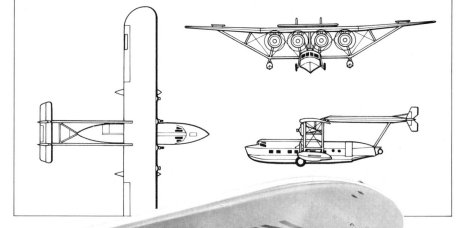

ANT-14, Tupolev

FIRST FLIGHT 1931

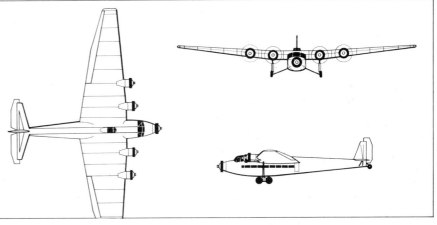

SOON after the 1914–18 war two events took place in the USSR which had a major influence on the design of Soviet aircraft. The first was the establishment of a Junkers factory near Moscow; the second, the appointment of Andrei Nikolaevich Tupolev (chief engineer of TsAGI [the Central Aero- and Hydrodynamic Institute]) to head the commission to organize the design and construction of metal aircraft in the USSR.

The outcome was a succession of aircraft designed on Junkers' principles, with multi-spar wings, metal-framed fuselages and tail units all covered with load-bearing corrugated metal skins. The early examples were small single-engined aircraft but from 1925 a series of bomber types emerged with the twin-engined ANT-4 (TB-1) and followed in 1930 by the four-engined ANT-6 (TB-3). Then in 1929 came the ANT-9 three-engined high-wing monoplane transport which served Deruluft (the Russo-German airline) and, in a number of versions including one with twin engines, the Soviet air services.

Looking rather like a much bigger ANT-9 but with five engines, the ANT-14 first flew on August 14, 1931. Its main claim to fame is its five-engined layout, very few aircraft ever having been designed for this number of engines.

The ANT-14 was a very large thick-winged aircraft with a fuselage wide enough to take pairs of seats on each side of the central aisle. The engines, four along the wing leading edge and one in the nose, were 480-hp Gnome-Rhône Jupiter VI radials, initially with a form of Townend ring

round the rear section of the engines. The propellers were two-blade wooden units. Later the engine cowlings were removed and two-blade metal propellers were fitted. The undercarriage was of the divided type, non-retractable, and fitted with large-diameter Palmer tyres. There was a sprung tail skid and the tail unit comprised single fin and rudder and wire-braced tailplane. Skis were fitted for winter operation.

The pilots' cabin was well forward, and above the wing was an engineer's position with streamlined canopy, reached by a ladder from the main cabin which had 36 seats.

The ANT-14 was named *Pravda*, used for propaganda tours and finally put on show in Moscow where the fuselage served as a cinema.

ANT-14

Type: passenger transport
Maker: Tupolev Design Bureau
Span: 40.4 m (132 ft 6½ in)
Length: 26.49 m (86 ft 11 in)
Height: 5.4 m (17 ft 8½ in)
Wing area: 240 m² (2583 sq ft)
Weight: maximum 17 530 kg (38 646 lb); empty 10 828 kg (23 871 lb)
Powerplant: five 480-hp Gnome-Rhône 9AKX Jupiter VI 9-cylinder air-cooled radial engines
Performance: cruising speed 195 km/h (121 mph); range 900 km (559 miles)
Payload: seats for 36 passengers
Crew: 3
Production: 1

Top: The ANT-14 *Pravda* which joined the Maxim Gorki Squadron on its prewar propaganda flights
Left: The versatile ANT-14 operated on skis as well as single and twin-wheeled undercarriages

Alpha, Northrop
FIRST FLIGHT 1930

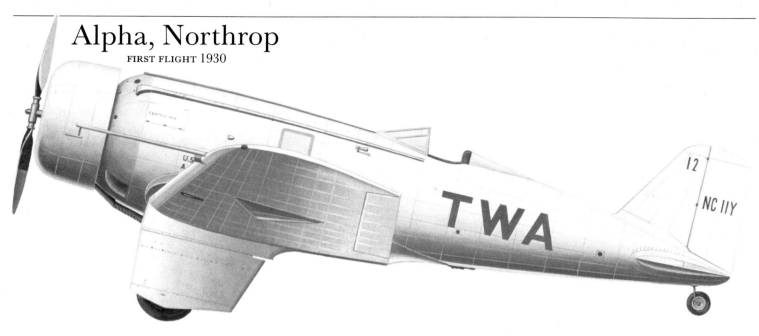

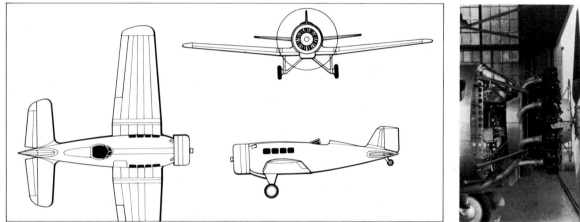

Alpha 3

Type: passenger, mail and cargo transport
Maker: Northrop Aircraft Inc; Stearman Aircraft Co
Span: 12.75 m (41 ft 10 in)
Length: 8.65 m (28 ft 4½ in)
Height: 2.74 m (9 ft)
Wing area: 27.4 m² (295 sq ft)
Weight: maximum 2041 kg (4500 lb); empty 1207 kg (2660 lb)
Powerplant: one 420-hp Pratt & Whitney R-1340-C Wasp C 9-cylinder air-cooled radial engine
Performance: cruising speed 233.3 km/h (145 mph); range 966 km (600 miles)
Payload: 211 kg (465 lb) and seats for up to 7 passengers
Crew: 1
Production: approx 17 (all models)

WHILST it was not particularly well known and built only in small numbers, the Northrop Alpha was an important aircraft because it set the pattern for the modern all-metal stressed-skin low-wing cantilever transport monoplane. It was designed by John K Northrop and embodied his multi-cellular wing construction.

Northrop had previously designed the wooden high-wing Lockheed Vega which was a very advanced aircraft, but in the Alpha design he switched to metal and a low-wing layout, with equally impressive results. The monocoque fuselage was of near circular section, the tail surfaces were cantilever and the undercarriage was of the divided non-retractable type. The original engine was a 420-hp Pratt & Whitney R-1340-C Wasp, driving a two-blade metal propeller.

The Alpha flew in May 1930 and the Alpha 2 and 3 were awarded their type certificates in November that year. The Alpha 2 could have six or seven passenger seats or be used as an all-cargo aircraft and the Alpha 3s were combination aircraft for three passengers and cargo. In both models the cabin was right forward, with the pilot occupying an open cockpit aft of the cabin.

One Alpha 2 went to National Air Transport, several were acquired by Transcontinental & Western Air (which in May 1950 became Trans World Airlines), three went to the US Army Air Corps as C-19s, and one was used by the US Assistant Secretary of Commerce for Aeronautics.

The Alpha was further refined and was certificated in September 1931 as the Alpha 4 with a 450-hp Wasp SC1 engine and cantilever main undercarriage enclosed in streamlined fairings. A few Alpha 4s were built as new aircraft and some of the early models were brought to this standard — several being used by TWA. In addition to the aerodynamic refinements these aircraft had increased span and wing area, greater maximum weight and better performance.

The final development of the type was the Alpha 4A. This had the passenger accommodation removed, most of the cabin windows blanked out and was used as a cargo and mail aircraft. A radio was fitted and there was a tall radio mast just aft of the cockpit. The Alpha 4As were certificated in February 1932 and were among the first aircraft to have leading-edge rubber-boot de-icing.

Top: One of the three Alpha 2s in service with TWA in 1931
Above: The Pratt & Whitney Wasp nine-cylinder radial engine, which had a long background of military and civil use
Below: Loading mail onto an Alpha 2

HP.42, Handley Page

FIRST FLIGHT 1930

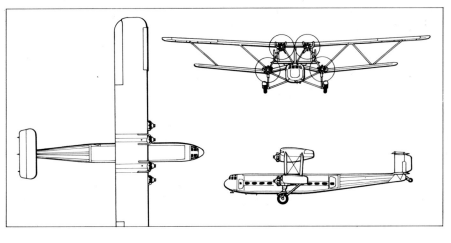

IN THE spring of 1928 Imperial Airways invited tenders from the British aircraft industry for the supply of three- and four-engined aircraft for service in Europe and the East. Handley Page tendered for batches of three, four and six aircraft to meet each of the requirements and received orders for eight four-engined aircraft.

The Handley Page design was for a large unequal-span biplane of metal construction with a metal-skinned forward fuselage but with a fabric-covered rear fuselage, wings and biplane tail unit with triple fins and rudders. The engines were arranged two on the upper centre section and two on the lower wing, the wings being braced by Warren girder struts. The propellers were wooden four-blade fixed-pitch units. The passenger accommodation was in two large cabins with crew compartment in the extreme nose.

The first aircraft flew on November 14, 1930. It was destined for the eastern and African routes, was named *Hannibal*, and bore the type number HP.42. There were six seats in the forward cabin and 12 in the rear, with large mail and baggage areas, lavatories, bar and steward's position amidships. Later, each cabin had 12 seats. *Hannibal* began the London-Paris route on June 11, 1931.

The European model, with 20 seats in the aft cabin and 18 in the front cabin, began service on the same route on September 11, 1931.

Throughout their working lives all these aircraft were known as HP.42s, the eastern examples being called HP.42Es, or Eastern Type, and having the class name Hannibal. The European aircraft were designated HP.42W, (Western Type) and known as the Heracles class. Much later it was discovered that the Hannibals were in fact HP.42s and the Heracles HP.45s.

Hannibals began working the Cairo-Kisumu sector of the African route early in 1932 and the Cairo-Karachi route sometime in the winter of 1931–32. Two of the Heracles class were converted to Hannibals and in 1937 *Hanno* was converted from eastern to western type.

These aircraft gave wonderful service and none was involved in a fatal accident until March 1940 when *Hannibal*, with eight people on board, was lost in the Gulf of Oman. *Hengist* was destroyed in a hangar fire in 1937 and the remainder were written off on war service.

HP.42

Type: passenger transport
Maker: Handley Page Ltd
Span: 39.62 m (130 ft)
Length: 27.35 m (89 ft 9 in)
Height: 7.62 m (25 ft)
Wing area: 277.8 m² (2990 sq ft)
Weight: maximum 12 701 kg (28 000 lb); empty 8047 kg (17 740 lb)
Powerplant: four 490-hp Bristol Jupiter XI.F 9-cylinder air-cooled radial engines
Performance: cruising speed 153 km/h (95 mph); range 805 km (500 miles)
Payload: seats for up to 24 passengers
Crew: 4 to 5
Production: 8 (HP.42 and 45)

Far left: *Heracles* which carried over 160 000 passengers in 8½ years
Left: The passenger cabins were well forward and aft of the wings to minimize noise and vibration
Below: Engine location was designed for smoother, silent flying

G-AAXC

Kent, Short

FIRST FLIGHT 1931

IN APRIL 1929 Imperial Airways began operating trans-Mediterranean flights as part of its England to India services, and used three-engined Short S.8 Calcutta flying boats. That autumn political problems enforced a change in the route and introduced a requirement for an aircraft capable of non-stop operation between Crete and Alexandria.

In outlining its specification the airline required four engines for greater security, improved seaworthiness, increased mail capacity and better passenger comfort. The resulting design was the Short S.17 Kent which was really a scaled-up and improved Calcutta. The structure was of metal but the flying and tail surfaces were fabric-covered. The four 555-hp Bristol Jupiter XFBM engines were arranged side-by-side between the wings, the crew accommodation was completely enclosed and the passenger cabin was well appointed.

Imperial Airways ordered three S.17s, *Scipio*, *Sylvanus* and *Satyrus*, and operated them under the class name Scipio. The first was launched onto the Medway at Rochester on February 24, 1931 and made its maiden flight the same day. The second aircraft flew on the last day of March and the third on May 2.

On May 16 Imperial Airways began flying a modified trans-Mediterranean route between Genoa and Alexandria and on that day introduced the S.17s into service, with *Satyrus* flying from Genoa and *Scipio* from Alexandria. Although suffering some mishaps, the Scipios continued to maintain the Mediterranean services, but on November 9, 1935, *Sylvanus* was sabotaged and burned out at Brindisi. The one fatal accident involving a Scipio happened on August 22, 1936, when *Scipio* herself alighted heavily at Mirabella in Crete, killing two and injuring nine. *Satyrus* maintained the services with assistance from the surviving Calcuttas until the introduction of the Empire C class flying boats two months later.

After its withdrawal from passenger service *Satyrus* was used to survey the routes on which the C class 'boats were to replace or supplement landplanes, flying to Lindi in Tanganyika (now Tanzania) in April 1937 and surveying the Alexandria-Singapore route in June and July 1937. A further Singapore flight, over a different route, was made in October and November 1937 after which *Satyrus* returned to the United Kingdom and was broken up at Hythe on Southampton Water in June 1938.

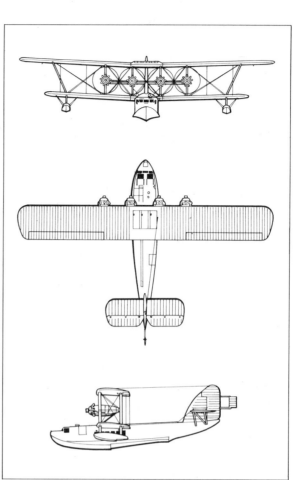

S.17 Kent

Type: transport flying boat
Maker: Short Brothers Ltd
Span: 34.4 m (113 ft)
Length: 23.9 m (78 ft 5 in)
Height: 8.5 m (28 ft)
Wing area: 245.3 m² (2640 sq ft)
Weight: maximum 14 515 kg (32 000 lb); empty 9280 kg (20 460 lb)
Powerplant: four 555-hp Bristol Jupiter XFBM 9-cylinder air-cooled radial engines
Performance: cruising speed 169 km/h (105 mph); range 724 km (450 miles)
Payload: seats for up to 16 passengers
Crew: 4
Production: 3

Above left: The interior of the S.17. It was considered the most comfortable transport of its time and had a galley for cooking hot meals in mid flight
Above: The Kent had four 555-hp Bristol Jupiter XFBM engines. The engine and wing structure was handed on to the landplane Scylla
Left: G-ABFB which was sabotaged by an Italian at Brindisi in November 1935

Tri-Motor Model A, Stinson

FIRST FLIGHT 1934

STINSON is best remembered for its long series of single-engined high-wing monoplanes, but the company built a number of three-engined transport aircraft, starting with the SM-6000 in 1930 and followed by the Model U in 1932.

American Airways had issued a specification for a nine-passenger aircraft with a take-off run of 244 m (800 ft), ability to clear 15 m (50 ft) in 366 m (1200 ft), and costing not more than $35 000. Stinson designed the Model A three-engined low-wing monoplane to meet the requirement and it easily met the take-off performance demanded and was within the price. After some trial hops the first proper flight was made on April 27, 1934.

The Stinson A was of metal construction, mostly fabric-covered, with a single-spar wing that had normal taper on the outer sections and inverse taper on the centre section, which was strut-braced to the top of the fuselage. Power was provided by three 260-hp Lycoming R-680 radial engines, and in the rear of the wing-engine nacelles were lockers for mail and baggage. The wing had trailing-edge flaps, and the main undercarriage units were retractable but with a portion of the wheels exposed to minimize damage in a wheels-up landing. Normal accommodation was for two crew and eight passengers.

American Airways demanded a number of changes in the Stinson A and as a result the first operator was the Delta Air Corporation (now Delta Air Lines) which introduced them on the Dallas-Atlanta-Charleston route in July 1935. Central Air Lines had five and American Airlines (successor to American Airways) had a fleet of 15. Delta withdrew the Stinsons in 1937 and American in 1938.

Airlines of Australia took delivery of four in 1936. Two were lost and the *City of Grafton* and *City of Townsville* passed to Australian National Airways (ANA) which, during the war, converted them to heavier twin-engined aircraft with 600-hp Pratt & Whitney Wasp engines.

CNAC in China and some private operators acquired Stinson As before production ended in 1937. As the aircraft began to be withdrawn by its original operators, it was passed to a number of other airlines.

Tata Air Lines (later Air-India) obtained four three-engined Stinson As in 1941 and kept the type in service until 1944. One Stinson A was restored to airworthy condition in 1979.

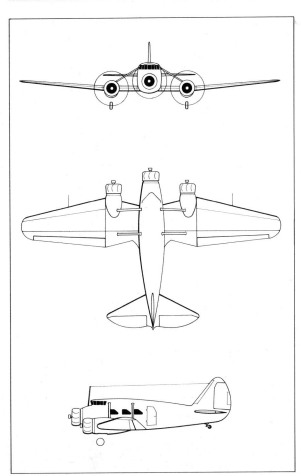

Top: An American Airlines Model A in 1936. The type was used by, amongst others, Central Airlines who operated it on a five-a-day each-way service between Detroit and Washington
Above: A Stinson on wartime service in India

Model A

Type: passenger transport
Maker: Stinson Division, Aircraft Manufacturing Corporation
Span: 18.29 m (60 ft)
Length: 11.23 m (36 ft 10 in)
Height: 3.89 m (12 ft 9 in)
Wing area: 46.45 m² (500 sq ft)
Weight: maximum 4513 kg (9950 lb); empty 3184 kg (7020 lb)
Powerplant: three 260-hp Lycoming R-680 or two 600-hp Pratt & Whitney Wasp S3H1 9-cylinder air-cooled radial engines
Performance: cruising speed 252.7 km/h (157 mph); range 644 km (400 miles)
Payload: seats for 8 passengers
Crew: 2
Production: 35

Atalanta, Armstrong Whitworth

FIRST FLIGHT 1932

IN 1930 Imperial Airways issued a specification for a four-engined aircraft to operate over the southern section of its planned route to South Africa. This was a particularly difficult route, with small aerodromes, mostly at high altitude and subject to high temperatures. The new aircraft had to be able to cope with these conditions, have accommodation for three crew and nine passengers, a payload of 1361 kg (3000 lb), cruise at a minimum of 185 km/h (115 mph), have a normal range of 644 km (400 miles) extendable to 966 km (600 miles), and be able to maintain an altitude of 2743 m (9000 ft) with one engine inoperative.

To meet this specification Armstrong Whitworth designed the AW.XV Atalanta as a high-wing cantilever monoplane with four 340-hp Armstrong Siddeley Double Mongoose engines mounted on the leading edge – later the engines were known as Serval IIIs. There was a single fin and rudder and initially the mainwheels were enclosed in streamlined spats. The main undercarriage structure was within the fuselage and the aircraft sat at a shallow angle and very close to the ground.

The AW.XVs were of a mixed construction with metal-framed fuselages covered with ply in the cabin area and fabric aft; the wing spars were metal but the ribs in the outer sections were of wood. The wing skin was ply back to the rear spar.

Eight AW.XVs were ordered and the first example flew on June 6, 1932, by which time the London to Cape Town service had been opened, with de Havilland Hercules biplanes operating the southern sector. On September 26, 1932, Imperial Airways introduced AW.XVs for a short time on the London to Brussels route and later between Paris and Basle and Zürich. Soon after the proving flight in January 1933, the type began working the Kisumu-Cape Town route.

On May 29, 1933, the *Astraea* left London on a proving flight to Australia before taking up duty on the trans-India route. Atalantas began operating between Karachi and Calcutta in July 1933, to Rangoon that September and to Singapore by the end of the year. When the route was extended to Australia in December 1934 the Atalantas worked to Darwin until Qantas was able to take over the complete Brisbane-Singapore sector with DH.86s.

During the war the surviving Atalantas were used by the RAF and the Indian Air Force. The last two were struck off charge in June 1944.

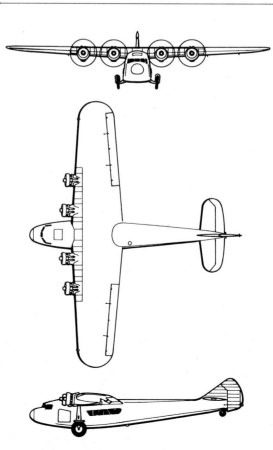

AW.XV Atalanta

Type: passenger and mail transport
Maker: Sir W G Armstrong Whitworth Aircraft Ltd
Span: 27.43 m (90 ft)
Length: 21.79 m (71 ft 6 in)
Height: 4.27 m (14 ft)
Wing area: 119.4 m² (1285 sq ft)
Weight: maximum 9526 kg (21 000 lb); empty 6728 kg (14 832 lb)
Powerplant: four 340-hp Armstrong Siddeley Serval III 10-cylinder air-cooled radial engines
Performance: cruising speed 190 km/h (118 mph); range 1030 km (640 miles)
Payload: 2495 kg (5500 lb); seats for up to 11 passengers
Crew: 3
Production: 8

Top: *Artemis* prior to take-off from an Indian airfield. The bulk of its service was seen in Africa
Above: *Atalanta* was taken over by the Indian Air Force in 1941 and damaged beyond repair at St Thomas' Mount, Madras in 1942

Orion, Lockheed

FIRST FLIGHT 1930

IN the late 1920s, Lockheed produced the Model 8 Sirius two-seat low-wing monoplane designed by Gerald Vultee but owing much to the Vega design. The best-known Sirius was that owned by Charles Lindbergh and used as a floatplane to survey Atlantic and Pacific air routes. From the Sirius was developed the Altair with retractable undercarriage.

To meet airline needs for an express airliner Lockheed designed the Model 9 Orion which appeared in 1930 and was certificated in May 1931. The Orion owed much to the Sirius and Altair and was known as the six-passenger Sirius and Altair D before being given its final name.

Like the earlier Lockheeds the Orion was of wooden construction with ply skinning, was of very clean design and capable of high performance. It had accommodation for a pilot and six passengers and was almost certainly the first transport aircraft with retractable undercarriage – the mainwheels retracting sideways and inwards into the wing.

There were 35 newly-built Orions and five converted from Sirius/Altair models. There were several versions, differing mainly in the type of engine fitted. The first aircraft had the 450-hp Pratt & Whitney Wasp C, the 9B had a 575-hp Wright Cyclone R-1820-E, the 9D a 550-hp Wasp, the 9E a 450-hp Wasp and the 9F a 645-hp Cyclone.

Bowen Air Lines was the first Orion operator, introducing the type in May 1931. The biggest United States operators were American Airways, Varney Speed Lanes, Northwest Airways, and

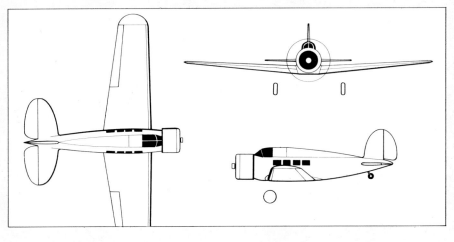

Wyoming Air Service. Transcontinental & Western Air (later Trans World Airlines) also used the Orion.

Varney used Orions between San Francisco and Los Angeles with a 1 hour 55 min schedule and is reported to have offered passengers a one dollar refund for every minute the Orion was behind schedule. Air Express used Orions on US transcontinental freight services in 1933–34 with average times of 16 to 17 hours.

It was Swissair that specified the 575-hp Cyclone when it ordered two Model 9Bs and put them onto high-speed Zürich-Munich-Vienna services in May 1932. One Orion found in the United States was restored in 1979 to represent one of these Swissair aircraft.

Model 9D

Type: express passenger transport
Maker: Lockheed Aircraft Corporation
Span: 13.05 m (42 ft 10 in)
Length: 8.48 m (27 ft 10 in)
Height: 2.95 m (9 ft 8 in)
Wing area: 24.3 m² (262 sq ft)
Weight: maximum 2449 kg (5400 lb); empty 1508 kg (3325 lb)
Powerplant: one 550-hp Pratt & Whitney Wasp S1D1 9-cylinder air-cooled radial engine
Performance: cruising speed 322 km/h (200 mph); range 1207 km (750 miles)
Payload: seats for 6 passengers
Crew: 1
Production: 35 plus 5 conversions

Far left: The Orion flown by the aviators Post and Rogers
Left: Orion was very probably the first transport aircraft to use a retracting undercarriage; the mainwheels retracted sideways and into the wing
Below: One of the two Swissair Orions

Delta, Northrop

FIRST FLIGHT 1933

IN AUGUST 1932 Northrop completed the first Gamma all-metal single-engined low-wing monoplane and developed it in parallel with the similar Delta which first flew in May 1933. The Delta had a larger fuselage than the Gamma and was intended to meet airline requirements for a high-speed transport; but a restriction was put on the use of single-engined aircraft for passenger operations at night and over difficult terrain, and as a result most examples were privately owned or used for executive transport.

Only 13 Deltas were built by Northrop – all Delta Is, with the suffixes A, B, C, D, and E. They had faired-in non-retractable undercarriages and most had six or eight passenger seats. They were fitted with a variety of nine-cylinder radial engines, including 775-hp Wright SR-1820s and 700-hp Pratt & Whitney Hornets. The pilot's cockpit was well forward and a fairing ran back from the cockpit to the base of the fin, but on later aircraft the depth of the fuselage was increased to incorporate a wider cockpit.

The first Delta, the 1A with 710-hp SR-1820-F3 engine, was leased to Transcontinental & Western Air and used as a mailplane between Kansas City and Los Angeles, but it had an inflight fire and crashed; the second, the 1B with 660-hp Hornet T2D-1 went to Aerovias Centrales in Mexico but that, too, was soon lost; the third, the 1C, went to ABA (Swedish Air Lines), and was named *Halland*; the fourth aircraft, a 1D, was an executive aircraft; and the fifth, the 1E with 660-hp Hornet, was much closer to the Gamma, having enclosed tandem cockpits over the trailing edge. It was used by ABA as a night mail aircraft.

The other Deltas were mostly privately owned; some passed to Spain during the Civil War where one was used by the Spanish airline LAPE. One went to the Royal Australian Air Force. The US Coast Guard purchased the 12th Delta as the RT-1 and the 13th was sold to Canadian Vickers who acquired a manufacturing licence and built 19 Deltas for the Royal Canadian Air Force. The Northrop-built example, used for photography, became the Delta I and two more were built.

Next came nine Delta IIs with additional windows and provision for armament, and finally eight Delta IIIs with modified tail units. These Deltas were operated with wheel, ski and float undercarriages and the last six were withdrawn in 1945.

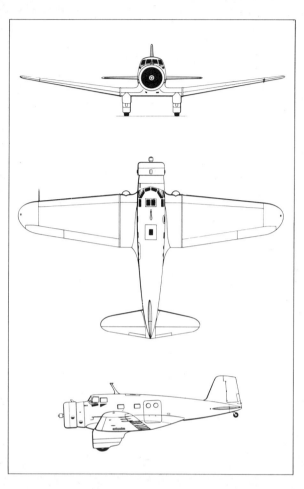

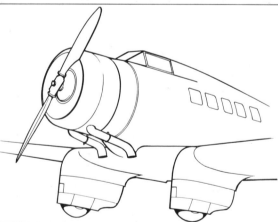

Delta 1B

Type: passenger/mail transport and photographic survey aircraft
Maker: Northrop Aircraft Inc; Canadian Vickers Ltd
Span: 14.55 m (47 ft 9 in)
Length: 10.44 m (34 ft 3 in)
Height: 2.95 m (9 ft 8 in)
Wing area: 33.7 m² (363 sq ft)
Weight: maximum 3175 kg (7000 lb); empty 1860 kg (4100 lb)
Powerplant: one 660-hp Pratt & Whitney Hornet T2D-1 9-cylinder air-cooled radial engine
Performance: cruising speed 300.9 km/h (187 mph); range 2494 km (1550 miles)
Payload: seats for 8 passengers
Crew: 1
Production: 13 (USA), 19 (Canada)

Left: The Delta had a fixed undercarriage which was almost completely enclosed by 'trousers'. Northrop pioneered modern stressed-skin cantilever monoplanes
Below: The Delta supplied to Aerovias Centrales SA of Mexico in 1933

Ju 52/3mho, Junkers

FIRST FLIGHT 1930

THE Junkers company was an early constructor of aero-engines as well as airframes. In 1923 Junkers Motorenbau was founded, and in July 1936 the airframe and engine companies merged as Junkers Flugzeug-und-Motorenwerke.

Apart from designing and building orthodox gasoline engines, Junkers embarked on a long development programme of what were known as Schweröl (heavy oil) or Rohöl (crude oil) engines – in other words diesels.

The five-cylinder FO-3 was produced in 1926 and this was followed in 1928 by the 750-hp six-cylinder FO-4 also known as the Jumo 4 and later Jumo 204, and the 545-hp Jumo 5 of 1932.

The Junkers diesel engines were flight-tested in a number of aircraft and in 1932 Jumo 4-powered Junkers F24s were put into service on Lufthansa's Berlin-Amsterdam route and nine of the airline's F24s were fitted with Jumos.

Jumo 204s were also installed in the Junkers G38 and later, Jumo 205s were used in a number of DLH flying boats and seaplanes and in the Junkers Ju 86. A Jumo 204 was also fitted to one of the single-engined Junkers Ju 52s.

Most of the many thousands of Ju 52/3ms were powered by air-cooled radial gasoline engines but two were fitted with 550-hp Jumo 205Cs. Changes to the airframe made them Ju 52/3mhs and, the Junkers suffix for the Jumo being the letter o, the correct designation became Ju 52/3mho.

One of these aircraft was the landplane *Emil Schaefer*. Apart from its Jumo engines and two-blade propellers it was a standard aircraft. Then at

the 1934 Paris Air Show a Jumo-powered Ju 52 twin-float seaplane was exhibited. After the show it was converted to a landplane and entered Lufthansa service as *W Höhndorf*. As far as is known these aircraft were identical and it is presumed that they were used to get operational experience of diesel engines and compare their performance with BMW-powered Ju 52/3ms.

There is evidence to suggest that *Emil Schaefer* was re-engined with BMW 132 radial engines and that the Jumo 205Cs in *W Höhndorf* were replaced by Jumo 206As, since these engines were listed as in the aircraft in 1940 and 1941.

The Jumo diesels, although having lower fuel consumption, were not an unqualified success and were noisy, heavy and smoky.

Above: D-ALAN *Eduard Dostler* in its prewar Lufthansa livery
Left: The three Junkers Jumo 5 heavy-oil engines of D-AJYR *Emil Schaefer*
Below left: *Södermanland*, a 12-seat floatplane version

Ju 52/3mho

Type: passenger transport
Maker: Junkers-Flugzeugwerk AG
Span: 29.25 m (95 ft 11½ in)
Length: 19 m (62 ft 4 in)
Height: 6.1 m (20 ft)
Wing area: 110.5 m² (1190 sq ft)
Weight: maximum 9500 kg (20 944 lb); empty 6050 kg (13 338 lb)
Powerplant: three 550-hp Junkers Jumo 205C 6-cylinder liquid-cooled diesel engines
Performance: cruising speed 240 km/h (149 mph); range not available
Payload: seats for 17 passengers
Crew: 2
Production: 2

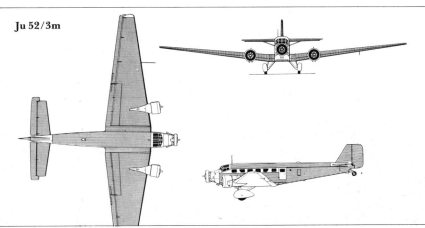

Ju 52/3m

He 70, Heinkel

FIRST FLIGHT 1932

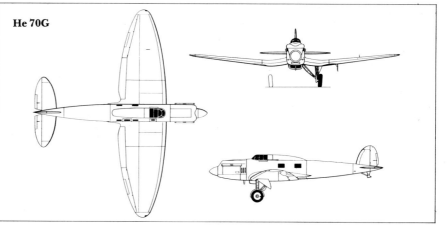

He 70G

THE He 70 was created to meet Deutsche
Lufthansa's requirements for faster aircraft
following the appearance of Lockheed's very advanced Orion in the autumn of 1931. Heinkel's first
design to meet this challenge was the 285-km/h
(177-mph) He 65 with non-retractable undercarriage, but this was abandoned when, in May 1932,
Swissair introduced Orions on the Zürich-Munich-
Vienna route. DLH then demanded an aircraft
capable of 300 km/h (186 mph) and the Günter
brothers designed the beautiful He 70 with elliptical planform wooden wing, streamlined metal
monocoque fuselage with flush riveting, single fin
and rudder and outward retracting main undercarriage.

The He 70 was originally powered by a 630-hp
BMW VI 6,0z glycol-cooled engine and its radiator
retracted into the underside of the fuselage just
ahead of the wing. There was a cabin for four
passengers and the pilot's cockpit was offset to the
left. The radio operator was at a lower level and to
the right. It first flew on December 1, 1932.

The second aircraft, the He 70A (V2) for
Lufthansa, carried the name *Blitz* ('Lightning')
and, although unofficial, this name was generally
applied to the type. The prototype achieved
377 km/h (234 mph) and the He 70 was claimed to
be Europe's fastest passenger aircraft.

Lufthansa had a mixed fleet of He 70As, Ds and
Gs. The D model had a 750-hp engine and the G
had a lengthened fuselage with the cockpit on the
centreline and no second crew member. The airline
operated 14 He 70s, introducing the type on

express services linking Berlin, Hamburg, Cologne
and Frankfurt-am-Main from June 15, 1934.

Although the He 70s had impressive performance, single-engined aircraft did not prove entirely
suitable for scheduled airline operation in Europe
and by the end of 1937 the fleet was reduced to five
and DLH withdrew its He 70s in 1938.

However, the He 70 had shown the potential of
the clean streamlined monoplane with retractable
undercarriage and in 1934, to provide increased
capacity with greater safety and reliability, Lufthansa had ordered the He 111 twin-engined development which could carry ten passengers.

Numerous military versions were produced of
both the He 70 and He 111 and there was a total of
324 He 70s built together with derivatives.

He 70G-1

Type: high-speed passenger
transport
Maker: Ernst Heinkel
Flugzeugwerke GmbH
Span: 14.8 m (48 ft 6¾ in)
Length: 12 m (39 ft 4½ in)
Height: 3.1 m (10 ft 2 in)
Wing area: 36.5 m² (393 sq
ft)
Weight: maximum 3460 kg
(7628 lb); empty 2530 kg
(5577 lb)
Powerplant: one 750-hp
BMW VI 7,3Z V-12 glycol-
cooled engine
Performance: cruising speed
305 km/h (189½ mph); range
1000 km (621 miles)
Payload: seats for 4
passengers
Crew: 1 to 2
Production: 28 (civil)

Top: In 1933, the He 70 was
named as the fastest
passenger transport in
Europe. Lufthansa operated
an express service on so-called
'Blitz routes'
Far left: One of the 28 He 70s
in Lufthansa service
Left: The small but
comfortable passenger cabin

Scion, Short

FIRST FLIGHT 1933

THE Scion was a rather unexpected aircraft to emerge from the works of a company specializing in large flying boats, but early in the 1930s the company decided that there was a market for a five-passenger light transport powered by two of the small 80-hp Pobjoy R radial engines.

One of the main concerns in designing the Scion was economy, both in original cost and flying costs and maintenance, and it was decided to use a fabric-covered steel-tube girder fuselage rather than the cleaner but more expensive monocoque form. A high-wing layout was chosen, with the engines slung from the leading edge. The tailwheel undercarriage was non-retractable.

The prototype S.16 first flew on August 18, 1933 and after some modifications and improvements, was granted its certificate of airworthiness on February 14, 1934. A batch of five production aircraft, with 90-hp Pobjoy Niagara III engines, was laid down, the first going to Aberdeen Airways and the third appearing as a twin-float seaplane for use in Papua. The last of the batch was produced as the Scion II with a number of improvements including six passenger seats.

Ten Scion IIs were put into production and the type saw some airline duties in the United Kingdom, including an hourly service on the Rochester to Southend ferry, and also in Australia. One of this batch of Scion IIs was kept by Shorts for experimental work and was fitted with a tapered wing with high-lift flaps in order to assess features of the C class flying boats that were then under construction. The wing was a scale model of that for the C class and the flaps proved that take-off run and alighting speed could be reduced.

As production of C class 'boats gathered momentum so the Scion became something of an embarrassment and an agreement was made whereby Pobjoy, as Pobjoy Airmotors & Aircraft, would take over licence production. The first two Pobjoy Scions were delivered to Palestine Air Transport in 1937 and the sixth, and last, was completed as a seaplane for Elders Colonial Airways' Bathurst to Freetown service.

Several Scions were impressed for RAF wartime service and none of these returned to civil use, but two in Australia remained airworthy until the mid 1960s, one belonging to Connellan Airways having been fitted with 90-hp DH Gipsy Minor inline engines in 1946.

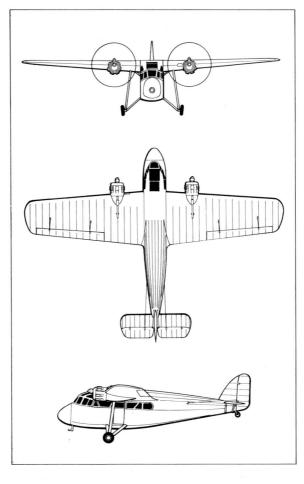

Top: G-ADDT, a Scion II which was operated by Pobjoy Airmotors and Aircraft Ltd. It crashed at Porthcawl in July 1936
Above: The Papuan Concessions Scion I floatplane, flying over the Medway, February 1935

Scion II

Type: light transport
Maker: Short Brothers Ltd; Pobjoy Airmotors & Aircraft Ltd
Span: 12.8 m (42 ft)
Length: 9.5 m (31 ft 4 in)
Height: 3.2 m (10 ft 4½ in)
Wing area: 23.8 m² (256 sq ft)
Weight: maximum 1452 kg (3200 lb); empty 851 kg (1875 lb)
Powerplant: two 90-hp Pobjoy Niagara III 7-cylinder air-cooled radial engines
Performance: cruising speed 186.7 km/h (116 mph); range 628 km (390 miles)
Payload: seats for up to 6 passengers
Crew: 1
Production: 22 (all Scions)

Boeing 247

FIRST FLIGHT 1933

IN May 1930, Boeing took a major step forward in the development of mail service operations when it flew the first Model 200 Monomail mail and cargo low-wing cantilever monoplane of all-metal construction and with retractable undercarriage. The Monomail was single-engined and it did not go into production although, as the Model 221A, it was fitted out for passengers.

To meet a specification for a bomber, Boeing designed and built the Models 214 and 215 (B-9). These were all-metal low-wing monoplanes with two engines and retractable undercarriages.

At about that time there was a requirement for a much improved aircraft to replace such types as the Ford Tri-Motor, Boeing 80 and the various Fokkers. It was decided to base a new design on the Monomail and B-9 and use the same all-metal structure with smooth duralumin skin.

The new type was the Boeing Model 247 powered by two 550-hp Pratt & Whitney Wasp engines and having a retractable main undercarriage. Boeing Air Transport was a component of United Aircraft & Transport which included Pacific Air Transport, National Air Transport and Varney, and early in 1932, while the 247 was still in the mock-up stage, this group ordered 59 of the new aircraft – a comparatively massive order for contemporary transport aircraft.

The Boeing 247 was a cantilever low-wing monoplane, and in planform its tapered wing and tailplane resembled those of the later B-17 Flying Fortress although the 247's wing had less taper. The wing was built in three sections and was not fitted with flaps. The semi-monocoque fuselage had accommodation for two pilots, a stewardess and ten passengers, plus mail and baggage.

The engines were enclosed in drag-reducing cowlings and drove three-blade fixed-pitch metal propellers. The mainwheels retracted into the engine nacelles and there was a non-retractable tailwheel. The windscreens were sloped forward from base to top, there were landing lights in the wing leading edge, radio communication was fitted and there were de-icers.

The first 247 flew at Seattle on February 8, 1933, received its type certificate on March 16, and is reported to have entered service with Boeing Air Transport on March 30, 1933.

On May 1, 1934, United Air Lines was formed out of the constituent airlines and it took over the

Boeing 247

1 Right elevator
2 Elevator tab
3 Tailplane construction
4 Tailcone
5 Tail navigation light
6 Rudder tab
7 Tab hinge control rod
8 Rudder construction
9 Rudder hinges
10 Sternpost
11 Tailfin construction
12 Rudder hinge control
13 Tailwheel shock absorber strut
14 Tailwheel mounting struts
15 Castoring tailwheel
16 Rear fuselage skin plating
17 Fin/tailplane fixing double frame
18 Left tailplane
19 Fuselage frame and stringer construction
20 Tailplane control cables
21 Access door to rear fuselage
22 Rear bulkhead
23 Left baggage compartment door
24 Baggage compartment
25 Water tank
26 Wash basin
27 Toilet compartment
28 Passenger entry door
29 Door latch
30 Trailing-edge wing root fillet
31 Toilet compartment door
32 First aid box
33 Rear aerial masts
34 Curtained passenger windows
35 Passenger compartment floor level
36 Right window panels
37 Centre/rear fuselage joint frame
38 Right wing fuel tank
39 Fuel filler cap
40 Main undercarriage wheel housing
41 Stub wing girder construction rib
42 Outer wing panel rear spar joint
43 Rear spar girder construction
44 Trailing-edge ribs
45 Right aileron
46 Wingtip construction
47 Right upper and lower navigation lights
48 Wing stringers
49 Leading-edge nose ribs
50 Front spar
51 Lattice rib construction
52 Right landing/taxiing lamp
53 Landing lamp glare shield
54 Outer wing panel front spar joint
55 Main undercarriage leg pivot point
56 Retraction strut
57 Main undercarriage leg struts
58 Wheel hub cover
59 Tyre valve access
60 Right mainwheel
61 Cabin heater intake
62 Exhaust pipe shroud
63 Exhaust collector ring
64 Pratt & Whitney S1H1-G Wasp supercharged radial engine
65 Propeller reduction gearbox
66 Three-bladed propeller
67 Propeller hub pitch change mechanism
68 Detachable engine cowlings
69 Oil cooler intake
70 engine bearer struts
71 Engine oil tank
72 Fireproof bulkhead
73 Oil cooler
74 Engine cowling support struts
75 Oil cooler outlet louvres
76 Centre/forward fuselage joint frame
77 Passenger seats
78 Fuselage main longeron
79 Cabin soundproofing and trim panels
80 Cabin heater air duct
81 Overhead luggage racks
82 Aerial cables
83 Left aileron trim tab
84 Aileron hinge control
85 Left aileron
86 Aluminium wing skin plating
87 Left wingtip
88 Left navigation light
89 Left engine nacelle
90 Landing/taxiing lamp
91 Front aerial mast
92 Cockpit roof emergency escape hatch
93 Sloping cockpit bulkhead
94 Sliding cockpit side windows
95 Co-pilot's seat
96 Control column
97 Pilot's seat
98 Forward raked windscreen panels (early model – later aircraft with rearward sloping windscreens)
99 Instrument panel
100 Rudder pedals
101 Cockpit floor level
102 Cockpit front bulkhead
103 Battery
104 Radio transmitter and receiver
105 Electrical equipment rack
106 Flare launchers
107 Left propeller
108 Nose compartment construction
109 Nose compartment mail locker
110 Ventral instrumentation mast
111 Pitot tube
112 Hinged nose cap access door

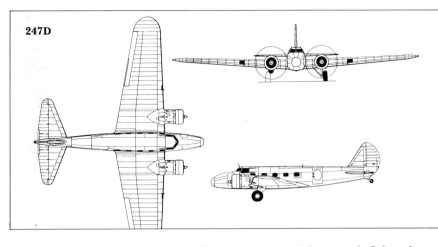

247D

Boeing 247

Type: passenger transport
Maker: Boeing Airplane Co
Span: 22.56 m (74 ft)
Length: 15.65 m (51 ft 4 in)
Height: 4.7 m (15 ft 5 in)
Wing area: 80.18 m² (863 sq ft)
Weight: maximum 5738 kg (12 650 lb); empty 3810 kg (8400 lb)
Powerplant: two 550-hp Pratt & Whitney Wasp S1D1 9-cylinder air-cooled radial engines
Performance: cruising speed 249.4 km/h (155 mph); range 781 km (485 miles)
Payload: seats for 10 passengers
Crew: 3
Production: 75

Left: The use of two engines and the modern structure of the Boeing 247 provided excellent aerodynamic qualities and also reduced operating costs, which was crucial to airline survival in the depression years
Below left: A 247 preserved at Boeing Field, Seattle and photographed in 1976

247s. The 30th example was converted to the Model 247A executive transport with 14-cylinder Twin Wasp Junior engines.

Although the Boeing 247, as the first of the modern all-metal twin-engined monoplane airliners, provided new standards and saw very widespread use, it had two disadvantages. The spars passed through the passenger cabin causing restricted movement and its performance at high elevation aerodromes left something to be desired. Nothing could be done about the spars but improvement in performance was achieved with the Model 247D which went into service with United in April 1934.

The Model 247D had geared Wasp engines with controllable-pitch propellers whch provided better take-off and a higher cruising speed. Other changes were the fitting of NACA engine cowlings, of backward sloping windscreens, and fabric- instead of metal-covered control surfaces. Thirteen 247Ds were built and many of the 247s were brought to D standard although not all had their windscreens changed.

As the 247Ds replaced 247s and as both were superseded by DC-2s, they passed to a variety of airlines, but United still had a fleet of the Boeings until 1942 when they were taken by the USAF as C-73s. One Model 247D flew in the England to Australia race and one was fitted with armament, as the 247Y, and sold to China.

At least one Boeing 247, in United Air Lines' livery, has been preserved in the United States.

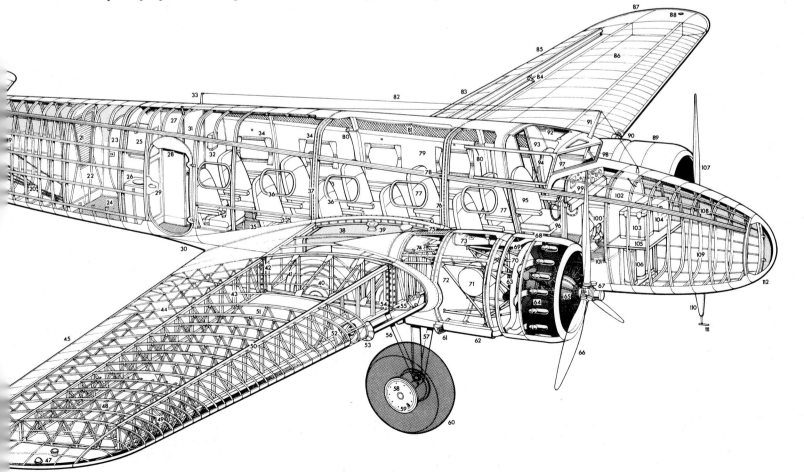

DC-2, Douglas

FIRST FLIGHT 1934

IN 1931 the US Bureau of Air Commerce issued a directive for frequent inspection of all transport aircraft with wooden wing spars. This led to a rapid phasing out of wooden aircraft and a search for metal-structures to replace them.

Although Transcontinental & Western Air (which in 1950 became Trans World Airlines) had been a very early negotiator with Boeing for its all-metal Model 247, Boeing would not supply the airline before completing the 59 ordered by the United group which included Boeing Air Transport. TWA's Jack Frye therefore decided that the airline would issue its own specification and drafted this for a three-engined all-metal monoplane with 550-hp engines, accommodation for two crew and at least 12 passengers to be carried over stages of 1738 km (1080 miles) at 241 km/h (150 mph). The performance requirements were very detailed but the most difficult was the demand that the aircraft should be able to take off at full load from any TWA-used airport with one engine inoperative – and some of the airports were at high altitude and experienced high temperatures.

In August 1932 TWA invited five companies to submit designs to its specification. Douglas accepted the challenge but decided to design a much more advanced twin-engined aircraft to be superior to the Boeing.

This first flew on July 1, 1933, as the DC-1 (Douglas Commercial No 1). It was an all-metal low-wing cantilever monoplane with taper on the leading edge of the outer wings, a single fin and rudder, retractable undercarriage and two 690-hp

Wright SGR-1820-F nine-cylinder air-cooled radial engines driving three-blade propellers. The DC-1 had seats for 12 passengers and from their point of view the great advantage over the Boeing 247 was the uninterrupted floor which was above the main spar. The wing employed Jack Northrop's extremely strong multi-cellular construction.

After some modifications and with more powerful engines, the DC-1 demonstrated its outstanding performance by flying from Los Angeles to Newark in 13 hours 4 min, and is said to have operated a few scheduled services with TWA. From October 1938 the sole DC-1 flew with LAPE in Spain and after passing to SATA was damaged beyond repair in December 1940.

TWA ordered 20 production aircraft. These

Above and below: NC13711 (serial number 1237) which made its maiden flight with TWA on May 11, 1934. It was the prototype DC-2 and was the first of 32 to be operated by TWA

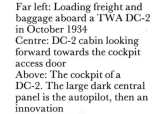

were designated DC-2, were powered by 710-hp Cyclone SGR-1820-F3s, had slightly longer fuselages, and seats for 14 passengers. The first DC-2 flew on May 11, 1934 and the type began service with TWA on May 18 with regular operation starting in July. About 200 DC-2s were built for civil and military use by Douglas and Nakajima.

DC-2s rapidly established themselves on United States domestic routes, American Airlines, Eastern Air Lines and TWA being the main operators of new aircraft. Pan American bought DC-2s, mainly for Panagra and CNAC. KLM and Swissair were the first European operators and it was the first KLM aircraft which made a great flight in the 1934 England to Australia race.

CLS in Czechoslovakia, LAPE in Spain, ALI in Italy, KNILM in the Netherlands East Indies and Holyman's in Australia all bought DC-2s. Lufthansa evaluated one, and the Polish airline LOT had two DC-2s powered by Bristol Pegasus engines. There were a number of privately owned DC-2s, and the type was supplied to the US Navy and Marine Corps as the R2D and to the air force under a number of designations, C-33 being the cargo version with enlarged tail surfaces. In addition, numerous airline DC-2s were taken over by the United States Army Air Force and redesignated.

DC-2s were hard-working and durable aircraft and remained in use for many years after World War II.

Far left: Loading freight and baggage aboard a TWA DC-2 in October 1934
Centre: DC-2 cabin looking forward towards the cockpit access door
Above: The cockpit of a DC-2. The large dark central panel is the autopilot, then an innovation

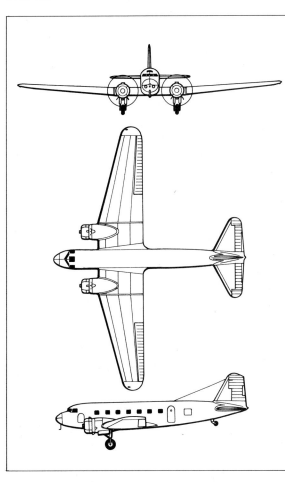

DC-2

Type: passenger transport
Maker: Douglas Aircraft Co Inc; Nakajima Hikoki Kabushiki Kaisha
Span: 25.91 m (85 ft)
Length: 18.89 m (61 ft 11¾ in)
Height: 4.97 m (16 ft 3¾ in)
Wing area: 87.2 m² (939 sq ft)
Weight: maximum 8419 kg (18 560 lb); empty 5628 kg (12 408 lb)
Powerplant: two 875-hp Wright Cyclone SGR-1820, 720-hp Pratt & Whitney Hornet R-1690 or 750-hp Bristol Pegasus VI 9-cylinder air-cooled radial engines
Performance: cruising speed 318 km/h (198 mph); range 1609 km (1000 miles)
Payload: seats for 14 passengers
Crew: 3
Production: approx 200

P.71A, Boulton Paul

FIRST FLIGHT 1934

THE Air Ministry, in 1932, placed an order for a high-speed mail carrier to carry a 454-kg (1000-lb) payload over a distance of 1609 km (1000 miles) at a cruising speed of not less than 241 km/h (150 mph). It was to be a landplane but capable of having floats fitted if required. This type was the Boulton Paul P.64 Mailplane which was intended to be tried out over the Empire routes.

The P.64 was an equal-span strut- and wire-braced biplane with deep fuselage occupying the entire gap between the wings, single fin and rudder and tailwheel undercarriage with the mainwheels partially enclosed in fairings attached to the lower wing. The engines, slung from the upper wing, were two 555-hp Bristol Pegasus radials in nine-sided cowlings and driving two-blade wooden propellers. The entire structure was of fabric-covered metal except for the ply covering on the nose.

The P.64 first flew in March 1933 and was claimed as the fastest British civil aircraft, but it crashed during a test flight that October. However, Imperial Airways had a requirement for a high-speed charter and secondary-route aircraft providing standards of comfort similar to those in the larger main-route aircraft. To meet this specification Boulton Paul designed the P.71A as a direct development of the P.64 Mailplane.

The two types were of similar layout, dimension and weight. The structures, too, were similar but the P.71A had metal skinning to the cabin area of the fuselage, triple rudders without fins, and 490-hp Armstrong Siddeley Jaguar engines in circular cowlings. In place of the mail hold there was a cabin for seven passengers which could be converted for ambulance work.

There were two P.71As, *Boadicea* and *Britomart*, delivered early in 1935. Although given considerable publicity because they were faster than most British transport aircraft of the time, they were not an outstanding success, neither were they particularly well liked. In fact, they were slower than the P.64 and had shorter range.

Britomart was damaged beyond repair in a landing accident at Brussels while carrying passengers on October 25, 1935. *Boadicea* continued in operation mainly as a mail carrier but was lost in the English Channel during a mail flight on September 25, 1936. Little of the wreckage was ever recovered.

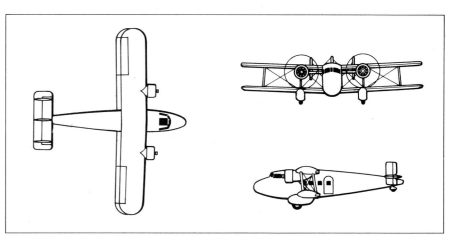

P.71A

Type: passenger and mail transport
Maker: Boulton Paul Aircraft Ltd
Span: 16.46 m (54 ft)
Length: 13.46 m (44 ft 2 in)
Height: 4.62 m (15 ft 2 in)
Wing area: 66.75 m² (718½ sq ft)
Weight: maximum 4309 kg (9500 lb); empty 2767 kg (6100 lb)
Powerplant: two 490-hp Armstrong Siddeley Jaguar VIA 14-cylinder air-cooled radial engines
Performance: cruising speed 241 km/h (150 mph); range 966 km (600 miles)
Payload: seats for 7 passengers
Crew: 2
Production: 2

Left: G-ACOY *Britomart* which was delivered to Imperial Airways at Croydon in 1935. It was damaged beyond repair when it crashed at Haren Aerodrome, Brussels later the same year

Scylla, Short
FIRST FLIGHT 1934

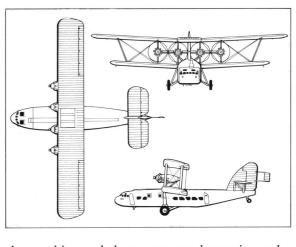

EARLY in 1933 Imperial Airways, due to accidents and increasing traffic, was extremely short of aircraft for its European routes. At that time there were no British production lines from which to order small numbers of proven aircraft. The airline tried to buy two more Handley Page Heracles-class aircraft but without success and therefore asked Short Brothers to build a land-plane version of the Short S.17 Kent flying boat which the airline was using as the Scipio class. The new landplanes were to use the wings, engines, engine mountings and tail unit of the Scipios combined with a new high-capacity fuselage and land undercarriage.

Short designed the 'new' aeroplane as the S.17/L (for S.17 landplane) but later simplified this to L.17. The fuselage mock-up for a 38-passenger landplane was approved in April 1933 and two examples were ordered.

The fuselages were of rectangular section and wide enough to contain pairs of seats on each side of a central aisle. In order to save time a braced structure with unstressed corrugated metal skin was adopted, and it was hoped that the two aircraft could go into service early in 1934.

Because of lack of facilities, the two large bi-planes had to be erected in the open; high winds and low temperatures delayed completion, but on March 26, 1934, the first aircraft, later named *Scylla*, made its first flight. The second example, *Syrinx*, flew on May 17, the day after *Scylla* had made its first London-Paris service flight.

Passenger accommodation was divided into three cabins and there were two lavatories and a steward's pantry. With the lower wing attached to the top of the fuselage the L.17s sat at quite a steep ground angle which made them vulnerable in strong winds. In the summer of 1935 *Syrinx* had its two inboard Jupiter engines replaced by Perseus sleeve-valve units but that November the aircraft was blown on its back by a gale after which it was rebuilt with Pegasus XC engines, as used in the C class flying boats, and its cabins used as trial mock-ups for those with seating increased to 39.

When the war started the L.17s were put to work on National Air Communications but *Scylla* was overturned and wrecked in a gale in April 1940. *Syrinx* had already been condemned and its fuse-lage served as offices at Exeter Airport.

L.17 Scylla

Type: passenger transport
Maker: Short Brothers Ltd
Span: 34.4 m (113 ft)
Length: 25.6 m (83 ft 10 in)
Height: 9.6 m (31 ft 7 in)
Wing area: 243 m² (2615 sq ft)
Weight: maximum 15 196 kg (33 500 lb); empty 10 274 kg (22 650 lb)
Powerplant: four 555-hp Bristol Jupiter XFBM 9-cylinder air-cooled radial engines
Performance: cruising speed 169 km/h (105 mph); range 724 km (450 miles)
Payload: seats for up to 39 passengers
Crew: 5
Production: 2

Below: *Scylla*, a Short L.17 which first flew in 1934 and after operating on the European service of Imperial Airways was wrecked at RAF Drem in Scotland during a storm in 1940

S-42, Sikorsky

FIRST FLIGHT 1934

IN 1932 the airline Pan American Airways issued a specification for a modern long-range trans-ocean flying boat. Sikorsky produced the S-42 to meet this specification, Pan American placed an order for three, and the first example made a short hop on March 29, 1934, and its first test flight was made the following day.

The S-42 broke with Sikorsky tradition in having a full-length two-step all-metal hull with the strut-braced wing mounted above the hull on a shallow superstructure. Another similar structure on the rear of the hull carried the strut-braced tailplane above which were mounted twin fins and rudders. The wingtip floats were carried on two struts and wire-braced. Power was supplied by four 700-hp Pratt & Whitney Hornet engines which were mounted side-by-side on the wing leading edge, enclosed in drag-reducing cowlings and driving three-blade controllable-pitch propellers. At a later stage flaps were fitted to improve the take-off and alighting approach.

The wing was a two-spar metal structure with metal skin except aft of the rear spar which was fabric-covered as were the tail surfaces. The passenger accommodation was divided into four compartments each with eight seats, and the crew accommodation was at a higher level and well forward.

On August 16, 1934, the S-42 entered service on the Miami-Rio de Janeiro route. Four improved S-42As and three S-42Bs were built, and ground was cleared at Hamble on Southampton Water for a factory for British Marine Aircraft to build S-42As under licence, but the project was abandoned.

In preparation for its trans-Pacific services, Pan American had one of its S-42s modified to increase its range and in the first half of 1935 it made a number of survey flights over the route. However, the type could not carry a payload over the long stages and did not operate services. The first S-42B, delivered in 1937, made a survey flight to New Zealand and then worked the Manila to Hong Kong extension of the Pacific route. On June 16, 1937, the S-42B *Bermuda Clipper* began working a regular New York-Bermuda service.

In 1937 the S-42B *Clipper III* undertook North Atlantic survey flights and in 1940 S-42s began operating Pan American's new Seattle to Alaska service. Four S-42s survived the war and were scrapped in mid 1946.

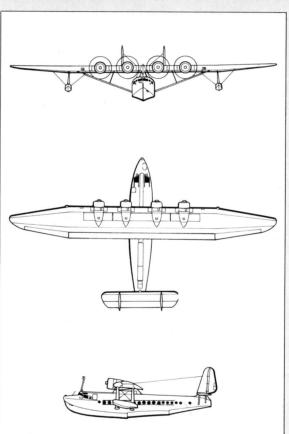

S-42

Type: passenger flying boat
Maker: Sikorsky Aircraft
Span: 34.79 m (114 ft 2 in)
Length: 21.08 m (69 ft 2 in)
Height: 5.28 m (17 ft 4 in)
Wing area: 124.5 m^2 (1340 sq ft)
Weight: maximum 17 237 kg (38 000 lb); empty 10 886 kg (24 000 lb)
Powerplant: four 700-hp Pratt & Whitney Hornet 9-cylinder air-cooled radial engines
Performance: cruising speed 273.6 km/h (170 mph); range 1931 km (1200 miles)
Payload: seats for 32 passengers
Crew: 4 to 5
Production: 10

Top: A Hornet-powered S-42 skims the water just before take-off
Below: A PanAm S-42 *Clipper III* at anchor in Lisbon after flying from New York via the Azores

L-10 Electra, Lockheed

FIRST FLIGHT 1934

THE first Model 10 Electra was flown on February 23, 1934, and on August 11 that year it entered service with Northwest Airlines as the third of the modern low-wing all-metal twin-engined airliners to go into service.

Unlike the earlier single-engined Lockheed transports, the Electra was of all-metal construction with monocoque fuselage and metal-skinned wing and tail surfaces. The inside of the wing covering was corrugated. The tail unit had twin fins and rudders, and the mainwheels retracted into the engine nacelles. The aircraft was laid out for two pilots and ten passengers.

There were four main versions – the Model 10A with Pratt & Whitney Wasp Junior SB engines, the Model 10B with Wright Whirlwind R-975-E3s, the Model 10C with Wasp Junior SC1s, and the Model 10E with Wasp R-1340 S3H1s. All had constant-speed two-blade metal propellers.

The first order for the Electra was placed by Northwest Airlines, previously an Orion operator, and the second customer was Pan American Airways with part of its order for Cubana. Braniff, Continental, Chicago & Southern, Delta, Mid-Continent and National all acquired Electras direct from Lockheed and British Airways, Aeroput, LARES and LOT were among the European customers. Ansett and Guinea Airways in Australia bought Electras; Trans-Canada Air Lines began operation using Electras; and LAV in Venezuela took a number of the aircraft. Lockheed built 148 between June 1934 and July 1941 and the last four were delivered to LAN in Chile.

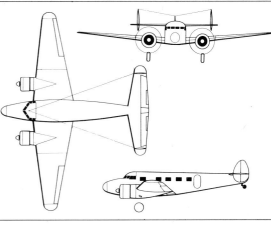

Four United States military Electras were designated C-36 and C-37 and the US Navy and Coast Guard each had one under the designations R2O and R3O.

A number of Electras were privately or corporately owned and some were used for long-distance flights. Major James Doolittle flew an Electra from Chicago to New Orleans in 5 hours 55 min in 1936 – two hours quicker than the previous fastest time – and it was in an Electra that Amelia Earhart was lost during an attempted round-the-world flight.

Pacific Alaska Airways and at least one Canadian operator had Electras with non-retractable ski undercarriages, and one very special Electra was the pressurized XC-35 used for high-altitude research.

Model 10A

Type: passenger transport
Maker: Lockheed Aircraft Corporation
Span: 16.76 m (55 ft)
Length: 11.76 m (38 ft 7 in)
Height: 3.07 m (10 ft 1 in)
Wing area: 42.6 m² (458 sq ft)
Weight: maximum 4581 kg (10 100 lb); empty 2869 kg (6325 lb)
Powerplant: two 450-hp Pratt & Whitney Wasp Junior SB 9-cylinder air-cooled radial engines
Performance: cruising speed 314 km/h (195 mph); range 1304 km (810 miles)
Payload: seats for 10 passengers
Crew: 2 to 3
Production: 148

Above: An Electra of Naples Airlines, a subsidiary of the Provincetown-Boston Airline formed in 1960 to operate between Naples and Fort Myers
Below left: Hanging the first Wasp Junior on the first Electra
Below: This aircraft was destroyed in a 1940 German night raid on Hendon

DH.84 Dragon, de Havilland

FIRST FLIGHT 1932

Dragon I

Type: light transport
Maker: de Havilland Aircraft Co
Span: 14.43 m (47 ft 4 in)
Length: 10.5 m (34 ft 6 in)
Height: 3.07 m (10 ft 1 in)
Wing area: 34.9 m² (376 sq ft)
Weight: maximum 1905 kg (4200 lb); empty 1043 kg (2300 lb)
Powerplant: two 130-hp de Havilland Gipsy Major 4-cylinder inverted air-cooled inline engines
Performance: cruising speed 175.4 km/h (109 mph); range 740 km (460 miles)
Payload: seats for 6 passengers
Crew: 1
Production: 202 (all Dragons)

THE first DH.83 Fox Moth was flown by de Havilland at the end of January 1932. It could carry a pilot and four passengers on the power of a single 120-hp de Havilland Gipsy III engine. Fox Moths, mostly with 130-hp Gipsy Majors, soon found favour as light transports but there was a need for a bigger 'double Fox Moth' to serve as an economic transport for small airlines. The newly created Royal Iraqi Air Force wanted a light transport capable of being used also for bombing, army cooperation and other duties.

The DH.84 was a simple wood and fabric equal-span biplane with two 130-hp Gipsy Majors, non-retractable undercarriage and folding wings. The simple cabin normally had six seats and the pilot's cabin was in the nose. The aircraft was originally known as the Dragon Moth but soon became simply the Dragon.

The prototype flew at Stag Lane on November 24, 1932, was delivered to Hillman's Airways on December 20 and the airline began London to Paris services with Dragons on April 1, 1933, with a return fare of £5.50 (then £5.10 shillings). The next two Dragons went to Hillman's and the eight DH.84Ms, with guns and bomb racks, made their delivery flight to Baghdad in May 1933.

The slightly improved Dragon II followed in 1934 and a total of 115 were built in the United Kingdom up to 1937, with a further 87 being built in Australia for the Royal Australian Air Force in 1942–43. The Australian Dragons were built as radio and navigational trainers, and had modified windows and wider doors.

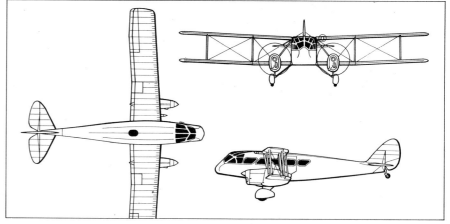

Dragons played a major role in developing British domestic air services and proved equally useful in Australia, New Zealand, Canada, East Africa and Egypt. They were cheap to operate, easy to fly and maintain, and could operate from small rough fields. A rare sight was the entire Jersey Airways fleet of eight flying across the English Channel in formation in order to land in Jersey at low tide – the beach serving as Jersey's airport until 1937.

Among the more notable flights made by Dragons were two with long-range tanks. The Mollisons' Dragon *Seafarer* made a 39-hour non-stop flight from Wales to Connecticut, and *Seafarer II*, renamed *Trail of the Caribou*, flew non-stop from Ontario to London in just under 31 hours.

DH.86 Express, de Havilland

FIRST FLIGHT 1934

Left: This aircraft completed the through scheduled route, for Qantas Empire Airways, from Britain to Australia, first from Singapore to Darwin and Brisbane and later to Sydney

DH.86 Express

Type: passenger transport
Maker: de Havilland Aircraft Co
Span: 19.66 m (64 ft 6 in)
Length: 14.05 m (46 ft 1¼ in)
Height: 3.96 m (13 ft)
Wing area: 59.55 m² (641 sq ft)
Weight: maximum 4649 kg (10 250 lb); empty 2859 kg (6303 lb)
Powerplant: four 205-hp de Havilland Gipsy Six 6-cylinder inverted air-cooled inline engines
Performance: cruising speed 233 km/h (145 mph); range 724 km (450 miles)
Payload: seats for up to 17 passengers
Crew: 2
Production: 62

FOLLOWING long negotiations, agreement was reached on the operation of an England to Australia air service and Qantas Empire Airways was the designated operator of the Singapore-Brisbane section, with other Australian airlines providing connecting services.

At that time de Havilland's new 200-hp Gipsy Six engine was being successfully developed and a simple economic ten-passenger wood and fabric biplane was designed to use four of the new engines.

The new aircraft was the DH.86 Express Air Liner, rather like an enlarged and refined Dragon with tapered wings and faired-in undercarriage. The prototype, with short nose and room only for one pilot, made its first flight on January 14, 1934 and achieved certification with one day to spare.

Qantas ordered six, under the class name Commonwealth, Holyman's Airways ordered some for the Melbourne-Tasmania service, and Imperial Airways ordered a batch including two for Railway Air Services.

The prototype was modified with a longer nose to accommodate two pilots and the undercarriage fairings were redesigned. All but the two Railway Air Services' aircraft were built with the longer nose but one of them was later modified.

Holyman's *Miss Hobart* was lost at sea in October 1934 and one of the Qantas aircraft crashed on its delivery flight the next month. As a result the trim tab on the rudder was removed. Thereafter the Qantas aircraft gave good service, the RAS aircraft maintained United Kingdom trunk routes

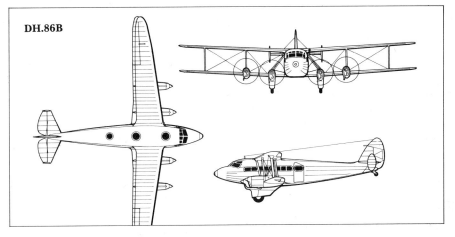

DH.86B

and the Imperial Airways DH.86s, known as the Diana class, worked European routes and the trunk route extensions to Hong Kong and West Africa.

A slightly improved model, the DH.86A, appeared in 1935, and in 1937 came the DH.86B with better controls including vertical fins attached to the outer ends of the tailplanes. Most of the A models were brought to B standard. The DH.86s saw much war service and particularly distinguished themselves with Qantas in New Guinea where they were used for evacuation from remote areas and for supply dropping.

A few DH.86s survived the war, some continued flying for RAS, but the last survivor was damaged beyond repair in September 1958.

DH.89 Dragon Rapide, de Havilland

FIRST FLIGHT 1934

THE prototype DH.89 was flown on April 17, 1934 as a development of the DH.84 Dragon but incorporated the experience gained in designing the DH.86 Express Air Liner to meet Australia's requirements.

In layout and size the DH.89 resembled the Dragon but had finely tapered wings and streamlined undercarriage housing as on the DH.86. Like the DH.86 it was powered by 200-hp Gipsy Six engines although like the Dragon it was twin-engined.

The new aircraft was initially known as the Dragon Six but was soon renamed Dragon Rapide and in time became known universally simply as the Rapide. The Rapide was heavier than the Dragon, could carry up to eight passengers, and had a higher cruising speed – the first production aircraft averaging 254 km/h (158 mph) in the 1934 King's Cup race.

The first three Rapides were delivered to Hillman's Airways and these were followed by two for Railway Air Services namely the *City of Bristol* and *City of Birmingham*. Orders quickly built up and Rapides were delivered to British internal airlines, LAPE in Spain, KNILM in the East Indies, Misr in Egypt, DHY in Turkey, and many other airlines, oil companies and private owners.

The Rapide did not have quite the same landing performance as the Dragon, so in 1937 a version was built with trailing-edge flaps under the lower wing. This was the DH.89A which became the standard aircraft, and many of the earlier examples were modified to conform.

Rapides saw worldwide service, a few on twin floats, and did much to develop air transport. Many of the British-owned Rapides were taken for war service in 1939 and 1940. A major boost to Rapide production came in 1940 with an order for 150 trainers for the RAF. Further orders for military Rapides followed, with a total of 523 of which 200 were built by Brush Coachworks. There were two versions, the radio and navigational trainer known as the Dominie Mk I and the communications version known as the Dominie Mk II. Incidentally, the RAF name for the Gipsy Six engine was Gipsy Queen and production of the aircraft ended in 1946.

Numerous Dominies were converted for civil use after the war and some Rapides were still flying at the end of 1979.

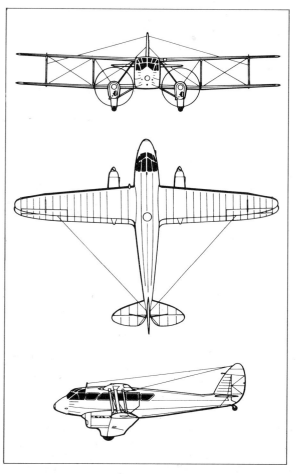

Above: G-AHKV was a DH.89B Dominie converted to a civil DH.89A. It first flew as such in 1946 and was withdrawn from service in 1969

Left: *Lord Shaftesbury* was part of the Islander class, which flew on the BEA Scottish, Scilly and Channel Islands routes. It ended its career in 1956 in the Laos Air Service

DH.89 Rapide

Type: light transport and radio and navigation trainer
Maker: de Havilland Aircraft Co; Brush Coachworks Ltd
Span: 14.63 m (48 ft)
Length: 10.5 m (34 ft 6 in)
Height: 3.12 m (10 ft 3 in)
Wing area: 31.3 m² (337 sq ft)
Weight: maximum 2495 kg (5500 lb); empty 1518 kg (3346 lb)
Powerplant: two 200-hp de Havilland Gipsy Six or Gipsy Queen 2 and 3 6-cylinder inverted air-cooled inline engines
Performance: cruising speed 212.43 km/h (132 mph); range 930 km (578 miles)
Payload: seats for up to 8 passengers
Crew: 1 to 2
Production: 731

DH.90 Dragonfly, de Havilland

FIRST FLIGHT 1935

DH.90 Dragonfly

Type: light transport
Maker: de Havilland Aircraft Co
Span: 13.1 m (43 ft)
Length: 9.65 m (31 ft 8 in)
Height: 2.79 m (9 ft 2 in)
Wing area: 23.78 m² (256 sq ft)
Weight: maximum 1814 kg (4000 lb); empty 1128 kg (2487 lb)
Powerplant: two 145-hp de Havilland Gipsy Major 4-cylinder inverted air-cooled inline engines
Performance: cruising speed 201 km/h (125 mph); range 1424 km (885 miles)
Payload: seats for 4 passengers
Crew: 1
Production: 67

HAVING produced a very successful series of light transport aircraft with the Dragon, Express Air Liner and Dragon Rapide, de Havilland decided to build a five-seat private owners' touring aircraft using the experience gained on the earlier types. This was the DH.90 Dragonfly.

Although the Dragonfly's ancestry was obvious, it was a very different aircraft to its predecessors. It was smaller and had unequal-span wings with an inverted V-strut arrangement aft of the engines and single outboard interplane struts. In order to give easy access to the cabin there were no bracing wires on the inner-wing bays. The Dragon, DH.86 and Dragon Rapides had fuselages constructed as wooden boxes with fabric covering stretched over the outside stiffening structure, but the Dragonfly had a monocoque shell of preformed plywood. The cabin had two pilot's seats, a double seat at the rear and a single seat on the right side.

The Dragonfly was powered by two 145-hp de Havilland Gipsy Major engines which were mounted on the lower wing and drove two-blade propellers. The mainwheels were housed in fairings similar to those of the Dragon Rapide. The first flight took place at Hatfield on August 12, 1935, and the prototype averaged 231.34 km/h (144 mph) in the 1936 King's Cup race.

The Dragonfly originally cost £2650, which was regarded as high at the time and initial sales on the home market were modest, but some were sold to overseas private owners including HM King Feisal of Iraq. Although the aircraft's capacity was strictly limited, the Dragonfly was ordered by a surpris-

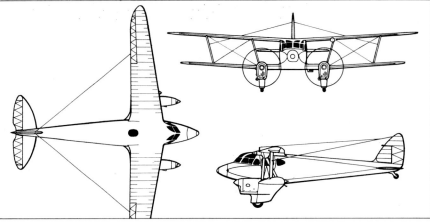

ingly large number of airlines including Qantas, LARES in Romania, DTA in Angola, Misr Airwork in Egypt, DHY in Turkey, Ala Littoria in Italy, Wearnes Air Services in Malaya, PLUNA in Uruguay, and RANA (Rhodesia and Nyasaland Airways). The Royal Canadian Mounted Police had four, and another Canadian Dragonfly, owned by Gold Belt Air Services, operated on twin floats.

Dragonfly production ended in 1938 and during the war some were impressed for military use. A small number survived the war and a few saw postwar airline service with Connellan Airways and Bush Pilots Airways in Australia and DETA in Africa. One continued to fly in the United Kingdom until 1961 but by the early 1970s only two of the type remained in flying condition.

Wibault

FIRST FLIGHT 1930

Left: F-AMHK was used by CIDNA on their Paris-Warsaw-Prague run
Below left: A Wibault-Penhöet 282 without the 'trousers' and central engine cowling common in the 282T
Below right: The 282T, *La Glorieux* F-AMYD

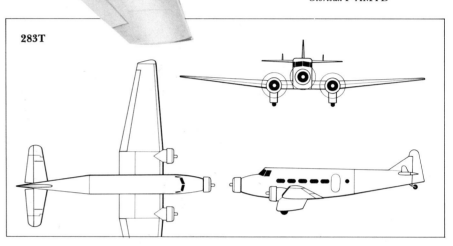

283T

WHEN the biplane was still in widespread airline service, Michel Wibault developed a very advanced all-metal three-engined low-wing monoplane which achieved a remarkable performance with low power. This was the Wibault 280.T10 which appeared in 1930.

Although the type numbers ranged from 280 to 283, these were essentially the same aircraft and individual aeroplanes were operated under varying designations. The prototype was powered by 300-hp Hispano Suiza 9Qa engines but the second aircraft had 350-hp Gnome-Rhône Titan Major 7Kd engines. Bringing the first aeroplane to this standard made it the 281.T10.

In 1931 the Wibault concern merged with Chantiers de Saint-Nazaire Penhoët and production of the 280 type began. Later the company was absorbed by Breguet but production continued with the first six 282.T12s. One aircraft entered service with CIDNA on the Paris-Prague-Istanbul route, and at least two, under the fleet name la Voile d'Or ('Golden Clipper'), went into service on the Paris-London route with Air Union in 1933. The whole batch had been delivered by the time Air France officially took over the earlier airlines in October 1933. The 282.T differed from the 281.T only in having cowlings on the engines.

In 1934 Air France took delivery of ten Wibault 283.T12s with increased fuel capacity, higher weights and different propellers, for its main European routes.

During their working lives the Wibaults underwent numerous modifications. Originally the en-gines were uncowled and there were no under-carriage fairings. Later, the wing engines and finally all three engines, were cowled, while at least seven were fitted with drag-reducing streamlined undercarriage fairings. One 282.T12 was for a time fitted with an experimental retractable undercarriage. There was also a number of tail changes which included increasing the rudder chord, strut-bracing the originally cantilever tailplane, and the addition of two small vertical fins above the tailplane. Two aircraft were converted to long-range versions with higher gross weight and accommodation for only two passengers.

In 1932 there was a twin-float version, soon written off, and a Wibault fuselage served as the first experimental rail-car on the French railways.

Wibault 282.T12

Type: passenger transport
Maker: Chantiers Aéronautiques Wibault; Wibault-Penhöet; Sociéte d'Aviation Louis Breguet
Span: 22.61 m (74 ft 2 in)
Length: 17 m (55 ft 9¼ in)
Height: 5.57 m (18 ft 3¼ in)
Wing area: 64.4 m² (693 sq ft)
Weight: maximum 6200 kg (13 668 lb); empty 4097 kg (9032 lb)
Powerplant: three 350-hp Gnome-Rhône Titan Major 7Kd 9-cylinder air-cooled radial engines
Performance: cruising speed 200 km/h (124 mph); range 1050 km (652 miles)
Payload: seats for 10 passengers
Crew: 2 to 3
Production: 18

F.XXXVI, Fokker

FIRST FLIGHT 1934

FOKKER built five three-engined F.XVIII monoplanes in 1932 for KLM and these went into service on the Amsterdam-Batavia (now Jakarta) route. Although larger, the F.XVIII followed the tradition of the early Fokker transports with rectangular-section straight-sided fuselages, and on the eastern route could carry only four passengers. KLM realized that bigger aircraft would be required and in 1932 placed an order for six four-engined monoplanes known as the F.Y. Construction began in 1933 and the first aircraft flew, as the F.XXXVI, on June 22, 1934. It was in fact the only example built, although the 1935 F.XXII was a scaled-down version.

The F.XXXVI was Fokker's first four-engined aircraft; it was the biggest until the appearance of the postwar F27 Friendship. In layout the F.XXXVI followed Fokker tradition in having a thick high-mounted all-wood cantilever wing, on the leading edge of which the engines were mounted. The fuselage was of welded steel-tube construction, like earlier Fokkers, but of elliptical section built up on a pyramidal girder framework as in the three-engined F.XX of 1933. There was a large single fin and rudder and the undercarriage, including the tailwheel, was non-retractable.

The passenger accommodation was divided into four eight-seat cabins and it was the total of 32 seats plus four crew members which provided the aircraft's type number. The flight-deck was designed to provide the best possible view for the pilots and resulted in a somewhat strange layout with the first pilot on the centreline and second pilot further aft and to the right. The radio operator was on a lower level on the left side. The fourth crew member was a steward.

The availability of the much more modern all-metal Douglas DC-2 led KLM to abandon its intention of using the F.XXXVI on the Indies route, the cancellation of the other five and the use of the sole example on European services, mainly on the London-Amsterdam-Berlin route. Actual delivery to KLM was in March 1935.

Shortly before World War II, having re-equipped with DC-2s and DC-3s, KLM sold the F.XXXVI to Scottish Aviation as a navigational trainer. It was damaged in 1940 and scrapped.

Of the smaller F.XXIIs, KLM had three and Swedish Air Lines (ABA) one. Two were lost in accidents and two passed to Scottish Aviation.

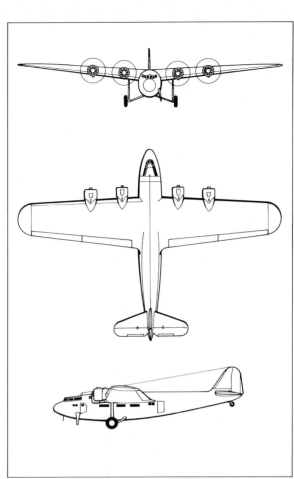

F.XXXVI

Type: passenger transport
Maker: NV Nederlandsche Vliegtuigenfabriek
Span: 33 m (108 ft 3¼ in)
Length: 23.6 m (77 ft 5¼ in)
Height: 6 m (19 ft 8¼ in)
Wing area: 170 m² (1830 sq ft)
Weight: maximum 16 500 kg (36 376 lb); empty 9900 kg (21 825 lb)
Powerplant: four 750-hp Wright Cyclone SGR-1820-F2 9-cylinder air-cooled radial engines
Performance: cruising speed 240 km/h (149 mph); range 1350 km (839 miles)
Payload: seats for 32 passengers
Crew: 4
Production: 1

Left and below: PH-AJA, built by Fokker for KLM, was eventually sold to a British firm and ended its days during World War II as a navigational trainer with the RAF in Scotland

V-1, Vultee

FIRST FLIGHT 1934

FOR many years US airlines made widespread use of single-engined aircraft and operated a wide variety of types. The last of the high-performance single-engined types, and the fastest, was the Vultee V-1A. This design had appeared in 1932 or 1933 as the V-1 designed by Gerard Vultee, formerly chief engineer of Lockheed, and built by the Airplane Development Corporation.

The V-1 was an all-metal low-wing cantilever monoplane with two-spar wing, stressed-skin covering and inward-retracting main undercarriage. The enclosed cockpit high in the nose had the pilot's seat on the left and a mail hold on the right. The passenger cabin had eight seats. The engine was a 700-hp Wright Cyclone F-2 enclosed in a NACA cowling. It appears that only one V-1 was built.

From the V-1 was developed the V-1A which was generally similar but slightly bigger and heavier, with 850-hp Cyclone R-1820-G2 and improved performance. It also had trailing-edge flaps. The V-1A maintained the accommodation for eight passengers but carried two crew.

American Airlines ordered 20 and introduced the type on September 9, 1934. Bowen Airlines also used the V-1A, and it was reported that at least one was sold to Canadian Colonial Airways.

The 1934 production programme contemplated the building of 50 V-1As a year but the days of the single-engined transport were nearly over and only limited numbers were built.

There were a number of V-1A variants and one, believed to have been the V-1A '8', was flown across the United States from Burbank, California, to Floyd Bennett Field, New York, in 11 hours 59 min by Major James Doolittle in 1935. Another of the same type, with long-range tanks and blanked-off windows, was flown across the North Atlantic by Dick Merrill and Harry Richman in 1936. This Vultee was the well known *Lady Peace*.

There was also a twin-float example known as the V-1A-S, and there were numbers of military developments including the V-11, V-12 and YA-19. The military Vultees were used by the United States Army and others were exported to Brazil, China, Turkey, and the USSR.

The V-1As did not long remain in airline service but at least seven of American Airlines' aircraft went to Spain during the Civil War.

Above: The Vultee V-1A, NC 16099 at Oshkosh, Wisconsin. After it had ceased to be used as a transport it remained popular as a racing and sporting aircraft

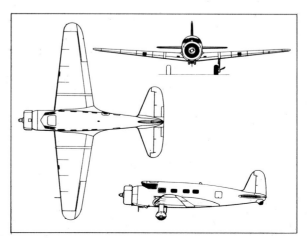

V-1A

Type: high-speed passenger transport
Maker: Airplane Development Corporation
Span: 15.24 m (50 ft)
Length: 11.28 m (37 ft)
Height: 3.09 m (10 ft 2 in)
Wing area: 35.67 m² (384 sq ft)
Weight: maximum 3856 kg (8500 lb); empty 2407 kg (5307 lb)
Powerplant: one 850-hp Wright Cyclone R-1820-G2 9-cylinder air-cooled radial engine
Performance: cruising speed 339.6 km/h (211 mph); range 1609 km (1000 miles)
Payload: seats for 8 passengers
Crew: 1 to 2
Production: not available

Potez 62

FIRST FLIGHT 1935

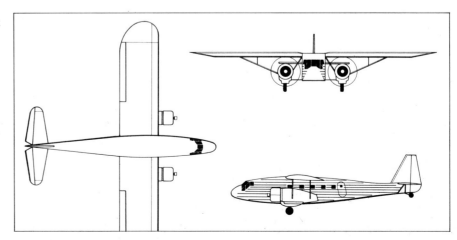

Above: F-ANPG *Albatros* which entered Air France service in 1935
Far left: F-AOTU, delightfully named *La Séduisante* (the Seductress)
Left: The spacious cabin was well decorated, soundproofed and had heating and air-conditioning systems

TOWARDS the end of 1933 the Potez 54 twin-engined military aircraft began flight testing and more than 200 were built. From this design was developed the Potez 62 civil transport which was very similar to the 54 bomber, but without the ugly and bulky lines. This aircraft was destined to form a major part of Air France's fleet, and saw service around the world in the years before the outbreak of World War II.

The Potez 62 had a high-mounted strut-braced wing, untapered except on the detachable tips, single fin and rudder, and retractable tailwheel undercarriage. The ply-covered wooden fuselage was rectangular in section but of streamlined profile; the wing was a metal structure with fabric covering except on the leading edge; and the tail surfaces were of wood with fabric covering.

The two 870-hp Gnome-Rhône 14Kirs Mistral Major supercharged radial engines were cowled and carried on a supporting structure attached to the fuselage lower longerons. They were strut-braced to the top of the fuselage. The engines drove three-blade propellers and the main undercarriage units retracted aft into the engine nacelles.

The Potez 62 had seats for 14 to 16 passengers in two cabins, smoking being allowed in one. The prototype flew on January 28, 1935, and in June, Air France began operating the type on its Paris-Marseilles-Rome services. The airline operated 12 of these aircraft under the designation Potez 62-0.

In 1935 Potez produced the 62-1 with slightly swept-back wing and 720-hp Hispano-Suiza 12Xrs liquid-cooled engines. Air France operated ten

Potez 62-1s and also had three 62-0s re-engined to 62-1 standard. In 1937 the unmodified 62-0s were fitted with 900-hp Gnome-Rhône 14N 16/17s with modified cowlings.

The Potez 62 fleet, in blue and silver livery, worked many of Air France's European services and in May 1936 two 62-1s began operating over the Buenos Aires to Santiago route which involved crossing the Andes.

For their period the Potez 62s were quite fast but had mostly been replaced by more modern aircraft by the start of World War II. One had been lost in India in 1938 and at least one served with the Free French forces.

The Potez 65 troop transport, flown in 1937, was a direct development of the Potez 62.

Potez 62-0

Type: passenger transport
Maker: Société des Aéroplanes Henri Potez
Span: 22.45 m (73 ft 7¾ in)
Length: 17.32 m (56 ft 10 in)
Height: 3.9 m (12 ft 9½ in)
Wing area: 76 m² (818 sq ft)
Weight: maximum 7500 kg (16 534 lb); empty 4895 kg (10 791 lb)
Powerplant: two 870-hp Gnome-Rhône 14Kirs Mistral Major 14-cylinder air-cooled radial engines
Performance: cruising speed 280 km/h (174 mph); range 1000 km (621 miles)
Payload: seats for up to 16 passengers
Crew: 2 to 3
Production: 23 (both versions)

SM.73, Savoia-Marchetti

FIRST FLIGHT 1934

Left: One of the 12 SM.73s in service with SABENA in the 1930s
Below: The robust spatted undercarriage of the SM.73

THE SM.73 was the first of the series of Savoia-Marchetti three-engined low-wing cantilever monoplanes to go into airline service. It had a thick wing, tapering in chord and thickness, built as a watertight three-spar wooden structure with plywood covering. The ailerons and flaps, like the tail surfaces, were of metal construction with fabric covering. The fuselage, also fabric-covered, was of welded steel-tube construction.

The main undercarriage was of the divided type with the wheels enclosed or partly enclosed in large streamlined spats. Passenger accommodation, for 18, was divided between two cabins, a main 14-seat cabin and a small forward cabin at a higher level over the wing spars. The crew normally consisted of two pilots, and one engineer, radio operator and steward. An interesting feature of the SM.73 was the unusually large amount of the fuselage occupied by payload, as the cabin extended well back towards the tailplane.

The prototype first flew on June 4, 1934. It had a continuous row of cabin windows, a tall S.71-type tail unit and four-blade propeller on the centre engine. Production aircraft had individual cabin windows, modified tails and three-blade propellers on each engine.

The first production batch of SM.73s went to Sabena which introduced them on European services in 1935. These SM.73s were powered by 600-hp Gnome-Rhône 9Kfr Mistral Major engines. There then followed a series of SM.73s for Ala Littoria and Avio Linee Italiane, and three types of engine were fitted to these Italian-owned examples – 700-hp Piaggio Stella X.RC, 800-hp Alfa Romeo 126 RC.10 and 760-hp Wright Cyclone GR-1820.

The Czechoslovak state airline ČSA took delivery of three SM.73s in 1937 and these were powered by 615-hp Czechoslovak Walter Pegasus IIM2 engines built under licence from Bristols.

It is believed that 40 SM.73s were built in Italy and in 1936 and 1937 the Belgian company SABCA built seven more Mistral Major-powered examples for Sabena. The acquisition of more SM.73s enabled Sabena to replace the elderly Fokker F.VIIb/3ms on the services linking Brussels with the Belgian Congo, from October 1936.

Some of the Italian examples were used during the war by the Regia Aeronautica and some Sabena SM.73s were used by the RAF. None appear to have survived the war.

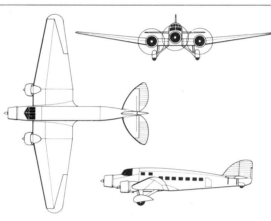

SM.73

Type: passenger transport
Maker: Società Idrovolanti Alta Italia; SABCA
Span: 24 m (78 ft 9 in)
Length: 17.45 m (57 ft 3 in)
Height: 4.6 m (15 ft 1 in)
Wing area: 93 m² (1001 sq ft)
Weight: maximum 10 430 kg (22 994 lb); empty 6930 kg (15 278 lb)
Powerplant: three 700-hp Piaggio Stella X.RC 9-cylinder air-cooled radial engines
Performance: cruising speed 280 km/h (174 mph); range 1600 km (994 miles)
Payload: seats for 18 passengers
Crew: 5
Production: 40 (Italy) 7 (Belgium)

SM.74, Savoia-Marchetti

FIRST FLIGHT 1934

SOCIETÀ Idrovolanti Alta Italia is probably best known for its series of three-engined low-wing monoplane transports and twin-hulled flying boats, but the company also built two types of high-wing monoplane that saw airline service. The first was the Savoia-Marchetti S.71 which generally resembled the three-engined Fokkers in widescale use when the S.71 first flew late in 1930.

The S.71 had accommodation for eight to ten passengers and was powered by three 240-hp Walter Castor or 370-hp Piaggio Stella radial engines. Then during the years 1934 and 1935 SIAI built three SM.74s. These were similar to the S.71s but much bigger and powered by four engines, 700-hp Piaggio Stella X.RCs in the first two aircraft and 845-hp Alfa Romeo Pegasus IIIs in the last one. The engines were enclosed in NACA cowlings and drove three-blade two-position controllable-pitch metal propellers. In 1938 Alfa Romeo 126 engines were fitted.

Like the S.71s, the SM.74s had thick one-piece three-spar wooden wings covered with plywood with a final covering of fabric; welded steel-tube fuselage with ply and fabric covering; and metal-framed tail unit with fabric covering. The wing was fitted with split flaps. The main undercarriage units were attached to the inboard engine mountings, and the wheels were fitted with brakes and partially enclosed in streamlined spats.

The crew cabin was high in the nose just forward of the wing and the main cabin, with full-length windows, had eight single seats on the left side and 16 on the right. There was a bar and lavatory aft

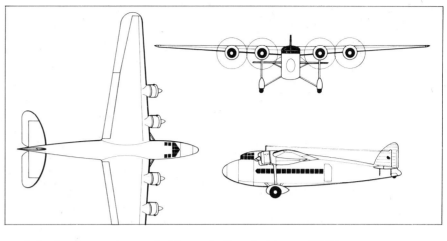

and the baggage was carried in underfloor holds.

The prototype SM.74 flew for the first time on November 16, 1934. All three aircraft were delivered to Ala Littoria during 1935 and were employed on the Rome to Paris route. This involved crossing the Alps and passengers were supplied with oxygen via leads hanging from the overhead baggage racks, the same system being used after World War II on the Savoia-Marchetti SM.95 four-engined low-wing monoplanes used by Alitalia.

During the war the SM.74s were used as military transports by the Regia Aeronautica, serving first with 616, and then later with 604 squadron. The last of the SM.74s was damaged in a bombing raid on Rome's old Urbe Airport on July 19, 1943.

SM.74

Type: passenger transport
Maker: Società Idrovolanti Alta Italia
Span: 29.68 m (97 ft 4½ in)
Length: 21.36 m (70 ft 1 in)
Height: 5.5 m (18 ft 0½ in)
Wing area: 118.54 m² (1276 sq ft)
Weight: maximum 14 000 kg (30 865 lb); empty 9600 kg (21 164 lb)
Powerplant: four 700-hp Piaggio Stella X.RC or 845-hp Alfa Romeo Pegasus III or 800-hp Alfa Romeo AR 126 9-cylinder air-cooled engines
Performance: cruising speed 300 km/h (186 mph); range 1000 km (621 miles)
Payload: seats for 24 passengers
Crew: 3 to 4
Production: 3

Left and below: I-URBE which, with I-ROMA and I-ALPE, made up the Ala Littoria SM.74 fleet. The aircraft's passengers had individual oxygen masks when the aircraft flew over the Alps

SM.83, Savoia-Marchetti

FIRST FLIGHT 1937

THE SM.83 was the smallest of the three-engined Savoia-Marchetti transports and was the civil airliner development of the Regia Aeronautica's standard bomber – the SM.79 Sparviero. The first civil example was described as an SM.83 but registered as an SM.79. The true civil prototype, I-LUCE, was exhibited at the 2nd Salone Aeronautico Internazionale in Milan in October 1937 and made its first flight on November 19 that year.

In general appearance the SM.83 resembled the SM.73 but had a retractable undercarriage. The three-spar watertight wing was of the traditional wooden construction and incorporated camber-changing flaps and Handley Page leading-edge slats. The fuselage also followed established Savoia-Marchetti principles but had a metal-skinned nose, and the top surface was covered partly by metal and partly by plywood. The sides and undersurfaces were fabric-covered.

Twenty-three SM.83s were built in three main versions – the standard type, the SM.83A and the SM.83T with increased fuel capacity.

The SM.83s were used on European services and originally had accommodation for ten passengers but the SM.83A and SM.83T were intended for operation of passenger and mail services between Italy and South America, the SM.83A having six seats and the SM.83T being a mail carrier.

It seems that at least 13 SM.83s were used by Ala Littoria SA Linee Atlantiche and LATI (Linee Aeree Transcontinentali Italiane) on South Atlantic operations. Three others were acquired by the Romanian airline LARES, and these and one owned by Prince Bibesco of Romania all appear to have been powered by 750-hp Alfa Romeo 126 RC.34 engines. However, the three operated by Sabena on its services between Brussels and the Congo had 1000-hp Wright Cyclone GR-1820-G2 engines. On the Congo route the SM.83s cut the flying time to 24 hours and the journey time to 3½ days.

On December 21, 1939, one of LATI's SM.83s left Rome to inaugurate the Italian mail service to Rio de Janeiro. The operation was maintained to a weekly schedule until 1942.

At least 16 of the SM.83s saw war service with the Regia Aeronautica, ten from LATI, three from Sabena and three Romanian. The last airworthy SM.83 made its final flight in 1945.

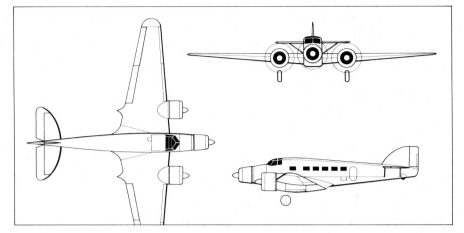

SM.83

Type: passenger and mail transport
Maker: Società Italiana Aeroplani Idrovolanti 'Savoia-Marchetti'
Span: 21.2 m (69 ft 6½ in)
Length: 16.2 m (53 ft 1¾ in)
Height: 4.6 m (15 ft 1 in)
Wing area: 60 m² (646 sq ft)
Weight: maximum 12 165 kg (26 819 lb); empty 6800 kg (14 991 lb)
Powerplant: three 750-hp Alfa Romeo 126 RC.34 or 1000-hp Wright Cyclone GR-1820-G2 9-cylinder air-cooled radial engines
Performance: cruising speed 400 km/h (249 mph); range 2000 km (1243 miles); range of Atlantic SM.83 4800 km (2983 miles)
Crew: 4
Payload: 1000 kg (2200 lb); seats for up to 10 passengers
Production: 23

Above left: The SM.83's crew access and hatches to the baggage area
Left and below: The civil SM.83 differed little from the bomber, except for the revised interior which could take ten passengers

Martin 130

FIRST FLIGHT 1934

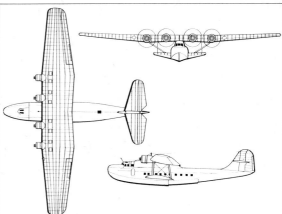

Martin 130

Type: long-range passenger
and mail flying boat
Maker: Glenn L Martin Co
Span: 39.62 m (130 ft)
Length: 27.7 m (90 ft 10½ in)
Height: 7.49 m (24 ft 7 in)
Wing area: 201.6 m² (2170 sq
ft)
Weight: maximum 23 702 kg
(52 252 lb); empty 11 164 kg
(24 611 lb)
Powerplant: four 950-hp
Pratt & Whitney R-1830
Twin Wasp 14-cylinder air-
cooled radial engines
Performance: cruising speed
252.7 km/h (157 mph); range
5150 km (3200 miles), (with
mail only) 6437 km (4000
miles)
Payload: seats for up to 41
passengers
Crew: 5
Production: 3

HAVING established a network of air services
in the Caribbean and South America, Pan
American Airways was eager to develop air services across the North Atlantic and the Pacific.
Charles Lindbergh made survey flights over both
routes and for the Pacific route to the Far East
recommended the northern way round. This was
ruled out because of political reasons and the
airline was faced with opening a mid-ocean route
with, for that time, very long stages.

In mid 1935 Pan American made route surveys
with a modified Sikorsky S-42 but this was incap-
able of carrying any payload over these long trans-
ocean stages. For the operation of the route Pan
American had issued a specification for a flying
boat capable of carrying four crew and at least
136 kg (300 lb) of mail over 4023-km (2500-mile)
stages against a 48-km/h (30-mph) wind. Martin's
M-130 design was given an order for three, and the
first flew on December 30, 1934.

The M-130 was a large strut-braced monoplane
of metal construction. It had a single fin and
rudder, sponsons or sea-wings instead of wingtip
floats, and used for the first time four 950-hp Pratt
& Whitney Twin Wasp radial engines driving
three-blade metal propellers.

Pan American normally employed a 14-seat
layout with triple seats on the right side and single
seats on the left side, but maximum seating was 41.
The crew accommodation was at a higher level.

The M-130s were originally named *China Clipper*, *Philippine Clipper* and *Hawaii Clipper* and the
first of them inaugurated trans-Pacific services
when it left Alameda, San Francisco, on November
22, 1935. The first service took 59 hours 48 min.

The renamed *Hawaiian Clipper* was lost in October 1938 and the other two passed to the US
Navy in 1942. *Philippine Clipper* crashed in California but *China Clipper* was returned to Pan American and used on South Atlantic operations until it
was destroyed whilst landing at night in Trinidad
in January 1945.

In 1937 Martin built a much larger development
of the M-130. This was the M-156 with twin fins
and rudders, four 1000-hp Wright Cyclone engines
and accommodation for 46 passengers. It went to
the Soviet Union where it was designated PS-30
and is believed to have been used by Aeroflot in
1942 on services between Vladivostock and Pet-
ropavlovsk-Kamchatski.

Farman F.224

FIRST FLIGHT 1937

ARLY in the 1930s Farman began development of a series of large high-wing braced monoplanes each with four engines mounted in tandem pairs on either side of the fuselage. The first of these rather ugly aircraft was the F.220 bomber powered with 600-hp Hispano-Suiza 12Lbr engines. One modified F.220, without military equipment, was used by Air France on South Atlantic mail services in 1935.

The heavier Gnome-Rhône-powered F.221 and 222 bombers followed, and Air France had four F.2200 and one F.2220 civil developments for its South Atlantic mail operations. After evaluating these aircraft Air France ordered six of a new development from these types. The F.224 was powered by four 815-hp Gnome-Rhône 14K 14-cylinder two-row air-cooled radials mounted in tandem. The wings, engine installation and undercarriage were similar to the F.222 but the F.224 had a larger tail due to its longer fuselage.

Passengers were accommodated in pairs of seats four abreast with a central aisle. Their baggage was stowed in a compartment in the nose and below the floor of the main cabin. The crew occupied a cockpit on a higher level.

The aircraft was exhibited at the Paris Salon in 1936 where its seating for 40 passengers provoked some interest. However Air France were disappointed with the F.224 and the Armée de l'Air took them into their transport groups in 1939. Their subsequent fate following the fall of France in 1940 is not known.

After the F.224 Farman built the aerodynamically cleaner F.2231 or 223-1 a high performance mail carrier.

The last of the line was the F.2234 which first flew on March 15, 1939. It was a direct development of the F.2231 but was cleaner and heavier. With a slender three-spar all-metal wing, braced to the fuselage by a single strut, it was fitted with full-span flaps and ailerons. The main undercarriage units retracted into the nacelles between the 1000-hp Hispano-Suiza engines which drove the three-blade propellers.

They were intended for experimental high-altitude North Atlantic flights by Air France-Transatlantique but the outbreak of war prevented these operations. They were modified as bombers and in June 1940 one became the first Allied aircraft to raid Berlin.

Above: The Farman 224 was very similar to the F.222 bomber, but due to its greater length it had a larger tail
Left: Cockpit interior, in which the crew positions were higher than the passenger cabin

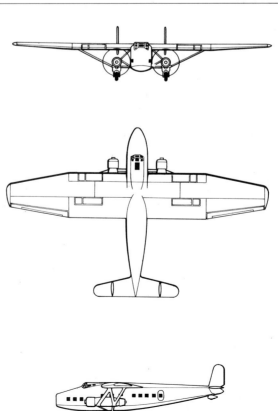

F.224

Type: passenger transport
Maker: Avions Farman (SNCAC)
Span: 36 m (118 ft 1 in)
Length: 23.35 m (76 ft 7 in)
Height: 5.19 m (17 ft)
Wing Area: 186 m² (2002 sq ft)
Weight: maximum 16 270 kg (35 869 lb); empty not available
Powerplant: four 815-hp Gnome-Rhône 14K 14-cylinder two-row air-cooled radials
Performance: maximum speed 300 to 310 km/h (186 to 193 mph); range up to 2000 km (1242 miles)
Crew: 4
Payload: seats for 40 passengers
Production: 6

D.338, Dewoitine

FIRST FLIGHT 1936

SOCIÉTÉ Aéronautique Française, formerly Constructions Aéronautiques E Dewoitine and nationalized in 1936 as Société Nationale de Constructions Aéronautiques du Midi, completed the D.332 in 1932. This was the first of a series of three-engined all-metal low-wing cantilever monoplane transports. It had eight seats, weighed 9350 kg (20 614 lb) loaded, cruised at 250 km/h (155 mph), had a range of 2000 km (1242 miles) and had three 575-hp Hispano-Suiza 9V radials.

The D.332 was followed by three eight- to ten-passenger D.333s which had increased wing area and greater maximum weight. The D.333s were required for the Toulouse-Dakar sector of the South America route. The first, *Antares*, was lost on that route in October 1937 and the other two were transferred to South America.

Sabena had planned to use a D.335 on its Brussels-Malmö services but it was not built and the next type to appear was the D.338 which first flew in the summer of 1936. This was slightly bigger than the earlier designs, heavier, more powerful and faster. The D.338 was essentially similar to the D.333 but had a longer fuselage, with accommodation for up to 22 passengers. In addition, its mainwheels retracted into the engine nacelles whereas the D.332 and D.333s had non-retractable undercarriages with large streamlined fairings.

Air France took delivery of the prototype D.338 in 1936 and soon ordered another 21, later increased to 29, requiring them for European, Far Eastern and South American services. The pro-totype went into service on the Paris-Marseilles-Cannes route in the summer of 1936, the first production aircraft flew in August 1937 and ten had been delivered by June 1938. It was a D.338 which opened Air France's Paris to Hong Kong service in August 1938.

For a short time after the start of World War II D.338s were operating the Paris to London (Heston) service. Two were at Beirut when the Franco-German armistice was signed and these were used for military transport between Beirut and the French Congo. Nine D.338s survived the war and Air France still had eight in December 1946. In Europe the D.338s had 22 seats, on African services 15 and on the Far East route 12 including six sleeper-seats.

Below: The D.338 *Ville d'Orleans* in Air France colours at Le Bourget in 1938. The type was used on routes to Africa and the Far East
Bottom: The slender elegance of the D.338 which was notably larger than its predecessors, the D.332 and 333

D.338

Type: passenger transport
Maker: Société Nationale de Constructions Aéronautiques du Midi
Span: 29.35 m (96 ft 3½ in)
Length: 22.13 m (72 ft 7¼ in)
Height: 5.57 m (18 ft 3¼ in)
Wing area: 99 m² (1066 sq ft)
Weight: maximum 11 150 kg (24 581 lb); empty 8053 kg (17 753 lb)
Powerplant: three 650-hp Hispano-Suiza 9V 16/17 9-cylinder air-cooled radial engines
Performance: cruising speed 260 km/h (161 mph); range 1950 km (1211 miles)
Payload: seats for up to 22 passengers
Crew: 3 to 4
Production: 31

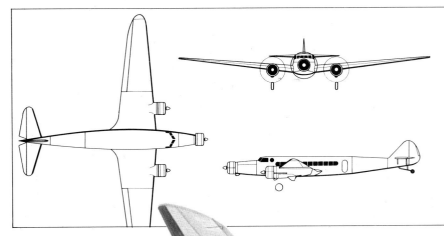

AIR FRANCE   F-AQBL

D.620, Dewoitine

FIRST FLIGHT 1936

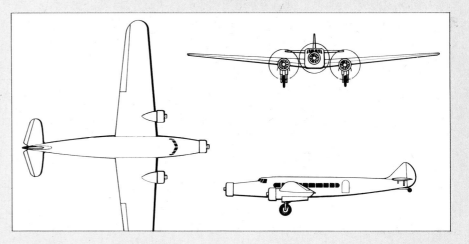

THE Dewoitine D.620 is something of a mystery. It appears to have been completed during 1936 just before the Société Aéronautique Française was nationalized, becoming part of the SNCAM (Société Nationale de Constructions Aéronautiques du Midi). This suggests that it came chronologically between the prototype and production D.338s, which were perhaps the finest civil transports built in France before World War II.

The D.620 had the same all-metal wing as the D.338, with trailing-edge flaps. The fuselage length of the two types was the same but initially the D.620 had eight square windows in each side of the fuselage instead of the D.338's long rectangular windows. Later, the D.620 was modified and had an almost continuous row of windows along each side of the cabin area.

It appears that the D.620 was designed for European routes because it had 30 seats. Nine of these seats were located in the forward cabin, and 21 in the main rear cabin which also contained a bar thus necessitating a steward, lavatory and baggage hold. Few airliners at that time had accommodation for so many passengers, and it is quite possible that this over-ambitious approach contributed in no small measure to the aircraft's lack of success.

The D.620 was powered by three 880-hp Gnome-Rhône 14Krsd 14-cylinder radial engines driving three-blade controllable-pitch propellers. There were close-fitting cowlings which were later changed for cowlings similar to those on the D.338. The mainwheels retracted into the engine nacelles and the undercarriage doors were hinged to let down in front of the wheels, but were later exchanged for side-hinged doors, which were found to be less drag-producing which in turn improved the performance of the aircraft.

The D.620 was heavier than the D.338 and slightly faster but it had less than half the range. With one engine inoperative it had a ceiling of 5200 m (17 060 ft). The aircraft was not put into production, was never used and its fate is unknown.

A last example of this Dewoitine layout was the D.342 of 1939. This was powered by three 915-hp Gnome-Rhône 14N engines, had accommodation for 24 passengers and was delivered to Air France in 1942.

D.620

Type: passenger transport
Maker: Société Aéronautique Française
Span: 29.36 m (96 ft 3¾ in)
Length: 23.59 m (77 ft 4½ in)
Height: 5.725 m (18 ft 9⅓ in)
Wing area: 99 m² (1065 sq ft)
Weight: maximum 12 760 kg (28 131 lb); empty 7800 kg (17 196 lb)
Powerplant: three 880-hp Gnome-Rhône 14N 14-cylinder air-cooled radial engines
Performance: cruising speed 270 km/h (168 mph); range 900 km (559 miles)
Payload: seats for 30 passengers
Crew: 4
Production: 1

Above left: The cockpit of a 620, with co-pilot's seat cushion removed
Left and below: The D.620 with the earlier landing-gear fairings

Monospar ST.4, General Aircraft

FIRST FLIGHT 1932

Left: G-ABUZ a privately owned Monospar ST.4, with experimental larger fin
Below left: G-AEDY after being rebuilt as the prototype ST.25 Universal, with twin fins and folding wings
Bottom: G-AEDY the prototype of the Monospar ST.25 De Luxe. There was only one other De Luxe built

THE ST.4 four-seat twin-engined monoplane was the first type to go into production with the patented 'Monospar' wing which had been designed by H J Stieger in the 1920s.

Stieger had been concerned with the problems of producing a cantilever metal-structured wing which combined adequate strength with an acceptably low weight. The result was a single spar built up as a tapering girder strengthened with a Warren girder system of tie-rods to prevent both blending and twisting.

The success of the ST.3, built by Gloster Aircraft, led to the setting up of General Aircraft and the design and production of the ST.4. The ST.4's entire structure was of metal with fabric covering and both the wing and fuselage were constructed on the Monospar system. The wing centre section had an untapered leading edge and reverse taper on the trailing edge. It tapered from the very thin section at the root to maximum thickness at the junction with the outer wings, which themselves were of normal taper in thickness and had taper in plan on both leading and trailing edges. The upper section of the spar was visible at the centre section, being revealed by the wing's thinning at the root. Aft of the spar, the centre-section panels folded upward against the fuselage to allow the main wing panels to fold aft.

There was a single fin and rudder, the undercarriage was non-retractable, and the engines were 85-hp Pobjoy R seven-cylinder radials driving four-blade wooden propellers.

The first ST.4 flew in May 1932, seven were built and these were followed by 22 improved ST.4 Mk IIs. E E Fresson's Highland Airways used one from Inverness to Wick and Orkney, VASP used two for airline work in Brazil, and Commercial Air Hire employed ST.4s on the Inner Circle airline linking Croydon and Heston.

Three ST.4s were converted to ST.6s with retractable undercarriages. Another development was the ST.10 which had a fixed undercarriage and was powered by Pobjoy Niagara I radials. Also built were two ST.11s, ten ST.12s and the one, much bigger, ST.18 Croydon.

The ST.25 was developed from the ST.10 and was the last built in numbers. There were three versions of the ST.25 – the ST.25 Jubilee, De Luxe and Universal. There were 30 Jubilees built, 29 Universals but only one De Luxe.

Monospar ST.4

Type: light transport
Maker: General Aircraft Ltd
Span: 12.24 m (40 ft 2 in)
Length: 8.02 m (26 ft 4 in)
Height: 2.13 m (7 ft)
Wing area: 20.3 m² (219 sq ft)
Weight: maximum 1157 kg (2550 lb); empty 617 kg (1360 lb)
Powerplant: two 85-hp Pobjoy R 7-cylinder air-cooled radial engines
Performance: cruising speed 185 km/h (115 mph); range 869 km (540 miles)
Payload: seats for 3 passengers
Crew: 1
Production: 29

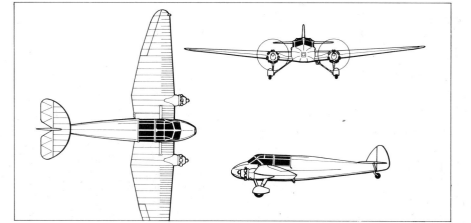

Ju 160, Junkers

FIRST FLIGHT 1934

THE Ju 160 stemmed from the same requirement as the Heinkel He 70, namely Lufthansa's need for an aircraft to match the performance of the Lockheed Orion. Junkers' first attempt to meet the specification was the Ju 60 which is thought to have been built in 1933.

The Ju 60 broke with Junkers' tradition in having a two-spar instead of multi-spar wing, although still covered with a corrugated metal skin, and a smooth-skinned metal fuselage with oval section. It had a single 600-hp BMW Hornet C radial engine, tandem seats for the two crew, and a cabin for six passengers. The only known example had a forward-retracting main undercarriage but there is some evidence of an earlier example with non-retractable undercarriage. The Ju 60 saw limited service with Lufthansa but did not go into production.

From the Ju 60 was developed the generally similar Ju 160 which can be regarded as the production version. The Ju 160's wing was of modified planform and smooth-skinned, as were the tail surfaces. The crew's cockpit was more cleanly faired into the fuselage, the main undercarriage retracted inwards and was completely enclosed, and the 660-hp BMW 132E was enclosed in a close-fitting NACA cowling. The prototype had a deep rudder and a tail skid but production aircraft had shorter rudders and were fitted with tailwheels. Full-span Junkers 'double wing' flaps and ailerons were fitted.

The prototype and 20 production aircraft, named after animals, were used by Lufthansa, the type entering service in 1935 and being used almost entirely on domestic routes. The type was operating over a dozen routes in 1937 and at least 16 were still in service when World War II began in September 1939.

Two Ju 160s are known to have been exported. They were to Manchurian Air Transport in 1937. The German Air Ministry operated Ju 160s, 26 are known to have been on the German civil register and total production according to reports, was as many as 48.

Just as the He 70 experience was embodied in the twin-engined He 111, so the experience gained in the design and development of the Ju 60 and Ju 160 was to prove useful to Junkers in producing the twin-engined Ju 86 which saw limited civil use and was produced in large numbers as a bomber.

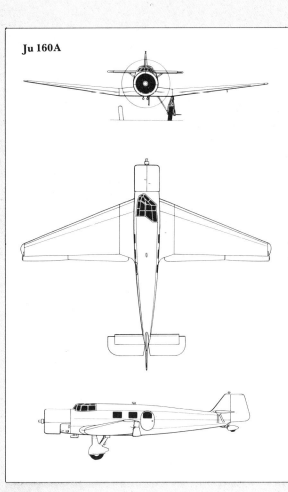

Ju 160A

Ju 160

Type: high-speed passenger transport
Maker: Junkers Flugzeug-und-Motorenwerke AG
Span: 14.32 m (46 ft 11¾ in)
Length: 12 m (39 ft 4½ in)
Height: 3.92 m (12 ft 10½ in)
Wing area: 34.8 m² (374½ sq ft)
Weight: maximum 3550 kg (7826 lb); empty 2320 kg (5115 lb)
Powerplant: one 660-hp BMW 132E 9-cylinder air-cooled radial engine
Performance: cruising speed 315 km/h (196 mph); range approx 1020 km (634 miles)
Payload: seats for 6 passengers
Crew: 2
Production: 48

Below: The slightly cranked wings of the Ju 160. Whereas in the Ju 60 the wing covering was of corrugated metal, in the 160 it was of polished aluminium sheet
Bottom: *Lion* opens up its engine prior to take-off

S-43, Sikorsky

FIRST FLIGHT 1935

Left: An S-43 in service with its largest operator, PanAm, with whom the type were nicknamed 'Baby Clippers'

THE Sikorsky S-43 made its first flight on June 1, 1935. It was a twin-engined amphibian of about half the weight and capacity of the four-engined S-42, although in appearance it resembled a much refined version of that aircraft. The S-43 was a high-wing monoplane with the wing supported on a pair of N struts above the hull; outboard of these struts, which were in line with the engines, the wing was a cantilever structure.

The hull, of pleasing shape, was a two-step all-metal structure into the sides of which the main-wheels retracted, the tailwheel being aft of the rear step. The wing was a metal structure but the trailing-edge flaps, occupying 48% of the span and 20% of the chord, were fabric-covered as were the tail surfaces which comprised strut-braced tail-plane, divided elevators and single fin and rudder.

The two engines, mounted ahead of the wing, were 750-hp Pratt & Whitney Hornets enclosed in NACA cowlings and driving three-blade constant-speed variable-pitch metal propellers. Normal accommodation was for two pilots, a steward, and 15 passengers in two separate cabins.

Pan American Airways bought 14 of these amphibians and put the first of them into service in April 1936 in Brazil where they replaced Commodore flying boats. Pan American called the S-43s 'Baby Clippers' and some were operated by the airline's associated Panair do Brasil. In August 1938 Pan American used the type on proving flights between Seattle and Juneau in Alaska.

Inter-Island Airways (later Hawaiian Airlines) operated four S-43s on internal services throughout

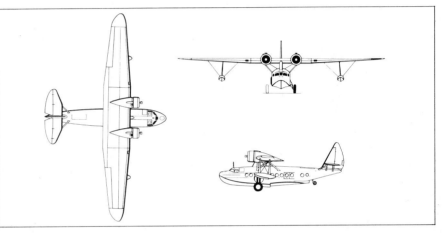

the Hawaiian Islands, Aéromaritime used four in West Africa, and DNL-Norwegian Air Lines had one. In addition, Iloilo-Negros Air Express operated Philippine inter-island services with S-43s, and one, operated in Alaska by Reeve Aleutian Airways, was still to be seen, although unairworthy, at Anchorage in 1958. One S-43 was sold to the Soviet Union and there was at least one privately owned example. During World War II, S-43s were used in Brazil to transport rubber.

Apart from the civil S-43s, the United States Army Air Forces had five, known as Y1OA-8s, for military transport work and bought one from a civil operator and redesignated it OA-11. The United States Navy had 15 S-43s and the US Marine Corps two.

S-43

Type: passenger amphibian
Maker: Sikorsky Aircraft
Span: 26.21 m (86 ft)
Length: 15.59 m (51 ft 2 in)
Height: 5.38 m (17 ft 8 in)
Wing area: 72.5 m² (781 sq ft)
Weight: maximum 8845 kg (19 500 lb); empty 5783 kg (12 750 lb)
Powerplant: two 750-hp Pratt & Whitney R-1690 Hornet 9-cylinder air-cooled radial engines
Performance: cruising speed 267 km/h (166 mph); range 1247 km (775 miles)
Payload: seats for up to 19 passengers
Crew: 3
Production: 53

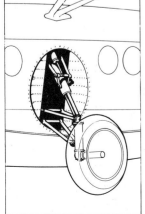

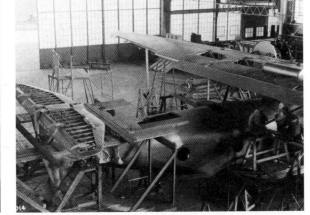

Far left: The retracting mainwheel of the S-43 which fitted snugly into the hull when the aircraft was in flight
Left: One of the 53 S-43s under construction in the mid 1930s

DC-3, Douglas

FIRST FLIGHT 1935

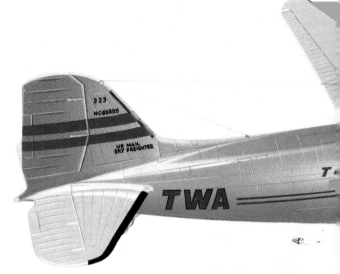

Left: A DC-3 of the Finnish airline Kar Air
Right: A DC-3 in the livery of TWA before the company's transition from Transcontinental & Western Air to Trans World Airlines. The 'S' was added to the word 'Airline' after May 17, 1950 when the company name changed officially
Below right: DC-3 night plane with Sleeper berths forward on each side of the aisle

THE Douglas DC-3 was one of the most important transport aircraft ever built. The type probably did more than any other to establish air transport as a normal means of travel and to open up communications in remote areas, while during the war variants had a vital world role.

The DC-3 was a direct development of the DC-2 and it came into being to meet the requirements of American Airlines. That airline and Transcontinental & Western Air (TWA) were both operating US transcontinental services. TWA was using DC-2s. But American's route was longer and it had to operate sleeper services with Curtiss Condor biplanes because the DC-2s did not have sufficient space for sleeping berths. However, the Condors were much slower than the DC-2s.

By the summer of 1934 American Airlines had foreseen this problem and decided that it required an aircraft with the performance and economics of the DC-2 combined with the space of the Condor, room for sleeping berths on each side of the aisle and the ability to fly non-stop in both directions over the New York to Chicago route.

Douglas was not anxious to embark on a new aircraft but American insisted and the result was the DST (Douglas Sleeper Transport) – an aircraft based on the DC-2 but with increased span and length, wider fuselage, more powerful engines and modified tail for better directional stability.

The new aircraft was to appear in two versions, namely the DST (sleeper) with 14 berths and the DC-3 (day plane) with, initially, 21 seats.

The first DST, with 1000-hp Wright Cyclone SGR-1820-G2 engines, made its first flight on December 17, 1935, and the type entered service with American on June 25, 1936, but initially as a day plane, between New York and Chicago. In August 1936 American Airlines began receiving DC-3s and this released DSTs which then, on September 18, began transcontinental sleeper services to a 16 hours eastbound and 17 hours 45 min westbound schedule.

The DC-3, or DST, was a very clean low-wing cantilever monoplane with single fin and rudder and retractable main undercarriage. It had the by then traditional Northrop multi-cellular wing structure and was very strong. The type was destined to be produced in many civil and military versions with a wide range of engines and suffered very few fatigue problems.

Forty DSTs were built, 21 with the original Cyclone engines and 19 as DST-As with 1000-hp Pratt & Whitney Twin Wasp R-1830s. Before the Japanese attack on Pearl Harbor, Douglas had built nearly 400 DC-3s of which about a quarter were exported. Wright Cyclones and Pratt & Whitney Twin Wasps were used as powerplant, with Cyclones finding most favour at that time.

The first 20 went to American Airlines, the 21st went to the USSR, and the next went to KLM – the first non-US airlines operator. Alternate batches then went to United Air Lines, Eastern Air Lines, American Airlines and TWA.

With the United States' entry into World War II large-scale military production of DC-3s began. These were to be used for almost every conceivable

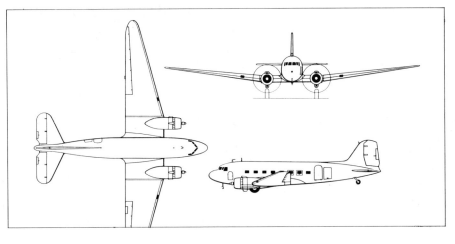

duty, fitted with a variety of engines and had many designations. Two of the most widely used were the C-47 Skytrain series with double loading doors and the C-53 Skytrooper. The US Navy designation was R4D.

Military DC-3s were used by most of the Allied air forces and after the war thousands became surplus and passed to civil operators with the result that almost every airline operating postwar services had DC-3s. In the UK BEA operated two with Rolls-Royce Dart turboprops.

Douglas built a total of 10 655 DC-3 series and about 2500 were built under licence in the Soviet Union (PS-84s later redesignated Li-2s) and in Japan (L2Ds) by Nakajima and Showa. Considerable numbers of DC-3s are still in service.

DC-3

Type: civil and military transport
Maker: Douglas Aircraft Co; Nakajima Hikoki KK; Showa Hikoki Kogyo KK; Soviet State Aircraft
Span: 28.96 m (95 ft)
Length: 19.65 m (64 ft 5½ in)
Height: 5.16 m (16 ft 11⅛ in)
Wing area: 91.692 m² (987 sq ft)
Weight: maximum 10 886 kg (24 000 lb); empty 7802 kg (17 200 lb)
Powerplant: two 1000-hp Wright Cyclone SGR-1820-G2 9-cylinder or 1000-hp Pratt & Whitney Twin Wasp R-1830-S1CG 14-cylinder air-cooled radial engines
Performance: cruising speed 333 km/h (207 mph); range 3420 km (2125 miles)
Payload: berths for 14 passengers (night) and up to 36 seats (day)
Crew: 4
Production: 10 655 (USA), approx 2500 (licence)

Above left: The cockpit of a typical prewar DC-3
Far left: BEA was one of a number of airlines who found that the DC-3 was not only reliable and safe but was the first airliner to return a profit without the support of mail contracts or subsidies
Centre left: The main landing gear was stronger than that of the DC-2 and operated more smoothly
Left: The nine-cylinder Wright Cyclone SGR-1820-G2 was by far the most popular DC-3 engine in the 1930s

FK.50, Koolhoven

FIRST FLIGHT 1935

Left: The Swiss airline Alpar
Luftverkehrs operated the
FK.50 on a route between
Berne and Geneva
Below: The last FK.50, which
had a modified fuselage and
twin rudders

FREDERICK Koolhoven was a designer of some reputation in the 1920s and 1930s. In 1922 he had designed the FK.31 two-seat fighter monoplane and later the FK.41 three-seat cabin monoplane. In 1934 the NV Koolhoven Vliegtuigen was formed and in the same year produced the six-passenger twin-engined FK.48 which was used by KLM on the Rotterdam-Eindhoven route and also for taxi work and training.

Only one FK.48 was built but in 1935 it was followed by the bigger FK.50 of similar layout and construction with two-spar all-wooden cantilever high-mounted wing, fabric-covered welded steel-tube fuselage and metal-framed tail unit, also fabric-covered. The tailwheel undercarriage was not retractable.

The FK.50's enclosed cockpit was ahead of the wing and housed a crew of two and the main cabin had seats for eight passengers. The engines were two 400-hp Pratt & Whitney Wasp Juniors driving two-blade adjustable-pitch propellers. The NACA cowlings enclosing the engines, however, gave the impression of being too large for the relatively small aircraft.

The first FK.50 left the factory in September 1935 and was delivered later that year to Alpar Luftverkehrs in Switzerland. A second FK.50 joined the Alpar fleet early in 1936.

In 1938 the third, and last, FK.50 was completed and this differed in a number of respects to the first two aircraft. It had twin fins and rudders instead of a large single fin and rudder, a longer nose, modified cockpit, larger-diameter wheels,

increased weight and much slimmer engine nacelles. The nacelle and tail changes suggest that the original aircraft had some shortcomings.

These unique aircraft served Alpar's domestic services based in Berne although only two were ever in service together, the second aircraft having crashed in September 1937. There were presumably adequate spares because the other two survived the war and in the summer of 1946 operated a weekly Berne-Paris-London (Croydon) service.

The original FK.50 was broken up in 1947 and the sole survivor crashed in Liberia in 1962. There is reason to believe that the third example with twin fins and rudders was known as the FK.50A. There was also a projected military version designated FK.50B but this was never built.

FK.50

Type: light transport
Maker: NV Koolhoven Vliegtuigen
Span: 18 m (59 ft 0¾ in)
Length: 14 m (45 ft 11¼ in)
Height: 3.7 m (12 ft 1½ in)
Wing area: 44.7 m² (481 sq ft)
Weight: maximum 4100 kg (9039 lb); empty 2505 kg (5522 lb)
Powerplant: two 400-hp Pratt & Whitney Wasp Junior T1B 9-cylinder air-cooled radial engines
Performance: cruising speed 260 km/h (161½ mph); range 1000 km (621 miles)
Payload: seats for 8 passengers
Crew: 2
Production: 3

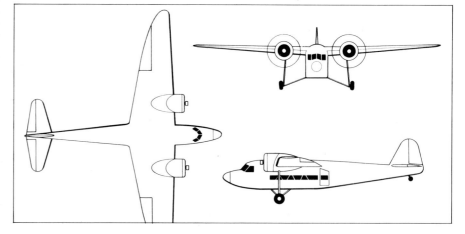

Empire Flying boat, Short

FIRST FLIGHT 1936

IN 1934 the British Government announced the Empire Air Mail Programme under which most first class mail for British territories was to be carried by air without surcharge. Imperial Airways invited Shorts' proposals for an improved Kent flying boat to carry 24 passengers and 1½ tons of mail, and cruise at 241 km/h (150 mph) over a 1287-km (800-mile) stage.

The Air Ministry had also invited Shorts to tender for a four-engined long-range flying boat. After studying biplane designs, Shorts submitted clean high-wing cantilever monoplanes to meet both requirements. These were the S.23 (later C class) and the S.25 (later the Sunderland). Impe-0rial Airways ordered 28 C class 'boats and the Air Ministry a prototype Sunderland.

The S.23 was of very advanced design with a deep hull, single fin and rudder, cantilever wing with camber-changing flaps, and fixed wingtip floats. The four fully-cowled 920-hp Bristol Pegasus XC engines were mounted on the leading edge and drove three-blade propellers. The lower deck contained four passenger cabins with an initial total of 24 seats and the flight-deck and mail hold were on the upper deck.

Canopus, the first S.23, flew on July 4, 1936 and the order was changed to provide a total of 31 of which six were for Qantas Empire Airways while two of Imperial Airways' 'boats, *Caledonia* and *Cambria*, were to be built as long-range aircraft for North Atlantic trials.

Canopus made the first C class scheduled flight, from Alexandria to Brindisi, on October 30, 1936

and the same aircraft flew the first through service from Southampton to Durban in June 1937. On June 26, 1938, *Camilla* and *Cordelia* left Southampton to inaugurate flying-boat services to Australia, *Challenger* taking over at Singapore on July 2.

The C class maintained essential services during the war, undertook some military duties in Europe and the Mediterranean and played a major role in the Pacific war.

Nine heavier Perseus-engined S.30s were built, and four were equipped to enable flight refuelling for North Atlantic operation.

In 1938 three high-weight S.33s were ordered to replace aircraft lost in accidents. Two were launched at the end of April 1940 but the third was not completed.

Above: *Canopus* takes off from the Medway with Rochester Castle keep in the background
Below: *Canopus* in wartime livery

S.23 C class

Type: passenger and mail flying boat
Maker: Short Brothers Ltd
Span: 34.7 m (114 ft)
Length: 26.8 m (88 ft)
Height: 9.7 m (31 ft 9¾ in)
Wing area: 139.4 m² (1500 sq ft)
Weight: maximum 18 371 kg (40 500 lb) S.23; 21 773 kg (48 000 lb) S.30 and S.33; empty 10 660 kg (23 500 lb) S.23; 12 239 kg (27 180 lb) S.30 and S.33
Powerplant: four 920-hp Bristol Pegasus XC, 890-hp Bristol Perseus XIIC or 1010-hp Pegasus XXII 9-cylinder air-cooled radial engines
Performance: cruising speed 265.5 km/h (165 mph); range 2414 km (1500 miles)
Payload: seats for up to 24
Crew: 5
Production: 42

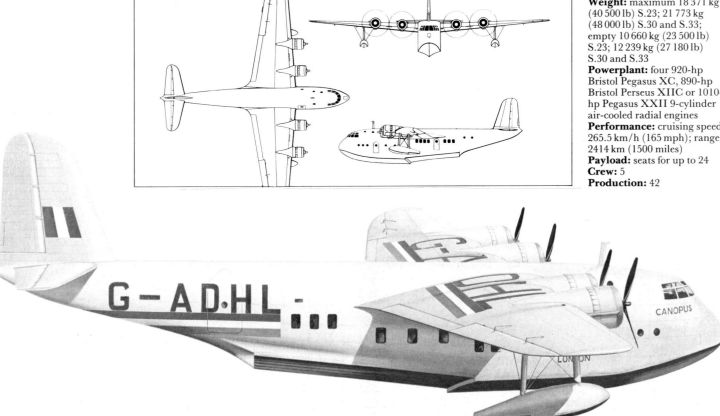

109

Ju 86, Junkers

FIRST FLIGHT 1934

THE German Air Ministry and Lufthansa col-laborated in 1933 on the specification for a twin-engined aircraft which could serve as a bomber for the still secret Luftwaffe and as a high-speed transport for the airline. The design to meet this specification was the Junkers Ju 86 which incorporated the experience gained in designing the single-engined Ju 60 and Ju 160.

The Ju 86 was a low-wing cantilever monoplane with the wing tapered in both chord and thickness. There were two main spars, between which were the fuel tanks, the covering was a smooth stressed metal skin and on the trailing edge were Junkers auxiliary-wing ailerons and flaps. The fuselage was of oval section and covered by a flush riveted duralumin skin. The tailplane was strut-braced and there were twin fins and rudders. The main undercarriage units retracted outwards to be housed in the wing.

In the civil aircraft there was accommodation for two crew and ten passengers. Because of the confined space the passenger seats were slightly staggered and turned inwards.

The Ju 86 was the first aircraft to be designed specifically for diesel power, 600-hp Junkers Jumo 205Cs being the chosen engines. But when the first prototype of the military version flew on November 4, 1934, it was powered by Siemens radial engines. The first civil aircraft, although the second proto-type, was the third to fly in April 1935, and the first with Jumo engines.

The first production Ju 86s were the Ju 86A bomber and the Ju 86B airliner which Lufthansa began operating on domestic services in 1936.

There were numerous versions of the civil Ju 86, and several types of engines were fitted. These included BMW 132s, Pratt & Whitney Hornets and Rolls-Royce Kestrel XVIs.

Swissair used both Jumo- and BMW-powered Ju 86s, ABA in Sweden used a Hornet-powered example on night mail services, and Southern Airlines and Freighters in Australia had a Jumo-powered Ju 86. LAN in Chile took three of the aircraft with Jumos, Lloyd Aereo Boliviano had two Hornet-powered Ju 86s and ten BMW-engined aircraft were used on Manchurian air services; three of them were re-engined with Mitsubishi Kinsei radials. A Jumo 205 Ju 86 made an endurance flight of 52 hours in 1939 but overall the type was not a great success.

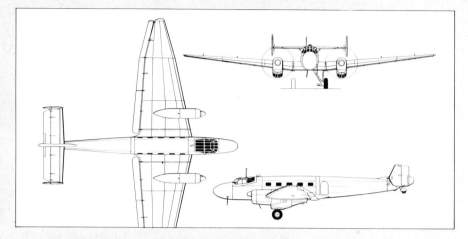

Ju 86

Type: passenger, freight and mail transport
Maker: Junkers Flugzeug-und-Motorenwerke AG
Span: 22.5 m (73 ft 10 in)
Length: 17.41 m (57 ft 1½ in)
Height: 4.7 m (15 ft 5 in)
Wing area: 82 m² (882 sq ft)
Weight: maximum 8000 kg (17 637 lb); empty 4960 kg (10 935 lb)
Powerplant: two 800-hp Pratt & Whitney Hornet S1E-G 9-cylinder air-cooled radial engines
Performance: cruising speed 360 km/h (224 mph); range 1100 km (684 miles)
Payload: seats for 10 passengers
Crew: 2
Production: approx 1000 (civil and military)

Above left: The accommodation for ten passengers in the Ju 86. Note the leather seats and the absence of head racks
Left: Lufthansa Ju 86 with the early Jumo 205 heavy-oil engines
Below: A Ju 86 of South African Airways

Z.506, Cant

FIRST FLIGHT 1935

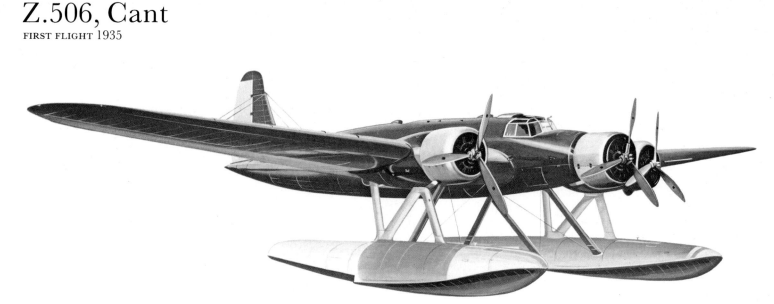

CANTIERI Riuniti dell'Adriatico built an attractive three-engined twin-float mail-carrying seaplane in 1935 to the designs of Ing Filippo Zappata. This was the Z.505, powered by Isotta-Fraschini Asso XI RC.15 liquid-cooled engines.

From the Z.505 design Cant developed the very similar Z.506 passenger carrier which first flew on August 19, 1935. The Z.506 was a low-wing monoplane with all-wood wing built round three box spars, divided into a number of watertight compartments and ply-covered. Long-span camber-changing flaps were fitted. The fuselage was a well proportioned wooden monocoque structure and the tail unit was also built of wood with ply covering; the tailplane was originally wire-braced to the fuselage and fin but later the lower wires were replaced by struts.

The large floats were single-step metal structures carried on N struts and strut- and wire-braced to the fuselage. Each float had a buoyancy equal to the maximum loaded weight of the aircraft.

Passenger accommodation was in two cabins divided by the entrance on the left side and lavatory to the right. Initially each cabin had six seats but later 15 or 16.

The prototype Z.506 had Pratt & Whitney Hornet engines but the first production batch, built for Ala Littoria, were powered by 760-hp Wright Cyclone GR-1820-F52s.

The production Z.506s were followed by the Z.506B which was produced in quantity as a torpedo bomber and the Z.506C civil airliner with 750-hp Alfa Romeo 126 RC.34 or 800-hp Alfa

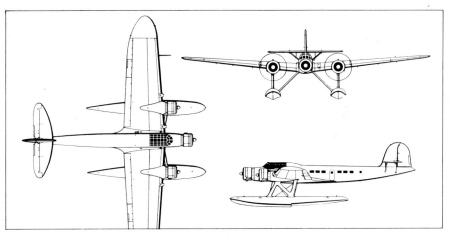

Romeo 126 RC.10 engines. Ala Littoria had a fleet of Z.506s and the type set a large number of speed, altitude and distance records.

In Ala Littoria service the Z.506s operated over the Rome-Benghazi, Rome-Palma-Melilla-Cadiz, Rome-Genoa-Marseilles and Trieste-Brindisi routes. There was not a standard colour scheme but all the seaplanes were brightly painted.

There were about 40 civil-registered Z.506s and Ala Littoria is believed to have operated at least 19 of them. Seventeen civil aircraft were operated under military serials during the war. Some of the military Z.506Bs were converted to Z.506S air-sea rescue aircraft. There was one Z.506 landplane, and one Z.506 derivative was the bigger Z.509 transatlantic mail floatplane.

Z.506

Type: passenger floatplane
Maker: Cantieri Riuniti dell'Adriatico
Span: 26.5 m (86 ft 11¼ in)
Length: 18.92 m (62 ft 1 in)
Height: 6.77 m (22 ft 2½ in)
Wing area: 85 m² (915 sq ft)
Weight: maximum 10 500 kg (23 148 lb); empty 7200 kg (15 873 lb)
Powerplant: three 760-hp Wright Cyclone GR-1820 F52 or 800-hp Alfa Romeo 126 RC.10 or 750-hp Alfa Romeo 126 RC.34 9-cylinder air-cooled radial engines
Performance: cruising speed 320 km/h (199 mph); range 1300 km (808 miles)
Payload: seats for up to 16 passengers
Crew: 3
Production: approx 40 (civil)

Above: The Cant Z.506 was one of the most successful designs of the talented Filippo Zappata
Left: I-FANO in service with Ala Littoria before the war

111

ANT-35, Tupolev

FIRST FLIGHT 1936

THE Soviet Union's first attempt at designing and building a clean twin-engined low-wing all-metal monoplane transport with retractable undercarriage resulted in the ANT-35. Although the aircraft bore Tupolev's initials, A A Arkangelskii was responsible for the design.

The ANT-35 had accommodation for two crew and ten passengers, the same as the Lockheed Electra, but in size it came somewhere between the Electra and the Douglas DC-2 and the Russian aircraft was faster than the American types.

The all-metal wing, with wide-span split flaps, was based on that of the SB-2 light bomber and the outer panels may have been the same on both types. There was a single fin and rudder and the rather stalky main undercarriage units retracted backwards into the engine nacelles. The powerplant comprised two 800-hp M-85 14-cylinder air-cooled radial engines based on the French Gnome-Rhône 14K series, and drove three-blade propellers.

The ANT-35 made its first flight on August 20, 1936, and on September 15 flew from Moscow to Leningrad and back in 3 hours 38 min at an average speed of 376 km/h (234 mph). At the end of that year it appeared at the Paris Salon, poorly finished and without any de-icing equipment, which was of course essential.

A small production batch was delivered to Aeroflot in 1937 and the type, as the PS-35, began working a Moscow-Riga-Stockholm service on July 1. PS-35s were also introduced on the Moscow to Prague route. The production aircraft were generally similar to the prototype but had 850-hp M-85A engines which were based on the Gnome-Rhône 14N engine.

PS-35s were considered to have too little capacity and were regarded as uneconomic and it is believed that only a few were built. However, it seems that a further attempt was made to improve the PS-35 and that a new version appeared in 1939 with 1000-hp M-62IR nine-cylinder engines based on the Wright Cyclone engine. This version was slightly heavier and had an improved payload but reduced range. There are reports of PS-35s, possibly the 1939 version, going into service between Moscow and Lvov and Moscow and Odessa in 1941. No further development of the PS-35 took place, although there were a few transport versions of the SB-2 series bombers.

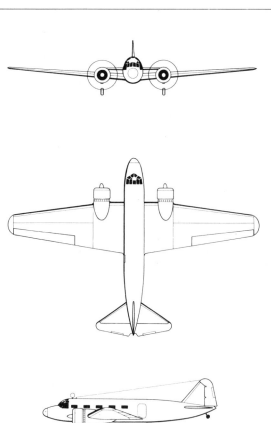

Above and below: The prototype ANT-35. Before the war it operated on Aeroflot's Moscow-Riga-Stockholm route

ANT-35

Type: passenger transport
Maker: Tupolev Design Bureau
Span: 20.8 m (68 ft 3 in)
Length: 15 m (49 ft 2½ in)
Height: not available
Wing area: 58 m² (624 sq ft)
Weight: maximum 6620 kg (14 594 lb); empty 4710 kg (10 384 lb)
Powerplant: two-800-hp M-85 14-cylinder air-cooled radial engines
Performance: cruising speed 350 km/h (217 mph); range 2000 km (1243 miles)
Payload: seats for 10 passengers
Crew: 2
Production: 11 (estimated)

DH.91 Albatross, de Havilland

FIRST FLIGHT 1937

THE fact that a standard DC-2 could only be beaten by a special DH.88 racing aircraft in the 1934 MacPherson Robertson race convinced de Havilland that Britain must produce a much more advanced transport aircraft. The Air Ministry placed an order for two experimental transatlantic mailplanes. These were the beautiful DH.91 Albatross airliners.

The Albatross was a low-wing monoplane with finely tapered wing, circular-section fuselage, four slim closely-cowled engines, retractable undercarriage and twin fins and rudders. The only jarring feature was the inset strut-braced fins and rudders, but the design was soon modified to incorporate endplate fins.

The structure owed much to the Comet racers and the wing was a one-piece cantilever structure with marked dihedral and comprised a wooden box-spar with two layers of spruce planking forming the skin. The fuselage was built as an unobstructed shell in the form of a sandwich with ply inner and outer skins and a balsa centre. The engines were specially developed 525-hp Gipsy Twelves created by joining two Gipsy Sixes to form an inverted V-12. They drove two-blade metal propellers.

The first aircraft flew on May 20, 1937, and although it suffered a few troubles, proved to have outstanding performance. Imperial Airways ordered five shorter-range 21-seat passenger aircraft for its European services and the first of these flew in June 1938.

As the first of the F class, *Frobisher* began

operation in November 1938 and promptly set a number of records including London to Paris in 53 min while the *Falcon* flew from London to Brussels in 48 min. Regrettably the F class suffered a number of problems, mainly connected with their retractable undercarriages, and they had not fully settled into service when the war began.

The passenger aircraft were then mainly used on Bristol-Shannon services, on flights to Lisbon, and for a short period operated military services between the United Kingdom and Egypt and India. The long-range pair went to No 271 (Transport) Squadron, RAF and operated between the United Kingdom and Iceland where both were destroyed in accidents. The Frobisher class was finally withdrawn in July 1943 and the survivors broken up.

Above and below: G-AFDI *Frobisher* which was delivered to Croydon in 1938 and became the flagship of the Imperial Airways F class. It was destroyed by a German air raid on the F class base at Whitchurch, Bristol in 1940

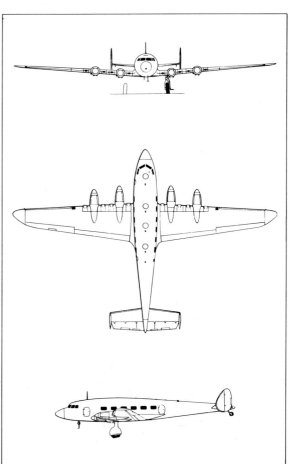

DH.91

Type: passenger transport and mailplane
Maker: de Havilland Aircraft Co
Span: 32 m (105 ft)
Length: 21.79 m (71 ft 6 in)
Height: 6.14 m (20 ft 2 in)
Wing area: 100.15 m² (1078 sq ft)
Weight: maximum 13 381 kg (29 500 lb); empty 9207 kg (20 298 lb)
Powerplant: four 525-hp de Havilland Gipsy Twelve inverted V-12 air-cooled engines
Performance: cruising speed 338 km/h (210 mph); range 1674 km (1040 miles)
Payload: seats for 21 passengers
Crew: 4
Production: 7

Envoy, Airspeed

Above: The seating was for six to eight passengers
Left: The prototype Envoy overflying the *Queen Mary*. It was modified to a series II aircraft and lost in 1936 when it crashed into a mountain in bad weather in Spain

WITH the AS.5 Courier of 1933, Airspeed had completed the first British aircraft with retractable undercarriage to go into production. From this type the company developed the larger twin-engined AS.6 Envoy and this first flew on June 26, 1934.

The Envoy was a low-wing cantilever monoplane of wooden construction with mixed plywood and fabric covering. The mainwheels retracted into the engine nacelles but were partially exposed in flight. The pilot's cabin provided very good visibility and the main cabin could seat eight passengers or six if a lavatory was provided.

The Airspeed design was based on the use of two Wolseley nine-cylinder radial engines and examples of the Envoy flew with Wolseley AR.9, Aries and Scorpio engines. But the development of the Wolseley engines was cancelled and most British-operated, as well as numbers of export Envoys, were powered by Armstrong Siddeley Lynx or Cheetah seven-cylinder engines. Envoys sold to Czechoslovakia had Walter Castor engines, one sold to Ansett in Australia was re-engined with Wright Whirlwinds, and at least some of the Envoys, built under licence by Mitsubishi as the Hina-Zuru (Young Crane), are thought to have had Mitsubishi-built Lynx engines.

Apart from the variety of engines fitted, and indicated by suffix letters to the type number, there were three main variants – the Series I without trailing-edge flaps, the Series II with flaps, and the Series III with split flaps and some other changes including stressed-ply wing skinning. There were

also the Convertible Envoys built for the South African Air Force. These, together with four sold to South African Airways, could be converted in about 30 hours from civil to military use, in the latter form having a dorsal gun turret, a fixed forward-firing gun and bomb racks.

In Britain a well-known Envoy was the King's Flight example in red, blue and silver. North Eastern Airways had Envoys on routes linking London with north-east England and Scotland; Japan Air Transport and Manchuria Air Transport used British and Japanese-built examples; CSA used them on Czechoslovak services.

For the 1934 England to Australia race the AS.8 Viceroy variant was built, and military Oxfords were a direct development of the Envoy.

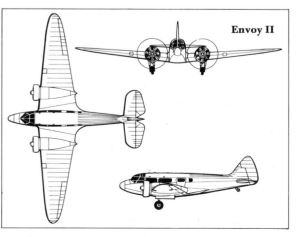

Envoy II

Envoy I

Type: light transport
Maker: Airspeed (1934) Ltd; Mitsubishi Jukogyo KK
Span: 15.95 m (52 ft 4 in)
Length: 10.52 m (34 ft 6 in)
Height: 2.9 m (9 ft 6 in)
Wing area: 31.5 m² (339 sq ft)
Weight: maximum 2404 kg (5300 lb); empty 1396 kg (3077 lb)
Powerplant: two 185-hp Wolseley A.R.9 Mk 1 9-cylinder or 220-hp Armstrong Siddeley Lynx IVC or 277-hp Cheetah V 7-cylinder radial engines
Performance: cruising speed 241 km/h (150 mph); range 644 km (400 miles)
Payload: seats for up to 8
Crew: 1
Production: 62 (all types)

Envoy III

Specification similar to Series I except in following particulars:
Weight: maximum 2994 kg (6600 lb); empty 1969 kg (4340 lb)
Powerplant: two 350-hp Armstrong Siddeley Cheetah IX 7-cylinder or 260-hp Walter Castor or 290-hp Wolseley Scorpio III 9-cylinder radial engines
Performance: cruising speed 274 km/h (170 mph); range 998 km (620 miles)

Bloch 120

FIRST FLIGHT 1934

THE Bloch 120 was one of the lesser known transport aircraft of the 1930s but it gave good service under very difficult operating conditions. It was a three-engined high-wing monoplane of all-metal construction, with non-retractable undercarriage, and the aircraft proved to be particularly hardy and robust.

France was anxious to develop its air services through Africa and in May 1934 the Government founded Régie Air Afrique to establish services across the Sahara into Black Africa, and the Bloch 120 was chosen to equip the airline, its characteristics of reliability and sturdiness being essential in the Africa of the 1930s.

A route was established from Algiers to the French Congo via Niamey and Fort Lamy, with numerous intermediate stops for refuelling, the longest sector being the 1207 km (750 miles) between Aoulef and Gao. Carrying only mail and cargo, the service began on September 7, 1934. After some experience was gained however, passengers were carried from April 27, 1935. The Bloch 120 was originally designed to accommodate ten passengers but because of the long stages and high temperatures only five seats were fitted and the passenger load was normally restricted to three or four with average payload 800 kg (1763 lb).

The crew compartment was beneath the leading edge of the wing and fully enclosed. Beneath the large passenger cabin windows, on the slab-sided fuselage, the Blochs carried the legend 'Ligne Alger Congo'.

In May 1935, to aid further development, the French Government made a Bloch 120 available to Service de la Navigation Aérienne de Madagascar for its Tananarive-Broken Hill route, a second Bloch being used from July of that year and passengers being carried from August. In November 1935 the service from Madagascar was extended to the Congo and by exchanging loads with Air Afrique, mail was flown over the entire route between Tananarive and Paris. Passengers were carried between Brazzaville and Tananarive from April 19, 1936.

In September 1937 Air Afrique took over the whole operation together with the two Madagascar Bloch 120s, giving the airline a fleet of at least seven, some of which served until September 1939. A total of 12 Bloch 120s was built.

Bloch 120

Type: passenger and mail transport
Maker: Avions Marcel Bloch
Span: 20.54 m (67 ft 4¾ in)
Length: 15.3 m (50 ft 2½ in)
Height: not available
Wing area: 61 m² (657 sq ft)
Weight: maximum 6000 kg (13 228 lb); empty 3600 to 3700 kg (7937 to 8157 lb)
Powerplant: three 300-hp Lorraine Algol 9Na 9-cylinder air-cooled radial engines
Performance: cruising speed 230 km/h (143 mph); range in excess of 1207 km (750 miles)
Payload: 800 kg (1763 lb); seats for up to 10 passengers
Crew: 3
Production: 12

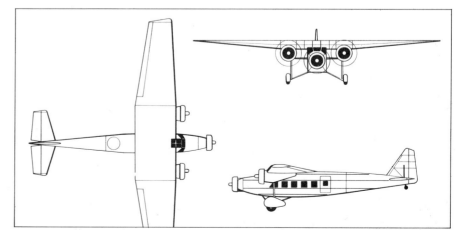

Bloch 220

FIRST FLIGHT 1935

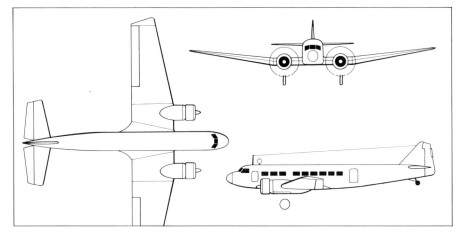

THIS clean all-metal low-wing monoplane designed for Air France's main European routes may be regarded as the French answer to the new Douglas transports. It flew first in December 1935, as did the DC-3, and in power and weight the Bloch 220 came somewhere between the DC-2 and DC-3.

The Bloch's span was shorter than that of the DC-2, the fuselage was close in size to the DC-2's, but performance was inferior to the American types. The Bloch had 16 passenger seats compared with the DC-2's 14.

The Bloch's wing had a flat untapered centre section while the outer panels had dihedral and taper on the leading edge. Split flaps were fitted. The two 985-hp Gnome-Rhône 14N 16/17 radial engines were mounted on the wing leading edge, enclosed in low-drag cowlings, and drove three-blade controllable-pitch propellers. The mainwheels retracted forward into the engine nacelles and were fully enclosed.

The rectangular-section fuselage and the tail surfaces were all metal-skinned. After some time in service rubber-boot leading-edge de-icers were fitted to the wings, tailplane and fin.

Air France ordered 14 Bloch 220s and introduced the type on the Paris-Marseilles route during the winter of 1937–38. When Bloch 220s began operating Paris to London services in the spring of 1938 they cut the scheduled time by 15 min to 1 hour 15 min.

By mid 1938 ten Bloch 220s had been delivered, which were operating as far as Stockholm and Bucharest, and Air France ordered two more. During World War II some of the Bloch 220s were seized and passed to Lufthansa, but at least 11 were registered as owned by the French State in 1943 and five were still in service six years later by which time they had been fitted with 1200-hp Wright Cyclone R-1820-97 engines and redesignated Bloch 221.

Air France used Bloch 221s on early postwar services between Paris and Geneva, Strasbourg and Prague, and four aircraft were being operated in 1949 by Société Auxiliaire de Navigation Aérienne (SANA).

Although 220s were mainline aircraft, none had flown 3000 hours by the autumn of 1945 – a low annual use for a modern airliner.

Bloch 220

Type: passenger transport
Maker: Avions Marcel Bloch; SNCASO
Span: 22.82 m (74 ft 10½ in)
Length: 19.25 m (63 ft 1¾ in)
Height: 3.9 m (12 ft 9½ in)
Wing area: 75 m² (807 sq ft)
Weight: maximum 9500 kg (20 944 lb); empty 6807 kg (15 007 lb)
Powerplant: two 985-hp Gnome-Rhône 14N 16/17 14-cylinder air-cooled radial engines
Performance: cruising speed 280 km/h (174 mph); range 1400 km (870 miles)
Payload: seats for 16 passengers
Crew: 4
Production: 16

Far left: The interior of a Bloch 220 on Air France's continental service
Left: Loading mail into F-AOHE *Saintonge*
Below: F-AQNM *Provence* part of the fleet which operated in the late 1930s

Ha 139, Blohm und Voss

FIRST FLIGHT 1937

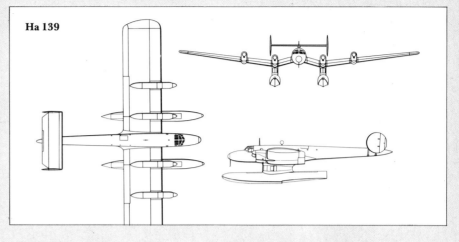

Ha 139

WHEN the airlines set out to operate the first transatlantic services they were severely handicapped by the limited range and payload of the contemporary aircraft. Lufthansa's answer was to catapult its aircraft from depot ships, thus enabling them to take off at greater weights than the aircraft could achieve under their own power and at the same time providing refuelling stations.

At first Lufthansa employed Dornier Wal flying boats but in 1935 and 1936 the technical director of Blohm und Voss's associate company, Hamburger Flugzeugbau, designed the Ha 139 long-range trans-ocean floatplane for the airline.

The Ha 139 was an all-metal low-wing monoplane with sharp anhedral angle on the inner sections of the wing, which was built up on a large-diameter tubular spar. There was a slender monocoque fuselage and a high-mounted tailplane with twin fins and rudders. The metal floats (each with 12 watertight compartments) were attached to the wings by streamlined mountings which carried the radiators for the inboard pair of the four 605-hp Junkers Jumo 205C heavy-oil engines.

It was required that the Ha 139 should be able to carry a 500-kg (1102-lb) payload over a stage of 5000 km (3107 miles) at 250 km/h (155 mph), be stressed for catapult launching and be able to alight on and take off from rough water at a weight high enough to allow a range of 1000 km (621 miles).

Two Ha 139s were built, *Nordwind* ('North Wind') and *Nordmeer* ('North Sea'). The first was completed in 1936, and in 1937 both made experimental flights between the Azores and New York,

operating from the depot ships *Schwabenland* and *Friesenland*. Seven return flights were made and in 1938 there were a further 13 return flights by the two Ha 139s and the bigger and aerodynamically improved Ha 139B *Nordstern* ('North Star').

Following these successful experimental North Atlantic operations, the three seaplanes were transferred to the South Atlantic where they shared regular operation of the mail service with the Dornier flying boats.

The war brought Lufthansa's South Atlantic operations to an end and the Bv 139s (as they became) were taken over by the Luftwaffe. The *Nordstern* was fitted with a magnetic degaussing ring for minesweeping and all three served as transports during the Norwegian campaign.

Ha 139A

Type: long-range mail-carrying seaplane
Maker: Blohm und Voss; Hamburger Flugzeugbau
Span: 27 m (88 ft 7 in)
Length: 19.5 m (63 ft 11¾ in)
Height: 4.8 m (15 ft 9 in)
Wing area: 117 m² (1259 sq ft)
Weight: maximum 17 500 kg (38 580 lb); empty 10 360 kg (22 840 lb)
Powerplant: four 605-hp Junkers Jumo 205C 6-cylinder upright liquid-cooled heavy-oil engines
Performance: cruising speed 260 km/h (162 mph); range 5300 km (3293 miles)
Crew: 4
Payload: 480 kg (1058 lb)
Production: 3

Far left: The view forward from the flight engineer's position behind the pilot
Left: The *Nordmeer* prepares to launch from her base ship the *Schwabenland* in autumn 1937.
Below: D-ASTA *Nordstern*, the third Ha 139 to be built

DC-4E, Douglas

FIRST FLIGHT 1938

EVEN before the DC-3 had made its first flight, Douglas and United Air Lines (now United Airlines) were discussing a four-engined aircraft of double the capacity – the first of the great United States family of metal four-engined transport monoplanes.

In 1936 American Airlines, Eastern Air Lines, Pan American Airways and Transcontinental & Western Air (TWA) decided to join United and each put up $100 000 towards the cost of designing and building one prototype DC-4. Later Pan American and TWA withdrew.

When it appeared, the DC-4 looked something like a big DC-3 but was a very big aircraft with four 1450-hp Pratt & Whitney Twin Hornet R-2180 two-row 14-cylinder closely cowled engines mounted on the swept-back leading edge of the wing centre section. Each engine drove a three-blade propeller. The wing was fitted with wide-span trailing-edge flaps. It was of multi-cellular construction with flush-riveted stressed-skin covering except for the fabric-covered ailerons.

The large-volume metal monocoque fuselage was divided into a number of compartments, the main cabin having seats for 40 passengers or berths for 28 on night flights. An aft stateroom, with its own lavatory and washbasins, could accommodate two day or night passengers. There were men's lavatories, washbasins and hand-baggage space forward and similar amenities for women between the main cabin and the stateroom, and also a galley and underfloor cargo and baggage holds. There were small sleeper windows high in the fuselage for the upper berths. Production aircraft were to be pressurized.

The tail unit comprised a dihedral tailplane with triple fins and rudders. These were of metal construction with metal-covered fixed surfaces and fabric-covered control surfaces.

An outstanding feature of the DC-4 was its retractable nosewheel undercarriage, the large single mainwheels retracting sideways and inward to be housed in the wing and the nosewheel retracting aft.

The DC-4 first flew on June 7, 1938 and, after certification in May 1939, was handed over to United Air Lines which had been scheduled to take delivery of the first six. The aircraft was painted in United's livery and began a series of demonstration

Below left: The prototype DC-4, later called DC-4E, comes in to land in autumn 1939. Note the inward-retracting single-wheel main gears

Below: The prototype at New York's Floyd Bennett Field in 1939. After receiving its Type Certificate it was painted in United Air Lines colours

and proving flights, frequently attracting large crowds at the places visited.

The big Douglas showed something of its performance when it took off from Cheyenne in Wyoming at an elevation of 1890 m (6200 ft) on the power of only two engines.

Although the DC-4 was an impressive aircraft, some aspects of its performance were disappointing. It was something of a maintenance nightmare, and its economics were not attractive even after seating capacity had been raised to 52 and the loaded weight increased. As a result of the trials with United, the sponsoring airlines favoured a smaller and less complicated derivative, also known as the DC-4. However, by the time the new aircraft was ready the US was in World War II

and the new DC-4 went into military service as the C-54 Skymaster.

After the decision to build the smaller DC-4, the original aeroplane was redesignated DC-4E, the suffix standing for Experimental.

United returned the DC-4E to Douglas and towards the end of 1939 it was sold to the Mitsui Trading Company allegedly for operation by Greater Japan Air Lines. There were reports that the DC-4E had crashed near Tokyo but apparently it was handed over to Nakajima for study and used as the basis for the Japanese Navy's Nakajima G5N1 Shinzan four-engined long-range bomber. Six prototypes were built but Shinzan was not a success. In Japan the DC-4E was known as the Navy Experimental Type D Transport.

DC-4E

Type: experimental passenger transport
Maker: Douglas Aircraft Co
Span: 42.14 m (138 ft 3 in)
Length: 29.74 m (97 ft 7 in)
Height: 7.48 m (24 ft 6½ in)
Wing area: 200 m² (2155 sq ft)
Weight: (during day) maximum 30 164 kg (66 500 lb); empty 19 307 kg (42 564 lb)
Powerplant: four 1450-hp Pratt & Whitney Twin Hornet R-2180-S1A1-G 14-cylinder air-cooled radial engines
Performance: cruising speed 322 km/h (200 mph); range 3540 km (2200 miles)
Payload: seats for 30 passengers (night) and for up to 52 (day)
Crew: 5
Production: 1

Ensign, Armstrong Whitworth
FIRST FLIGHT 1938

WHEN the British Government announced the Empire Air Mail Programme in 1934, Imperial Airways had to plan for an adequate fleet to carry the extra mail as well as to cater for increasing passenger traffic. The main operations were to be undertaken with flying boats but it was decided to maintain a landplane route between the Middle East and India and it was necessary to acquire a suitable, large aircraft.

A specification for an eastern route aircraft was issued in May 1934 and to meet this Armstrong Whitworth designed the AW.27 four-engined high-wing cantilever monoplane which, when it entered service, was known as the Ensign class. Imperial Airways ordered one AW.27 in September 1934 and specified that it should be delivered within two

years. At the end of May 1935 the order was increased to 12, with delivery of the extra 11 at a rate of one a month from March 1937. Finally, in January 1937, two more AW.27s were ordered to provide a fleet of 14.

It had been decided that there should be two versions, one with accommodation for 27 passengers for the eastern route and the other capable of carrying 40 passengers on European services. The aircraft became known as Eastern and Western but did not have separate type numbers.

The thick cantilever wing was a metal structure built up on a box spar. It had split flaps and was metal-covered back to the aft face of the rear spar, with fabric on the rear surfaces. The fuselage was a fairly slender metal monocoque structure and the

Above: The AW.27 Ensign 1 G-ADSR had a comparatively unproductive career flying 2099 hours before it was withdrawn from service at Almaza, Cairo in September 1944 and scrapped in 1945
Below right: *Euterpe* is loaded with first-class Empire mail prior to a flight in the days before World War II
Bottom right: *Ensign*, flagship of the Imperial Airways Fleet. It was scrapped at Cairo in 1945

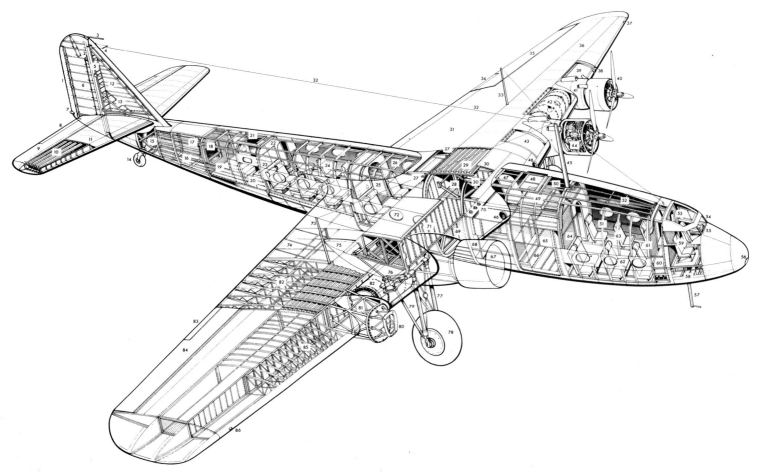

tail unit was of metal with fabric-covered control surfaces. Four closely cowled 800-hp Armstrong Siddeley Tiger IX moderately supercharged 14-cylinder radial engines were mounted on the leading edge and drove the three-blade metal propellers. The massive mainwheels retracted into the inboard engine nacelles.

In the Eastern type there were three nine-seat cabins and on the left side a 'promenade deck' linking the mid and forward cabins. On the right side was a large mail and freight hold. In the Western type there were 12-seat cabins, and a four-seat coupé behind the main aft cabin.

Although Imperial Airways had taken adequate steps to acquire a modern landplane fleet ready for the Empire Air Mail Programme, things went very wrong. Britain was being forced to re-arm to meet the German threat and priority had to be given to production of Armstrong Whitworth's Whitley bomber. Eventually the prototype AW.27 made its first flight, at Hamble, on January 24, 1938.

The AW.27 proved to have a number of shortcomings including a very poor initial climb due to the length of time taken to retract the undercarriage. Some improvements were made and on October 24, 1938, *Ensign* began operating *ad hoc* London to Paris services following a demonstration flight over the route on October 20. That December *Egeria, Elsinore* and *Euterpe* were selected to help with the heavy Christmas mail loads to Australia but all three suffered failures and none got beyond India.

All the AW.27s so far delivered were returned to Armstrong Whitworth for improvement and the

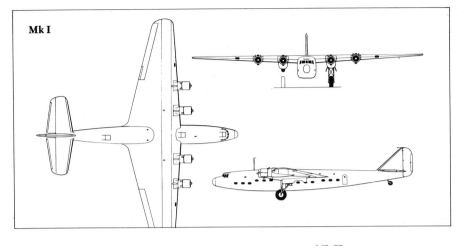

Mk I

engines were changed for 850-hp Tiger IXCs. Delivery of modified aircraft began in the summer of 1939 and 11 were received before the start of World War II.

The Tiger engine continued to give trouble and it was decided to install 950-hp Wright Cyclone engines. The last two aircraft had still not been delivered and one of them first flew, with Cyclones, as the prototype Mk II on June 20, 1941.

The re-engined aircraft served BOAC in Africa, the Middle East and India but still gave trouble. *Eddystone* flew the last AW.27 passenger service, from Cairo to Hurn, in June 1946. The seven survivors returned to the United Kingdom in 1946 and were all broken up at Hamble, where they had been built, in 1947.

Mk II

Type: passenger transport
Maker: Sir W G Armstrong Whitworth Aircraft Ltd
Span: 37.49 m (123 ft)
Length: 33.83 m (111 ft)
Height: 7 m (23 ft)
Wing area: 227.6 m² (2450 sq ft)
Weight: maximum 25 175 kg (55 500 lb); empty 16 597 kg (36 590 lb)
Powerplant: four 950-hp Wright Cyclone GR-1820-G102A 9-cylinder air-cooled radial engines
Performance: cruising speed 289.7 km/h (180 mph); range 2205 km (1370 miles)
Payload: 5443 kg (12 000 lb)
Crew: 5
Production: 14 (total)

Mk I

Specification similar to Mk II except in following:
Weight: maximum 22 000 kg (48 500 lb); empty 14 932 kg (32 920 lb)
Powerplant: four 800-hp Armstrong Siddeley Tiger IX or 850-hp Tiger IXC 14-cylinder radials
Performance: cruising speed 274 km/h (170 mph); range 1384 km (860 miles)
Payload: seats for 27 (Eastern); 40 (Western)

Ensign

1 Rudder servo and trim tab
2 Tail bias mechanism
3 Mass balance
4 Aerial attachment point
5 Rudder post
6 Rudder structure, fabric-covered
7 Tail lamp
8 Elevator trim tab
9 Right elevator, spring balanced
10 Tailplane box-spar construction
11 Tailplane metal skinning
12 Fin structure, fabric-covered
13 Box-spar/fin brace
14 Non-retractable tailwheel
15 Shock-absorber strut
16 Catwalk access to tail
17 Aft fuselage construction
18 Corrugated bulkhead (with hatch)
19 Aft freight hold (right loading)
20 Aft toilet/washroom
21 Dorsal hatch
22 Aft passenger entry door (left)
23 Aft passenger cabin bulkhead
24 Aft cabin (9 passengers)
25 Aft midships cabin door
26 Midships cabin (9 passengers)
27 Wing fixing points
28 Box-spar internal bracing
29 Box-spar corrugated skin
30 Wing fixing points
31 Wing fabric covering (aft of spar)
32 Aerial
33 Aerial post
34 Left aileron servo and trim tab
35 Left aileron, mass-balanced Frise type
36 Wing light-alloy skinning torsion box and leading edges
37 Left navigation lamp
38 Landing lamp
39 Left outer oil tank
40 De Havilland variable-pitch propeller
41 Engine exhaust stubs
42 Left fuel tank
43 Left inner oil tank
44 Armstrong Siddeley Tiger IX engine
45 Aerial mast
46 Cabin ventilation intakes
47 Forward passenger/crew entry door
48 Dorsal freight hatch
49 Upper freight compartment
50 Promenade deck (left)
51 Forward cabin (9 passengers)
52 Control cables (above false cabin ceiling)
53 Flight-deck door
54 Flat windscreen
55 Control yoke
56 Nose landing lamp
57 Pitot head
58 Corrugated bulkheads and flooring
59 Pilot/co-pilot seats
60 Radio-operator's position
61 Forward cabin bulkhead
62 Double seats to right throughout
63 Single seats to left throughout
64 Forward cabin/freight bulkhead
65 Main freight hold
66 Right freight loading hatch
67 Pantry/galley position
68 Forward toilet/washroom
69 Mail compartment beneath wing-spar
70 Fuel cocks
71 Box-spar/undercarriage attachment
72 Individual oval windows per seat row
73 Aerial post
74 Split flaps
75 Undercarriage nacelle
76 Retraction jack
77 Main undercarriage legs
78 Mainwheel
79 Radius rods
80 Engine mounting
81 Engine-bearer frame
82 Wing construction
83 Right aileron servo tab
84 Right aileron
85 Wing ribs
86 Right navigation lamp

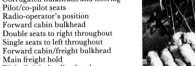

L-14, Lockheed

FIRST FLIGHT 1937

THE Model 10 Electra having proved successful, Lockheed designed a larger, heavier, faster and more refined aircraft of similar layout. This was the Model 14 which first flew on July 29, 1937. In its early days the Lockheed 14 was known as the Super Electra, Electra Senior and Sky Zephyr, but these names were soon abandoned and throughout its working life the aircraft was generally known by its type number.

The L-14 had a deep elliptical-section fuselage, a wing with compound taper on the trailing edge, twin fins and rudders and retractable undercarriage. Unlike the Electra, the L-14 was a mid-wing monoplane and it had Fowler trailing-edge area-increasing flaps. Slots were built into the wing near the leading edge of the outer sections. Normal accommodation was for two crew and 12 passengers.

The Lockheed 14 was available in a number of versions, the main differences being the engine installation – Pratt & Whitney Hornets and Wright Cyclones being the original installations.

Northwest Airlines introduced Lockheed 14s on its Twin Cities-Chicago services in October 1937, and the type was adopted by a number of airlines in the United States, Canada, Europe, Australia and Asia. British Airways operated a mixed fleet of Lockheed 14s and Electras on its main services and some passed to BOAC.

In 1938 Howard Hughes flew a Lockheed 14 round the world in 3 days 19 hours 14 min, and Air Afrique set a record by flying one from Paris to Algeria in 3 hours 55 min. Also in 1938, it was in an L-14 that Chamberlain flew to Munich for his historic meeting with Hitler.

Lockheed built 112 Model 14s and Japan acquired a licence for manufacture. Kawasaki and Tachikawa built these with 900-hp Mitsubishi Ha-26-II engines. The Japanese designation for the Lockheed 14 was LO. In addition the Japanese companies developed the aircraft and built 121 under the designation Ki-56.

From the Lockheed 14 was developed the Hudson maritime reconnaissance bomber for the Royal Air Force. The USAAF operated Hudsons as A-28s, A-29s and AT-18s and the US Navy used the type under the designation PBO. A further development of the model was the L-18 Lodestar, which had a longer fuselage but was basically very similar to the L-14.

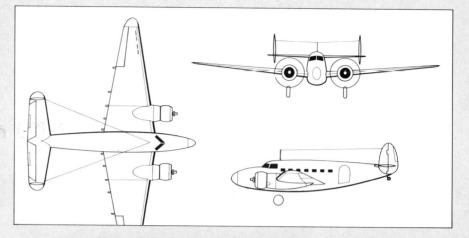

Model 14

Type: passenger transport
Maker: Lockheed Aircraft Corporation; Kawasaki Kokuki Kogyo Kabushiki Kaisha; Tachikawa Hikoki Kabushiki Kaisha
Span: 19.96 m (65 ft 6 in)
Length: 13.47 m (44 ft 2½ in)
Height: 3.49 m (11 ft 5½ in)
Wing area: 51.2 m² (551 sq ft)
Weight: maximum 6804 kg (15 000 lb); empty 4393 kg (9685 lb)
Powerplant: two 750-hp Pratt & Whitney Hornet S1E2G or 760-hp Wright Cyclone GR-1820-F62 or 820-hp Cyclone GR-1820-G3 9-cylinder air-cooled radial engines
Performance: cruising speed 387.8 km/h (241 mph); range 1609 km (1000 miles)
Payload: seats for 12 passengers
Crew: 2 to 3
Production: 112 (USA) 119 (Japan)

Above left: Checking the Cyclone engines on a Northwest Model 14
Left: Part of the accommodation for 14 passengers
Below: The Model 14 used by Chamberlain in 1938

L-18 Lodestar, Lockheed

FIRST FLIGHT 1939

THE Lockheed 18 Lodestar was generally similar to the Model 14 but with a longer fuselage with accommodation for two pilots, a stewardess and 14 passengers. The prototype first flew on September 21, 1939.

The Lodestar was a mid-wing all-metal monoplane with single-spar three-piece wing fitted with Fowler flaps and built-in leading-edge slots. Like the 14, the Lodestar had an elliptical-section monocoque fuselage and twin fins and rudders. The mainwheels retracted into the engine nacelles.

There were six main production models – the 18-07 with 750-hp Pratt & Whitney Hornet engines; the 18-08 with 900-hp Twin Wasps; the 18-14 with 1050-hp Twin Wasps; the 18-40 with 900-hp Wright Cyclones; the 18-50 with 1000-hp Cyclone G202As; and the 18-56 with 1000-hp Cyclone G205As. All versions had three-blade controllable-pitch fully-feathering metal propellers.

Lodestars entered service in March 1940 with Mid-Continent Airlines. Although in Europe World War II was already in progress, in the US airlines were still operating under peacetime conditions and Continental Airlines, National, Pennsylvania-Central and Pan American all bought Lodestars. Alaska Star Airlines and Pacific Alaska Airways also acquired the L-18. In Canada CPA and TCA operated the type, BWIA took them and other Lodestar operators in the Americas were Panair do Brasil, TACA and LAV.

Sabena, Régie Air Afrique and South African Airways used Lodestars in Africa, BOAC operated a total of 38 mostly in the Middle East and Africa, and postwar operators included East African Airways, New Zealand National, Trans-Australia, Kar-Air in Finland and Airtaco in Sweden.

Although most airlines used the orthodox 14-passenger layout, National Airlines converted at least one to carry 26 passengers on bench seats along the fuselage walls. This layout was for Puerto Rican operations by Caribbean-Atlantic Airlines. It was also National Airlines that in 1940 flew a Lodestar from Burbank to Jacksonville, with one stop, in 9 hours 29 min.

Apart from civil operations, military Lodestars were operated by the USAAF as C-56s, 57s, 59s and 60s and by the US Navy and Marine Corps as R5Os. In military service some Lodestars served as glider tugs. The 1940 Vega Ventura bomber was a direct development of the Lodestar.

Above: A Lockheed Model 18 Lodestar of Star Lines, Anchorage
Left: Preparing aircraft for delivery in 1941
Below: Fowler flaps, one of the innovations which earned the designer the 1937 Lawrence Sperry Award

L-18 Lodestar

Type: passenger transport
Maker: Lockheed Aircraft Corporation
Span: 19.96 m (65 ft 6 in)
Length: 15.18 m (49 ft 9⅞ in)
Height: 3.62 m (11 ft 10½ in)
Wing area: 51.2 m² (551 sq ft)
Weight: maximum 7938 kg (17 500 lb); empty 5532 kg (12 195 lb)
Powerplant: (amongst others) two 1000-hp Wright Cyclone GR-1820-G205A (18-56) 9-cylinder air-cooled radial engines
Performance: cruising speed 344 to 404 km/h (214 to 251 mph); range 2736 to 3267 km (1700 to 2030 miles)
Payload: seats for up to 26 passengers
Crew: 3
Production: 624 (480 USAAF and US Navy)

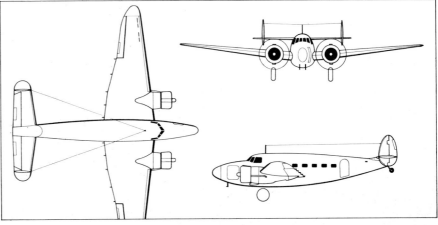

Fw 200 Condor, Focke-Wulf

FIRST FLIGHT 1937

THE Focke-Wulf Fw 200 Condors are probably best remembered for their attacks on Allied shipping during World War II when operating from bases in France and Norway. But the type began as a request from Lufthansa for an airliner and its design was begun in 1936.

The Condor was a rather beautiful four-engined low-wing cantilever monoplane with single fin and rudder and retractable undercarriage. It was of metal construction with metal skin except for the control surfaces which were fabric-covered. The fuselage was quite slim, and seating was arranged in pairs on the left side with single seats to the right. The main cabin had 16 or 17 seats and there was a forward smoking cabin with nine seats.

The prototype Condor was powered by 760-hp Pratt & Whitney Hornet S1E-G engines and first flew on July 27, 1937. It was followed by the second prototype and a batch of Fw 200As with 720-hp BMW 132G engines. The second prototype went to Lufthansa which also took delivery of five Fw 200As. The second of the pre-production batch became Hitler's personal aircraft D-2600, two others went to DDL (Danish Air Lines) as *Dania* and *Jutlandia* and were delivered in July and November 1938, and two went to Syndicato Condor in Brazil.

DDL and Lufthansa both began operating Condor services in the summer of 1938 but it is not known which was first to introduce the type.

The Fw 200A was followed by the Fw 200B with 830-hp BMW 132H engines, three-blade propellers instead of the two-blade previously used, and increased weight. Lufthansa took at least three.

Aero O/Y, now Finnair, ordered two Condors but the war prevented their delivery. A Condor operated Lufthansa's last scheduled flight in April 1945, one of DDL's models flew until 1947, and the Brazilian Condors passed to Cruzeiro do Sol, were fitted with Pratt & Whitney engines and remained in service until April 1947.

In August 1938 the modified first prototype showed its potential by flying non-stop from Berlin to New York in under 25 hours and in November that year flew from Berlin to Tokyo in 46 hours 18 min. The Japanese were interested in a bomber-reconnaissance version and the Fw 200 V10 was produced as a long-range prototype for the military Fw 200C – one at least of which served Lufthansa as a transport.

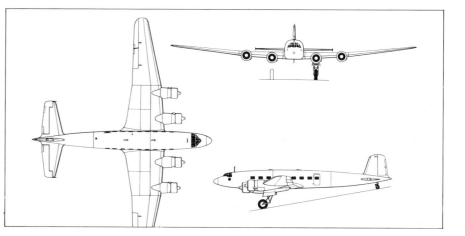

Fw 200 Condor

Type: passenger transport
Maker: Focke-Wulf Flugzeugbau GmbH
Span: 33 m (108 ft 3¼ in)
Length: 23.85 m (78 ft 3 in)
Height: 6 m (19 ft 8¼ in)
Wing area: 120 m² (1292 sq ft)
Weight: maximum 17 000 kg (37 478 lb); empty 11 300 kg (24 912 lb)
Powerplant: four 830-hp BMW 132H 9-cylinder air-cooled radial engines
Performance: cruising speed 365 km/h (228 mph); range 1500 km (932 miles)
Payload: seats for up to 26 passengers
Crew: 3 to 4
Production: minimum 280 (civil and military)

Top: *Nordmark*, a Condor powered by 750-hp BMW 132L engines, was allocated the Versuchs number 6
Above left: D-ACON at New York's Floyd Bennett Field in 1938
Left: The compact cockpit of the Fw 200 Condor

124

Ju 90, Junkers

FIRST FLIGHT 1937

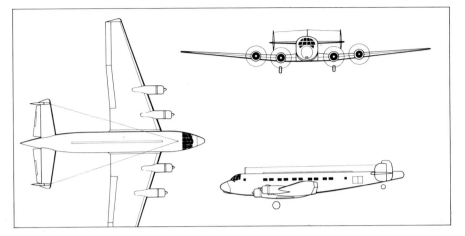

IN 1935 a Luftwaffe strategic bomber force was proposed and orders were placed for prototype Dornier Do 19 and Junkers Ju 89 four-engined bombers. The Ju 89 flew in December 1936 and was followed by a second prototype but before the third aircraft was completed the strategic bomber programme was cancelled.

Junkers obtained permission to embody the main components of the third Ju 89 in a large transport for Lufthansa, and this first flew in the summer of 1937 as the Ju 90 V1 *Der Grosse Dessauer*. It was powered by four 1100-hp Daimler-Benz DB 600 engines and broke up in flight.

Nevertheless, Junkers went ahead with the Ju 90B version powered by 830-hp BMW 132H radial engines and these began flight trials early in 1938. The second Ju 90B, *Bayern*, went into service with Lufthansa on the Berlin to Vienna route in the summer of 1938 and a few Ju 90s were seen at Croydon in the following summer. The type did not become fully operational before the start of World War II, however. Lufthansa did have 10 or 11 Ju 90s but two ordered by South African Airways were never delivered. These aircraft would have had Pratt & Whitney Twin Wasps.

The Ju 90 was a large aircraft with a loaded weight of 23 tonnes. It was a low-wing monoplane of all-metal construction, with the wing built in five sections. There was marked sweepback on the leading edge and on the trailing edge of the outersections. The typical Junkers 'double wing' flaps and ailerons were fitted.

The fuselage of the Ju 90 had parallel sides throughout the length of the cabin, where the interior width was 2.83 m (9 ft 3½ in). There were two interior layouts. One had five equal-sized cabins in which there were pairs of facing seats on each side and the other had a main cabin with six rows of forward-facing seats (pairs each side of the aisle) and a forward smoking cabin with 16 seats arranged in facing pairs on each side. The normal operating crew consisted of two pilots and a radio operator. There were large holds fore and aft and under the cabin between the centre-section spars.

Ju 90s were operating Berlin to Belgrade services in 1940 but all the Lufthansa aircraft were taken over as military transports – operating in Norway, the USSR and the Mediterranean theatre. Developments of the Ju 90 were the Ju 290 and six-engined Ju 390 military transports.

Ju 90

Type: passenger transport
Maker: Junkers Flugzeug-und-Motorenwerke AG
Span: 35.02 m (114 ft 10¾ in)
Length: 26.3 m (86 ft 3½ in)
Height: 7.3 m (23 ft 11½ in)
Wing area: 184 m² (1981 sq ft)
Weight: maximum 23 000 kg (50 706 lb); empty 16 000 kg (35 273 lb)
Powerplant: four 830-hp BMW 132H 9-cylinder air-cooled radial engines
Performance: cruising speed 320 km/h (199 mph); range 2092 km (1300 miles)
Payload: seats for 40 passengers
Crew: 3 to 5
Production: 14

Above left: D-AALU *Der Grosse Dessauer*, the prototype Ju 90
Left: The capacious cockpit of the Ju 90
Below: The third prototype which had 830-hp BMW 132 H engines

AT-2, Nakajima

FIRST FLIGHT 1936

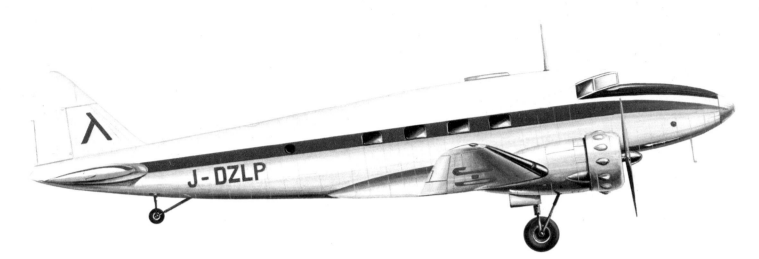

IN 1935 Nakajima began design of a small twin-engined transport for use on routes where traffic potential was limited. Japan had already bought manufacturing rights for the Douglas DC-2, and the Japanese design resembled a scaled-down DC-2 and which employed the same multi-cellular wing construction.

The design began as the AT-1 but underwent extensive changes and the prototype appeared in 1936 as the AT-2, making its first flight on September 12. The aircraft was of metal construction and metal-skinned except for plywood control surfaces. It was a low-wing cantilever monoplane with two 580-hp Nakajima Kotobuki 2-1 radial engines, had a retractable tailwheel undercarriage and accommodation for three crew and eight passengers.

After curing some minor shortcomings, the AT-2 was put into production with 710-hp Nakajima Kotobuki 41 engines and 32 were built for Dai Nippon Koku KK (Greater Japan Air Lines) and Manchuria Air Transport. They remained in service until 1945. These production aircraft had variable-pitch two-blade metal propellers in place of the fixed-pitch wooden units of the prototype.

In 1937 the Japanese army air force adopted the Nakajima AT-2 as a paratroop transport and communications aircraft. The AT-2 was given the army designations Ki-34 and Army Type 97 Transport. This version had 710-hp Nakajima Ha-1b engines with modified cowlings and 19 were built by Nakajima from 1937 to 1940.

The total requirement for military AT-2s was

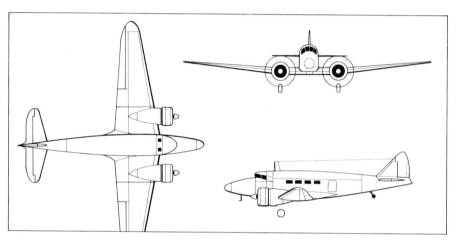

318 and of these 299 were built by Tachikawa with production continuing until 1942.

The Nakajima AT-2 received further designation changes when some of the army's Ki-34s were handed over to the Japanese navy which called them Navy Type AT-2 Transport and Nakajima L1N1. All versions of the aircraft were known to the Allies by the codename Thora.

The Ki-34s retained the small left-side entrance door and, compared with most types of aircraft used for paratroop dropping, must have been difficult aircraft from which to jump, the technique used being a power reduction and shallow descent.

At least one Ki-34 which had been based in China was given Chinese markings and used by the Chinese air force.

AT-2

Type: civil and military transport
Maker: Nakajima Hikoki Kabushiki Kaisha; Tachikawa Hikoki Kabushiki Kaisha
Span: 19.91 m (65 ft 4 in)
Length: 15.3 m (50 ft 2¼ in)
Height: 4.15 m (13 ft 7½ in)
Wing area: 49.2 m² (530 sq ft)
Weight: maximum 5250 kg (11 574 lb); empty 3500 kg (7716 lb)
Powerplant: two 710-hp Nakajima Kotobuki 41 or Ha-1b 9-cylinder air-cooled radial engines
Performance: cruising speed 310 km/h (193 mph); range 1200 km (746 miles)
Payload: seats for 8 passengers
Crew: 3
Production: 351

Top: The AT-2 was used by Dai Nippon, Koku KK and Manchurian Air Lines for short-range commercial flights. It was the first twin-engined commercial transport built in Japan to an entirely original design
Left: A line-up of AT-2s before the war

DH.95 Flamingo, de Havilland

FIRST FLIGHT 1938

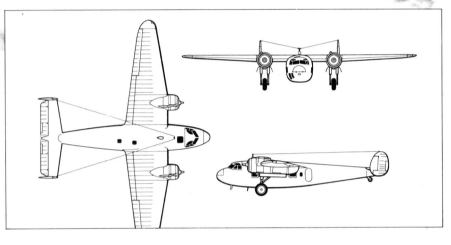

THE DH.95 Flamingo was a complete break with de Havilland tradition, being an all-metal aircraft resembling a high-wing version of the Lockheed Electra, and it was probably designed as a result of the import of Lockheed Electras and Model 14s by the prewar British Airways.

The wing was a cantilever metal structure with slotted flaps, the fuselage had a stressed-skin metal covering and the tail unit was also of metal. The control surfaces and the rear part of the wing were fabric-covered. The tail unit comprised a cantilever tailplane with endplate fins and rudders but for initial flight trials there was also a central fin.

The two 890-hp Bristol Perseus XIIC sleeve-valve radial engines were closely cowled and drove three-blade constant-speed controllable-pitch propellers. The mainwheels retracted aft into the engine nacelles. The flight-deck housed two pilots and a radio officer and the main cabin could have 12 to 17 seats and possibly 20 if required.

The prototype flew on December 28, 1938, obviously too late for the Flamingo to achieve any worthwhile success before the start of the war, although Jersey Airways and Guernsey Airways each ordered one. Jersey Airways used the prototype during the summer of 1939 and in less than two months carried 1373 passengers in it with 71.25% load factor.

There was an unfulfilled Egyptian order for the Flamingo and a batch of 13 was built, three going to the RAF with two of them to the King's Flight, and seven went to BOAC in 1940–41. Eventually BOAC was to have eight and they were operated,

as the King class, mainly in the Middle and Near East and East Africa. These aircraft had 930-hp Perseus XVI engines.

The first two aircraft were operated by No 24 Squadron RAF, mainly for the use of the Prime Minister and other Government officials. The RAF was also interested in a troop-carrying version and 30 were ordered as the Hertfordshire, with circular windows instead of rectangular, but there was only one prototype built and four production aircraft started before the order was cancelled.

At least six of the 16 DH.95s built were lost in accidents and most of the others scrapped during or soon after the war, but one BOAC aircraft was passed on to British Air Transport and used for charter work until withdrawn in 1949.

DH.95 Flamingo

Type: passenger transport
Maker: de Havilland Aircraft Co
Span: 21.34 m (70 ft)
Length: 15.72 m (51 ft 7 in)
Height: 4.67 m (15 ft 4 in)
Wing area: 60.48 m² (651 sq ft)
Weight: maximum 7983 kg (17 600 lb); empty 5137 kg (11 325 lb)
Powerplant: two 890-hp Bristol Perseus XIIC or 930-hp Perseus XVI 9-cylinder air-cooled radial engines
Performance: cruising speed 328.3 km/h (204 mph); range 2165 km (1345 miles)
Payload: seats for up to 17 passengers
Crew: 3
Production: 16

Top: G-AFYH which was first flown in 1940 and was finally scrapped at Redhill in May 1954
Left: G-AFUE of Guernsey and Jersey Airways, was impressed into RAF service in 1939 and struck off after an accident in October 1940

LeO H.242, Lioré et Olivier

FIRST FLIGHT 1934

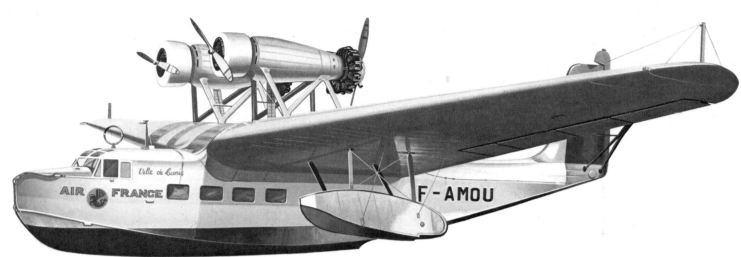

UNTIL World War II a high proportion of the trans-Mediterranean air services were operated by flying boats and seaplanes. In 1928 Aéropostale had introduced the CAMS 53 twin-engined four-passenger biplane on its Marseilles to Algiers route. Air Orient and Air Union also acquired fleets of these flying boats.

Although the CAMS flying boats gave good service they were of wooden construction and had limited capacity and performance. Air Union had ordered a replacement fleet of ten to 15-passenger four-engined Lioré et Olivier H.242 flying boats with metal hulls although the thick-section cantilever wings were built of wood.

The first H.242 was completed in 1933 but by the time the type was ready for service in 1934, Air France had succeeded Air Union. Two H.242s were built, *Ville de Tunis* and *Ville d'Alger*, and their four 350-hp Gnome Rhône Titan Major engines were uncowled and mounted above the wing in tandem pairs, the nacelles being flat-sided. A number of minor modifications were made to the H.242 and the type was followed by a production batch of 12 H.242-1s with increased weight and range. These had circular-section engine nacelles. Originally the front engines had NACA cowlings but these were later removed and replaced with exhaust collector rings.

Until the war brought the trans-Mediterranean services to a halt, the H.242 series gave good service and operated between Marseilles and Algiers; Marseilles, Ajaccio and Tunis; and on the Marseilles-Athens-Tripoli-Beirut sector of the Far East route. Four were lost in accidents but the fate of the remainder is not known.

In 1935 a specification was issued for a LeO H.242 replacement and this was designed as the 31.72-m (104 ft 0¾-in) span, 9800-kg (21 605-lb) Lioré et Olivier H.246 which was a development of the H.47 transatlantic 'boat which never went into airline service. With metal two-step hull and cantilever wooden wing, the prototype H.246 flew in September 1937, and Air France ordered six production H.246-1s fron SNCASE of which Lioré had become a constituent. These could take up to 26 passengers and were powered by four 720-hp Hispano-Suiza 12Xir engines.

The war prevented full operation of the H.246s, three were taken to Germany, but two were still on the Marseilles to Algiers route late in 1945.

H.246

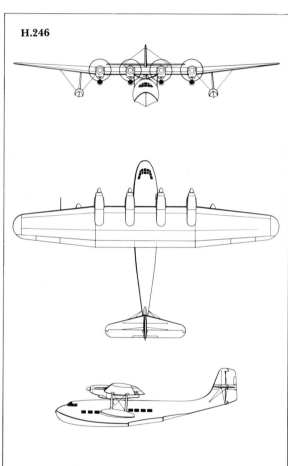

LeO H.242

Type: passenger transport flying boat
Maker: Lioré et Olivier
Span: 28 m (91 ft 10½ in)
Length: 18.45 m (60 ft 7½ in)
Height: 6.1 m (20 ft)
Wing area: 116.25 m² (1251 sq ft)
Weight: maximum 8400 kg (18 519 lb); empty 5056 kg (11 146 lb)
Powerplant: four 350-hp Gnome-Rhône Titan Major 7Kd 7-cylinder air-cooled radial engines
Performance: cruising speed 180 km/h (112 mph); range 750 km (466 miles)
Payload: seats for up to 15 passengers
Crew: 4 to 5
Production: 14

Above: An Air France Lioré et Olivier 242 which operated on the Mediterranean routes
Below: An LeO 246 over Marseilles

Boeing 307 Stratoliner

FIRST FLIGHT 1938

THE Boeing 307 Stratoliner was the first production airliner with a pressurized cabin. Full-scale development of the Model 300 (as the Model 307 was originally known), began towards the end of 1934. This emerged as a transport version of the Model 299H/B-17C bomber. The wings, engines, nacelles and original tail surfaces all came from the B-17, and an enormous new fuselage of circular cross-section gave the 307 a distinctive whale-like appearance.

The prototype, one of four 307s ordered by Pan American Airways and registered NX19901, made its maiden flight on December 31, 1938. Unfortunately, NX19901 broke up pulling out of an unintentional spin with a KLM delegation on board. Boeing added a new fin and rudder of greatly increased area to improve directional stability. Later the B-17E introduced this tail to the bomber.

Pan American's remaining three aircraft (designated PAA307/S-307) were delivered in 1940 and named *Clipper Flying Cloud*, *Clipper Comet* and *Clipper Rainbow*. Externally, these aircraft could be distinguished from other 307s by the absence of external flap hinges. All three PAA307s were based at Miami, for use on Latin American routes. The five SA-307Bs ordered by TWA (Transcontinental & Western Air) were also delivered in 1940. In 1942 all five were impressed as C-75s into the Army Air Transport Command and flown by TWA crews.

In 1944 the SA-307Bs went back to the factory for rebuilding. They were returned to TWA as SA-307B-1s with B-17G wings, nacelles and tail-surfaces. More powerful Wright Cyclone engines were introduced, the cabin pressurization system was removed and a B-29 type electrical system was installed. The Stratoliners were later sold to the French airline Aigle Azur in 1951. They then entered a decade of intensive work flying to Indo-China and on other routes, several with Aéromaritime.

The single SB-307B was purchased by Howard Hughes and specially equipped to his specific requirements. He wanted to beat his own 3-day 18-hour record for a flight around the world set in July 1938, using a Lockheed Model 14. The outbreak of World War II cancelled this project and Hughes spent $250 000 converting the SB-307B into a flying palace.

Boeing 307

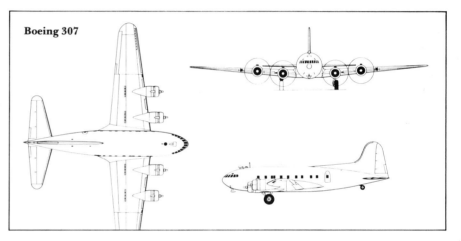

Boeing 307B

Type: long-range transport
Maker: Boeing Airplane Co
Span: 32.69 m (107 ft 3 in)
Length: 22.65 m (74 ft 4 in)
Height: 6.33 m (20 ft 9 in)
Wing area: 138 m² (1486 sq ft)
Weight: maximum 20 415 kg (45 000 lb); empty 13 610 kg (30 000 lb)
Powerplant: four 1100-hp Wright Cyclone GR-1820-G102 (Model 307) or 1200-hp GR-1820-G666 (Model SA-307-B1) engines
Performance: maximum speed 387.8 km/h (241 mph) at 1830 m (6000 ft); range 2815 km (1750 miles)
Payload: 2990 kg (6590 lb); seats for up to 38 passengers
Crew: 5
Production: 10

Top: A Transcontinental & Western Air Stratoliner; production started after orders from TWA and PanAm
Above left: Loading mail into a PanAm Boeing 307
Left: The flight-deck of the Stratoliner showing pilot, co-pilot and flight engineer

MC-20, Mitsubishi

FIRST FLIGHT 1940

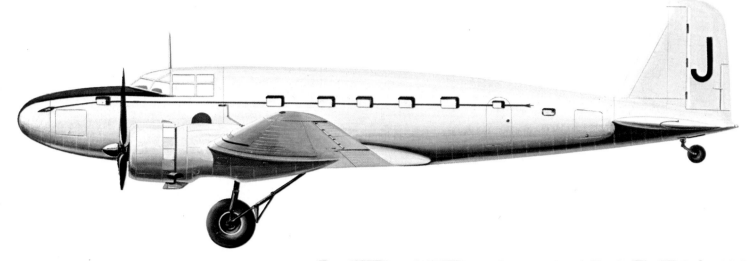

THE Mitsubishi MC-20 had its origins in a bomber design, in common with several other transport aircraft developed in Japan before World War II. The basis of the design lay in a requirement, issued early in 1939, by Nippon Koku KK (Japan Air Lines), for an airliner based on the Mitsubishi Ki-21 and able to operate on the airline's international route network.

In August 1939, the Imperial Japanese Army Air Force took the opportunity to capitalize on the work already done by Mitsubishi. It called for an aircraft able to operate as an airliner and also as a military staff transport or paratroop aircraft.

The basic joint requirement called for an aircraft able to carry 11 passengers and 300 kg (661 lb) of cargo over a range of 1400 km (870 miles) at a cruising speed of 300 km/h (186 mph). In civil service the new aircraft was to be designated MC-20, and in military service Ki-57. The new transport was based on the Ki-21-I, from which it inherited its wings, tail, cockpit section, landing gear and powerplant. The new fuselage was sleeker than that of the Ki-21-I, and was without the bomber's dorsal 'glasshouse'. To provide an unimpeded fuselage, the wing of the MC-20 was mounted in the low position, rather than in the mid position of the bomber. Accommodation for the 11 passengers was provided in rows of single seats along each side of the aircraft.

The prototype was rolled out in July 1940, and flight trials started in August. Despite the loss of an early aircraft, the type was adjudged highly satisfactory, and ordered into production, initially in the MC-20-I form with a pair of 850-hp Army Type 97 radial engines. Some of the aircraft were transferred to the Imperial Japanese Navy Air Force with the designation Mitsubishi L4M1.

In May 1942 there appeared an improved variant, the MC-20-II. This had some detail improvements to equipment, but differed from its predecessor in having two 1050-hp Army Type 100 (Mitsubishi Ha-102) radials in place of the earlier Army Type 97 (Nakajima Ha-5 KAI) radials. Weights rose slightly, but maximum speed was increased from 430 km/h (267 mph) to 470 km/h (292 mph), and service ceiling was increased by 1000 to 8000 m (3280 to 26 240 ft).

Only a few of the type survived the war, operated by Dai Nippon Koku KK until all Japanese flying was banned on October 10, 1945.

MC-20

Top and above: The Mitsubishi MC-20 was used by Dai Nippon Koku KK (Greater Japan Air Line Co Ltd). During the war, these aircraft operated in camouflage and, as shown, with military Hinomaru (The Sun's Red Disc) markings

MC-20-II

Type: light transport
Maker: Mitsubishi Jukogyo KK
Span: 22.6 m (74 ft 1¾ in)
Length: 16.1 m (52 ft 10 in)
Height: 4.86 m (15 ft 11½ in)
Wing area: 70.08 m² (754 sq ft)
Weight: maximum 9120 kg (20 106 lb); empty 5585 kg (12 313 lb)
Powerplant: two 1050-hp Army Type 100 (Mitsubishi Ha-102) 14-cylinder radial engines
Performance: maximum speed 470 km/h (292 mph) at 5800 m (19 030 ft); range 3000 km (1865 miles)
Payload: seats for up to 11 passengers
Crew: 4
Production: 101 (MC-20-Is/Ki-57-Is); 406 (MC-20-IIs/Ki-57-IIs)

G Class, Short

FIRST FLIGHT 1939

FOLLOWING the complete success of the S.23 Empire Flying Boat, Imperial Airways in late 1937 discussed with the Air Ministry the possibility of using the powerful new Bristol Hercules 14-cylinder sleeve-valve engine in aircraft with transatlantic range. Three S.26 flying boats were ordered. The first was flown in June 1939. Named *Golden Hind* it was the first of the so-called G class, the sisters becoming *Golden Fleece* and *Golden Horn* (G-AFCI to CK).

Though strikingly similar to the S.23 and relatives, the S.26 was a much larger and heavier boat and had more than double the range/payload capability. Among the more important changes was the four-man flight-deck of the Sunderland and the latter's tall vertical rear step and higher stern.

These fine boats had not entered revenue service when World War II broke out. Though they would have been valuable civil transports the need for long-range Atlantic patrol aircraft was pressing. They were impressed into the RAF in 1940, with their crews, and given serial numbers X8273-5. Major rebuild followed in the course of which they were equipped with Boulton Paul four-gun turrets at the tail and two dorsal positions, a large Sunderland-type weapon bay under the wing in the hull and a complex ASV.II radar installation.

At the end of 1941 the two survivors were re-civilianized (though their tailcones had been lost, so the rear turret was simply faired over). They began the long Poole-Lisbon-Bathurst-Accra-Freetown-Lagos service, Lisbon-Bathurst alone

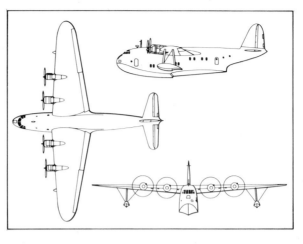

being a 13-hour sector. On the northbound run from Lisbon refugees and RAF escapees were aboard on every trip, but on January 9, 1943, *Golden Horn* caught fire in the air on an air-test and crashed into the Tagus losing 12 lives.

The survivor, the original boat, was completely rebuilt in 1944 and as a 38-seater with crew of seven operated the route Durban-Lourenço Marques-Beira-Mombasa and Kisumu-Mombasa-Pamanzi-Madagascar-Seychelles, the latter soon extended via the Maldives to Ceylon. In late 1945 she was rebuilt again by Short & Harland at Belfast as a luxurious 24-seater with Hercules XIVs and flew Poole-Augusta-Cairo until 21 September 1947. She was sunk in a gale at Harty Ferry, England, in May 1954.

S.26

Type: long-range flying boat
Maker: Short Brothers (Rochester and Bedford) Ltd
Span: 40.94 m (134 ft 4 in)
Length: 30.89 m (101 ft 4 in)
Height: 11.45 m (37 ft 7 in)
Wing area: 201 m² (2160 sq ft)
Weight: maximum 33 340 kg (73 500 lb); empty 17 100 kg (37 700 lb)
Powerplant: four 1380-hp Bristol Hercules IV or XIV air-cooled radial engines
Performance: cruising speed 290 km/h (180 mph); range 5150 km (3200 miles)
Payload: seats for 38 passengers
Crew: 4
Production: 3

Below: G-AFCI *Golden Hind* on the Medway following her maiden flight in June 1939. She was piloted by J Lankester Parker. This 'boat was retired in 1947 and it was planned to use her on tourist flights abroad. However she sank in a gale in May 1954

SE. 161 Languedoc, SNCASE

FIRST FLIGHT 1945

THE origins of the Languedoc can be traced back to a short-range passenger airliner, the MB 160. This was a short-range transport for use in the colonies and powered by four 720-hp Hispano-Suiza 12 Xirs engines. However, it did not enter production. Instead, the MB 161 was adopted for use by Air France as a 33-seat passenger airliner on their medium-range routes.

It was developed in parallel with the MB 162 heavy bomber and wartime production of the MB 161 was taken over by the Germans and plans for 20-seat and 16-seat variants of this model had to be abandoned. Twenty were ordered to be built at the SNCASE factory at Toulouse for use by Lufthansa but no production aircraft were completed until the war ended.

The first SE. 161 was flown on September 17, 1945 and was powered by four 1150-hp Gnome-Rhône 14N 44/45 engines. France at this time was eager to modernize its air services and Air France ordered 40 Languedocs for use on their European and North African routes. The first 13, which were delivered in late 1945 and early 1946, were used in experimental services to the United Kingdom and Africa and by late 1946 Languedocs were being used on all major European and African routes.

At the end of 1946 several improvements were made, including the replacement of the Gnome-Rhône engines by 1200-hp Pratt & Whitney R-1830-S1C3-G engines. De-icing equipment and interior cabin heating was also installed. The modified aircraft designated SE. 161-P7 was popular with several other operators. These included Air Atlas, Air Liban, Iberia, Misrair, LOT and Tunis Air. Several of the aircraft supplied to the export customers retained their Gnome-Rhône engines.

In the late 1940s several Languedocs were employed in the flying testbed role for experiments with aero engines. Four SE. 161s were used for carrying the Leduc ramjet research aircraft mounted on top of their fuselages.

By the end of 1947, 62 Languedocs had been completed and several were ordered by the Armée de l'Air and Aéronavale. Some of these were still in service with Aéronavale for aircrew training as late as 1960. By this time Air France had withdrawn its SE. 161s from all major passenger routes and the Languedocs in service with Aviaco of Spain were the only ones left in civil use.

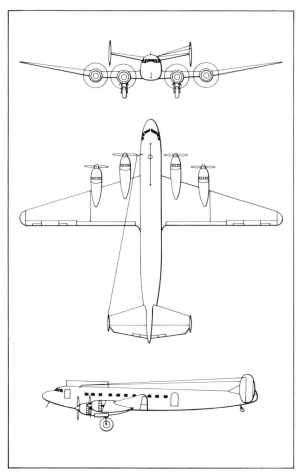

Top and above: The Sud Est SE. 161 Languedoc was used by Air France on routes to North Africa and later on European flights, including London to Paris. With Pratt & Whitney Twin Wasp engines it was sold to the Polish airline LOT which took delivery of five between 1947 and 1948

SE. 161

Type: medium-range passenger transport
Maker: SNCASE
Span: 29.38 m (96 ft 4¾ in)
Length: 24.25 m (79 ft 6¾ in)
Height: 5.13 m (16 ft 10 in)
Wing area: 111.3 m² (1198 sq ft)
Weight: maximum 22 940 kg (50 573 lb); empty 12 651 kg (27 890 lb)
Powerplant: four 1200-hp Gnome-Rhône 14N 68/69 14-cylinder air-cooled radial engines
Performance: cruising speed 405 km/h (252 mph); range 1000 km (620 miles)
Payload: 3970 kg (8752 lb); seats for 33 passengers
Crew: 4
Production: 67

Boeing 314

FIRST FLIGHT 1938

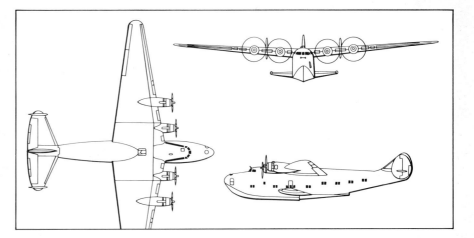

SUCH was the rate of progress with large long-range flying boats in the United States in the mid 1930s that within two years the Martin 130 made the Sikorsky S-42 obsolete, and within a year of the 1935 maiden flight of the great Martin, Pan American Airways was talking with Boeing about a boat to eclipse the Martin. By December 1936 the Boeing Model 314 had a firm specification.

Structure was to be entirely of light-alloy stressed skin. The chosen engine was the new 1500-hp 14-cylinder Wright two-row Cyclone GR-2600, the most powerful then available. The wing was similar to that of the giant XB-15 bomber.

By late 1937 the seating had been revised to 50 sleeping and 75 by day, (previously 82 and 40), with a crew of ten, with sleeping quarters above the passenger cabins and just under the wing. Behind this crew sleeping compartment were baggage holds along the upper rear of the hull. The forward part of the upper level had a flight-deck, navigation compartment, radio officer's cabin, chartroom, map and library room, and a large compartment for engineers. Stability on the water was provided by two-spar sponsons, called sea wings, from which fuel was pumped up to the main wing tanks.

The first flight took place in June 1938. Directional stability was the chief problem and eventually two additional fins and rudders were added to the tail. All six 314s were delivered in 1939. One, *Dixie Clipper*, opened the first regular non-stop North Atlantic service on June 28, 1939; *Yankee Clipper* and *American Clipper* soon joined. The other three operated on the Pacific, with conspicuous success and passenger appeal.

In 1940 Boeing sold six improved 314A Clippers to PanAm, and three were turned over to BOAC (which had ordered from Boeing anyway). The 314A had many changes including more powerful versions of the GR-2600 engines, larger HamStan propellers of improved efficiency, and greater fuel capacity making possible unprecedented ranges. (The original *Dixie Clipper* had flown non-stop Lisbon to New York in 25 hours in 1939.) PanAm's three 314As were requisitioned by the USAAF as C-98s in 1942, soon being transferred to the navy where as B-314s they operated with PanAm crews. BOAC named their aircraft *Bristol*, *Berwick* and *Bangor*, the first taking Prime Minister Churchill to the US and back in 27 hours in mid 1942. Six were scrapped in 1950.

Boeing 314A

Type: long-range flying boat
Maker: Boeing Airplane Co
Span: 46.33 m (152 ft)
Length: 32.31 m (106 ft)
Height: 8.41 m (27 ft 7 in)
Wing area: 266.3 m² (2867 sq ft)
Weight: maximum 38 102 kg (84 000 lb); empty 21 930 kg (48 400 lb)
Powerplant: four 1600-hp Wright GR-2600 Cyclone 14-cylinder two-row radial engines
Performance: cruising speed 303 km/h (188 mph); range 5930 km (3685 miles)
Payload: 74 day passengers or 40 with sleeping berths
Crew: 10
Production: 12

Above left: Assembling the engines of the first Boeing Model 314 at Seattle
Left: The flight-deck of a Clipper with the pilot, co-pilot, navigator, radio operator and flight engineer
Below: G-AGCA *Berwick* in BOAC service on the Atlantic route during World War II

C-46 Commando, Curtiss

FIRST FLIGHT 1940

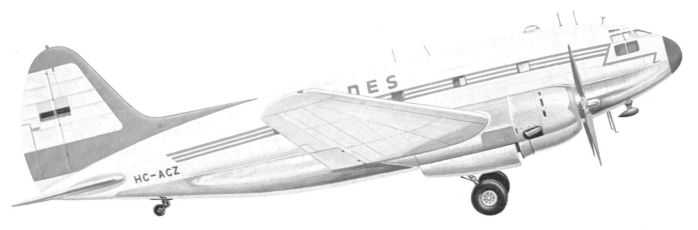

HC-ACZ

THE Curtiss C-46 Commando will always be associated with the 'Hump' run from India to China during World War II. After overcoming early mechanical problems caused by low technical support and high utilization, the Commando became a prime mover of material in every Allied theatre of operations. A total of 3182 C-46/R5Cs were delivered to the US Army, Navy and Marines between 1942 and 1945.

The Commando began life as the CW-20 commercial airliner. Designed to operate on routes around 1000 km (600 miles) in distance (90% of the US domestic network), the CW-20 would have competed head-on with the Douglas DC-3. Designated CW-20T, the prototype (NX19436) made its maiden flight on March 26, 1940. The CW-20

featured a double lobe or 'double-bubble' fuselage with accommodation for 36 passengers in the upper lobe and 3719 kg (8200 lb) of cargo in the lower. Two of the new Wright Cyclone R-2600 two-row radial engines were installed, each developing 1700 hp for take-off. Rather surprisingly, a tailwheel landing gear was chosen.

In July 1940, the US Army ordered 40 unpressurized cargo versions of the CW-20. The C-46 Commando was born. The Army also bought the CW-20T as the C-55 for $361 556 in June 1941. Strangely, the C-55 was soon returned to Curtiss, who then sold it to British Overseas Airways (BOAC) in September 1941. Registered G-AGDI, the aircraft was named *St Louis* after its birthplace, and was scrapped in Britain on October 29, 1943.

Above: An Andes Airline C-46, HC-AC2. An all-cargo carrier, this airline was established in 1961 by Captain Alfredo Franco. In its first few years various freight charters were undertaken in South America using DC-3s and C-46s

Above: This C-46 Cargo Clipper was inaugurated into Pan American service on December 1, 1948
Right: Fred Olsen of Norway operated the C-46 on cargo services. The airline company was a subsidiary of the massive shipping consortium of the same name
Far right: A Rich International Airways C-46A. The airline began operating in January 1971 and by 1980 worked five aircraft on Charter services from Miami, Florida, mainly to the Bahamas

The first C-46 was delivered to the US Army in July 1942. Early production aircraft were little different from the CW-20T. Cabin windows were reduced to four on the left side and five on the right. Except for a small section at the rear, the fairing over the fuselage 'crease' was dropped for lack of any aerodynamic advantage. Four-bladed Curtiss fully-feathering electric propellers were fitted. The C-46A (CW-20B) had a reinforced floor for 6804 kg (15 000 lb) of cargo, loaded through a large two-segment cargo door on the left side. Power was provided by two 2000-hp Pratt & Whitney R-2800-51 engines. Subsequent versions differed chiefly in door configuration (eg paratroop door on C-46D) and stepped windscreens. Some versions featured the R-2800-34W engine with water injection.

After the war Curtiss tried to launch a new passenger transport version of the Commando – the CW-20E. With thousands of surplus transports on the market, this project never stood any real chance of success. Even civil C-46 conversions failed to attract orders from US trunk carriers. They preferred newly demobbed DC-4s, Constellations and DC-3s. The majority of C-46s bought by US operators were used as freighters. US cargo operators in the 1970s included Rich International (3), American Flyers (1), Miami Air (1) and Trans Continental (4).

One Curtiss project that literally never got off the ground was the XC-113 – a C-46 converted to test the new General Electric TG-100 turboprop. The TG-100 could not be installed in the nose

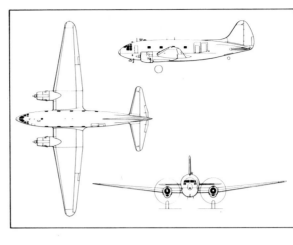

because the cockpit was too far forward, so the engine was mounted in the right nacelle. The left R-2800 was retained, but the power gap between the two powerplants and their different reaction times to throttle movements combined to make the aircraft virtually uncontrollable.

Passenger and freighter versions sold very well in South America. There were over 600 working there in 1959 and around 50 machines remain active there. LACSA, the Costa Rican national airline, is unique among other operations in that its three C-46s carry passengers according to daily domestic schedules. One C-46 has been flying with LACSA for 31 years. In 1980, 80 Commandos were still in regular operation, the largest fleet being operated by Air Haiti (5).

C-46

Type: medium-range transport
Maker: Curtiss-Wright Corporation
Span: 32.92 m (108 ft)
Length: 23.26 m (76 ft 4 in)
Height: 6.62 m (21 ft 9 in)
Wing area: 126.34 m² (1360 sq ft)
Weight: maximum 21 772 kg (48 000 lb); empty 13 608 kg (30 000 lb)
Powerplant: two 2000-hp Pratt & Whitney R-2800-51 Double Wasp 18-cylinder radial engines
Performance: cruising speed 278 km/h (173 mph) at 3050 m (10 000 ft); range 5069 km (3150 miles)
Payload: 4536 kg (10 000 lb); seats for 40 to 62 passengers
Crew: 4
Production: 3341 (originally military)

Above: The CW-20 version of the C-46 had a pressurized fuselage in a double-bubble configuration with the floor acting as a tie between the two arcs. Though it had been designed for pressurization, the CW-20 at first appeared without it

York, Avro

FIRST FLIGHT 1942

THE Avro 685 York was a high-wing transport derivative of the Lancaster bomber, Roy Chadwick designing a new square-section fuselage with twice the volume of the original. The prototype LV626 made its maiden flight on July 5, 1942 –only five months after the drawings were delivered to Avro's experimental department.

Only three prototypes were built in 1943 however, and most early production aircraft were VIP transports; LV633 *Ascalon*, for example, became Winston Churchill's flying conference room. (*Ascalon* was replaced in 1946 by MW295 *Ascalon II* – destined to become the RAF's last operational York.) All Yorks built after the second prototype incorporated a central fin to compensate for the increased fuselage side-area forward of the CG (centre of gravity). The prototype also collected a central fin when it became the only York powered by Bristol Hercules VI engines.

Yorks were produced at three per month in 1944, and BOAC were allowed to take five from Royal Air Force production. These aircraft carried 12 passengers in the rear cabin with mixed freight forward, and inaugurated the first UK to Cairo route on April 22, 1944. After World War II, BOAC shared 25 Yorks with the RAF until joint services were handed over to the corporation. Full BOAC livery was applied and M class names (such as *Mersey*, *Manchester* and *Montgomery*) were allotted. Thirteen were equipped as 12-berth sleepers for the UK-Johannesburg 'Springbok' service. The entire fleet was withdrawn from passenger services on October 7, 1950, but York freighters remained with BOAC until November 22, 1957. The York carried 90 000 passengers and flew 71 million km (44 million miles) with BOAC, and their discarded fleet joined the surplus RAF Yorks bought by smaller operators. Overseas operators included South African Airways and FAMA.

War Office trooping contracts provided Skyways, Surrey Flying Services, Air Charter and Scottish Airlines with valuable revenue. Hunting-Clan Air Transport and Dan-Air Services also acquired Yorks. During the Berlin Air Lift, military and civil Yorks flew thousands of sorties, G-AHFI *Skyway* flying 147 sorties before crashing at Gatow on March 16, 1949 and G-AHLV flying 467 sorties. Another York which flew 467 sorties was G-ALBX *Sky Dominion*, the only York built by Victory Aircraft (later Avro Aircraft) of Canada.

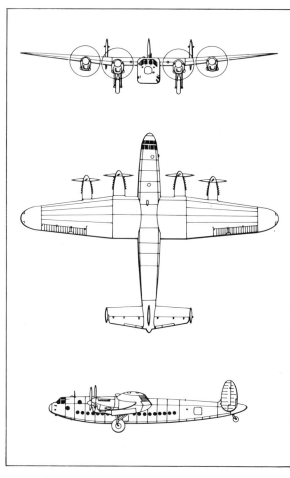

Top: A BOAC Avro 685 York G-AGNL *Mersey* which, after service with Lancashire Aircraft Corporation Ltd, was used for trooping
Above: A clear view of the slab-sided fuselage and three fins of an Avro York

685 York

Type: long-range transport
Maker: A V Roe Ltd
Span: 31.09 m (102 ft)
Length: 23.92 m (78 ft 6 in)
Height: 5.44 m (17 ft 10 in)
Wing area: 120.5 m² (1297 sq ft)
Weight: maximum (passenger-freighter version) 32 206 kg (71 000 lb); empty 18 872 kg (41 605 lb)
Powerplant: four 1610-hp Rolls-Royce Merlin 502 V-12 liquid-cooled engines
Performance: cruising speed 404 km/h (251 mph) at 4572 m (15 000 ft); range 4345 km (2700 miles)
Payload: 14 307 kg (31 542 lb); seats for 12 to 65 passengers
Crew: 4
Production: 257

DH.98 Mosquito transport, de Havilland

FIRST FLIGHT 1940

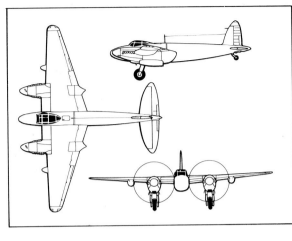

DURING World War II, British Overseas Airways Corporation operated a 'commercial' service between the UK and neutral Sweden. By 1942, BOAC's Lockheed Hudsons and Lodestars were becoming increasingly vulnerable to intense enemy activity along their routes, and the airline badly needed a new light merchantman with sufficient speed and altitude performance to elude prowling German fighters, and flak batteries.

On August 6, 1942, a Royal Air Force Mosquito from 105 Squadron made a secret flight to Sweden with a consignment of special mail. To BOAC the possibilities were obvious, but the Air Ministry were less than enthusiastic.

For the corporation it was Mosquitos or nothing. Finally a B Mk IV, DZ411, was allotted. Registered G-AGFV, the aircraft was delivered on December 15, 1942, and Captain Houlder and R/O Frape guided 'FV to Stockholm for the first time on February 4, 1943. (Houlder went on to train all BOAC's Mosquito captains.) On April 12, BOAC was allotted six more Mosquitos (FB Mk VIs) registered respectively G-AGGC to AGGH. The introduction of the Mosquito 'airliner' did not pass unnoticed by the Luftwaffe. An Fw 190 intercepted G-AGFV over the Skagerrak, and though his aircraft was severely damaged, Captain Gilbert Rae made a successful wheels-up landing at Barkaby near Stockholm. Services promptly ceased until the Mk VIs arrived.

Following the American bombing raid on the German ball-bearing works at Schweinfurt, two Mosquitos were hastily modified to take one passenger each in the bomb bay. The two British negotiators flown to Stockholm purchased Sweden's entire production of ball-bearings; thereby eliminating an alternative source of supply to the Germans. Previously, BOAC's Mosquitos had carried only small freight and special mail, but priority passengers now became a regular feature of operations. Passengers wore full flying-kit and reclined on a mattress. A reading lamp, headphones, (for communication with the pilot) and temperature control was provided. On average, the flight from Leuchars to Stockholm lasted 3 hours, compared with up to 9 hours for slower aircraft such as the Dakota. Some crews made three single trips in one night. All BOAC's Mosquitos were returned to the RAF or scrapped.

FB Mk VI

Type: high-speed transport
Maker: de Havilland Aircraft Co Ltd
Span: 16.51 m (54 ft 2 in)
Length: 12.34 m (40 ft 6 in)
Height: 3.81 m (12 ft 6 in)
Wing area: 41.99 m² (452 sq ft)
Weight: maximum 10 096 kg (22 258 lb); empty 6506 kg (14 344 lb)
Powerplant: two 1460-hp Rolls-Royce Merlin 21 or 23, or two 1635-hp Merlin 25 liquid-cooled V-12 engines
Performance: cruising speed 410 km/h (255 mph); range 3035 km (1885 miles)
Payload: up to 907 kg (2000 lb); 1 passenger
Crew: 2
Production: 7 (conversions)

Below: The first civil Mosquito which was delivered to BOAC in 1943. It was operated from Leuchars airfield, in Scotland, on the Stockholm route, and returned to the RAF in 1945

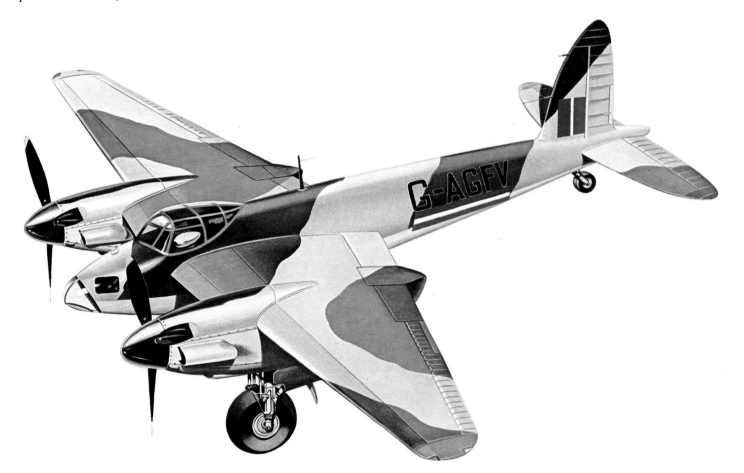

DC-4, Douglas

FIRST FLIGHT 1942

BOTH the five sponsoring airlines and Douglas Aircraft lost rather heavily on the original DC-4, later called DC-4E (for Experimental), which was judged too big and uneconomic after prolonged service testing in 1939. Undaunted, and recognizing it had to build a four-engined transport, a team under Edward F Burton at Santa Monica started again and drafted a much neater and rather smaller design, using the R-2000 version of the familiar Twin Wasp engine.

Other modern features included the first transport fuselage with a long parallel section of constant diameter (years later this was to prove a boon in 'stretching' the same aircraft, first into the various types of DC-6, and then into the even longer DC-7 family). The tail had a tall single fin and rudder and the main landing gears had twin wheels and retracted forwards, as did the steerable nose unit.

In 1940 the same sponsoring airlines placed combined orders for 60 of the re-born DC-4 off the drawing board. Though still larger than any existing equipment, with seating for 42 day passengers and sleeping berths for 30 by night, it looked so attractive that with rising traffic it seemed well-matched to future needs. Production began in 1941 but even before Pearl Harbor, on 7 December that year, the project was slowed by urgent expansion of military output. In December 1941 the programme was taken over by the USAAF and the designation changed to C-54, as a long-range military transport. By late 1942 nearly 1000 had been ordered by the USAAF and Navy.

During World War II there were nine military and naval versions, while Douglas planned for civil variants to be sold after the war. The standard postwar DC-4 was planned to be a 44-seater, with a crew of five, though for a time the old idea of a sleeper persisted and Douglas offered (but did not sell) a model with 22 passengers in sleeping berths. Little space was then accorded to cargo in civil airliners, and though there were two small under-floor compartments, the main freight hold was a small cubicle just in front of the passenger cabin on the right side. Postwar DC-4s, and the Merlin-powered version built under licence by Victory aircraft at Montreal (later taken over by Canadair), were without pressurization. Later Canadair did build a pressurized DC-4M version, the Argonaut for BOAC.

In 1945–46 the US government sold or leased approximately 500 wartime C-54 and R5D Skymasters to the civilian market, and this obviously had a major effect on sales prospects for new aircraft from Douglas. Despite this the Santa Monica plant did manage to build 74 new civil DC-4s – the Douglas Model 1109 – after VJ-Day, the last going to South African Airways in August 1947. The civil DC-4 followed exactly the structure and systems of the wartime machines, though without a freight floor or large loading doors. Usually the fuel capacity was reduced, though zero-fuel weight and maximum landing weights were raised to allow payload to increase. For the next 20 years civil DC-4s worked alongside the vastly more numerous civilianized C-54s and R5Ds, externally almost indistinguishable.

138

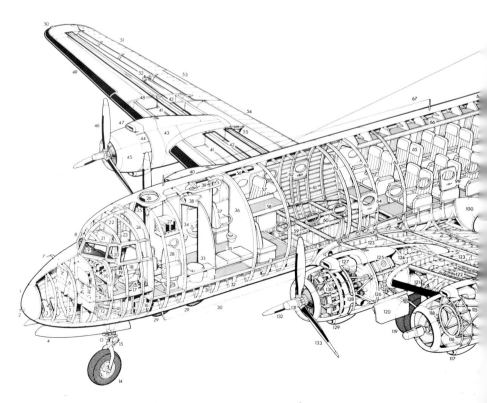

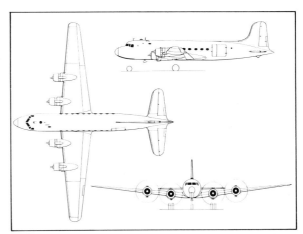

DC-4-1009

Type: long-range transport
Maker: Douglas Aircraft Co
Span: 35.81 m (117 ft 6 in)
Length: 28.6 m (93 ft 10 in)
Height: 8.38 m (27 ft 6 in)
Wing area: 135.639 m² (1460 sq ft)
Weight: maximum 33 113 kg (73 000 lb); empty 19 641 kg (43 300 lb)
Powerplant: four 1450-hp Pratt & Whitney Twin Wasp R-2000 14-cylinder air-cooled radial engines
Performance: cruising speed 451 km/h (280 mph) at 4265 m (14 000 ft); range 4025 km (2500 miles)
Payload: 5190 kg (11 440 lb); seats for 44 passengers
Crew: 4
Production: 79 (civil)

Above: This Qantas DC-4 was operated on the airline's trans-Pacific routes. With the opening of a route through Manila on April 24, 1950, Qantas was represented in every major city in South-East Asia
Left: A Balair DC-4 cargo aircraft. This Swiss company was formed in 1953, initially as a flying school
Right: A DC-4 night plane complete with American Airlines booklets and blankets. It could carry 28 passengers

DC-4

1 Nose cone
2 Radio homing aerial
3 Fire extinguisher bottles
4 Nosewheel doors
5 Nose undercarriage bay
6 Cockpit front bulkhead
7 Pitot tubes
8 Windscreen panels
9 Instrument panel shroud
10 Instrument panel
11 Rudded pedals
12 Nosewheel hydraulic retraction jack
13 Steering jacks
14 Nosewheel
15 Torque scissors
16 Battery bay
17 Cockpit floor level
18 Control column handwheel
19 Captain's seat
20 Opening side window panel
21 1st Officer's seat
22 Right side crew entry door
23 Navigator's folding chart table
24 Cockpit bulkhead
25 Forward upper deck cargo hold
26 Astrodome observation hatch
27 Radio racks
28 Radio operator's seat
29 D/F loop aerials
30 ADF sense aerial cable
31 Forward underfloor cargo hold
32 Lower section fuselage frames
33 Forward toilet
34 Wash basin
35 Men's cloakroom
36 Cabin bulkhead
37 Aft facing forward seat row
38 Heater intake
39 Cabin combustion heater
40 Right inner engine air intake duct
41 Right wing integral fuel tanks
42 Wing panel walkways
43 Right outer engine nacelle
44 Engine-cooling air outlet flaps
45 Detachable engine cowlings
46 Hamilton standard, 3-bladed propeller
47 Engine air intake
48 Outer wing panel joint rib
49 Leading-edge de-icing boots

50 Right navigation light
51 Right fabric-covered aileron
52 Aileron hinge control
53 Aileron tab
54 Right single-slotted flap
55 Flap hydraulic jack
56 Cabin heater air distribution roof duct
57 Forward cabin seats
58 Left overhead luggage rack
59 Floor beam construction
60 Wing centre-section carry through
61 Fuselage frame and stringer construction
62 Right emergency exit window
63 Wing/fuselage attachment main frames
64 Left emergency exit window
65 Main cabin, 4-abreast passenger seating, 44-seat layout
66 Right overhead luggage rack
67 HF aerial cable
68 Fuselage skin plating
69 Food and coat stowage locker
70 Aft toilet
71 Fin root fillet
72 Right tailplane
73 Right elevator
74 Leading-edge de-icing boots
75 Tailfin construction
76 VHF aerial cable
77 Fin tip fairing
78 Fabric-covered rudder construction
79 Rudder tab
80 Rudder and elevator hinge controls
81 Tailcone fairing
82 Tail navigation light
83 Elevator tab
84 Left fabric-covered elevator
85 Leading-edge de-icing boot
86 Tailplane construction
87 Tail bumper
88 Tailplane centre-section carry-through
89 Fin mounting frame
90 Tailplane fillet
91 Rear fuselage frame and stringer construction
92 Aft cabin bulkhead
93 Wash basin
94 Ladies cloakroom
95 Wardrobe
96 Buffet unit

97 Passenger entry door
98 Rear underfloor freight hold
99 Aft emergency exit window
100 Wing root trailing-edge fillet
101 Left single-slotted flap construction
102 Flap shroud ribs
103 Inner wing panel rear spar
104 Left fabric-covered aileron
105 Aileron hinge control
106 Single-spar outer wing panel construction
107 Wingtip fairing
108 Left navigation light
109 Leading-edge de-icing boots
110 Wing rib construction
111 Outer wing panel joint rib
112 Inner wing panel 3-spar construction
113 Nacelle tail fairing
114 Nacelle firewall
115 Engine bearers
116 Engine mounting ring
117 Oil-cooler air duct
118 Left outer engine nacelle
119 Twin mainwheels
120 Mainwheel doors
121 Main undercarriage leg strut
122 Wing stringers
123 Left wing integral fuel tanks
124 Left inner engine nacelle
125 Nacelle oil tank
126 Main undercarriage hydraulic retraction jack
127 Engine air intake
128 Exhaust collector ring
129 Oil-cooler air duct
130 Pratt & Whitney R-2000-SD13G Twin Wasp, 14-cylinder, two-row radial engine
131 Propeller hub pitch change mechanism
132 Propeller-blade de-icing boots
133 Hamilton-Standard three-bladed, variable pitch propeller

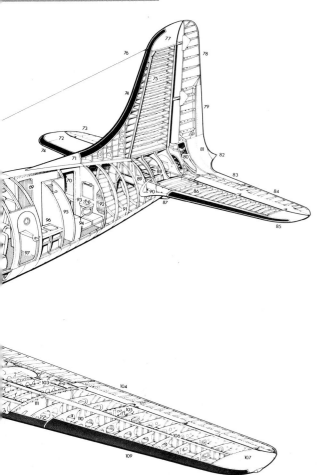

SO.30, SNCASO

FIRST FLIGHT 1946

THE SO.30 was the largest of the projects tackled by the Groupe Technique de Cannes, and was started at Châteauroux in March 1941. The idea was to create the first French pressurized airliner, using the same kind of ultra-streamlined fuselage as that adopted for the SO.90 on a bigger scale. Stressed-skin construction was adopted throughout, and the chosen engines were the Gnome-Rhône N48/49s. Designated SO.30N, the N reflecting the engine model, it was tailored to carry 23 passengers and 1200 kg (2640 lb) freight. The prototype was ready for tests in November 1942, but the Italo-German Armistice Commission refused permission for flight.

Undeterred the group continued with a much more powerful development, the SO.30R Bellatrix. This had Gnome-Rhône 14R-5 engines, each rated at 1650 hp, and a larger wing, tricycle landing gear and single fin and rudder instead of a twin-finned tail. Another change was incorporation of hot-air anti-icing on wings and tail. The 30R abounded with novel or up-to-date features, such as large hinged cowl panels giving access all round each engine. It was fitted with 30 passenger seats (or 16 sleeping berths) in three pressurized cabins. First flight took place in March 1946.

By 1948 however, the SO.30P Bretagne was coming off the assembly line, with Pratt & Whitney Double Wasp R-2800-B43 engines of 2000 hp, driving Curtiss electric propellers. In September 1949, with the tenth aircraft, the engine changed to the 2400 hp R-2800-CA18, driving HamStan paddle-blade propellers. This was ordered by Air

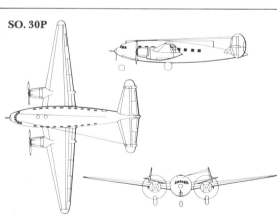

SO. 30P

France as a passenger airliner with luxurious seating for 30 but with usual accommodation for up to 45 in 'coach' comfort. Goodrich pulsating-rubber or thermal de-icing on wings and tail was backed up by electric anti-icing of propellers and engines. The tail went back to a twin-finned form, and for the first time the pilots' windscreen had upright panels giving a better forward view than those of the perfectly streamlined nose on previous variants.

Several operators including Air France used Bretagnes from 1951 until at least 1959. One oddball was the SO.30C cargo model, offered with GR 14R or R-2800 engines, in which the lower rear part of the fuselage was a pair of large doors, like those for a bomb bay.

SO.30P-2

Type: medium-range passenger transport
Maker: Société Nationale de Constructions Aéronautiques du Sud-Ouest (SNCASO)
Span: 26.9 m (88 ft 2 in)
Length: 18.95 m (62 ft 2 in)
Height: 5.9 m (19 ft 4 in)
Wing area: 86.2 m² (927.5 sq ft)
Weight: maximum 19 500 kg (42 900 lb); empty 13 600 kg (30 000 lb)
Powerplant: two 2000-hp Pratt & Whitney R-2800-B43 Double Wasp 18-cylinder radial engines
Performance: cruising speed 415 kmh (258 mph); range 1200 km (746 miles)
Payload: 4350 kg (9570 lb); seats for 45 passengers
Crew: 5
Production: 45 (all types)

SO.90, SNCASO

FIRST FLIGHT 1943

Left: The SO.90 Cassiopée. The SO.90 was a larger version of the SO.80 which first flew in July 1942
Below left: An SO.94 in the livery of the French navy. The SO.94 is instantly distinguishable from the SO.95 in having a nosewheel, the latter being equipped with a tailwheel landing gear

THE clandestine GTC (Groupe Technique de Cannes) carried through five major aircraft projects during World War II under extreme difficulty. One was a neat twin-engined light transport, powered by two 375-hp Béarn six-cylinder inverted inline engines, with crew of three and payload of 1200 kg (2640 lb). Except for the control surfaces the skin was entirely of stressed light alloy, and the landing gear and flaps were operated hydraulically. The type was intended as a replacement for the Caudron 440 Goeland, and it was called the SO.80.

This flew in July 1942, before the south of France had been occupied. It was successful, but the GTC decided it should be made larger, and the result was the SO.90 Cassiopée. The prototype was wheeled out into the sun in August 1943, but by this time Cannes was occupied by Italian troops. The latter looked on as no fewer than nine engineers, and much baggage, went on board for the first taxi test. At the controls was M Hurel, chief engineer of the former CAMS company and a leading French designer. He opened up the engines and took straight off. Italian fighters were scrambled but failed to catch the new aircraft, which on its first flight crossed the Mediterranean to Philippeville, North Africa, and the Allies.

From April 1946 SNCASO built 25 Cassiopées, while via the 93 the much more powerful 94 and 95 were derived. Both were powered by the former German Argus As 410 inverted V-12 air-cooled engine, which the nationalized group SNECMA was preparing to build as the Renault 12S (later SNECMA 12S). While the SO.94 had a nosewheel,

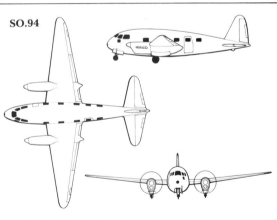

SO.94

the SO.95 had a tailwheel landing gear. Both could carry up to 13 passengers, with separate toilet forward and baggage compartment aft, making them considerably larger than the otherwise similar British Dove. By 1947 a total of 75 SO.94 and smaller numbers of SO.95 Corse II transports had been ordered, some being for military training and liaison duties, notably with the Aéronavale (French navy). Both the 94 and 95 saw considerable service in the 1950s, the Corse II being the predominant civil transport version. Production aircraft, delivered in 1948–52, had a large extended dorsal fin, prominent direction-finding loop area above the humpbacked fuselage, and extensive provision for flight at night or in icing conditions.

SO.95

Type: light commercial transport
Maker: Société Nationale de Constructions Aéronautiques du Sud Ouest (SNCASO)
Span: 17.9 m (59 ft)
Length: 12.35 m (40 ft 5 in)
Height: 4.29 m (14 ft 1 in)
Wing area: 376 m² (4047 sq ft)
Weight: maximum 5605 kg (12 346 lb); empty 4024 kg (8863 lb)
Powerplant: two 590-hp Renault 12S-02-201 inverted V-12 air-cooled engines
Performance: cruising speed 335 kmh (208 mph) at 2700 m (8860 ft); range 1300 km (810 miles)
Payload: 882 kg (1943 lb); seats for 13 passengers
Crew: 2
Production: minimum 60

VS-44A, Vought-Sikorsky

FIRST FLIGHT 1937

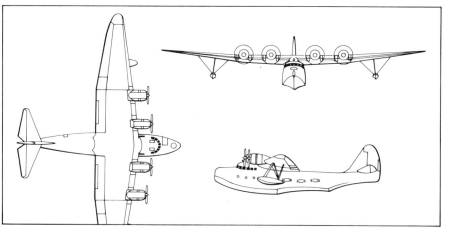

THE origins of the Vought-Sikorsky VS-44A civil flying boat lay in a 1935 United States Navy requirement for a four-engined long-range patrol boat. Powered by four 1050-hp Pratt & Whitney XR-1830-68 Twin Wasp radials, the single XPBS-1 prototype first flew in August 1937, and although it was in every way adequate, the company received no further US Navy orders. The XPBS-1, armed with single 12.7-mm (0.5-in) machine-guns in the nose and tail positions and one 7.62-mm (0.3-in) gun in each of the two waist positions, remained in US Navy service until it sank in San Francisco Bay during 1942.

Further development of the basic type resulted from the ambitions of a major US shipping company, American Export Lines, to break into the increasingly lucrative long-haul airline business, to which end it had formed American Export Airlines in April 1937. In May 1939 this company applied for a licence to operate a flying-boat service from New York to the United Kingdom and France. The chosen boat was a civil development of the XPBS-1, designated the VS-44A Excalibur. American Export Airlines ordered three examples.

The outbreak of World War II led to a postponement of American Export Airlines' plans, but in July 1940 the airline secured presidential permission to operate a transatlantic service from New York to Lisbon. American Export Airlines confirmed its order with accommodation for up to 16 passengers over transatlantic routes.

The situation was once again changed when the United States entered World War II as a result of Japan's attack on Pearl Harbor in December 1941. On January 12, 1942 the US Navy thus contracted with American Export Airlines to operate its VS-44s on behalf of the Naval Air Transport Service on the North Atlantic route, operating from New York to Foynes in Ireland. The three VS-44As were designated JR2S-1 by the US Navy, but flew in civil markings, the first transatlantic flight being made on June 20, 1942. The first VS-44A had flown on January 18, 1942 and all three had been delivered by June 1942.

One VS-44A crashed on take-off on October 3, 1942, but the other two made 405 transatlantic crossings before being retired by American Export Airlines in October 1945, to be sold to smaller operators. The two boats survived for some time as short-haul transports seating up to 47 passengers.

VS-44A

Type: transport flying boat
Maker: Vought-Sikorsky Division, United Aircraft Corporation
Span: 37.8 m (124 ft)
Length: 23.21 m (76 ft 2 in)
Height: 8.4 m (27 ft 7 in)
Wing area: 155.14 m² (1670 sq ft)
Weight: maximum 22 018 kg (48 540 lb); empty 11 978 kg (26 407 lb)
Powerplant: four 1200-hp Pratt & Whitney R-1830-S1C3-G Twin Wasp radial engines
Performance: crusing speed 282 km/h (175 mph) at 3048 m (10 000 ft); range 7314 km (4545 miles)
Payload: seats for up to 16 (later 47) passengers
Crew: 6
Production: 1 (XPBS-1), 3 (VS-44A)

Top: NC-41881 *Excambian* which was renamed *Excalibur* when it was operated by Avalon Air Transport from 1957 to 1967
Above left and left: NC-41881 at Long Beach, California, where it was overhauled and converted to carry 47 passengers

Bv 144, Blohm und Voss

FIRST FLIGHT 1944

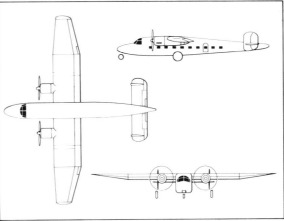

THE Blohm und Voss Bv 144 was one of the few German civil aircraft to undergo any real measure of development during World War II. The aircraft was designed in the early part of the war, and its origins lay in a Deutsche Lufthansa requirement for a Junkers Ju 52/3m replacement on the airline's short- and medium-range routes.

In 1942 Deutsche Lufthansa ordered two prototypes of this interesting Blohm und Voss aircraft, which was basically conventional but with two particularly notable features. The wing, of typical Blohm und Voss design, was located in the shoulder position, giving the propellers of the two wing-mounted radial engines adequate ground clearance, even with the adoption of a relatively short tricycle landing gear configuration.

The net effect of such a design was that the bottom of the fuselage was close to the ground, facilitating passenger boarding, and the straight lower fuselage was also parallel with the ground.

There were difficulties at take-off and landing. Blohm und Voss selected the unusual solution of a variable-incidence wing. By means of electrically actuated jacks under the centre-section leading edge the angle of incidence could be increased from the low-angle low-drag cruising position to the high-lift high-drag position for take-off and landing. This feature was extensively tested, during 1940, on the Blohm und Voss Ha 140 V3 seaplane prototype. In practice, the outer wing panels could be moved through 9° of incidence, apparently with highly successful results.

The other unusual feature of the Bv 144's design was the use of the tubular main spar patented by Dr Richard Vogt, the chief designer of Blohm und Voss. Light in weight but possessing admirable load-carrying characteristics, such a spar could also be used as the aircraft's main fuel tank, with consequent saving in weight.

Construction of the two prototype Bv 144s was at the Louis Breguet factory. It is hardly surprising that progress was slow. The first prototype Bv 144 V1 made its maiden flight in August 1944. By this time, however, the German engineers were in the process of evacuating the plant and little flying was accomplished before the French took over. Breguet continued the programme and completed the second aircraft but it is not known whether it flew before the project was abandoned.

Bv 144

Type: short-and medium-range transport
Maker: Blohm und Voss Schiffswerft, Abteilung Flugzeugbau
Span: 27 m (88 ft 7 in)
Length: 21.8 m (71 ft 6¼ in)
Height: 5.01 m (16 ft 5¼ in)
Wing area: 88 m² (947 sq ft)
Weight: maximum 13 000 kg (28 660 lb); empty not available
Powerplant: two 1600-hp BMW 801 MA 18-cylinder radial engines
Performance: estimated maximum speed 470 km/h (292 mph); estimated range 1550 km (963 miles)
Payload: seats for 18 passengers
Crew: 3
Production: 2 (prototypes)

Top: The Bv 144 after the Liberation, sporting French markings and the Cross of Lorraine

143

Boeing 377 Stratocruiser

FIRST FLIGHT 1944

THE Boeing B-29 Superfortress programme catapulted aviation on to a new plateau of technology, and it was natural to translate it into transport aircraft, just as had been done with the B-17 (307 Stratoliner) and XB-15 (314 Clipper).

Boeing began working on studies of transport derivatives of the B-29 in 1941, but 1942 opened the floodgates of military money and in January of that year the USAAF ordered three XC-97 prototypes. Called Model 367 by Boeing, they were designed in the course of 1942, using as many B-29 parts as possible but with a completely new fuselage, pressurized throughout, whose dimensions at that time looked fantastic. The front looked bluff and unstreamlined, but in fact maximum speed was calculated to be as high as for the bomber. Boeing had to tailor the basic machine to military needs, but from the start had one or two engineers working on the differences needed for civil applications after the war under the designation Model 377.

Little effort could be spared until VJ-Day in August 1945, by which time the military XC-97 was flying. Pan American suggested the bold move of fitting the new Wasp Major engine (already ordered by the airline for its intended fleet of DC-7s, the civil version of the C-74 Globemaster). By 1946 Boeing had refined the 377 with this engine, increased gross weight and fuel capacity, full airframe anti-icing, structure of 75ST high-strength light alloy and modified and augmented systems, tall and foldable vertical tail (as on the XB-50) and an attractive two-deck interior with

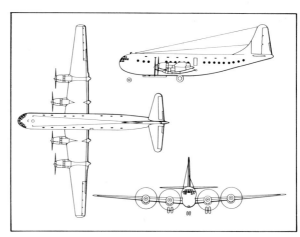

luxurious furnishing and spiral staircase to a downstairs bar/lounge. Typical day seating was for up to 100 passengers, though sleeper versions were studied.

PanAm ordered 20, to be named Stratocruiser, in June 1946, cancelling its DC-7s. Further orders came from Northwest, American Overseas, SAS, BOAC (after battles in Parliament) and United. The Northwest and United aircraft were built to a slightly different standard, the most obvious change being that passenger windows were square. Total production of the 377 was only 55, most airlines fighting shy of the complex Wasp Major with its twin General Electric turbos and HamStan hollow-steel square-tipped propellers.

The airlines that did operate this aircraft suf-

Boeing 377

Type: long-range transport
Maker: Boeing Airplane Co
Span: 43.05 m (141 ft 3 in)
Length: 33.63 m (110 ft 4 in)
Height: 11.66 m (38 ft 3 in)
Wing area: 164.35 m^2 (1769 sq ft)
Weight: maximum 64 638 kg (142 500 lb); empty 37 876 kg (83 500 lb)
Powerplant: four 3500-hp Pratt & Whitney R-4360-B6 Wasp Major 28-cylinder radial engines
Performance: cruising speed 547 km/h (340 mph); range 4426 km (2750 miles)
Payload: 10 855 kg (23 930 lb); seats for up to 112 passengers
Crew: 5
Production: 55 (civil)

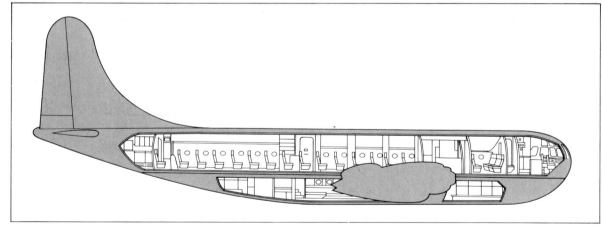

fered many problems, though these were no worse
than those that caused prolonged groundings of the
rival Constellation and DC-6. SAS never in fact
took delivery, preferring a succession of DC-4, DC-
6 and DC-7 versions; their four aircraft were added
to the BOAC order, which eventually grew from
the original (controversial) six to no fewer than 17
by the mid 1950s. Apart from United nearly all the
377s were initially fitted with folding sleeper bunks
for at least some of the passengers. PanAm used
their 20 aircraft, soon supplemented by the ex-
AOA machines plus the prototype, for all their
chief trunk routes including 'The President' first-
class service, as did BOAC with its rival service
called 'The Monarch'. Both operators installed
extra tankage for non-stop North Atlantic services

in 1950–55, BOAC even buying one aircraft from
PanAm in 1954 to help fill the gap caused by the
grounding of the Comets. By 1956 Stratocruisers
were fast being replaced by jets on the original
routes, but most continued with new owners, often
with as many as 112 passenger seats. Among the
more important second-hand operators were
RANSA of Venezuela, which used three converted
for all-cargo operations with weather radar like a
C-97, and Transocean whose fleet of ten remained
in service until 1963. In 1962 five Stratocruisers
were bought by Israel Aircraft Industries which
rebuilt them as refuelling tanker/transport/elec-
tronic-warfare aircraft with the Israeli air force.
Others were grossly rebuilt as the outsize 'Guppy'
freighters.

Lancaster transport, Avro
FIRST FLIGHT 1941

IN production as a bomber in 1942, the Lancaster was notable for its reliability, good altitude performance and excellent handling. In 1943 British Overseas Airways (BOAC) created a Development Unit to conduct research to support civil operations after the war, and one of its first aircraft was a Lancaster I delivered to the unit at Hurn in January 1944. Though camouflaged, it had its three turrets replaced by metal fairings, and for 2½ years carried out many test and trials programmes including proving the Merlin 102 powerplants of the Tudor I.

Soon after VJ-Day six of the vast number of surplus nearly new Lancasters were handed to the now British South American Airways. They looked rather like Lancastrians, with long pointed noses for carrying cargo, but had bluff faired tails and no fuselage windows. Only four were put into service, freighting between Hurn and then Heathrow and South America until the end of 1947. One of the other pair went to BOAC, and the last BSAA machine was taken over by Airtech at Thame and fitted with a large ventral freight pannier for carrying bulky loads on the Berlin Air Lift.

Flight Refuelling Ltd at Tarrant Rushton, Dorset, took over four ex-RAF Lancaster IIIs in 1946 (G-AHJT to JW). They put in a great deal of valuable development flying with the looped-hose method of aerial refuelling, and routinely made non-stop flights between Heathrow and Bermuda with a refuelling (by one of their number) based in the Azores. By mid 1948 they were heavily involved in the Berlin Air Lift, making 757 round trips.

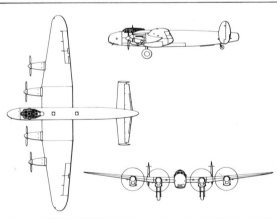

However, the 'Lanc' was even less of an economic peacetime vehicle than the redesigned bombers such as the Lancastrian and Halton.

Various other civil Lancasters were used as trainers, notably G-AJWM and AKAB. The former was one of the Lancaster Is with a bulged weapon bay with a capacity of 9979 kg (22 000 lb); it did not have provision for the Earthquake bomb which was carried semi-externally. With turrets still fitted it was flown out to Rome in summer 1947 by BEA to train crews of Alitalia Lancastrians. At the end of 1948 it passed into Alitalia ownership, having long since been repainted in their livery. AKAB was operated as a conversion trainer at Dunsfold by Skyways, one of the new British independents, and named *Sky Trainer*.

683 Lancaster

Type: medium- and long-range transport
Maker: A V Roe and Co Ltd
Span: 31.09 m (102 ft)
Length: 21.18 m (69 ft 6 in)
Height: 6.09 m (20 ft)
Wing area: 120.5 m² (1297 sq ft)
Weight: maximum 29 484 kg (65 000 lb); empty 16 738 kg (36 900 lb)
Powerplant: four 1640-hp Rolls-Royce Merlin T.24 liquid-cooled V-12 engines
Performance: cruising speed 338 km/h (210 mph); range 2670 km (1660 miles)
Payload: 10 000 kg (22 000 lb)
Crew: 4
Production: 20

Above: A Canadian Lancaster transport built at the Victory Aircraft plant at Toronto. Seven of these aircraft were used on a wartime transatlantic route carrying mail, high priority passengers and freight

Halton, Handley Page

FIRST FLIGHT 1946

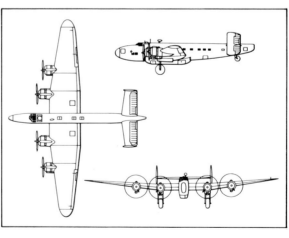

IN late 1945 it became clear that the Avro Tudor would not be ready for BOAC operational service in 1946 as planned. It was therefore imperative that the airline should receive an interim type enabling it to meet its route targets for the year.

The model selected was the Halifax C.8, and during the first half of 1946 12 such aircraft were converted in Belfast by Short & Harland into Halton Is. An entrance door was fitted into the right side of the rear fuselage, which was fitted with seating for 12 passengers and with small rectangular windows. The large ventral pannier was retained for the carriage of up to 3629 kg (8000 lb) of baggage, freight and mail, this stowage being supplemented by space in the nose where the glazed nose of the C.8 was replaced by metal skin. The pannier, which produced little extra drag, allowed the volume of what had been the bomb bay to be more than doubled.

The first Halton I, G-AHDU, was christened at the Handley Page airfield at Radlett on July 18, 1946. The 12 Halton Is were soon in service with BOAC, operating the difficult route from London to Accra in the Gold Coast, flying over the inhospitable Sahara. The Halton Is proved their worth in one year of operations with BOAC, after which they were retired.

The Halton Is were then kept at London Airport, one subsequently being sold to the French manufacturer Louis Breguet, and the others went to Aviation Traders Ltd for servicing before sale to the Egyptian air force together with 22 Halifax A.9 paratroop aircraft. During 1950, however, an em-

bargo was placed on the sale of weapons to Egypt, and the deal fell through. The Haltons had meanwhile been used in the Berlin Air Lift: between June 24, 1948 and August 15, 1949 seven freight operators used some 41 civil Halifax conversions, including the Haltons, to make 4653 freight sorties into Berlin – a major share of the total British civil contribution. The survivors were mostly scrapped in Southend.

There was also a single Halton II, registered G-AGZP. This was originally a VIP Halifax used by the Maharajah Gaekwar of Baroda, which was converted into the special Halton II in 1946. It then spent some time in South Africa, and was then operated by Lancashire Aircraft Corporation before being scrapped in 1953.

Halton I

Type: interim civil transport
Maker: Handley Page Ltd
Span: 31.6 m (103 ft 8 in)
Length: 22.43 m (73 ft 7 in)
Height: 6.91 m (22 ft 8 in)
Wing area: 118.4 m² (1275 sq ft)
Weight: maximum 30 845 kg (68 000 lb); empty 17 123 kg (37 750 lb)
Powerplant: four 1800-hp Bristol Hercules 100 14-cylinder radial sleeve-valve engines
Performance: cruising speed 418 km/h (260 mph); range 4072 km (2530 miles)
Payload: 3629 kg (8000 lb); seats for up to 12 passengers
Crew: 5
Production: 13

Liberator Express, Consolidated

FIRST FLIGHT 1944

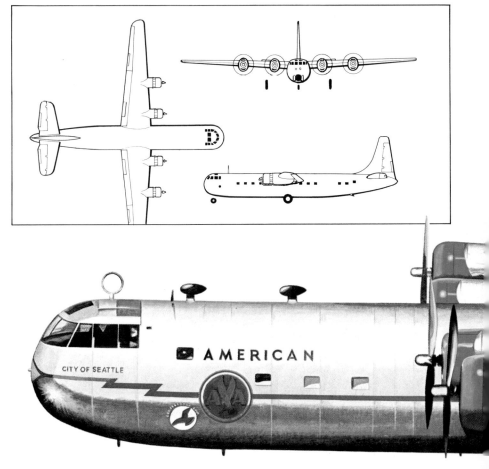

DURING World War II the US aircraft industry supplied the bulk of transport aircraft to the Allied air forces, and towards the end of hostilities it was clear that in their C-54 and C-69 Douglas and Lockheed had the makings of excellent four-engined heavy transports for civil operators.

The two designs eventually appeared in civil guise as the DC-4 and L-049 Constellation. Consolidated-Vultee tried to develop another airliner for the civil market, in the form of the Model 39. Of the four types, the Model 39 was the least successful, only a single prototype being built.

This is all the more surprising in that the basic Liberator bomber had been adapted as a transport aircraft of notable success used in large numbers during World War II. The LB-30 and the LB-30A were unarmed *ad hoc* transport conversions of the Liberator II and Liberator I (B-24A) respectively, only small numbers being converted. Properly executed conversions of the B-24 series were produced for the USAAF as the C-87 series, for the US Navy as the RY series, and for the RAF as the Liberator C.VII and C.IX. The C-87 was a modification of the B-24D with a crew of five and accommodation for 20 passengers or large tanks of fuel; 276 were produced for the USAAF. The RAF's C.VII, of which 24 were supplied under the terms of the Lend-Lease Act, was basically similar, as were the five RY-2s supplied to the US Navy. The C-87 was succeeded by the C-87A, of which six were supplied to the USAAF. This model was derived from the B-24D again, but was powered by Pratt & Whitney R-1830-45s instead of R-1830-43s, and was used as a VIP transport with ten sleeper berths. The US Navy used three similar aircraft under the designation RY-1. The C-87C was to have been a transport version of the single-finned B-24N, but no production under this designation took place.

Given this background, therefore, it was not unreasonable for Consolidated-Vultee to regard with optimism a specialized civil derivative of the Liberator bomber, especially as the wing of the bomber and its derivatives was still highly efficient. Designed for Consolidated-Vultee by David R Davis, for the XP4Y-1 flying boat (Consolidated 31), this wing was of high aspect ratio, with constant taper in chord and thickness from root to tip, and offered very low drag at both low and high speeds. The Model 39 thus had the wings, powerplant and landing gear of the Liberator, and single-finned tail surfaces of the PB4Y-2 Privateer, but a totally new fuselage of circular section with the cockpit let into the hemispherical nose in a fashion similar to that pioneered on the Boeing B-29 Superfortress.

The single prototype was moderately successful, being used by American Airlines for air-freight operations with a maximum load of 5443 kg (12 000 lb), but the type could not compete in performance with current civil aircraft, and was much less powerful than the DC-6, Constellation and the more advanced Boeing Model 377. In passenger configuration the Model 39 was to have carried 48 passengers and 544 kg (1200 lb) of mail over a range of 4023 km (2500 miles).

Model 39

Type: long-range transport
Maker: Consolidated-Vultee
Aircraft Corporation
Span: 33.55 m (110 ft)
Length: 27.45 m (90 ft)
Height: 9.14 m (30 ft)
Wing area: 97.36 m² (1048 sq
ft)

Weight: maximum 29 030 kg
(64 000 lb); empty not
available
Powerplant: four 1200-hp
Pratt & Whitney R-1830-65
Twin Wasp radial engines
Performance: cruising speed
386 km/h (240 mph);
maximum range 6437 km
(4000 miles) at 322 km/h
(200 mph)
Payload: 5443 kg (12 000 lb);
seating for up to 48
passengers
Production: 1

Above: The Model 39 during
evaluation flights from
Salinas and El Centro
California to cities east of the
Mississippi including New
York and Boston. Cargo
included soft fruit and
engineering parts which could
be loaded direct from trucks
through large fuselage doors
Left: One of the many
Liberator bombers which
were converted after the war.
Unlike the Liberator Express
these aircraft had been built
as bombers and after 1945
had their turrets removed and
the nose position faired over.
This aircraft has a British
registration and was in service
with Scottish Airlines

Tudor, Avro

FIRST FLIGHT 1945

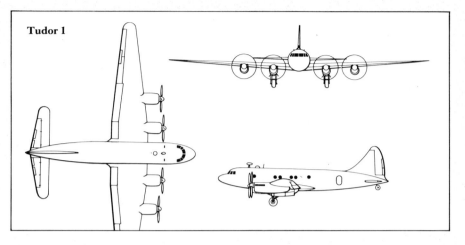

THE Avro Tudor originated in 1943 as an idea for a postwar transatlantic transport derived from the Avro Lincoln bomber. Detail design began in 1944, but the Tudor then developed into a significantly different aircraft, retaining only the general configuration of the Lincoln, with a single-fin tail.

The first prototype flew on June 14, 1945 and was soon followed by two production aircraft, all of which underwent rigorous testing, which revealed the need for extensive modification to the nacelles, undercarriage, wing root fillets, empennage, engines and the airframe generally. Apart from these government-inspired modifications, moreover, the British Overseas Airways Corporation insisted on another 343 alterations at the final development meeting held on March 12, 1946, finally cancelling its order on April 11, 1947.

Apart from the three development aircraft, another 21 Tudors ordered in April 1945 were then in production, and in an attempt to find a niche for the type development was diversified within the two main strands already in existence. Under the overall designation Avro 688 appeared the Tudor 1, Tudor 3, and Tudors 4 and 4B; under the designation Avro 689 appeared the Tudor 2, Tudor 5, Tudor 6 and Tudor 7.

The Avro 688 Tudors were all powered by the 1770-hp Merlin 621. The two Tudor 3s were nine-seat government VIP transports converted by Armstrong Whitworth and so used between 1950 and 1953 when they went to Aviation Traders for conversion into Tudor 1s for charter work up to 1956. The main Avro 688 variant was the Tudor 4, lengthened by 1.83 m (6 ft) and with the flight engineer's position removed to accommodate 32 passengers.

The Avro 688 Tudor was designed to carry a small payload over a long range; the Avro 689 Tudor, on the other hand, was intended to carry a large payload over a shorter range.

Original orders totalled 79, but these were eventually reduced to six, of which only five were completed. The prototype crashed in 1947, one was re-engined with 1715-hp Bristol Hercules radials as the prototype (and single) Tudor 7, one was used as a testbed and the other two were used for trooping up to 1959. The six Tudor 5s were used for miscellaneous trooping, freighting and charter work up to the mid 1950s.

Tudor 4

Type: commercial transport
Maker: A V Roe and Co Ltd
Span: 36.58 m (120 ft)
Length: 25.98 m (85 ft 3 in)
Height: 6.38 m (20 ft 11 in)
Wing area: 132.02 m² (1421 sq ft)
Weight: maximum 36 288 kg (80 000 lb); empty 22 426 kg (49 441 lb)
Powerplant: four 1770-hp Rolls-Royce Merlin 621 V-12 liquid-cooled engines
Performance: cruising speed 338 km/h (210 mph); range 6437 km (4000 miles)
Payload: seats for up to 32 passengers
Crew: 5
Production: 31

Above left: The British South American Airways G-AHNK *Star Lion*, a Tudor 4 initially used on the London to Bermuda route until the unexplained loss of the two other BSAA Tudors in 1949, when it was relegated to freighting duties
Left: Interior of a BSAA Tudor 4 typical of late 1940s furnishing
Below: The BSAA Tudor 4 *Star Leopard*

Sandringham, Short

FIRST FLIGHT 1946

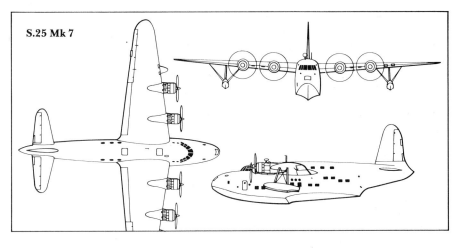

S.25 Mk 7

BY the end of World War II the conversion of the Sunderland III flying boats into the S.25 transports proved that superior operating economics could be gained by the development of the basic Sunderland design along the lines of the prewar Empire class flying boats. In 1945, therefore, the Hythe class boat G-AGKX *Himalaya* was extensively rebuilt by Short Brothers. By the time it made its appearance at the Victory Air Pageant on June 22, 1946 this single S.25 Sandringham Mk 1 had smoothly faired nose lines, a neat tailcone replacing the rear gun turret, and accommodation for 22 passengers on two decks, together with a promenade deck, dining room and cocktail bar. This single aircraft, powered by four 1030-hp Bristol Pegasus 38s, was retained by BOAC, which did not order any more of the type.

With a plethora of war-surplus aircraft to hand, however, Short set about producing a number of Sandringhams, all basically identical on the outside, but varying considerably in internal dispositions and flying equipment. There were three Sandringham Mk 2s (*Argentina*, *Paraguay* and *Uruguay*) for the Argentinian operator Dodero, with seating for 45 passengers and a cocktail bar. This version was powered by four 1200-hp Pratt & Whitney Twin Wasps. Dodero also received two Sandringham Mk 3s (*Brasil* and *Inglaterra*) with seating for 21 on the lower deck, and a galley and dining room on the upper deck. Four Sandringham Mk 4s were produced to the order of Tasman Empire Airways, with seating for 30, with a pantry and bar on the upper deck. Despite its earlier

refusal to accept more of the type, BOAC found itself so short of aircraft in 1947 that it took nine Sandringham Mk 5s as the Plymouth class, these boats having accommodation for 22 day or 16 night passengers on the routes from the UK to the Middle and Far East, and that between Hong Kong and Singapore. Four Sandringham Mk 6s were produced for Norwegian Air Lines, with seating for 37 passengers on two decks for service on the route between Oslo and Tromso. The final variant was the Sandringham Mk 7, of which three were produced for BOAC in 1948 as the Bermuda class with seating for 30 passengers.

After successful careers with these airlines the survivors were generally passed on to lesser operators, the type remaining in service up to the 1960s.

S.25 Mk 5

Type: long-range passenger flying boat
Maker: Short Brothers Ltd
Span: 34.37 m (112 ft 9½ in)
Length: 26.28 m (86 ft 3 in)
Height: 6.97 m (22 ft 10½ in)
Wing area: 156.7 m² (1687 sq ft)
Weight: maximum 27 216 kg (60 000 lb); empty 17 917 kg (39 498 lb)
Powerplant: four 1200-hp Pratt & Whitney R-1830-92D Twin Wasp 14-cylinder two-row radial engines
Performance: cruising speed 283 km/h (176 mph); range 3943 km (2450 miles)
Payload: seats for up to 22 passengers
Crew: 5
Production: 26 (all types)

Right: LN-IAV, a Sandringham Mk 6, was delivered as the *Kvitbjorn* to the Norwegian airline DNL in 1948, for the Oslo-Tromso service, and later lost in a crash
Below: *Southern Cross* a Short Sandringham of Antilles Air Boats

Solent, Short

FIRST FLIGHT 1946

THE Short S.45A Solent was the civil version of the S.45 Seaford, itself originally known as the Sunderland IV and intended for service largely in the Pacific theatre. The Seaford was too late to see service in World War II, and the 30 originally ordered were cut back to six. One of these aircraft was lent to BOAC in 1946 for evaluation as a civil transport, and so successful was this that the airline ordered 12 production Solents from Short Brothers.

The conversion from Seaford to Solent resembled that of the Sunderland to Sandringham, with a sleek nose replacing the bluff lines of the turreted military nose, a new tailcone replacing the rear turret, and all military equipment removed. At the same time the 1800-hp Bristol Hercules 100s of the Seaford were replaced by civil 1680-hp Hercules 637s on the production Solent 2, the first of which was launched on November 11, 1946.

The Solent was the most powerful British civil flying boat to enter service, and was thus well appointed: accommodation was on two decks for a maximum of 34 passengers. On the upper deck were a cocktail bar, a large cabin and lounge combined, a steward's compartment and a galley; on the lower deck were three passenger cabins, a promenade, a library, wardrobe compartments, dressing rooms and lavatories. A spiral staircase connected the two decks, whose upper one had the flight-deck at the forward end.

All the Solent 2s were owned by the Ministry of Transport and Civil Aviation, and leased to BOAC for the airline's route from Southampton to Johannesburg. In November 1950 BOAC ended its flying-boat operations, but by this time the 12 Solent 2s had been joined by six Solent 3s converted on the production line from Seafords and able to carry 39 passengers.

The last Solent type was the 4, introduced on the route between Auckland and Sydney by Tasman Empire Airways in 1949. The four Solent 4s were produced specifically for long-range operations, and could carry 44 passengers on the power of their four 2040-hp Hercules 733 radials.

Aquila Airways ceased operating Solents on its Madeira route on September 30, 1950, ending British commercial flying boat services. The three boats were taken over by Aerovias Aquila and the Madeira route was re-opened by the Portuguese.

Solent 2

Type: long-range passenger flying boat
Maker: Short Brothers Ltd
Span: 34.36 m (112 ft 9 in)
Length: 26.7 m (87 ft 8 in)
Height: 11.46 m (37 ft 7 in)
Wing area: 156.7 m² (1687 sq ft)
Weight: maximum 35 381 kg (78 000 lb); empty 21 664 kg (47 760 lb)
Powerplant: four 1690-hp Bristol Hercules 637 radial engines
Performance: cruising speed 393 km/h (244 mph); range 2897 km (1800 miles)
Payload: seats for up to 34 passengers
Crew: 7
Production: 22 (all types)

Above: A Short S.45 Solent 4 G-AOBL, which was re-registered ZK-AMC when it was sold to Portugal in 1958. Abandoned in the Tagus estuary, it was finally scrapped in August 1971
Below: A Short Solent 4 of Ansett, the Australian airline started in 1936 by Reginald Miles Ansett. This freight and passenger carrier now operates services throughout Australia in competition with TAA

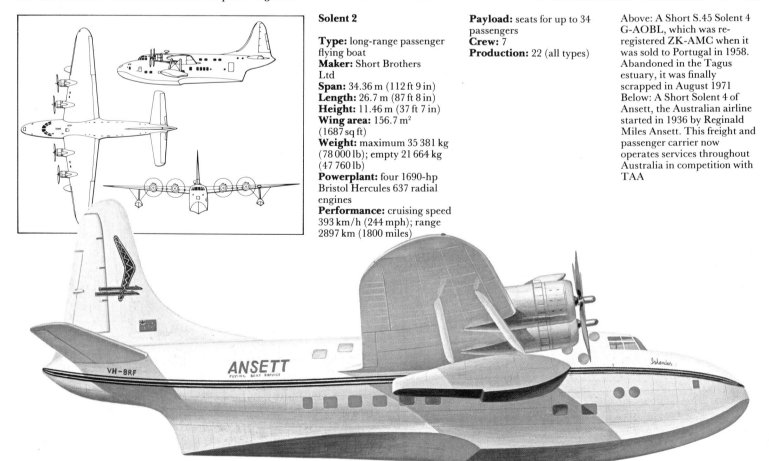

Viking, Vickers-Armstrongs
FIRST FLIGHT 1945

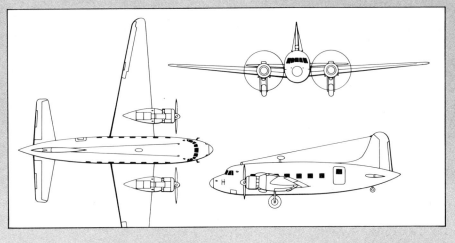

WITH an end to World War II in sight, there was an urgent need for Britain to produce an interim short-haul airliner to supplement the Douglas DC-3. In 1944 Vickers studied three civil developments of existing bomber designs – the Windsor Empire, the Warwick Continental and the Wellington Continental. The latter was considered the most promising and duly designated VC.1 (Vickers Commercial One), and later named Viking.

Being an interim type, the Viking did not come under the auspices of the Brabazon Committee, and Government Specification 17/44 was issued in October 1944. Construction of the prototype began in early 1945, and lead time was kept to a minimum by using Wellington wings and Warwick Mk V tail surfaces. Bristol Hercules 100 radial engines were selected after successful trials in a Wellington. Vickers' design team knew that a fabric-covered geodetic fuselage would be unacceptable to postwar airlines, and a new stressed-skin fuselage was introduced. The Viking became Britain's first postwar airliner to fly when Mutt Summers took the prototype, G-AGOK, aloft for the first time on June 22, 1945.

The first 19 production aircraft were delivered with fabric-covered wings (of geodetic type derived from the Wellington) and tail surfaces. These aircraft were later designated Mk 1As, 11 of which were operated by British European Airways. The cabin was unpressurized but controlled for temperature and ventilation. Apart from the ramp across the main spar, the accommodation was of a

Viking 1B

Type: medium-range passenger transport
Maker: Vickers-Armstrongs Ltd
Span: 27.2 m (89 ft 3 in)
Length: 19.86 m (65 ft 2 in)
Height: 7.32 m (24 ft)
Wing area: 81.92 m² (882 sq ft)
Weight: maximum 15 422 kg (34 000 lb); empty 10 433 kg (23 000 lb)
Powerplant: two 1690-hp Bristol Hercules 634 14-cylinder sleeve-valve radial engines

Performance: cruising speed 423 km/h (263 mph) at 3048 m (10 000 ft); range 2736 km (1700 miles)
Payload: 4989 kg (11 000 lb); seats for up to 36 passengers
Crew: 3 to 5
Production: 163

Below: The Vickers Type 610 Viking IB in BEA markings. Designated G-AIVM, it entered service in July 1947 and was called Vigorous (as here), and later George Monck, before being transferred to Germany in December 1955

CUNARD EAGLE AIRWAYS

G-AJPH

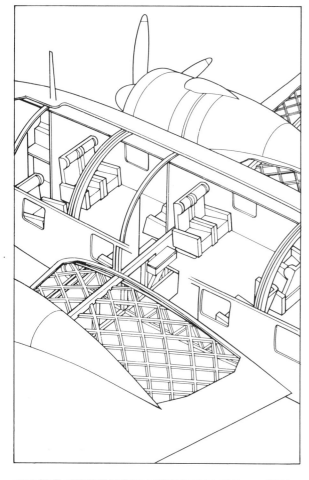

Above left: The Viking used a geodetic-construction wing fixed to the fuselage near the leading and trailing edges
Left: The passenger cabins of a BEA Viking 1B, photographed in April 1947. Note the seats facing each other at the forward end of both cabins
Right: The relatively spartan interior cockpit of an Admiral Class Viking. The class represented a new departure for BEA in October 1952, and carried 36 instead of 27 passengers
Far right: Two BEA engineers checking a 1690-hp Bristol Hercules sleeve-valve radial

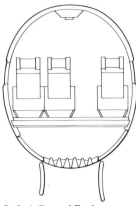

Cunard Steamship Company joined with British Eagle International Airways
Left: The Viking had the usual underfloor stowage area, and was notable for its passenger comfort and freedom from vibration
Right: A Type 635 Viking 1B G-AMGG which entered service with BEA in 1951 as *Sir Robert Calder*, and was passed on to Eagle Aviation Ltd in 1955
Below: G-AMNR, a Vickers Type 635 Viking 1B which first flew in 1952 and was withdrawn from Service in 1961. In BEA service it was named *Lord Beresford*
Left: A Cunard Eagle Airways Viking; in 1960 the

high standard. The flight-deck was spacious, modern, and provided very good visibility – particularly important when taxiing the tail-wheeled Viking at busy airports. The Viking was the first postwar design to comply with new Icao (International Civil Aviation Organization) regulations governing engine-out performance during take-off.

On April 5, 1946, the Ministry of Aircraft Production ordered 50 Vikings and certification followed on April 24. On September 1, BEA (formed only a month earlier), operated its first Viking service from Northolt to Copenhagen with G-AHOP *Valerie*. Services to Stavanger, Oslo and Amsterdam began the day after.

In December 1946 a serious icing problem forced BEA to ground its Viking fleet. Heavy ice accretion on the leading edge of the tailplane had been found to cause overbalanced elevators. Altering the asymmetrical horn balance areas of both elevators and increasing the flow rate of de-icing fluid cured the problem, and BEA resumed normal services during April 1947.

The first of 45 Viking 1Bs were introduced by BEA in April 1947, and these began to replace 'Pionair' class DC-3s on main routes. The lengthened fuselage of the Mk 1B increased passenger capacity from 21 to 27 and later 36.

A dramatic incident occurred on April 13, 1950, when a saboteur's bomb exploded in the rear toilet of *Vigilant* over the English Channel. After successfully bringing his passengers back to Northolt Captain Harvey was awarded the George Medal.

The Viking became BEA's workhorse and laid the foundations of its route network and operating procedures. When replaced by Viscounts in 1954, the type had flown nearly 500 000 hours and carried 3 million passengers. For some 18 years the Viking had been the backbone of the British aviation industry.

Other UK Viking operators included: Airwork, Eagle Aviation, Hunting Air Transport, Air Safaris, East Anglian Flying Services, Pegasus Airlines, Orion, Invicta Airways, Field Aircraft Services, Autair and the King's Flight. Vikings were also sold to many other airlines including Aer Lingus, British West Indian Airways, Indian National Airways, DDL (Danish Air Lines), Central African Airways, South African Airways, Iraqi Airways and the air forces of Pakistan, Argentina and Jordan.

Bristol 170

FIRST FLIGHT 1945

WORK was begun on the Bristol 170 by technical director L G Frise (of aileron fame), and A E Russell, in 1944. It was to be a private venture design, suitable for short-range general duty transport work. The Mk I Series employed a wing of the same section and taper ratio as the 1936 Bombay, but with a swept-back leading edge, and a straight trailing edge of simplified two-spar construction. Power was to be provided by an improved model of the sleeve-valve Perseus. The fuselage was flat-sided, the aircraft being loaded through a trap door in the nose, and the undercarriage was fixed.

When the design came to the attention of the Air Staff, they recalled recommendations made a few weeks earlier by Orde Wingate for a transport capable of carrying vehicles and supplies to jungle airstrips in Burma during World War II. Accordingly, two prototypes were ordered. An enlarged fuselage allowed a standard 3-ton (3048-kg) truck or equivalent load to be carried. More powerful Hercules 630 engines were specified.

The prototype Freighter, G-AGPV, made its maiden flight from Filton on December 2, 1945 – a little late to have any effect on the Burma Campaign. The second prototype, G-AGVB, configured as a 32-seat Wayfarer, received the first unrestricted Certificate of Airworthiness granted to a new postwar aircraft.

Wayfarer customers included British-American Air Services (who operated 2), REAL of Sao Paulo (2), Dalmia Jain Airways of Delhi (3), Bharat Airways (2), Skytravel (2) and Indian National

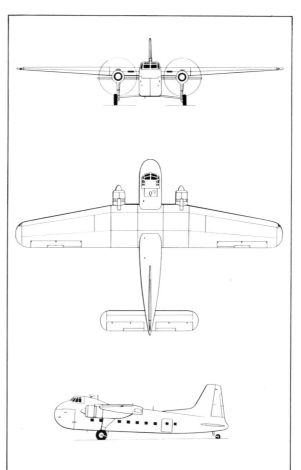

Mk 31

Type: short-range specialized transport
Maker: Bristol Aeroplane Co
Span: 32.92 m (108 ft)
Length: 20.83 m (68 ft 4 in)
Height: 6.56 m (21 ft 6 in)
Wing area: 138 m² (1485 sq ft)
Weight: maximum 19 958 kg (44 000 lb); empty 12 247 kg (27 000 lb)
Powerplant: two 1980-hp Bristol Hercules 734 14-cylinder sleeve-valve radial engines
Performance: cruising speed 311 km/h (193 mph) at 3048 m (10 000 ft); range with maximum payload 1320 km (820 miles)
Payload: 5670 kg (12 500 lb); seats for 15 to 23 passengers depending on configuration; up to 60 in Mk 32
Crew: 2 to 3
Production: 214 (all types)

Airways (2). The first of 15 Freighters were delivered to the Argentine government on October 25, 1946. Other Mk I Series Freighters went to Hunting Air Survey, Airwork and Shell. Silver City chartered a Mk IIA Wayfarer for evacuating refugees following the partition of India.

At the 1947 SBAC Show at Radlett, the Mark XI (later Mk 21) was unveiled. This featured the 32.92-m (108-ft) span round-tipped wing tested on the prototype, which together with the availability of Hercules 672 engines, increased gross weight by 1361 kg (3000 lb). Two versions were offered; the unfurnished Mk 21 and the convertible Mk 21E, which had seating for 32 passengers and the comforts of cabin heating and sound insulation. The Pakistan air force ordered 30 Mk 21s, and

Left: The Mk 32 *Voyager*, originally a 31E, was used for short-haul trooping in 1954 with military serial XH385, and converted to Mk 32 standard in 1958 with lengthened nose and increased fin area. It was finally scrapped in 1967
Top: A Channel Airways Freighter 21E, which saw service with Central African Airways in 1948 and then with West African Airways, until 1957. It was finally withdrawn in 1966
Above: This 170 Mk 32 began life as the Silver City *City of Leicester* before being transferred to Cie Air

Transport of France in May 1961 as F-BKBD *Quatorze Juillet*
Right: The clamshell doors of the Bristol Freighter which could take two cars with their occupants seated to the rear. Silver City Airways Ltd ran a 25-minute flight between Lympne and Le Touquet which was inaugurated on July 13, 1948 and proved very successful. The hold of the Bristol Freighter was used to accommodate less than peaceful cargo when a chartered aircraft ferried light tanks into the French fortress of Dien Bien Phu in Vietnam in 1953

the Royal Australian Air Force three Mk 21Es.

Certification of the Mk 31 was delayed when G-AHJJ crashed on March 21, 1950, after the rudder had locked during single-engined climb. G-AIFF was lost off Portland Bill on May 6, 1949 in similar circumstances. Freighter G-AGVC was modified to Mk 31 standard with Hercules 734 engines, and a new fin prevented rudder-locking in the extreme yaw condition. The Pakistan air force bought 38 Mk 31Ms – the largest single order for Freighters. Other Freighter Mk 31 operators included: Air Vietnam, Silver City, Aviation Traders, Iberia, Wardair, SAFE, and the air forces of Canada, Iraq and New Zealand. The last Mk 31 delivered new, went to Dan-Air on March 25, 1950.

The last variant of the Bristol 170, the Mk 32, was developed at the request of Silver City Airways. Silver City inaugurated the first Lympne to Le Touquet car ferry service with G-AGVC on July 13, 1948. Volumetric capacity was increased by lengthening the nose, to carry not two cars but three, plus passengers. Silver City took delivery of the first of the 14 Mk 31s, on March 31, 1953. This aircraft was later converted into a Super Wayfarer with accommodation for 60 passengers. In October 1962, Silver City and Air Charter were merged into British United Air Ferries with many intensive routes between Britain and Europe.

In 1980, Bristol 170s were still being operated by Safe Air (9), Norcanair (1) and Air Express (1). It was a tough, dependable performer, and it is unfortunate that Bristol, and later BAC, never produced a modern version.

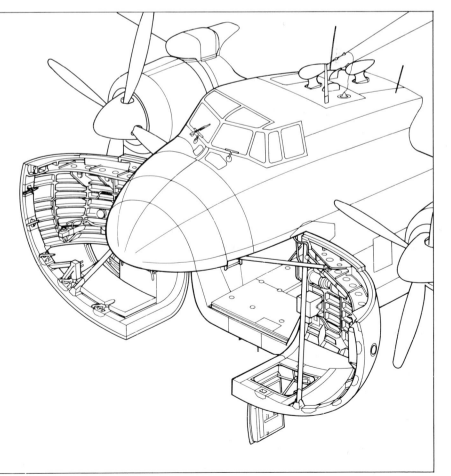

DH.104 Dove, de Havilland

FIRST FLIGHT 1945

UNTIL the advent of the Britten-Norman BN-2 Islander, the de Havilland DH.104 Dove was the most successful civil transport ever produced in the UK. It was conceived in 1943 as a replacement for the prewar DH.89 Dragon Rapide, to serve as a feederliner on British internal routes with a load of eight passengers. The type was produced in conformity with the Brabazon Committee's Type 5B specification, and was thus a smaller contemporary of the Miles M.60 Marathon, with the emphasis placed on low operating costs combined with good air and field performance.

The prototype, G-AGPJ, appeared in 1945, and immediately impressed with its attractive lines and obviously functional configuration: low-set cantilever wings, neat retractable landing gear (based on that of the Vampire), twin de Havilland Gipsy Queen 71 engines and an all-metal stress-skinned structure. This prototype flew at Hatfield on September 25, 1945. Flight trials were completely satisfactory apart from the need to increase fin area to remedy asymmetric control problems.

Despite de Havilland's intention of supplying a DH.89 replacement for British customers, the high purchase cost of some £20 000 made this impossible for all but a few British operators in the difficult years immediately after World War II. Nevertheless, the Dove entered wide-scale production despite the fatal crashes of the second prototype and third production aircraft. Early users were the Iraq Petroleum Transport Company and Sudan Airways, and the first British Dove in commercial

service was G-AHRB of Skyways, which received its certificate of airworthiness on October 7, 1946. Other early British users were Hunting, Olley and Morton Air Services, and BOAC.

These initial production aircraft, with seating for eight passengers, were Series 1 machines. The next model to appear, in 1948, was the Series 2, configured as a six-seat executive aircraft. The type proved immediately popular with large industrial concerns. Series 1 and 2 Doves were powered by two 330-hp Queen 70-3s, while the 340-hp Queen 70-4s led to the designations Series 1B and 2B.

The Series 4 took physical form as a military communications aircraft, entering service with the RAF as the Devon C.1 and with the Royal Navy as the Sea Devon C.20.

Left: A de Havilland Dove 6 which served as a demonstration aircraft for Smiths Industries' Para-Visual Director system. This machine made its first flight in September 1959 and was used by Smiths for over 13 years

Far left: The tall Heron-type cockpit canopy of a Royal Jordanian Air Force Dove 8. The engines of the Dove 8 are recognizable by their oil-cooler intakes above and thrust augmentor tubes below

Left: The Dove had a nose which gave easy access to the wiring for the controls and radio, and the pneumatic system which operated the nosewheel. The wheel was fully castoring, but non-steerable. Ground crew could also reach the batteries and electrical junction box with ease

Above: A DH.104 Dove 1 of Trans National Airlines, an American operator absorbed by the North American Airlines Agency in 1950
Right: A DH.104 Dove of Balair, photographed at Berne in July 1964. Based at Basel-Mulhouse, this small airline does passenger, cargo charter and inclusive-tour flights. It also flies extensively for the Red Cross

The Dove 5 and 6 of 1953 were essentially similar to the Series 1 and 2, but engined with the Queen 70-2, rated at 380 hp. The use of two such engines allowed an increase in maximum take-off weight of 136 kg (300 lb) to 3992 kg (8800 lb), and allowed the Series 5 and 6 to carry 20% more payload over a stage length of approximately 805 km (500 miles).

The final Dove models were the Series 7 and 8, similar to the Series 1 and 2 but powered by the 400-hp Queen 70-3. A sub-variant of the Series 8 was the 8A, sold in the United States as the Dove Custom 600. These final models were externally similar to their predecessors, with the exception of a higher cockpit roof modelled on that of the DH.114 Heron, but the increased power available from the uprated engines permitted yet another increase in maximum weight, this time to 4060 kg (8950 lb), while still increasing speed and range: the maximum speed of the Dove Series 1 and 2 was 323 km/h (201 mph) compared with the 378 km/h (235 mph) of the 7 and 8, the equivalent range figures being 1609 km (1000 miles) and 1891 km (1175 miles).

The success of the Dove is attested by the fact that production lasted almost 25 years, the 542nd (the last Dove), a Series 8, being delivered to Dowty Group Services on September 20, 1967; it should be noted that the penultimate Dove, also a Series 8, was delivered to Martin-Baker Ltd only in February 1968, bringing to an end the production of this classic type. Today, most Doves have American engines.

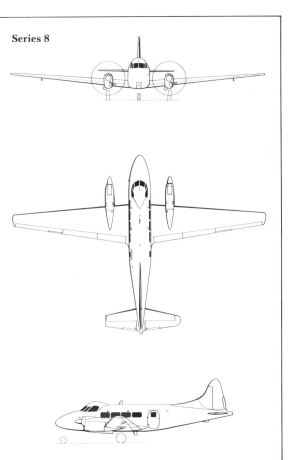

Series 8

Series 7

Type: feederliner and executive aircraft
Maker: de Havilland Aircraft Co Ltd
Span: 17.37 m (57 ft)
Length: 11.99 m (39 ft 4 in)
Height: 4.06 m (13 ft 4 in)
Wing area: 31.12 m^2 (335 sq ft)
Weight: maximum 4060 kg (8950 lb); empty 2985 kg (6580 lb)
Powerplant: two 400-hp de Havilland Gipsy Queen 70-3 six-cylinder inverted inline air-cooled engines
Performance: cruising speed 261 km/h (162 mph); range 1891 km (1175 miles)
Payload: seats for up to 8 passengers
Crew: 1 or 2
Production: 542 (all types)

Consul, Airspeed

FIRST FLIGHT 1946

EVERY Airspeed Consul was a civil conversion of a surplus Oxford trainer, itself derived from the civil Envoy. The Consul retained all major Oxford components, but the cabin was redesigned to accommodate six passengers. Other changes included the installation of extra windows, double doors fitted to the cockpit bulkhead and luggage space at the rear of the cabin. Thus modified, the prototype G-AGVY (converted from the de Havilland-built Oxford V3679), was certificated on March 15, 1946.

Baggage space was transferred into an elongated nose in all subsequent Consuls, and this arrangement provided more cabin space and extended the CG range (limits within which the centre of gravity must be located for safe flight). This modification also gave the Consul a more pleasing appearance. Airwork were appointed official distributors, and their demonstrator, G-AHEG, was delivered to Heston in April, 1946.

Despite an obvious lack of refinement, the Consul came on the market at the right time, at the right price, and satisfied the immediate postwar need for charter-class aircraft, until the arrival of more modern equipment. Cockpit layout resembled the Oxford, and single-engined performance was poor. Points in its favour, however, were good visibility from the cockpit, low maintenance requirements and reliable operation.

Large UK Consul fleets were operated by the following: Morton Air Services (who flew 8), British Air Transport (5), Chartair (9), Atlas Aviation (4), Westminster Airways (7), Lancashire

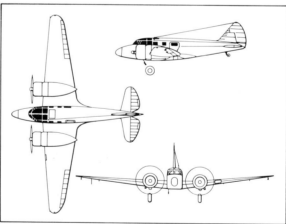

Aircraft Corporation (6), International Airways (5), Air Enterprises (7), British Aviation Services (4), Hornton Airways (3), Steiner's Air Service (6), Transair (5) and the Ministry of Aviation.

The Consul was also popular overseas. Air Malta leased several for services to North Africa, Sicily and Rome. Eight were sold outright to Air Jordan. Consuls operated in the Near East, Burma, Central Africa and French Indo-China. Two were refitted with Oxford noses and exported to French West Africa for aerial survey work. The sole ambulance version, G-AJWR, was displayed at the 1947 SBAC (Society of British Aircraft Constructors) Show at Radlett, and later sold to French Indo-China. Consul G-AKCW undertook the original flight testing of the Alvis Leonides engine.

AS.65 Consul

Type: light-transport and business aircraft
Maker: Airspeed (1934) Ltd
Span: 16.25 m (53 ft 4 in)
Length: 10.77 m (35 ft 4 in)
Height: 3.09 m (10 ft 1½ in)
Wing area: 32.33 m² (348 sq ft)
Weight: maximum 3742 kg (8250 lb); empty 2743 kg (6047 lb)
Powerplant: two 395-hp Armstrong Siddeley Cheetah X 7-cylinder radials
Performance: cruising speed 251 km/h (156 mph); range 1448 km (900 miles)
Payload: 997 kg (2203 lb); seats for 6 passengers
Crew: 2
Production: minimum 150 Oxford conversions

Top: G-AJWR, an ambulance version of the Consul, which was re-registered F-BEDP when it was passed to the Société Indochinoise de Transports Aériens. It was destroyed by fire at Saigon in October 1950

G.212, Fiat

FIRST FLIGHT 1947

THE Fiat G.212 was a logical evolution from the Fiat G.12, which had first flown on October 15, 1940 as the G.12C tri-motor civil transport. The G.12 was produced in a number of variants, all notable for their high speed and long range.

The G.212CA prototype first flew on January 19, 1947 and immediately revealed a close family resemblance to the G.12 series. The main points of difference between the two types were the G.212's increased span, considerably larger fuselage and bigger tail. The G.212CA had a typical flight crew of three, and could accommodate up to 30 passengers seated three-abreast, compared with the G.12's 14 passengers seated two-abreast. Power was provided by a trio of 860-hp Alfa Romeo 128RC18 radial engines, and maximum take-off weight was 16 000 kg (35 274 lb).

During 1947 the G.212CA was followed by the first examples of the two planned production variants, the G.212CP Aeropullman Monterosa and the G.212TP Aviocargo Monviso. The G.212CP, which was the only variant to enter commercial service, was the definitive passenger model, with seating for 34 passengers; aft of the passenger compartment were a lavatory, galley and baggage hold, this last supplemented by three large freight holds under the floor and extra compartments in the wing leading edges outboard of the engines. The G.212TP did not enter service, but was planned as a pure freighter. Both models were powered by three 1065-hp Pratt & Whitney R-1830-S1C3-G Twin Wasp radials.

The first and main operator of the G.212CP was

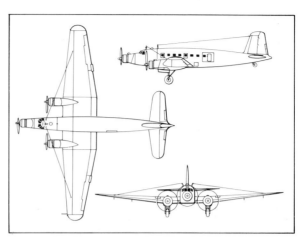

Avio Linee Italiane, which received six in 1947–48, four subsequently going to Ali Flotte Riunite. The only other airline to use new G.212CP airliners was Services Aériens Internationaux d'Egypte (SAIDE), which accepted three of the type in 1948 for use on the North African littoral route from Cairo to Tunis via Benghazi and Tripoli. The only other two G.212s for civil use were bought by the Compagnie Air Transport, but were apparently not actually placed in service. Other G.212s were procured by the Italian air force for transport and training duties.

The G.212 was the last civil air transport aircraft to be developed by Fiat until the early 1960s, when work began on design of the twin-engined Aeritalia G.222.

G.212

Type: passenger transport
Maker: Fiat SpA
Span: 29.34 m (96 ft 3 in)
Length: 23.05 m (75 ft 7½ in)
Height: 6.5 m (21 ft 4 in)
Wing area: 116.6 m² (1255 sq ft)
Weight: maximum 17 400 kg (38 360 lb); empty 11 200 kg (24 692 lb)
Powerplant: three 1065-hp Pratt & Whitney R-1830-S1C3-G 14-cylinder radial engines
Performance: cruising speed 300 km/h (186 mph) at 4500 m (14 764 ft); range 3000 km (1864 miles)
Payload: 3250 kg (7165 lb); seats for up to 34 passengers
Crew: 3
Production: 12 (civil)

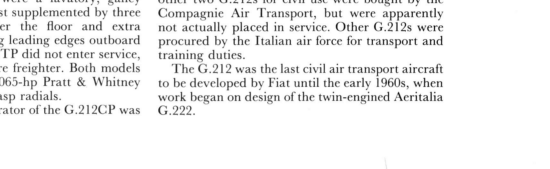

Above: A 1949 Spanish Freight Company G.212
Left: The Fiat G.212 CP Monterosa, which was designed for commercial use. It differed from the prototype mainly in having three Pratt & Whitney R-1830-S1C3-G Twin Wasps. The G.212 CP went into service with ALI in 1948 and operated mainly on international freights, from Milan

DC-6, Douglas

FIRST FLIGHT 1946

THE DC-4 had been designed for civil use, but it was overtaken by World War II, and the bulk of DC-4 production was therefore of the C-54 transport version, many of which were de-militarized after the war for airline use. Douglas realized in the closing stages of the war that although the type was a considerable improvement on prewar types, and would certainly enjoy a rosy commercial future, the presence of rivals such as the L-049 made it essential to stretch and improve the basic DC-4. Thus there appeared the DC-6, which was essentially the DC-4 with much more powerful R-2800 engines, a fuselage stretch of 2.11 m (6 ft 11 in), providing accommodation for another ten passengers, and with the essential advantage of pressurization to enable the aircraft to fly at fuel-economical high altitude, where it also avoided the worst weather. At the same time the Douglas design team introduced other refinements. As these improvements were planned during the war, it is not surprising that the DC-6 prototype was in fact produced to a USAAF requirement, under the designation XC-112. But by the time this aircraft first flew, on February 15, 1946, the military's finances for such an aircraft had disap-peared, and so the bulk of Douglas production was available for the civil market, for which the initial orders had started to come in during September 1944. First off the mark was American Airlines, which ordered 50 DC-6s, soon followed by United Air Lines with an order for 20.

Douglas flew its first production DC-6 in June 1946, with deliveries to the first two customers following in November of the same year. United had the honour of introducing the DC-6 in sched-uled operations, with the launch of its transconti-nental service on April 27, 1947: this service had a single stop, and the coast-to-coast flight took only 10 hours, compared with the 11 hours taken by the new Constellation in service with TWA, and the 14 hours needed by the DC-4. Production of the DC-6 reached 175, the last going to Braniff on November 2, 1951. As the type was replaced by later models it was relegated to freight operations, modified with large doors in the rear fuselage. The one drawback in the DC-6's early career was a four-month grounding from November 12, 1947 following two internal fuselage fires. The problem was eventu-ally solved however, and no permanent damage

Left: A DC-6B of Alitalia's former charter subsidiary Società Aerea Mediterranea (SAM). The DC-6B was without the reinforced floor and main deck cargo doors of the DC-6A and was produced in larger numbers than any other version in the DC-6 series

Below: A Guest Aerovias Mexico DC-6 on the runway at Paris in 1959

was done to the DC-6's overall sales prospects.

In 1948 the availability of a more powerful version of the Pratt & Whitney R-2800 with water/methanol injection persuaded Douglas to introduce yet another stretch, this time of 1.52 m (5 ft), to produce the DC-6A Liftmaster. This was an all-cargo model without windows, and the more powerful R-2800-CB16 engines with 'paddle-blade' propellers allowed an increase in maximum take-off weight from 44 090 kg (97 200 lb) to 48 535 kg (107 000 lb), the payload being 12 786 kg (28 188 lb). The first DC-6A flew on September 29, 1949; the last of 74 was delivered in early 1959.

Produced in parallel with the DC-6A was the DC-6B passenger equivalent. Original standard accommodation was for 54 passengers, although 102 could be seated in high-density configuration, compared with the 52 and 86 of the DC-6. The first DC-6B flew on February 2, 1951 and the first scheduled operator was American, which introduced the type on its transcontinental route on April 29, 1951. Production of the DC-6B reached 288, the last being delivered on November 17, 1958. The type was the most successful of the whole DC-4, 6, 7 series, and its operating economics were the best ever recorded for a piston-engined airliner in the 1940s and 1950s. Passengers also appreciated the type for its quietness, smoothness and general comfort.

The DC-6C was basically a convertible version of the DC-6A. Cabin windows were fitted, and the interior was designed for the easy installation and stripping of passenger facilities.

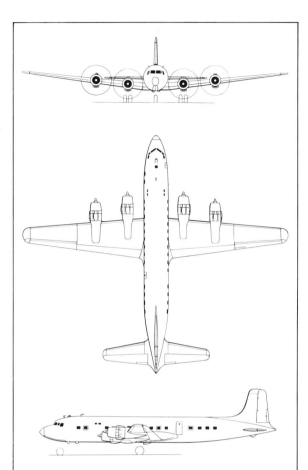

DC-6B

Type: long-range passenger transport
Maker: Douglas Aircraft Co
Span: 35.81 m (117 ft 6 in)
Length: 32.18 m (105 ft 7 in)
Height: 8.74 m (28 ft 8 in)
Wing area: 135.91 m² (1463 sq ft)
Weight: maximum 48 535 kg (107 000 lb); empty 26 595 kg (58 635 lb)
Powerplant: four 2400-hp Pratt & Whitney R-2800-CB16 Double Wasp or 2500-hp R-2800-CB17 Double Wasp 18-cylinder two-row radial engines
Performance: cruising speed 507 km/h (315 mph) at 6279 m (20 600 ft); range with maximum payload 4835 km (3005 miles)
Payload: 11 143 kg (24 565 lb); seats for up to 102 passengers
Crew: 5
Production: 175 (DC-6), 74 (DC-6A and DC-6C), 288 (DC-6B)

Above: HK-1276, a DC-6A of Tampa Colombia photographed in February 1978. Several DC-6As and -Bs are still in service for small South African airlines. There are no fuselage windows and two upward-opening freight doors on this aircraft
Left: An American Airlines DC-6A freighter with its water-methanol injection 2400-hp Double Wasp CB16 engines

SM.95, Savoia-Marchetti

FIRST FLIGHT 1942

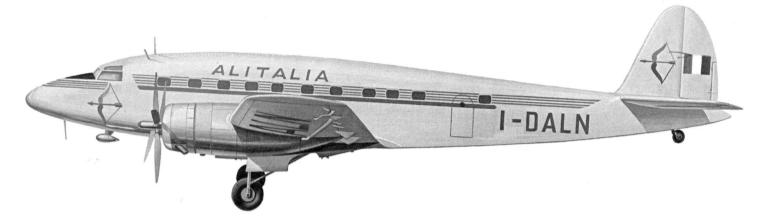

THE origins of the SM.95 began in World War II, when SIAI Marchetti initiated preliminary studies for the production of a four-engined long-range transport, capable of being used as both a military and civil aircraft. By May 8, 1943, the first of four ordered by the Italian air force was ready for its maiden flight.

Before the end of the war, however, only two other examples were completed, by SAI Ambrosini at Perugia. In the civilian role, these were equipped to carry 18 passengers on transatlantic routes and were, in fact, requisitioned by the German Luftwaffe. One of these wartime aircraft operated for a while in 1945–46 between the United Kingdom and the continent of Europe bearing postwar Italian air force insignia.

The initial powerplant of the prototype SM.95 comprised four 850-hp Alfa Romeo 131RC14/50 radials, but these were later replaced by four 930-hp Alfa Romeo 128RC18 engines which were also used to power the two other wartime aircraft.

After the war the SM.95s were built with a longer fuselage (increased from 22.25 m [73 ft] to 24.77 m [81 ft 3¼ in]), to operate over short-range continental routes; the aircraft was now designed to accommodate up to 30 passengers. These aircraft handled well and had, as interchangeable engines, Alfa Romeo 128s, 740-hp Bristol Pegasus 48s or 1065-hp Pratt & Whitney R-1830-S1C3-Gs. Six of the updated SM.95s were ordered by the Italian air force, but this order was cancelled and the newly created national airline Alitalia acquired

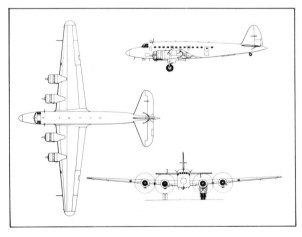

them and they were redesignated SM.95C.

On August 6, 1947 *Marco Polo* (I-DALM) inaugurated the first Alitalia international service from Rome to Oslo. On April 3, 1948, the Rome to London (Northolt) route was started. In July 1949 three SM.95Cs inaugurated a weekly flight to Caracas, Venezuela, with an extremely testing last leg. Alitalia later acquired three ex-LATI Twin-Wasp-engined SM.95s, and continued to operate them until 1951. Three SM.95s, reportedly seating as many as 38 passengers were also operated by SAIDE of Egypt.

The SM.95C proved itself to be a robust aircraft. Despite this, production of the aircraft was extremely limited, and probably totalled little more than 12 civilian aircraft.

SM.95

Type: long-range transport
Maker: Societa Italiana Aeroplani Idrovolanti 'Savoia-Marchetti'
Span: 34.28 m (112 ft 5½ in)
Length: 24.77 m (81 ft 3¼ in)
Height: 5.25 m (17 ft 2½ in)
Wing area: 128.3 m² (1381 sq ft)
Weight: maximum 24 000 kg (52 910 lb); empty 14 500 kg (31 970 lb)
Powerplant: four 1050-hp Pratt & Whitney R-1830-S1C3-G Twin Wasp 14-cylinder two-row radial engines
Performance: cruising speed 344 km/h (215 mph) at 3500 m (11 480 ft); range with 4072 kg (8977 lb) payload, 2000 km (1242 miles)
Payload: 5540 kg (12 215 lb); seats for up to 30 passengers
Crew: 5
Production: 12

Top: The SIAI Marchetti SM.95 inaugurated the first international run by Alitalia from Rome to Oslo in 1948
Above left: One of the first four machines to enter service with Alitalia in 1947
Above: An Egyptian-operated SM.95; the mixed-construction airframe was able to accommodate three different powerplants

164

L-749 Constellation, Lockheed

FIRST FLIGHT 1947

THE design of the Constellation originated in 1939 when Trans Continental and Western Air (later Trans World Airlines) submitted requirements for a 40-passenger airliner. TWA ordered 40, and later Pan American announced their interest but the United States had entered World War II before the first prototype, NX25600, was flown on January 9, 1943.

The early career of the Constellation was therefore as a military transport, designated C-69. The USAAF initially ordered 180 aircraft, but by VJ-day in 1945, only 15 had been accepted.

The remainder were quickly converted for civilian use and allocated to commercial customers, the first two of which were Pan American and TWA as before. Lockheed foresaw the bitter com-

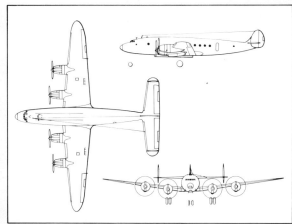

L-749A

Type: long-range civil transport
Maker: Lockheed Aircraft Corporation
Span: 37.49 m (123 ft)
Length: 29 m (95 ft 2 in)
Height: 7.21 m (23 ft 8 in)
Wing area: 153.3 m² (1650 sq ft)
Weight: maximum 48 535 kg (107 000 lb); empty 27 280 kg (60 140 lb)
Powerplant: four 2200-hp Wright Cyclone R-3350-C18-BA1 18-cylinder radial engines
Performance: cruising speed 480 km/h (298 mph); range 4828 km (3000 miles)
Payload: seats for 43 passengers
Crew: 7
Production: 233 (all Constellations)

Left: A Lockheed L-749 Constellation at Miami in November 1977. The nose has been extended to accommodate a radar installation
Below: An open-air production line of Constellations in the livery of Eastern Air Lines and Pan American. It was, however, interest from TWA that gave Lockheed the go ahead

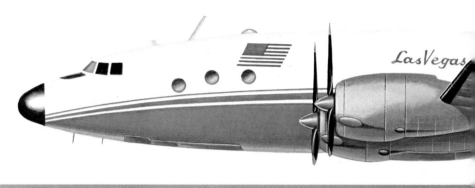

petition which was to develop between the giants of the American aircraft industry to resupply the airlines in peacetime, and so decided to modify their existing C-69 aircraft, which had already given proof of their validity. This was a good decision, and valuable time was thus gained over their closest rivals, Douglas and Boeing.

Civil Aviation Authority (CAA) approval was granted on December 11, 1945, and the early version was known as the L-049 Constellation. Pan American operated the L-049 first, on its New York to Bermuda route, in February 1946. Meanwhile TWA opened the first United States to Europe service, flying to Paris on February 6, 1946. On July 1, 1946, the first of five L-049s for BOAC, G-AHEJ *Bristol II*, opened the London–New York transatlantic service.

The L-049 was basically a 43 to 48-seat aircraft, with a high-density capacity for up to 60 passengers. The first entirely civil Constellation was the 'gold plate' Model L-649, which was flown for the first time on October 19, 1946, and entered service with Eastern Air Lines in May 1947. Powerplant comprised four Wright R-3350-C18-BD1 engines, rated at 2500 hp, which enabled the aircraft to accommodate a maximum of 81 passengers. The more usual number was between 48 and 64, however.

In 1947 the L-749 became the next version of the Constellation in production. It was basically similar to the 649, with the same seating capacity, but with additional fuel storage in the wings, thus enabling non-stop flights between New York and Paris, though not fully laden. In June 1947, the first round-the-world service was started by PanAm's *Clipper America*.

The L-749A was a variant which incorporated sturdier landing gear, permitting the gross take-off weight to be increased by 2268 kg (5000 lb) to 48 534 kg (107 000 lb), and was therefore useful in a military capacity.

The total production of all Constellation variants, excluding 12 military L-749As, was 221 with 22 C-69/L-049 conversions, 66 L-049s, 20 L-649/649As and 113 L-749/749As. The L-749 was superseded by the Super Constellation in 1951. The Constellation and its descendants performed stoic service and were veterans of the transatlantic and other long-haul air routes during the 20-year period after 1945.

Above: A Lockheed 049 Constellation of Modern Air in January 1965
Right: *Friesland*, an L-749 of KLM's *Flying Dutchman* service. The 749 was similar to the 649 but had a larger fuel capacity and consequently longer range

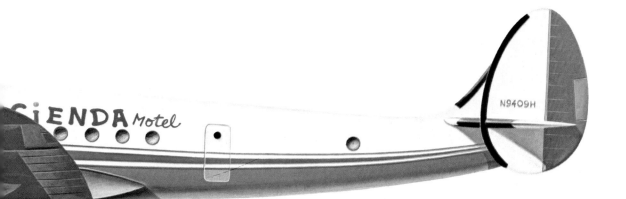

Far left: Air France
Lockheed Constellations; it
was not until the L-749 was
introduced that non-stop
flights could be made between
New York and Paris, a
distance of 5990 km (3660
miles)
Left: The Lockheed L-049;
first used on a New York-
Bermuda run within months
of the end of World War II, it
was to become the pioneer of
postwar aviation on all the
major routes

Above: Part of the flight-deck
of a BOAC 749A
Constellation. The 17 aircraft
acquired by BOAC in 1948
were still in use nearly 20
years later with various
freight carriers
Left: Checking the outboard
right-side R-3350 engine of a
'Connie', as the Constellation
became affectionately known

Canadair 4

FIRST FLIGHT 1946

CANADAIR was formed in 1944 to take over and develop the Canadian Vickers aircraft factory at Cartierville near Montreal, and the new company's first objective was the development of the Douglas C-54 Skymaster (the military DC-4) with four Rolls-Royce Merlin engines in place of the original Pratt & Whitney R-2000 Twin Wasp radials. Trans-Canada Air Lines proposed that this Canadian derivative should be pressurized (American C-54s were unpressurized) and use Merlin engines, as these could be imported from the UK without duty, whereas the Twin Wasps would incur such a financial penalty.

When Canadair inherited this project in 1944, they decided to concentrate first on the aerodynamic and structural problems of mating Merlin engines to the airframe of the C-54, and so a C-54G airframe was imported for the development. Only production models of what was to be designated the Canadair DC-4M were to be pressurized and include a wide variety of Douglas-developed improvements. Progress with the first aircraft, designated DC-4M-X (Experimental Merlin-powered DC-4), was without serious problems, and the aircraft took to the air for its initial flight in July 1946, powered by four 1725-hp Merlin 620s with chin radiators in place of the annular radiators first proposed by Trans-Canada Air Lines.

This prototype and the subsequent 23 production aircraft were all unpressurized transports for the Royal Canadian Air Force: the last 23 comprised 17 C-54 GMs taken on charge between September 1947 and April 1948 with the name

North Star Mark I and five C-54 GMs named North Star Mark MI. The former were powered by Merlin 620s and the latter by Merlin 622s. Trans-Canada Air Lines had ordered 20 DC-4M-2 pressurized models, but pending the development of these more advanced aircraft, distinguishable by their round rather than square fuselage windows, the six Merlin 622-powered aircraft were lent by the Royal Canadian Air Force to the airline, which designated the aircraft DC-4M-1s. These entered scheduled service with Trans-Canada Air Lines on April 15, 1947 on the route between Montreal and London. The DC-4M-1s were later retrofitted with DC-6 undercarriages, which allowed an increase in maximum take-off weight from 33 112 kg (73 000 lb) to 35 380 kg (78 000 lb).

Below: A Canadair Four in Canadair livery during a demonstration flight
Bottom: A member of the ground crew crawls onto the wing of a DC-4M North Star to insert the fuel hose. Trans-Canada Airlines operated these aircraft on domestic and international routes in the early 1950s. They were replaced by Super Constellations on the Atlantic run in 1954

Delivery of the pressurized DC-4M-2s to Trans-Canada Air Lines was made between October 1947 and June 1948, allowing the airline to return the DC-4M-1s between March and October 1949. The DC-4M-2 appeared in two variants: the DC-4M-2/3 had Merlin 622s with three-blade propellers and a maximum take-off weight of 36 106 kg (79 600 lb), while the DC-4M-2/4 had Merlin 624s with four-blade propellers and a maximum take-off weight of 36 378 kg (80 200 lb). Both models carried 40 first-class or 62 economy-class passengers, at speeds up to 145 km/h (80 mph) greater than those possible with the DC-4, although the noise levels of the Canadair aircraft were higher. The problem was alleviated somewhat, however, by the adoption of a cross-over exhaust system, and Trans-Canada's last DC-4M-2s were not withdrawn until June 1961.

BOAC ordered 22 Canadair C-4s basically similar to the DC-4M-2 apart from having 1760-hp Merlin 626 engines. These 22 aircraft were delivered between March and November 1949, and the first scheduled service by a member of this Argonaut class was flown on August 23, 1949.

Canadian Pacific Air Lines received four C-4-1 aircraft between May and July 1949 for use on its trans-Pacific routes from Vancouver. The C-4-1s were basically similar to BOAC's C-4. The three survivors of this small fleet were sold to Trans-Canada Air Lines in the autumn of 1951. With the type's relegation from main airline use the aircraft were sold to smaller airlines, but all had been scrapped by the mid 1970s.

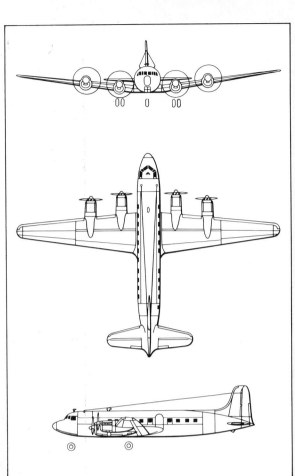

C-4

Type: long-range transport
Maker: Canadair Ltd
Span: 35.81 m (117 ft 6 in)
Length: 28.54 m (93 ft 7½ in)
Height: 8.39 m (27 ft 6¼ in)
Wing area: 135.64 m² (1460 sq ft)
Weight: maximum 37 331 kg (82 300 lb); empty 21 243 kg (46 832 lb)
Powerplant: four 1760-hp Rolls-Royce Merlin 626 V-12 liquid-cooled engines
Performance: cruising speed 465 km/h (289 mph) at 3720 m (12 200 ft); range 6244 km (3880 miles)
Payload: seats for up to 62 passengers
Crew: 4
Production: 46 (civil)

Martin 2-0-2

FIRST FLIGHT 1946

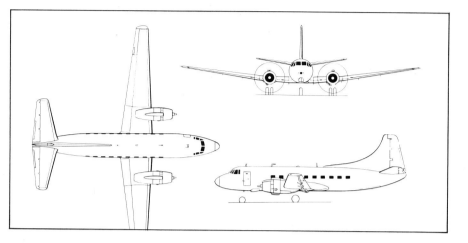

TOWARDS the end of World War II a number of US aircraft manufacturers turned their attention to the possibility of a new airliner which would, they hoped, replace the Douglas DC-3/C-47 family in service with the secondary airlines. The early pacemaker in what was clearly to be a keen struggle was Martin, the prototype 2-0-2 first flying on November 22, 1946, some four months before the CV-240 made its initial flight. Flight-test results were highly satisfactory, and the order book looked most healthy when Northwest Airlines launched the inaugural 2-0-2 service on November 15, 1947, some 6½ months before American Airlines could reply with the CV-240. The 2-0-2 was a less ambitious aircraft than the CV-240, but could carry up to 52 passengers over longer stage lengths at about the same speed, albeit without the comfort of cabin pressurization. Disaster struck the 2-0-2 in 1948, however, when accident investigation revealed the cause of a fatal crash to have been a major structural problem in the wings. All 2-0-2s were withdrawn for extensive strengthening and re-engining, in which form the aircraft were designated Martin 2-0-2As. TWA was the first airline to start operations with the revised aircraft, on September 1, 1950, but by this time many possible users of the 2-0-2 had suffered a change of heart and ordered the CV-240. Other airlines who had ordered the improved and pressurized 3-0-3, notably United Air Lines, also pulled out of the Martin camp. The manufacturer was able to profit from the disaster to a certain extent, however, for much valuable test flying was done with the sole 3-0-3, which first flew on June 20, 1947.

The fruits of experience with the 2-0-2 and 3-0-3 led Martin to develop the 4-0-4, a pressurized aircraft with a fuselage some 0.991 m (39 in) longer than that of the 2-0-2. The first 4-0-4 flew on October 21, 1950, and the relative success of the type was assured when Eastern Air Lines took 40 examples and TWA another 61, the last two going to the US Coast Guard under the designation RM-1. The 4-0-4 entered service with TWA and Eastern Air Lines in October 1951 and January 1952 respectively. The utility of the design is indicated by the fact that Eastern Air Lines used its 4-0-4s for some ten years, and the type was then handed on to smaller local-service operators.

4-0-4

Type: short-haul passenger transport
Maker: Glenn L Martin Co
Span: 28.44 m (93 ft 3½ in)
Length: 22.73 m (74 ft 7 in)
Height: 8.58 m (28 ft 2 in)
Wing area: 80.26 m² (864 sq ft)
Weight: maximum 20 367 kg (44 900 lb); empty 13 212 kg (29 126 lb)
Powerplant: two 2400-hp Pratt & Whitney R-2800-CB-16 Double Wasp 18-cylinder radial engines
Performance: cruising speed 444 km/h (276 mph) at 5486 m (18 000 ft); range with a payload of 4629 kg (10 205 lb) 500 km (310 miles)
Payload: 5304 kg (11 692 lb); seats for up to 40 passengers
Crew: 2
Production: 43 (civil 2-0-2), 1 (3-0-3), 101 (civil 4-0-4)

Left: The Martin 2-0-2 demonstration model
Below: A Martin 4-0-4 flying at the peak of the piston-engined age, in the years immediately prior to 1956, when TWA began to order Boeing 707 jets

L-1049 Super Constellation, Lockheed

FIRST FLIGHT 1950

THE mildly critical airline attitude to the Douglas DC-4 and the Lockheed L-049 Constellation in the later 1940s had given Lockheed warning of the need to increase payload while reducing seat-mile costs, and to this end No 1961 was taken in hand during 1949 for extensive modification: the fuselage was lengthened by 5.59 m (18 ft 4 in), and the 2300-hp Wright R-3350 radials replaced with 2700-hp Wright R-3350-CA1 Cyclones. Extra fuel was added in tip tanks. The result was the prototype L-1049, with a maximum take-off weight which had risen from 39 123 kg (86 250 lb) to 54 432 kg (120 000 lb), allowing a 40% increase in payload. This was one of the first and greatest examples of stretching, made more difficult by the curving fish-like profile of the 'Connie's' fuselage.

In its revised form, 1961 first flew on October 13, 1950. Given its previous involvement in the Constellation's history, it is hardly surprising that the airline behind this move was TWA, although the first airline to order the new L-1049 was Eastern, which signed for ten in April 1950. Of the 24 L-1049 Super Constellations built, Eastern operated 14, and TWA the other ten; the two airlines brought their new aircraft into service on December 15, 1951 (New York to Miami) and September 10, 1952 (New York to Los Angeles) respectively. Rectangular windows, well placed in relation to seats, replaced the previous circular openings.

The L-1049B was a purely military version of the Super Constellation, and so the next civil variant was the L-1049C, the first of which flew on February 17, 1953. This model put new life into the design, for the original piston engines of earlier models were replaced by 3250-hp Wright R-3350-DA1 Turbo-Compound engines. The extra power increased speed by some 16 km/h (10 mph), but more importantly allowed higher take-off weights. The wing structure was considerably strengthened to cater for maximum weights in the order of 60 328 kg (133 000 lb), which allowed extra fuel to be carried, and so greatly extended range. KLM put the L-1049C into service on its route from Amsterdam to New York in August 1953, and Trans World Airlines started its Ambassador non-stop service from Los Angeles to New York on October 19, 1953. Production of the Lockheed

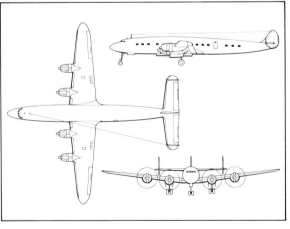

Above: A Central American Airways L-1049G. Nicknamed the Super G, the aircraft had optional 3400-hp Turbo-Compound engines and better payload/range capabilities

L-1049C

Type: long-range commercial transport
Maker: Lockheed Aircraft Corporation
Span: 37.49 m (123 ft)
Length: 34.62 m (113 ft 7 in)
Height: 7.54 m (24 ft 9 in)
Wing area: 153.3 m² (1650 sq ft)
Weight: maximum 62 370 kg (137 500 lb); empty 33 120 kg (73 016 lb)
Powerplant: four 3250-hp Wright R-3350-DA3 Turbo-Compound 18-cylinder radial engines
Performance: cruising speed 571 km/h (355 mph) at 6889 m (22 600 ft); range 7435 km (4620 miles)
Payload: seats for up to 95 passengers
Crew: 9
Production: 24 (L-1049), 60 (L-1049C), 26 (L-1049D), 18 (L-1049E), 99 (L-1049G), 53 (L-1049H)

171

L-1049C totalled 60 aircraft, and the type was operated by ten airlines.

The L-1049D was a freight version of the Super Constellation, the first flying in September 1954. The main operator of the type, which could carry a payload of 16 329 kg (36 000 lb) was Seaboard & Western Airlines. The next model was the L-1049E improved model, of which 38 were ordered. However, only 18 were completed as such, the other 20 being finished as L-1049Gs when the manufacturer offered the customers this option.

The L-1049G, of which 99 were built, was in essence the airframe of the L-1049C allied with four 3250-hp Wright R-3350-DA3 Turbo-Compound engines offering better climb performance than the R-3350-CA1. Intended for long-range routes, the L-1049G could be fitted with 2271-litre (500-Imp gal) tip-tanks as pioneered on the first L-1049. Accommodation was provided for 71 first-class or 95 coach-class passengers. The first L-1049G flew on December 17, 1954 and the type entered service with Northwest Airlines in January 1955.

The final Super Constellation variant was the L-1049H, which first flew on September 20, 1956. The L-1049H, of which 53 were built, was basically a convertible model of the L-1049G, with the fuselage stressed to carry loads of over 20 312 kg (44 780 lb), or alternatively up to 94 passengers. The last Super Constellation, an L-1049H, was delivered to The Flying Tiger Line in November 1958.

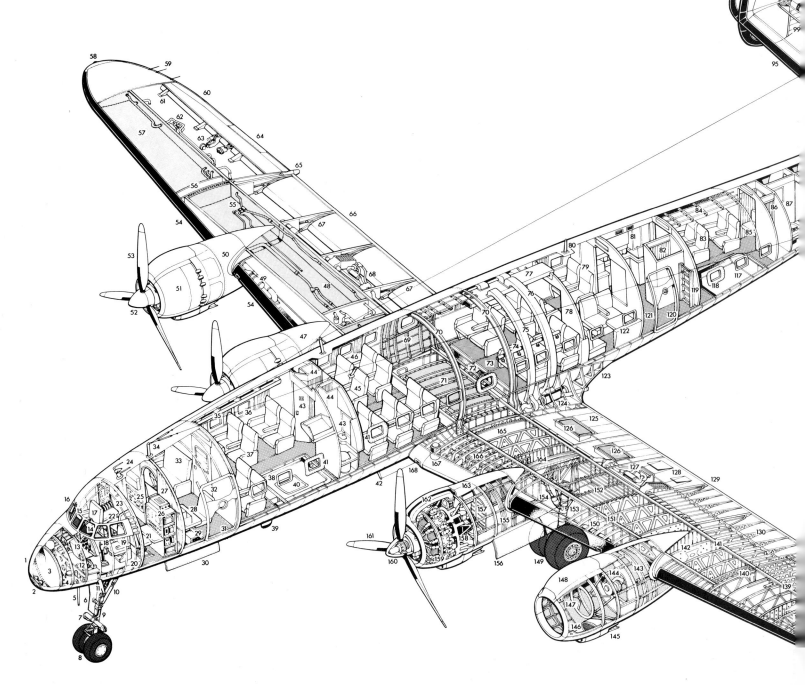

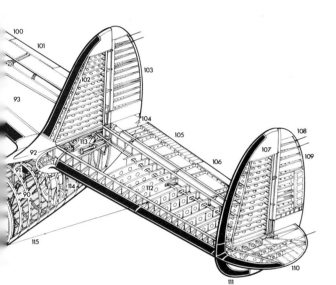

L.1049C Super Constellation

1 Nose cone
2 Landing and taxiing lamps
3 Front pressure bulkhead
4 Hydraulic brake accumulator
5 Radio mast
6 Nosewheel leg door
7 Steering jacks
8 Twin nosewheels
9 Nosewheel leg strut
10 Retraction linkages
11 Pitot tube mast
12 Rudder pedals
13 Instrument panel
14 Instrument panel shroud
15 Windscreen wipers
16 Windscreen panels
17 Co-pilot's seat
18 Control column
19 Pilot's seat
20 Flight-deck floor level
21 Radio operator's station
22 Flight engineer's station
23 Right-hand crew door
24 VOR aerial
25 Engineer's instrument panel
26 Radio racks
27 Cockpit bulkhead
28 Navigator's chart table
29 Underfloor battery bay
30 Nosewheel doors
31 Forward entry door
32 Cabin bulkhead
33 Crew rest area
34 Radio aerial mast
35 Overhead luggage racks
36 Right emergency exit window
37 Forward cabin seating
38 Forward underfloor freight hold, total freight hold volume 20.6 m³ (728 cu ft)
39 Radio altimeter
40 Ventral freight door
41 Left emergency exit windows
42 Ventral ADF sense aerial
43 Toilet compartments, left and right
44 Wardrobes
45 Main cabin, 4-abreast seating
46 Cabin wall trim panels
47 Right inner engine nacelle
48 Right wing integral fuel tank, total fuel capacity 24 760 litres (5433 Imp gal)
49 Supercharger oil cooler
50 Right outer engine nacelle
51 Detachable engine cowling panels
52 Spinner
53 Hamilton Standard three-bladed propeller
54 Leading-edge de-icing boots
55 Fuel system piping
56 Outer wing panel joint rib
57 Outboard integral fuel tank
58 Right navigation light
59 Static dischargers
60 Right aileron
61 Aileron balance weights
62 Fuel venting system piping
63 Aileron control hydraulic booster
64 Aileron tab
65 Fuel jettison pipe
66 Right Fowler-type flap
67 Flap guide rails
68 Right air-conditioning plant
69 Fuselage centre-section construction
70 Wing/fuselage attachment main frames
71 Centre-section bag-type fuel tanks

72 Central flap control motor
73 Cabin floor panels
74 Fresh air distribution ducting
75 Air-conditioning system overhead ducting
76 Heating system overhead ducting
77 Cabin roof air distribution duct
78 Cabin partition
79 Lounge area
80 VHF aerial
81 Galley
82 Wardrobe
83 Aft cabin seating
84 Fuselage frame and stringer construction
85 Cabin attendants' folding seats
86 Wardrobes, left and right
87 Left and right washrooms
88 Cabin pressurization valves
89 Rear pressure bulkhead
90 Tailcone construction
91 Elevator mass balance weight
92 Fin/tailplane fillets
93 Right tailplane
94 Rudder control rods
95 Leading-edge de-icing boots
96 Right tailfin
97 Fabric-covered rudder
98 Rudder trim tab
99 Lower rudder segment
100 Right elevator
101 Elevator trim tab
102 Centre fin construction
103 Centre rudder
104 Tail navigation light
105 Left elevator construction
106 Elevator tab
107 Left tailfin construction
108 Static dischargers
109 Left rudder construction
110 Tailplane tip fairing
111 Leading-edge de-icing boots
112 Tailplane construction
113 Rudder and elevator hydraulic boosters
114 Tailplane attachment frame
115 HF aerial cable
116 Aft toilet compartments, left and right
117 Rear underfloor freight hold
118 Rear cabin emergency exit window
119 Ladder stowage
120 Passenger entry door
121 Entry lobby
122 Folding table
123 Wing root fillet construction
124 Cabin heater unit
125 Left flap shroud panels
126 Life raft stowage bays
127 Left air-conditioning plant
128 Heat exchanger air exhaust ducts
129 Left Fowler-type flap
130 Flap shroud ribs
131 Fuel jettison pipe
132 Aileron tab
133 Left aileron construction
134 Static dischargers
135 Wingtip construction
136 Left navigation light
137 Leading-edge de-icing boots
138 Left outboard fuel tank bay
139 Outer wing panel main spar
140 Outer wing panel joint rib
141 Rear spar
142 Wing rib construction
143 Engine nacelle construction
144 Air conditioning system turbine
145 Oil-cooler air duct
146 Oil cooler
147 Engine mounting ring
148 Carburettor intake duct fairing

149 Twin mainwheels
150 Leading-edge nose ribs
151 Front spar
152 Wing stringer construction
153 Main undercarriage leg strut
154 Retraction linkage
155 Main undercarriage wheel well
156 Mainwheel doors
157 Engine firewall
158 Exhaust collector ring
159 Wright R-3350-DA1 Turbo-Compound, 18-cylinder, two-row, radial engine
160 Propeller hub pitch change mechanism
161 Hamilton Standard three-bladed propeller
162 Carburettor intake duct
163 Engine oil tank
164 Main undercarriage mounting ribs
165 Inner wing integral fuel tank
166 Leading-edge construction
167 Hydraulic reservoir
168 Cabin fresh air intake

CV-240, Convair

THE Convair CV-240 Convair-Liner owed much to the single CV-110, first flown on July 8, 1946 at San Diego. The experience gained with the CV-110, combined with careful examination of airline recommendations, persuaded Convair to launch their DC-3 replacement. The result was probably the most advanced twin-engined passenger airliner of its day.

American Airlines greatly influenced the thinking of I M Laddon's design team, which was reflected by the size of their original order – 100 aircraft. Construction began in late 1945, and the first flight of the prototype CV-240 (NX90849), took place on March 16, 1947. During its flight-test programme the aircraft displayed excellent flying qualities, and the high standard of its engineering ensured that only minor changes would be necessary before certification.

In construction the CV-240 was conventional by American standards. It did, however, feature glass-fibre rudder and elevator trailing edges, and it was the first commercial twin-engined transport to be pressurized The two Pratt & Whitney Double Wasp engines incorporated exhaust-augmented cooling. This system decreased cooling drag and produced some jet thrust; the additional air was drawn through by the exhaust expelled from twin circular stacks at the end of each nacelle. This allowed a very clean shape, but the performance improvement was paid for by increased cabin noise.

On June 1, 1948, the CV-240 entered service with American Airlines. Seventy-five were eventually delivered to the airline, and designated CV-

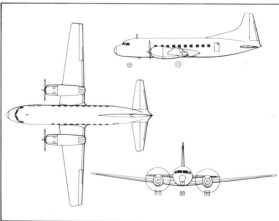

240-0. Western, PanAm, Continental and North East shared 40 more. For accommodation, ten rows of seats, four-abreast were fitted. Ventral passenger loading stairs – a major innovation – and carry-on luggage racks embodied the degree of refinement which typified the Convair-Liner.

The CV-240 survived the postwar slump and the glut of war-surplus DC-3s better than any comparable type. It filled the short-haul slot admirably, complementing the DC-4 and Constellation. Fittingly, the last variant delivered was the CV-240-26, four of which were absorbed into the American Airlines fleet. The USAF received 272 as T-29s and C-131s. Fewer than 50 airworthy CV-240s were still in existence in 1980, mainly flown as corporate transports in the USA.

CV-240

Type: medium-range passenger transport
Maker: Convair Division, General Dynamics Corporation
Span: 27.97 m (91 ft 9 in)
Length: 22.76 m (74 ft 8 in)
Height: 8.2 m (26 ft 11 in)
Wing area: 75.9 m² (817 sq ft)
Weight: maximum 18 956 kg (41 790 lb); empty 12 520 kg (27 600 lb)
Powerplant: two 2000-hp Pratt & Whitney R-2800-CA18 Double Wasp 18-cylinder radial engines
Performance: cruising speed 435 km/h (270 mph) at 4880 m (16 000 ft); range with maximum payload 2900 km (1800 miles)
Payload: 4240 kg (9350 lb); seats for up to 40 passengers
Crew: 3 to 4
Production: 176

Above: A privately-owned CV-240 photographed in the United States in November 1976. The 240 was to lead to a successful series of Convair airliners of the 1950s which totalled well over 1000 aircraft

CV-340, Convair

FIRST FLIGHT 1951

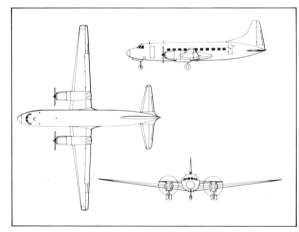

THE year 1950 proved to be a beneficial one for the Glenn L Martin Company. Eastern Air Lines and Trans World Airlines between them ordered 65 Martin 4-0-4s. Consequently, Convair saw their market-share threatened, and responded by launching the CV-240A, (subsequently designated CV-340). The prototype, N3401, made its first flight on October 5, 1951, and certification followed on March 27, 1952.

No radical changes were necessary to improve on the successful CV-240 formula, but the fuselage was stretched to make room for another row of seats. The same wing aerofoil section was used but span was increased, providing extra lift, less drag and additional fuel capacity. The powerplants used were developed versions of the Pratt & Whitney Double Wasp, and these retained the augmentor engine-cooling system. The nacelles were lengthened slightly, placing the propeller discs 17.8 cm (7 in) further forward.

United Air Lines took 55 CV-340-31s after cancelling an order for 50 Martin 3-0-3s, and rejecting the CV-240 and Martin 4-0-4, the hot-and-high performance of the CV-340 being a crucial factor. More orders came in from Braniff (20), Continental (10), Delta (20), Northeast (5) and National (8). After delays caused by Allied trade restrictions, four CV-340-68s were delivered to Lufthansa, and five were operated by KLM on its Netherlands Antilles routes.

With the CV-340 firmly established in production, Convair considered building a version with Wright R-3350 Turbo-Compound engines.

This would have offered customers a coach configuration for 60 to 65 passengers but the proposal was dropped. The CV-340 achieved an enviable reputation for reliability and profitability.

South American operators included Aeronaves de Mexico (4), Servicios Aereos Cruzeiro do Sul (4) and REAL Transportes Aereos (8). The USAF received the last version built (the CV-340-79), and after cancelling the YT38-powered T-29E, evaluated two YC-131Cs powered by Allison 501-D13 (T38) turboprops. Development of these versions paved the way for hundreds of CV-340/440 turboprop conversions.

The USN and RCAF also operated CV-340s. Most surviving CV-340s operate as corporate aircraft.

CV-340

Type: short-haul passenger transport
Maker: Convair Division, General Dynamics Corporation
Span: 32.1 m (105 ft 4 in)
Length: 24.13 m (79 ft 2 in)
Height: 8.58 m (28 ft 2 in)
Wing area: 85.5 m² (920 sq ft)
Weight: maximum 21 319 kg (47 000 lb); empty 13 375 kg (29 486 lb)
Powerplant: two 2400-hp Pratt & Whitney R-2800-CB16 Double Wasp 18-cylinder radial engines
Performance: cruising speed 457 km/h (284 mph) at 5490 m (18 000 ft); normal range with maximum payload 933 km (580 miles)
Payload: 6075 kg (13 391 lb); seats for up to 52 passengers
Crew: 3 to 4
Production: 113 civil, 99 military

Above: A Convair CV-340 in Lufthansa service; the German airline bought four aircraft and used them to re-open services after the war. Other operators included KLM, on its Netherlands Antilles routes

CV-440 Metropolitan, Convair

FIRST FLIGHT 1955

THE CV-440, a development from the earlier Convair CV-340, reflected concern over the impact of the British Vickers Viscount turboprop on American airlines.

The CV-440 Metropolitan first flew on October 6, 1955. It was outwardly very similar to the CV-340 but modifications made it 8 km/h (5 mph) faster and reduced the noise level in the cabin. The engine cowling baffles and 'aspirated cooling' exhaust were redesigned and aileron and flap seals were fitted. The exhaust exit became one single rectangular opening instead of the two circular exits – one for each pipe – in the 340 and 240.

The CV-440 could be fitted with either Pratt & Whitney R-2800-CB16 or CB17 (Double Wasp) engines. These powered three-blade Hamilton Standard Hydromatic automatic fully-feathering and reversing propellers.

The fuselage was a circular-section aluminium alloy structure with a stressed-skin covering. The wings and tail unit had thermal (hot air) de-icing for the leading edges, and the wings were fitted with aluminium-alloy ailerons and Fowler flaps. The landing gear was basically the same as for the CV-240 and 340 but locally strengthened for long life with frequent landings.

As in the CV-340 the CV-440 could accommodate 44 or 52 passengers in pairs each side of a central aisle. There was an integral self-contained stairway forward of the wings on the left side. The cabin was pressurized with radiant wall heating and refrigeration to keep a constant air temperature in the air and on the ground. There were cargo compartments ahead of and behind the cabin and below the floor forward of the wings. As part of the improved soundproofing the cabin was fitted with special inner window assemblies for the first eight rows of seats.

Civil Airworthiness requirements for CB16-powered aircraft were similar to the CV-340, and included an operating height of 2895 m (9500 ft), with one engine feathered and at a weight of 20 412 kg (45 000 lb). With a maximum take-off weight of 22 271 kg (49 100 lb) the CV-440 was cleared to use runways of 1503 m (4930 ft).

The CV-440 entered service on April 1, 1956 with Continental Airlines. It proved successful in the USA, but most of the 153 aircraft built were exported to European operators. Even before the production was fully under way Convair had received considerable orders, among them REAL (Brazil) (4), Continental Airlines (3), SAS (16), Aero O/Y (Finland) (2), Sabena (12), Swissair (11), National Airlines (6), Braniff International Airways (5), Delta Air Lines (8), Eastern Air Lines (15), Alitalia (2), Iberia (5), Yugoslav Airlines (1), Deutsche Lufthansa (2), Air Carrier Service (2), US Air Force (6), Royal Australian Air Force (2), and nine for private customers.

Many CV-440s have been re-engined with turboprops and a common improvement was the installation of weather radar in the nose. This increased the fuselage length by 71.1 cm (2 ft 4 in).

Air Sea of Basle, Switzerland, currently uses ex-Sabena aircraft in a 44-seat configuration for charter flights. However, many of the surviving 440 aircraft are now in use with minor airlines as cargo carriers.

Right: A CV-440 of Aspen Airways Inc based in Denver, Colorado. The airline was started in 1962 to provide a fast air-taxi service between Denver and the skiing resort of Aspen, Colorado
Below: A Convair CV-440 of Great Lakes Airlines Ltd, a Canadian operator based at London, Ontario, photographed at Toronto in March 1971

176

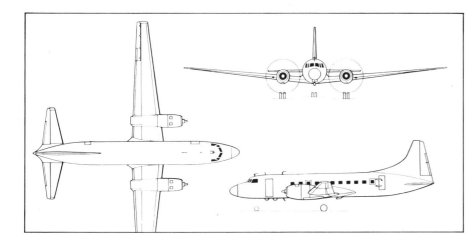

CV-440

Type: medium-range passenger transport
Maker: Convair Division, General Dynamics Corporation
Span: 32.12 m (105 ft 4 in)
Length: 24.84 m (81 ft 6 in)
Height: 8.59 m (28 ft 2 in)
Wing area: 85.5 m² (920 sq ft)
Weight: maximum 22 544 kg (49 700 lb); empty 15 110 kg (33 314 lb)
Powerplant: two 2500-hp Pratt & Whitney R-2800-CB16 or -CB17 18-cylinder radial engines

Performance: cruising speed 483 km/h (300 mph) at 3962 m (13 000 ft); range with maximum payload 459 km (285 miles)
Payload: 5820 kg (12 836 lb); seats for up to 52 passengers
Crew: 2
Production: 153

Saab Scandia

FIRST FLIGHT 1946

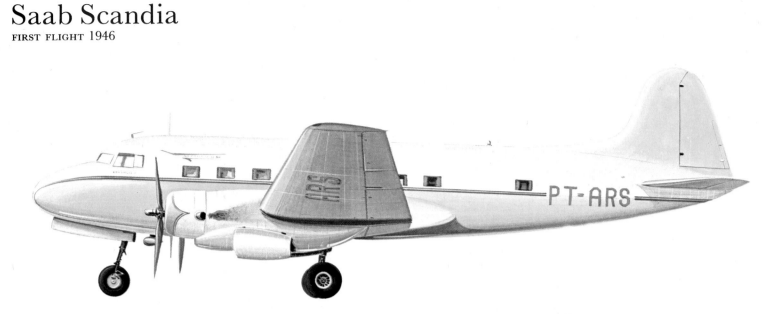

S VENSKA Aeroplan AB (Saab) began work on
an aircraft which could serve in a similar role to
the Convair 240, the Ilushin Il-12 and the Vickers
Viking. The Scandia, as it was called, remains the
only airliner of Swedish design to enter regular
commercial service. Design work began in 1944
under the title Project CT and it was only later that
it was designated the Saab 90. Designed by a team
under F Likmalm, the prototype Scandia, SE-
BCA, made its first flight on November 16, 1946.
The aircraft was designed to meet ICAO standards
and was a low-wing cantilever monoplane with a
fully-retractable tricycle undercarriage. A pair of
Pratt & Whitney R-2000 Twin Wasp radials (of
the enlarged type fitted to the DC-4) rated at
1350 hp for take-off were fitted, but production
aircraft had 1800-hp Twin Wasps of the R-2180
type (fitted to no other aircraft). Deep oval cowlings were soon replaced by the conventional circular type. The oval-section fuselage was of stressed-
skin, semi-monocoque construction and built as a
single unit.

Saab had high hopes for the Scandia, but the
cheap, war-surplus DC-3's hold on the market was
almost total. Two years after its first flight, the
Scandia finally attracted an order from AB Aerotransport (Swedish Air Lines) for ten aircraft. In
fact, the first four went to Aerovias Brasil and the
remaining six were delivered to Scandinavian
Airlines Systems (SAS). Aerovias Brasil was absorbed into VASP who ordered five more and SAS
reordered two aircraft. Ironically, heavy defence
commitments allowed Saab to build only one of
these; the remaining six being produced with the
assistance of Aviolanda, de Schelde and Fokker.

In November 1950 SAS introduced the Scandia
on its domestic network. Regular services linked
Oslo and Bodø in Arctic Norway and Stockholm
and Luleå at the head of the Gulf of Bothnia. In
1957 SAS sold their fleet to VASP who also
acquired the prototype. The Brazilian carrier
therefore operated all of the 18 Scandias built and
they were all employed usefully throughout their
lengthy careers. All production aircraft were designated Saab 90A-2s. The Saab 90A-2 had seats for
24 to 32 passengers in an unpressurized fuselage.
This passenger capacity was later increased to 36
and the flight crew of four was reduced to three.
The Saab 90A-3, which was to accommodate 38
passengers, was never built.

Saab 90

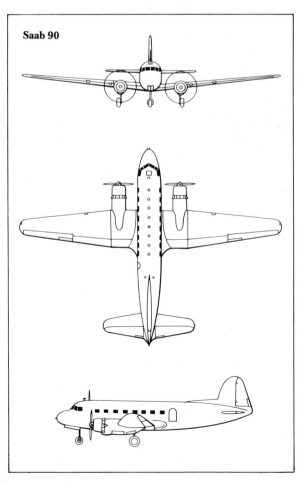

Top: The Saab 90A-2 Scandia
was externally very similar to
the DC-4. After seeing a
decade of service with SAS,
Scandias were withdrawn in
1957, but continued lengthy
flying careers in Brazil
Above: A good view of the
Scandia's two 1800-hp Pratt
& Whitney R-2180-El Twin
Wasps (larger than other
Twin Wasps)

Saab 90A-2

Type: medium-range
passenger transport
Maker: Svenska Aeroplan AB
(SAAB)
Span: 28 m (91 ft 10 in)
Length: 21.3 m (69 ft 11 in)
Height: 7.08 m (23 ft 3 in)
Wing area: 85.7 m² (922 sq
ft)
Weight: maximum 16 000 kg
(35 275 lb); empty 9960 kg
(21 960 lb)
Powerplant: two 1800-hp
Pratt & Whitney R-2180-El
Twin Wasp radial engines
Performance: cruising speed
391 km/h (242 mph) at
3048 m (10 000 ft); range
1480 km (920 miles)
Payload: 2800 kg (6172 lb);
seats for 24 to 32 passengers
Crew: 4
Production: 18

Il-12, Ilyushin

FIRST FLIGHT 1946

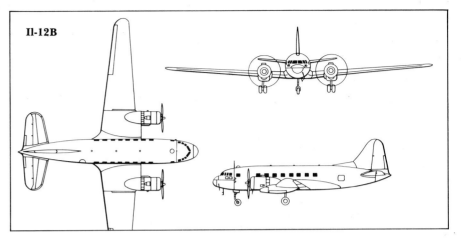

Il-12B

FROM the late 1930s right up to the end of World War II, the Soviet Union relied almost exclusively for transport aircraft on the Douglas DC-3, built under licence in the USSR as the Lisunov Li-2. With the end of the war in sight during 1944, the Russians started to consider the production of a new transport aircraft of indigenous design, incorporating the aeronautical lessons of World War II. Given the scope of air transport in the vastnesses of the Soviet Union, and the need to operate from grass runways in many areas, an official requirement issued in 1944 called for a twin-engined Li-2 replacement able to operate from unpaved strips.

The Ilyushin design bureau began work on what was to be designated the Il-12 during 1944. As conceived, the Il-12 was to be powered by a pair of Charomsky diesel engines, which offered low fuel consumption and simplicity of maintenance.

The prototype first flew in 1946, and was revealed publicly on August 18 of that year. Production got under way quickly, and Il-12s began to operate in Aeroflot colours on August 22, 1947. The type had been designed largely for internal routes, but by 1948 Aeroflot was operating its Il-12s on both national and international networks. Accommodation on these early aircraft was for 27 passengers, and a large crew of five (four on the flight-deck) was normal.

The Il-12 was a conventional low-wing all-metal monoplane, and powered by a pair of Shvetsov ASh-82FNV radials. The use of a strut to support the tail while the aircraft was being loaded suggests that the Il-12 was designed with a tailwheel-type undercarriage.

Early operations led to a number of modifications: a small dorsal fin was added, the nosewheel leg was strengthened, the oil-cooler air intake was moved from the wing leading edge to the engine cowling, the thermal de-icing equipment replaced the initial pulsating rubber boots. With these modifications the Il-12 became the Il-12B, unmodified aircraft being graced with the retrospective designation Il-12A. In later models accommodation was increased to 32, and some were convertible freight/passenger aircraft. Problems with single-engine safety dictated a reduction in gross weight in the later years of the Il-12's useful airline life.

Il-12

Type: medium-range transport
Maker: Ilyushin Design Bureau
Span: 31.7 m (104 ft 3 in)
Length: 21.31 m (69 ft 11 in)
Height: 8 m (26 ft 3 in)
Wing area: 100 m² (1076.4 sq ft)
Weight: maximum 17 250 kg (38 029 lb); empty 11 000 kg (24 250 lb)
Powerplant: two 1830-hp Shvetsov ASh-82FNV 18-cylinder two-row radial engines
Performance: cruising speed 350 km/h (217 mph) at 2500 m (8202 ft); range with 32 passengers 1250 km (777 miles)
Payload: 3000 kg (6614 lb); seats for up to 32 passengers
Crew: 5
Production: approx 3000 (250 civil and 2750 military)

Left: An Ilyushin Il-12, which had to fulfil both civil and military requirements and therefore had high fuel consumption
Below: An Il-12B with the Czechoslovak airline CSA. Il-12s were the standard medium-range aircraft of the 1940s Aeroflot fleet, but were also exported

Il-14, Ilyushin

FIRST FLIGHT 1950

THE Ilyushin design bureau during the late 1940s reworked the basic Il-12 concept to produce a safer and more economical aircraft. Particular attention was paid to single-engined performance, safety in icing conditions, fire control and the problems of instrument flight. At the same time various aerodynamic improvements were made, the structure was revised, and more powerful engines were installed. The result of the programme was the Il-14, which first flew in 1950.

The new aircraft was ordered into large-scale production for the Soviet air force as the Il-14 and for Aeroflot as the Il-14P (*Passazhirskii*, or passenger), both models apparently entering service in 1954. That safety standards were still fairly marginal is indicated by the fact that although the Il-14 had engines of slightly more power than those of the Il-12, structure weight was also greater but take-off weight had to be reduced, necessitating a reduction in passenger capacity to 26.

This resulted in operating economics that were, even by Russian standards, very poor, and in 1955 Ilyushin produced a stretched variant, the Il-14M (*Modifikatsyi*, or modification), with the fuselage lengthened by 1 m (3 ft 3½ in). This allowed the Il-14M to carry up to 36 passengers in high-density configuration, although a payload of 30 passengers was more usual. It also seems that some Il-14Ps were later brought up to Il-14M standard.

For specialized freighting operations, Ilyushin also developed the Il-14G (*Gruzovoi*, or freight). These were built as such or converted from standard Il-14s, with large double loading doors in the left side of the rear fuselage, and a floor strengthened to carry a maximum payload of 3000 kg (6614 lb).

Licence production of the Il-14 was also undertaken in Czechoslovakia and East Germany, while plans for the type to be built in China were ultimately unsuccessful. In Czechoslovakia the Il-14 entered production at the Dimitrov works near Prague as the Avia 14P, this model being basically identical with the Il-14P. Production began in 1957, and in 1958 the Avia 14-32A equivalent of the Il-14M followed it on the production line. The Avia 14-32A was extensively recast within the fuselage to provide seating for up to 32 passengers. Avia also went on to develop other models of the basic Il-14: the Avia 14T was a specialized freighter with one large loading door and the ability to carry 3494 kg (7703 lb) of freight over a range of 860 km (534 miles); the Avia 14-40 Super of 1960 introduced a pressurized fuselage for up to 42 passengers, identifiable by its circular rather than rectangular windows; and the Avia 14 Salon was similar to the Avia 14-32A but configured as an executive aircraft. Total Czech production was approximately 120 aircraft of the Avia 14 type, of which some 50 were supplied to the USSR.

In East Germany production of the Il-14P was undertaken by the VEB Kooperationszentrale für die Flugzeugindustrie at Dresden-Klötzsche.

Aeroflot operation of the Il-14P began on November 30, 1954, and the Il-14 is still in service in the early 1980s, an eloquent testimony of its longevity if not its economic viability. The type was widely used in the USSR and its satellites.

Right: Polish and Hungarian Il-14s; they were still in use in the mid 1970s with a variety of operators, including CAAC, CSA, Cubana, Mongolian and Tarom
Below: An Il-14 taxies onto the runway of a Soviet airfield in the late 1950s
Below right: An Avia-built Il-14 in Czech service at Paris in the summer of 1959
Bottom: An Il-14 of the Polish Airline LOT; it was also used by 20 Aeroflot directories

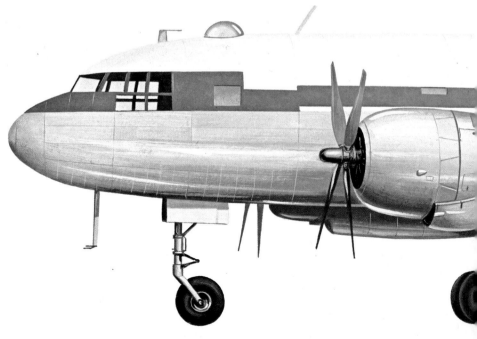

Il-14M

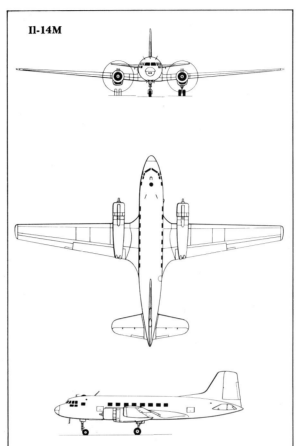

Il-14

Type: medium-range transport
Maker: Ilyushin Design Bureau; Avia; VEB
Span: 31.7 m (104 ft)
Length: 22.31 m (73 ft 2¼ in)
Height: 8 m (26 ft 3 in)
Wing area: 100 m² (1076.4 sq ft)
Weight: maximum 18 250 kg (40 234 lb); empty 12 700 kg (27 998 lb)
Powerplant: two 1900-hp Shvetsov ASh-82T 18-cylinder two-row radial engines
Performance: cruising speed 350 km/h (217 mph) at 3000 m (9842 ft); range with maximum payload 400 km (249 miles)
Payload: 3300 kg (7275 lb); seats for up to 36 passengers
Crew: 4
Production: minimum 3700 (civil and military)

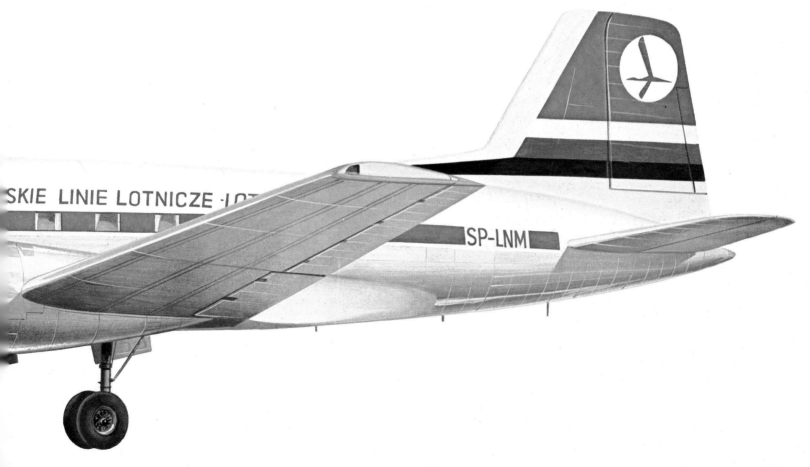

Br 763 Provence, Breguet

FIRST FLIGHT 1949

THE Breguet Provence had its origins in a 1944 design for a large aircraft to be used in either the passenger or cargo role. However, the prototype of this aircraft, the Br 761 Deux Ponts (two decks), did not fly until February 15, 1949. It was powered by four 1580-hp SNECMA-built Gnome-Rhône 14R engines but the three Br 761s which followed it were powered by four 2020-hp Pratt & Whitney R-2800-B31s. These aircraft differed from the prototype only in that they had modified wingtips and three tail fins.

These three pre-production aircraft were used to conclude the outstanding flight tests, and, despite the fact that they seemed to do this satisfactorily, Air France were not particularly impressed. The reason for this was probably the use of unsatisfactory war surplus Pratt & Whitney engines, although one aircraft was leased to Air Algérie and one was in service with Silver City for a short period before being transferred to the French Armée de l'Air.

In 1951 a structurally improved version, with 2400-hp R-2800 engines, was put forward, designated Br 763. Air France ordered 12 Provences, as the new version had been christened, and the first of these flew on July 20, 1951. Air France received its first example in August 1952 and this was put into regular service on the Lyons-Algiers route on March 16, 1953. In 1964, six of these aircraft went to the Armée de l'Air for service in the Far East, but Air France continued to use the type as a freighter up to 1971. Although not a particularly handsome aircraft, the Br 763 had a reputation for

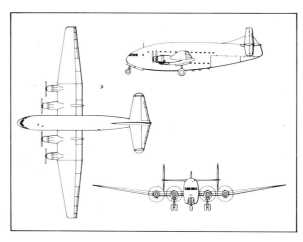

being extremely capable. It had a double-decker layout, with 59 passengers on the upper deck and 48 on the lower deck, although 135 passengers could be carried in high-density configuration. Known as a 'hard worker', the Provence could be used for carrying both cargo and passengers. In fact the all-cargo version could carry 11 tonnes (11 000 kg) of freight or it could be used for ferrying vehicles, loaded through clamshell doors under the rear fuselage.

The six aircraft used in the military transport role were renamed Saharas and saw service with the 64e Escadre de Transport, together with four Br 765s with removable cargo doors, and the three Br 7615S. The last of these aircraft was in service with Groupe Aérien Mixte 82 until late 1972.

Br 763

Type: passenger/cargo transport
Maker: Société Anonyme des Ateliers d'Aviation Louis Breguet
Span: 42.99 m (141 ft)
Length: 28.94 m (94 ft 11½ in)
Height: 9.65 m (31 ft 8 in)
Wing area: 185.4 m² (1995½ sq ft)
Weight: maximum 51 600 kg (113 757 lb); empty 25 350 kg (55 890 lb)
Powerplant: four 2400-hp Pratt & Whitney R-2800-CA18 Double Wasp 18-cylinder radial engines
Performance: cruising speed 351 km/h (218 mph); range with maximum payload 2165 km (1345 miles)
Payload: 12 228 kg (26 960 lb); seats for up to 135 passengers
Crew: 4
Production: 16

Above: An Air France Breguet Br 763 Provence photographed in March 1967. Despite its fat fuselage and slightly ungainly appearance, it was widely used on routes to France's colonies in the 1960s

Armagnac, SNCASE

FIRST FLIGHT 1949

DESPITE the difficulties in which France found herself during the German occupation in World War II, design work on many military and civil aircraft continued relatively unabated.

Full-scale design of the Armagnac did not begin until 1945, when the Société Nationale de Constructions Aéronautiques de Sud-Est (SNCASE) was selected as prime contractor for the SE.2000. It was intended to be capable of North Atlantic service at a cruising altitude of 4000 m (13 123 ft) on the power of four 2100-hp Gnome-Rhône 18R radials.

It was soon realized that the wartime origins of the design meant that it was approaching obsolescence, and so the basic concept was scaled up to produce a pressurized airliner capable of carrying 64 passengers across the North Atlantic, some 107 being accommodated on shorter routes. The larger aircraft was clearly beyond the capabilities of the Gnome-Rhône 18R, and so the SE.2010 Armagnac was to be powered by four 3500-hp Pratt & Whitney R-4360 Wasp Majors. In this form the first SE.2010 Armagnac flew on April 2, 1949, and production of 15 definitive Armagnacs (eight for Air France) was instituted. However, to accommodate three levels of bunks the fuselage of the Armagnac was very deep, so that, when sleeper accommodation fell from favour at about this time, Air France felt that the Armagnac had too great an interior volume and so cancelled its order. SNCASE decided to press ahead with the construction of nine, the first four being delivered to Transports Aériens Intercontinentaux).

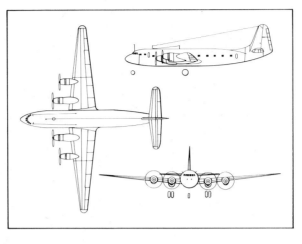

The Armagnac entered service on December 8, 1952 but was soon found to be operationally uneconomic. The four aircraft were then returned to SNCASE and placed in store at Toulouse. The type's chance came in 1953 when the outbreak of full-scale war in Indo-China led to a greater demand for air transport from France. Seven Armagnacs were thus allocated to the Société Auxiliaire de Gerence et de Transports Aériens (SAGETA) for operation between Toulouse and Saigon via Beirut, Karachi and Calcutta.

There were two passenger cabins: the forward cabin could accommodate 24 first-class passengers, the rear cabin seating 60 first-class passengers; total accommodation in second-class configuration was 107, and in high-density configuration 160.

SE.2010

Type: long-range transport
Maker: Société Nationale de Constructions Aéronautiques de Sud-Est
Span: 48.95 m (160 ft 7 in)
Length: 39.63 m (130 ft)
Height: 13.5 m (44 ft 3½ in)
Wing area: 236 m² (2540.3 sq ft)
Weight: maximum 77 500 kg (170 855 lb); empty 44 922 kg (99 035 lb)
Powerplant: four 3500-hp Pratt & Whitney R-4360-B13 Wasp Major 28-cylinder radial engines
Performance: cruising speed 454 km/h (282 mph); range with maximum payload 2450 km (1522 miles)
Payload: seats for up to 160 passengers
Crew: 5
Production: 9

Above left: An SE.2010 in service with TAI (Cie de Transports Aériens Intercontinentaux) – they bought four but grounded them due to high running costs
Far left: Two of the four 3500-hp Pratt & Whitney Wasp Major engines
Left: Seating for transatlantic passengers – the aircraft ended its career as a troop carrier in Indo-China
Above: The nosewheels with navigation and landing lights on an SNCASE *Armagnac*

Marathon, Miles
FIRST FLIGHT 1946

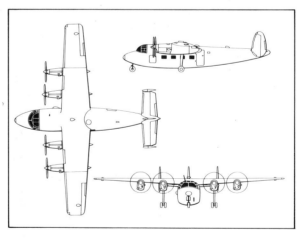

Above: The first production Marathon built at Reading for the Ministry of Supply in 1950. It entered BEA service where it was named *Rob Roy* and was finally passed to the RAF in 1952
Left: G-AMGX as a flying show room with Balfour Marine Engineering

FROM 1943 onwards, much thought was given in British aeronautical circles to the possibilities of the civil market after the end of World War II. Key to this thinking was the powerful Brabazon Committee, whose job it was to decide the types of aircraft that would be needed to meet British civil aviation requirements. During 1944 the Miles design team came up with the M.60, a high-wing aircraft powered by four de Havilland Gipsy Queen inline engines and intended as a feederliner. The concept was sufficiently attractive for the Brabazon Committee's Type 5A specification to be written round it. After fierce competition, Miles, in October 1944, received instructions to build three prototype M.60s, the first of these flying on May 19, 1946. As was frequently the case with British aircraft, then as now, the situation was made extremely difficult by the involvement of several interested parties, which led to delay.

In these circumstances it was inevitable that Miles should have to wait apparently interminably for a production order, despite the consensus of those who had flown a prototype that the M.60 was attractive and generally satisfactory. In the event the Miles company collapsed before an order was placed, and so the order went instead to Handley Page, which took over Miles on July 5, 1948 in the form of Handley Page (Reading) Ltd. The new company received an order for 50 HPR.1 Marathon 1s, revised at a cost of 227 kg (500 lb) extra weight to accommodate 18 passengers instead of 14. Of the 50 Marathons, 30 were intended for British European Airways and the other 20 for

British Overseas Airways to offer to its subsidiaries and associates in other parts of the world. In 1951 the first production Marathon was handed over to BEA after an extensive sales tour of Australia and New Zealand, but was rejected by the airline, which then reduced its order from an already cut order of 25 to a mere seven. In February 1952 BEA decided not to accept any Marathons at all. The 30 Marathons left in the hands of the Ministry of Supply then went to the RAF as Marathon T.11 navigation trainers, with a crew of two, and accommodation in the fuselage for one instructor.

The other main operators of the Marathon were West African Airways Corporation, which had six, Far East Air Lines with two, and Union of Burma Airways which had three.

HPR.1

Type: feedliner
Maker: Handley Page (Reading) Ltd
Span: 19.81 m (65 ft)
Length: 15.93 m (52 ft 3 in)
Height: 4.27 m (14 ft)
Wing area: 46.45 m² (500 sq ft)
Weight: maximum 8278 kg (18 250 lb); empty 5302 kg (11 688 lb)
Powerplant: four 330-hp de Havilland Gipsy Queen 70-3 inverted six inline air-cooled engines
Performance: cruising speed 282 km/h (175 mph); range 1505 km (935 miles)
Payload: seats for up to 18 passengers
Crew: 2
Production: 42

Hermes IV, Handley Page

FIRST FLIGHT 1948

DESIGN work on the Handley Page HP.68 Hermes I continued slowly throughout World War II. By 1944 the design had been fixed as a rather old-fashioned low-wing monoplane with single mainwheels and a tailwheel, to be powered by four Bristol Hercules radials and capable of accommodating up to 50 passengers in its pressurized fuselage. The prototype, G-AGSS, crashed because of elevator overbalance on its maiden flight on December 3, 1945.

Although the company's main effort was then devoted to the type's military counterpart, the HP.67 Hastings transport, work progressed on the HP.74 Hermes II, generally similar to its predecessor apart from a 3.96-m (13-ft) fuselage stretch, but much development was yet to be done on the definitive model, the HP.81 Hermes IV. British Overseas Airways had in April 1947 ordered, through the Ministry of Supply, 25 Hermes IVs which differed from the two earlier aircraft in having a more modern tricycle landing gear with twin wheels. The Hermes IV prototype first took to the air on September 5, 1948 and soon vindicated its advertising claim of being able to accommodate 63 passengers over ultimate ranges which were approximately 5633 km (3500 miles).

Deliveries of the Hermes IV to BOAC began in 1950, the type flying its first scheduled service on August 6, 1950. The type soon proved its worth, but its systems engineering was insufficiently developed and most were replaced by Canadair Argonaut C-4s in 1952. However, the grounding of the de Havilland Comet in 1954 led to the recom-

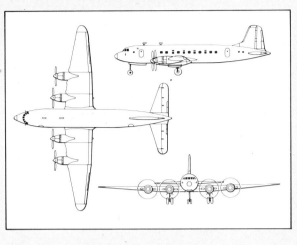

missioning of BOAC's Hermes IVs for the period between July and December of that year, with seating for 56 passengers on the route between London and Africa.

During 1952, however, Hermes IVs had begun a new type of operation, serving with Airwork Ltd on commercial trooping flights. Airwork was later joined by Skyways Ltd in such operations, and the Hermes IVs (designated Hermes IVAs when fitted with Hercules 763 engines to run on 100-octane rather than 115-octane fuel) served long and profitably in this role. In the late 1950s the type was also used for charter work, carrying up to 78 passengers. The survivors were mostly scrapped in 1961 and 1962, although the last Hermes IV made its ultimate commercial flight as late as December 13, 1964.

Hermes IV

Type: medium-range passenger transport
Maker: Handley Page Ltd
Span: 34.44 m (113 ft)
Length: 29.52 m (96 ft 10 in)
Height: 9.09 m (29 ft 11 in)
Wing area: 130.8 m² (1408 sq ft)
Weight: maximum 39 009 kg (86 000 lb); empty 25 107 kg (55 350 lb)
Powerplant: four 2100-hp Bristol Hercules 763 14-cylinder radial sleeve-valve engines
Performance: cruising speed 444 km/h (276 mph) at 3048 m (10 000 ft); range with maximum payload 3219 km (2000 miles)
Payload: seats for up to 82 passengers
Crew: 7
Production: 25

Left: The BOAC Handley Page Hermes IV *Hero* flying over the Needles, Isle of Wight
Below: *Hannibal* in BOAC service at Nairobi airport in the early 1950s. It ended its career at Stansted when it was scrapped in September 1962

Ambassador, Airspeed

FIRST FLIGHT 1947

THE Airspeed AS.57 was a product of the Brabazon II specification of 1943. It was defined as a large medium-haul airliner with twice the payload of a DC-3. More power was obviously needed and Bristol produced a commercial version of the two-row Centaurus.

Development flying of the engine was undertaken by Airspeed in a Warwick testbed. The AS.57 emerged as a high-wing cantilever monoplane of all-metal stressed-skin construction, with a fully pressurized cabin and a tricycle undercarriage. Close attention was given to aerodynamic form of the aircraft to achieve economic operation through sheer speed and competitive range.

The Ministry of Aircraft Production ordered two prototypes in September 1945 and the name Ambassador was bestowed. Nearly two years later Airspeed's chief test-pilot G B S Errington took the first, G-AGUA, into the air for its maiden flight on July 10, 1947. Not surprisingly, the Ambassador comfortably met all ICAO airworthiness requirements. Centaurus 630 engines replaced the 130 series units fitted to G-AGUA.

Production problems lost Airspeed valuable orders, but on September 22, 1948, British European Airways signed for 20 Ambassador 2s, costing £3 million. The airline specified Centaurus 661s with two-stage superchargers and slotted flaps replaced the earlier split type to improve runway performance. After intensive trials G-ALZN inaugurated the first scheduled London to Paris service on March 13, 1952. The service entry of the Ambassador coincided with the succession of Queen Elizabeth II, and BEA named every aircraft after a famous figure in the reign of Elizabeth I: *Sir Francis Drake*, *Sir Walter Raleigh* and *William Shakespeare* are examples.

Services expanded rapidly. Most of Europe was served by the end of 1952, and the route network had spread to Benghazi, Cairo, Malta and Tripoli by 1955. In 1956 the Vickers Viscount began to replace BEA's largest and last piston-engined airliner on major routes. On June 30, 1958, BEA's final scheduled Ambassador flight arrived at London from Cologne.

Small charter operators bought the majority of BEA's redundant fleet and others were used as engine testbeds. The sole surviving Ambassador (G-ALZO) is maintained in non-flying condition by the Dan-Air Preservation Group.

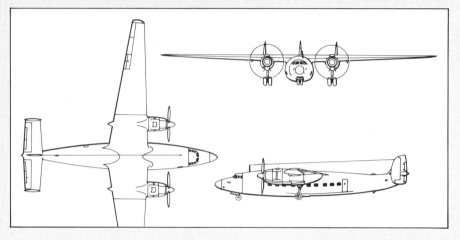

Ambassador 2

Type: medium-range passenger transport
Maker: Airspeed Division, de Havilland Aircraft Co
Span: 35 m (115 ft)
Length: 25 m (82 ft)
Height: 5.56 m (18 ft 3 in)
Wing area: 111 m² (1200 sq ft)
Weight: maximum 23 814 kg (52 500 lb); empty 16 230 kg (35 781 lb)
Powerplant: two 2625-hp Bristol Centaurus 661 18-cylinder sleeve-valve radial engines
Performance: cruising speed 438 km/h (272 mph); range 2494 km (1550 miles)
Payload: 5280 kg (11 645 lb); seats for 47 to 60 passengers
Crew: 3
Production: 20

Above: The Airspeed AS. 57 Ambassador 2 G-ALZP during its service with the Decca Navigator company at Gatwick Airport. During its career it was operated by, amongst others, BEA and the Royal Jordanian Air Force. It ended its career in New Zealand
Below: The Ambassador 2 *William Shakespeare* of BEA which was later named *Vogel Gryf* when it passed into Swiss service

Carvair, Aviation Traders

FIRST FLIGHT 1961

Left: An Aviation Traders ATL 98 Carvair of Falcon Airways, a Texas-based all-cargo airline which links towns in the mid western and southern states
Below: G-APNH *Menai Bridge* with British Air Ferries at Southend; it was lost when the nosewheel collapsed at Le Touquet in March 1971

ONE of the most interesting developments of the basic Douglas DC-4 transport was the specialized carry-ferry version developed by Aviation Traders (Engineering) Ltd under the designation A T L 98 Carvair. The origins of the type lay with the far-sighted Freddie Laker, managing director of Aviation Traders and its associated company Channel Air Bridge: the latter was seeking a replacement for its Bristol Superfreighter 32 car ferries, and Laker stipulated that the small market requirement for such an aircraft prohibited the development of a new aircraft, although the conversion of secondhand (and very cheap) DC-4s offered distinct possibilities.

The result was an extraordinary hybrid: to a basic DC-4 fuselage, wings and powerplant, were mated a tail unit derived from that of the DC-7, DC-6 wheel brakes, and a new forward fuselage. This last used the same constructional method as that of the DC-4, but the new section lengthened the nose by 2.64 m (8 ft 8 in) while raising the cockpit by 2.08 m (6 ft 10 in), so allowing a hydraulically operated nose door to be fitted. At the same time the nose unit of the undercarriage was arranged to retract into an underfuselage blister, allowing the loading of five cars straight through the nose. Passenger accommodation was 25, and the whole conversion added only 1043 kg (2300 lb) to the weight.

After a mock-up had proved the engineering feasibility of the project, the first conversion of a C-54 was begun in October 1960, and this initial Carvair, as it was to be called, took to the air for its maiden flight on June 21, 1961. Full certification was obtained on January 31, 1962, allowing Channel Air Bridge to begin a scheduled service from Southend to Rotterdam on March 1, 1962. The company acquired another two Carvairs, and, after its merger with Silver City Airways in 1962 as British United Air Ferries, the company eventually bought another seven. Total Carvair production was 21, and the other main users of the type were: Aer Lingus, operating three with accommodation for racehorses; Ansett-ANA, operating three, two of which had enlarged nose doors; Aviaco, operating three between France, Spain and the Balearic Islands. In 1974 there were still 13 Carvairs in service, nine with British Air Ferries, two with Ansett, one with Air Cambodge and one with Dominicana.

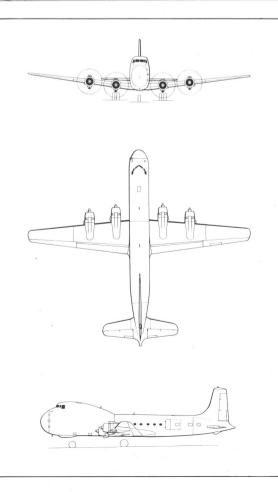

ATL 98

Type: medium-range car/passenger ferry
Maker: Aviation Traders (Engineering) Ltd
Span: 35.81 m (117 ft 6 in)
Length: 31.27 m (102 ft 7 in)
Height: 9.09 m (29 ft 10 in)
Wing area: 135.83 m² (1462 sq ft)
Weight: maximum 33 475 kg (73 800 lb); empty 18 763 kg (41 365 lb)
Powerplant: four 1450-hp Pratt & Whitney R-2000-7M2 Twin Wasp radial engines
Performance: cruising speed 296 km/h (184 mph) at 3048 m (10 000 ft); range 3330 km (2070 miles) with a payload of 8000 kg (17 635 lb)
Payload: up to 5 cars and 23 passengers; or up to 65 passengers
Crew: 4
Production: 21

DC-7, Douglas

FIRST FLIGHT 1953

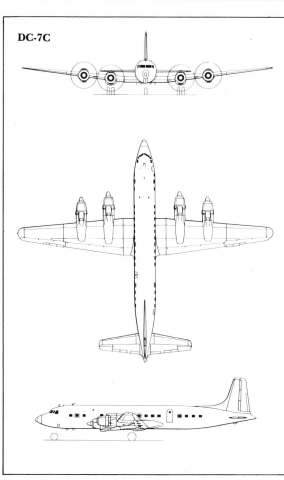

Left: A Douglas DC-7B finds strange employment as a flying country club with the Atlanta (Georgia) Skylarks
Below left: A DC-7C at Chicago in March 1976. The type is still widely used by third-level airlines
Below: The flight-deck of G-AOIF, a DC-7C operated by BOAC in the late 1950s and early 60s

THE development of the DC-7 was prompted by American Airlines whose transcontinental market was being threatened by Trans World Airlines. In the early 1950's TWA ordered the faster, longer-ranged L-1049 Super Constellation, powered by the R-3350 Turbo-Compound, which enabled it to operate across the USA non-stop.

Accordingly, in 1951, American Airlines attempted to convince a reluctant Douglas of the need to build a competitive aircraft, powered by four of the new Turbo-Compounds. To help persuade Douglas, American offered to pay $40 million for 25 of the projected aircraft to complement its fleet of 50 DC-6s, six DC-6As and 25 DC-6Bs.

Comforted by this substantial order, which paid for most of the development costs, Douglas began production of the DC-7 on the same line as the DC-6A and -B. Eventually they sold 338 DC-7s, -7Bs, and -7Cs, making a substantial profit.

The DC-7 was sold exclusively to US trunk carriers: United (57), American (34), Delta (10) and National (4). The aircraft was a direct development of the DC-6B with its fuselage stretched by 1.02 m (40 in) to add one row of seats. While retaining the DC-6B's 20 914-litre (4600-Imp gal) fuel tank arrangement, the DC-7 introduced a number of design changes. These included the use of titanium in the engine nacelles for increased fire resistance, and a strengthened landing gear whose main units could be lowered at high air speeds to be used as an airbrake during quick descents.

The first DC-7 was flown on May 18, 1953, and entered service with American Airlines on

DC-7C

DC-7

Type: long-range transport
Maker: Douglas Aircraft Co
Span: 35.81 m (117 ft 6 in)
Length: 33.2 m (108 ft 11 in)
Height: 8.71 m (28 ft 7 in)
Wing area: 135.92 m² (1463 sq ft)
Weight: maximum 55 429 kg (122 200 lb); empty 30 076 kg (66 306 lb)
Powerplant: four 3250-hp Wright R-3350-18DA-2 Turbo-Compound engines
Performance: cruising speed 578 km/h (359 mph); range with maximum payload 4585 km (2850 miles)
Payload: 16 000 kg (35 275 lb)
Crew: 3
Production: 338 (DC-7, -7B, -7C)

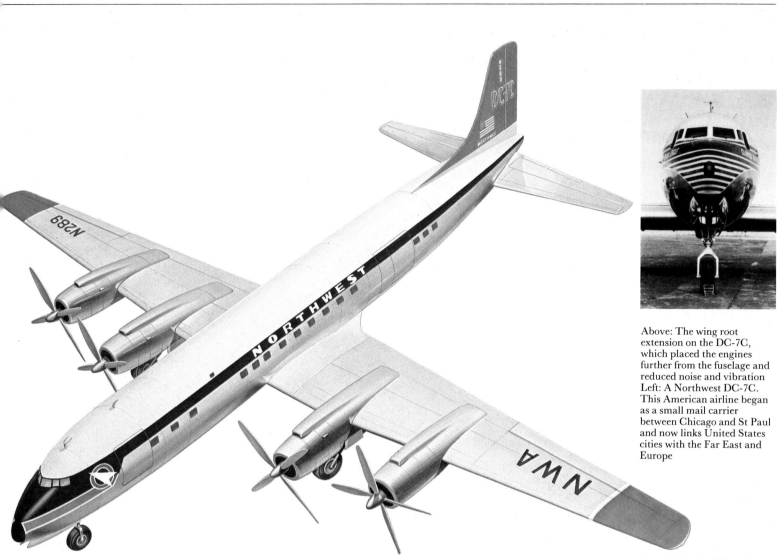

November 29 of that year. All of the 105 DC-7s were powered by four 3250-hp Wright R-3350-18DA-2 Turbo-Compounds driving four-blade propellers. In 1959–60 Douglas modified some of their DC-7s, -7Bs and -7Cs as freighters by fitting reinforced flooring and cargo doors.

The DC-7B was externally identical to the DC-7 except for longer engine nacelles filled with fuel. A total of 112 were sold, and the versions purchased by Pan American and South African Airways were slightly heavier than the rest because of an increased fuel tankage of 24 453 litres (5380 Imp gal). Pan American introduced it on June 13, 1955, on non-stop New York to London services.

Because the DC-7B could not fly non-stop westbound against average winds, however, the DC-7C was developed to a PanAm requirement for an aircraft capable of flying services in either transatlantic direction. Aptly named Seven Seas, the DC-7C was the world's first true long-range commercial transport. Its span was increased 3.05 m (10 ft) by adding sections between the fuselage and inner nacelles. The result of this was two-fold. Total fuel carried was now 29 620 litres (6515 Imp gal), and the engines were moved further outboard which reduced noise and vibration in the passenger cabins, an important consideration during long flights.

The first Seven Seas was flown on December 20, 1955, and Pan American introduced the type into service on June 1, 1956. The fuselage was stretched a further 1.1 m (42 in) in relation to the DC-7B and maximum take-off weight was increased to

64 864 kg (143 000 lb). All DC-7Cs were powered by 3400-hp R-3350-18EA-1 Turbo-Compounds. A total of 121 DC-7Cs were sold to US and foreign airlines, and, when phased out of passenger service, many were converted to freighters.

The importance of the DC-7 lay in its use in developing scheduled, non-stop commercial operations across the United States, over the Atlantic and Pacific and over the North Pole. However, in the long run, for the airlines, the DC-7 series was not as successful as anticipated. Its timing, together with the unreliability of its engines, proved that it had been developed too far from a basic design which originated in the 1930s. By the time the last DC-7C was delivered to KLM in December 1958, the Boeing 707 was in service.

DH.114 Heron, de Havilland

FIRST FLIGHT 1950

THE DH.104 Dove was conceived by de Havilland as a successor to the DH.89 Dragon Rapide. Similarly the larger DH.114 was seen as a replacement for the DH.86B feederliner. Although de Havilland came up with the concept of the DH.114, later named Heron, shortly after the end of World War II, they sensibly appreciated that postwar austerity and slow market growth left little room for such an aircraft, capable of accommodating up to 17 passengers, and so postponed development.

It was in 1949 that the company decided the time was ripe for what was essentially a scaled-up Dove with four unsupercharged engines and a fixed tricycle undercarriage. Such an aircraft, de Havilland reasoned, would be admirably suited for small-field operation, in undeveloped countries. The prototype, registered G-ALZL, was completed in early 1950 thanks to the use of many standard and modified Dove components, and first flew on May 10, 1950.

This prototype completed a successful test programme, and was then used quite extensively as a promotional aircraft in the liveries of several prospective operators.

Orders had already started to come in, and the first production aircraft left for delivery to New Zealand National Airways in April 1952. Only the first seven production Herons were built at the company's headquarters at Hatfield before production was switched to the vast (former Wellington) factory at Hawarden outside Chester. The last Heron built at Hatfield, it should be noted, was the

prototype Series 2. This featured retractable landing gear, the reduced drag increasing speed by 32 km/h (20 mph) and increasing range. It is clear, therefore, that de Havilland had erred slightly in their assessment of the desirability of a fixed undercarriage for its simplicity and slight saving in weight, and good evidence of this is given by the fact that Series 1 production totalled only 51 aircraft compared with 97 production Series 2 Herons.

Both the Series 1 and 2 were produced in a major sub-variant, the Series 1B and 2B with four de Havilland Gipsy Queen 30-2 inlines in place of the similarly rated (250-hp) Gipsy Queen 30s of the Series 1. Other modifications have been minimal: in 1955 wider rudders were fitted to all Herons to

Left: A Scottish Airways de Havilland DH.114 Heron 1. This aircraft was based at Renfrew where it had the name *John Hunter*, but later at Glasgow Abbotsinch it operated under the name *Sister Jean Kennedy*
Below: A DH.114 Heron of East African DCA based in Kenya. In 1969 this aircraft was converted by Executive Air Engineering at Baginton and fitted with turbocharged Lycoming engines

cure directional problems; the suffixes C and E indicate aircraft specially modified for the fulfilment of executive roles, and the suffix D indicates that the aircraft is fitted with the optional de Havilland fully feathering propeller, which replaced the variable-pitch unit of the standard Heron aircraft.

The basic worth of the Heron is in no way better attested than in the number of re-engined modifications that have been made in many countries. The first of these was the Heron Series 2C of the Banco Nacional de Mexico, delivered in October 1957 and later modified by Riley Aeronautics of Florida into the first Riley Heron: the standard 250-hp Gipsy Queens were ultimately replaced by four 340-hp Lycoming GSO-480-B1A6 piston engines and then by 290-hp Lycoming IO-540-G1A5 turbocharged piston engines. The effect of these changes was to improve quite considerably the payload and cruising performance of the Riley Heron, alternatively known as the Turbo-Liner. At least 16 Herons received the Riley modification, and a similar conversion was undertaken during 1969 by Executive Air Engineering at Baginton in England.

Production of the Heron reached 148 examples, the last of these being completed in 1963 and kept in store until 1966 when it became the Hawker Siddeley Group's utility aircraft at Hatfield. Obviously, the de Havilland company erred inexcusably in failing to produce a modern successor both to the DH.114 Heron aircraft and, especially, its Gipsy Queen powerplant.

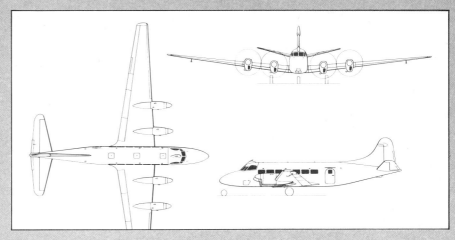

Series 2D

Type: feederliner
Maker: de Havilland Aircraft Co Ltd
Span: 21.79 m (71 ft 6 in)
Length: 14.78 m (48 ft 6 in)
Height: 4.75 m (15 ft 7 in)
Wing area: 46.36 m² (499 sq ft)
Weight: maximum 6124 kg (13 500 lb); empty 3697 kg (8150 lb)
Powerplant: four 250-hp de Havilland Gipsy Queen 30-2 inverted six inline engines
Performance: cruising speed 295 km/h (183 mph) at 2438 m (8000 ft); range 1473 km (915 miles)
Payload: seats for up to 17 passengers
Crew: 2
Production: 148

5Y-KVC

L-1649A Starliner, Lockheed

FIRST FLIGHT 1956

THE Lockheed L-049 Constellation like the other four-engined transports developed during World War II, proved well suited to the ever increasing demands made on it for performance and payload. The basic design evolved through 11 other variants before arriving at its final expression in the L-1649A Starliner, the ultimate piston-engined civil transport.

The immediate spur to the development of the L-1649A was the success being enjoyed by Pan American on the North Atlantic route with its fleet of Douglas DC-7Cs. This final development of the DC-4 had both customer and operator appeal in the high level of comfort it could offer, and also in the fact that it could cross the Atlantic without any refuelling stops. The main US rival to Pan American World Airways on the 'blue riband' North Atlantic route was TWA, and for this operator Lockheed had to develop the long-range L-1649A Starliner, with an entirely new wing.

Of thinner section than the wing of the earlier Constellations, this new structure was built up on long machined panels and spanned a remarkable 45.72 m (150 ft) instead of the previous 37.47 m (123 ft) or 37.62 m (123 ft 5 in). Fuel capacity was a prodigious 36 378 litres (8002 Imp gal), giving the L-1649A Starliner a maximum range, with reserves of 10 170 km (6320 miles).

Also important was the fact that the increase in span allowed the engines to be moved 1.52 m (5 ft) farther from the fuselage, with a consequent reduction in cabin noise levels. This improvement was also aided by the inclusion of extra soundproofing

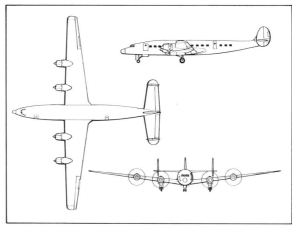

material in the way pioneered by TWA and Lockheed for the L-1049G Super Constellation, and by the synchrophasing of the Hamilton Standard propellers.

The Starliner at first accommodated 58 first-class or 75 coach-class passengers (this soon grew to 92), and also had 16.8 m³ (593 cu ft) of cargo space. With its excellent range, the Starliner was a natural for the North Atlantic route, TWA – which called it the Jetstream – being able to inaugurate services from New York to London and Paris on June 1, 1957. But by this time the 707 and DC-8 were piling up orders and the Starliner was too late. Only 43 were built, of which 42 served with Air France, Condor Flugdienst, Lufthansa, Trek Airways, TWA and World Airways.

L-1649A

Type: long-range transport
Maker: Lockheed Aircraft Corporation
Span: 45.72 m (150 ft)
Length: 34.62 m (113 ft 7 in)
Height: 7.14 m (23 ft 5 in)
Wing area: 171.87 m² (1850 sq ft)
Weight: maximum 70 761 kg (156 000 lb); empty 38 675 kg (85 262 lb)
Powerplant: four 3400-hp Wright R-3350-EA2 Turbo-Compound 18-cylinder radial engines
Performance: cruising speed 550 km/h (342 mph) at 6890 m (22 600 ft); range 10 170 km (6320 miles)
Payload: seats for up to 75 passengers, later increased to 92
Crew: 5
Production: 43

Trent-Meteor, Gloster

FIRST FLIGHT 1945

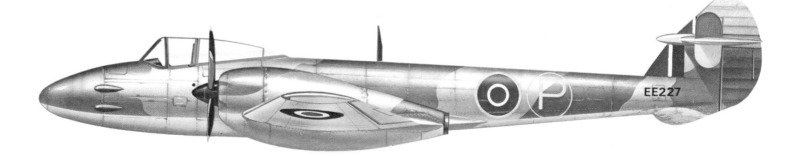

THE Gloster Trent-Meteor, although in no way an airliner, has a unique place in aviation history as the aircraft which pioneered turboprop power, and this type of powerplant has since become one of the standard types of engine used on short- and medium-range airliners.

The aircraft used for the Trent conversion was one of the first batch of production Gloster Meteor F.1 fighters, EE227, modified for trials.

In February 1945, with the RAF's immediate needs catered for by the delivery of the improved Meteor F.3, EE227 was converted back to F.1 standard and handed over to the Rolls-Royce facility at Hucknall as a flying testbed for the newly developed RB.50 Trent propeller-turbine, or turboprop. Such a powerplant seemed to offer many of the advantages of turbine power (relative simplicity, high power and lack of vibration) combined with the proven capabilities of the propeller (high aerodynamic efficiency even up to quite high Mach numbers). Rolls-Royce therefore began to develop the experimental Trent in May 1944, using as the basis of the engine the centrifugal-flow Derwent turbojet which was to power the F.3 and later marks of the Meteor.

The Trent-Meteor needed little modification for the accommodation of the Trent powerplant, though the nacelles were somewhat larger, which, with the extra side area of the propellers, entailed the fitting of two small auxiliary fins towards the outboard ends of the tailplane to ensure directional stability. The Gloster Trent-Meteor first flew on September 20, 1945 and thereafter contributed greatly to the development of turbine engines as pure turbojets and as turboprops. In its first form, the Trent-Meteor was fitted with five-blade Rotol propellers, each having a diameter of 2.41 m (7 ft 11 in), though some reports claim a propeller with a diameter of 2.31 m (7 ft 7 in) absorbing 750 hp and leaving 454 kg (1000 lb) of residual thrust. Later, the aircraft was modified to accommodate propellers with a diameter of 1.49 m (4 ft 10½ in), absorbing only 350 hp and leaving a residual thrust of 635 kg (1400 lb) to emerge from a squeezed orifice.

The Trent was intended only as a research engine, and valuable results were obtained, especially in determining the effect of a propeller hub on the efficiency of the turbine's air intake, and in the development of suitable reduction gears.

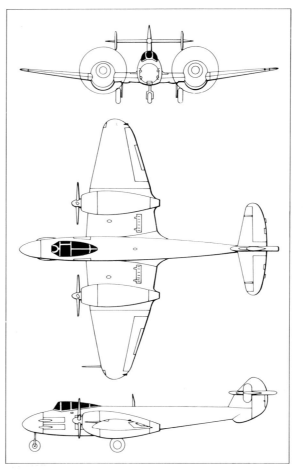

Trent Meteor

Type: experimental aircraft
Maker: Gloster Aircraft Co
Span: 13.12 m (43 ft)
Length: 12.57 m (41 ft 3 in)
Height: 3.96 m (13 ft)
Wing area: 34.75 m² (374 sq ft)
Weight: not available
Powerplant: two 1750-ehp Rolls-Royce RB.50 Trent turboprops
Performance: not available
Payload: none
Crew: 1
Production: 1

Above: The Trent-Meteor, flying testbed to explore the concept of the turboprop. Below: Flying on one engine

Hermes V, Handley Page

FIRST FLIGHT 1949

VARIOUS delays in the development of the HP.64 Passenger Version, Freighter Version and Military Transport, slowed the 1943 Handley Page programme, but the type finally emerged as the Handley Page Hastings transport for the RAF, and the Hermes airliner for the British Overseas Airways Corporation.

The possibility of producing a turboprop-powered version of the Hermes II was first considered in February 1946, with the Bristol Theseus as the prospective engine. Consideration was also given to a nosewheel-version of the aircraft. At this time the names for the family were Hermes I for the prototype which had crashed on December 3, 1945 on its first flight; Hermes II for the proposed lengthened version of the Hermes I, the HP.74; and Hermes III for the Theseus-engined HP.74. The types were to have basic seating for 64 passengers five-abreast, but on June 25, 1946 it was decided to reduce seating to 52, increase fuel capacity by the addition of outer-wing bag tanks, and redesignate the Hermes III as the HP.79. Finally, in September 1946 it was resolved to develop a nosewheel version of the Hermes, the model with piston engines to be the HP.81 Hermes IV and that with turboprops the HP.82 Hermes V. Official approval for the building of the initial run of Hermes IVs and the prototype Hermes V was given on October 5, 1946.

The first Hermes V, registered G-ALEU, took off on its maiden flight from Radlett in Hertfordshire on August 23, 1949. Intended for trial purposes, the aircraft was unfurnished internally, but did have production-standard soundproofing. In external appearance the type was identical with the Hermes IV, apart from the nacelles and Theseus turboprops in place of the Hermes IV's Bristol Hercules 763 radials. Considerable trouble was experienced with the bifurcated jet pipes, but the Hermes V had the distinction of being the largest and fastest turboprop airliner of its day. Development continued, but was plagued by the never-ending series of problems with the Theseus engines. The aircraft was finally written off after a wheels-up landing on April 10, 1951.

The only other Hermes V (G-ALEV) first flew on December 6, 1950 and had a similar test career until grounded as a fatigue-test airframe at Farnborough in September 1953.

Below: G-ALEU, the first prototype HP.82 Hermes V, at Farnborough in September 1949

HP.82 Hermes

Type: medium- and long-range transport
Maker: Handley Page Ltd
Span: 36.6 m (113 ft)
Length: 29.55 m (96 ft 10 in)
Height: 9.14 m (30 ft)
Wing area: 131.6 m² (1408 sq ft)
Weight: maximum 38 566 kg (85 000 lb); empty 23 088 kg (50 900 lb)
Powerplant: four 2490-hp Bristol Theseus 502 turboprops

Performance: maximum speed 565 km/h (351 mph); range 4023 km (2500 miles)
Payload: seats for up to 74 passengers
Crew: 7
Production: 2

Mamba-Marathon, Handley Page

FIRST FLIGHT 1946

THE development of the Handley Page Mamba-Marathon owes a lot, to the celebrated Brabazon Committee. During its 1943 deliberations about the type of aircraft which would be needed by a renascent British civil aviation industry, the Brabazon Committee had formulated the concept for a twin-engined feederliner to replace the DH.84 Dragon and DH.89 Dragon Rapide.

This requirement emerged as the Type 5, but in 1944 pressure from Miles Aircraft Limited resulted in a slight recasting of the requirement to include four-engined aircraft. After specification C.18/44 had been issued in the spring of 1944 to cover a high-wing monoplane able to carry 14 passengers on routes with small, inaccessible airfields on the power of four 330-hp de Havilland Gipsy Queen inline piston engines, the Miles M.60 Marathon was adopted as the Brabazon Committee Type 5A, and the DH.104 Dove as the Type 5B.

The Marathon was intended for use by both the BOAC and BEA, though the latter was also interested in a turboprop-powered derivative. Specification C.15/46 had accordingly been issued on May 19, 1947, resulting in the M.69 Marathon II.

By this time the Miles concern was in deep financial trouble, and on July 5, 1948, Handley Page, seeking a means to stay in the airliner business after the HP.86's failure against the Bristol Type 175 (Britannia), bought out Miles, whose Marathon was momentarily expected to be ordered into production, to the tune of some 50 aircraft. Handley Page also inherited the Marathon II, of which the single prototype was rapidly approaching completion at that time.

The Marathon II first flew on July 21, 1949 and almost ended its career on that same date: the left undercarriage leg refused to come down as the pilot prepared to land, and it was only very skilful flying that finally persuaded the leg to drop. The BEA trials of the aircraft were short: the Mamba-powered aircraft was more noisy than the Gipsy Queen-engined variant, and in early 1950 BEA cancelled its order for the type. The Mamba-Marathon was then used for experimental and racing work before being taken over by the Ministry of Supply early in 1951 as a test aircraft for de Havilland Propellers. In 1953 this sole example of its kind was converted into a testbed for the Alvis Leonides Major radial piston engine.

Below: The Mamba-Marathon 2 in Ministry of Supply markings
Bottom: The Mamba-Marathon, which was eventually broken up at Bitteswell in October 1959

HPR.1 Marathon II

Type: short-range transport
Maker: Handley Page (Reading) Ltd
Span: 19.84 m (65 ft)
Length: 15.93 m (52 ft 3 in)
Height: 4.32 m (14 ft 2 in)
Wing area: 46.4 m² (498 sq ft)
Weight: maximum 8165 kg (18 000 lb); empty 4922 kg (10 850 lb)
Powerplant: two 1010-shp Armstrong Siddeley Mamba turboprops
Performance: cruising speed 418 km/h (260 mph); range 1448 km (900 miles)
Payload: seats for up to 18 passengers
Crew: 2
Production: 1

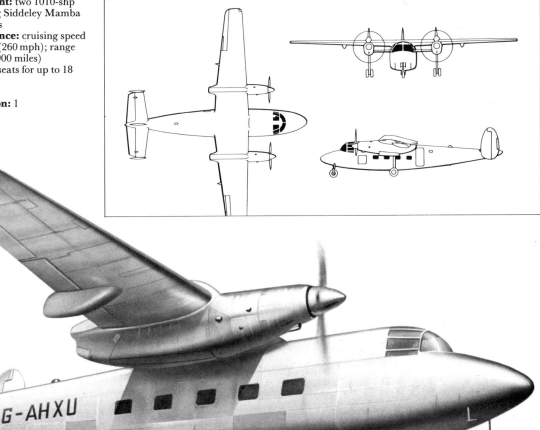

Apollo, Armstrong Whitworth

FIRST FLIGHT 1949

THE Armstrong Whitworth AW.55 Apollo was designed as a competitor to the Vickers Viscount in response to the requirement outlined in the wartime Brabazon Committee's Type II civil transport. It was a short- and medium-range airliner intended for operations in Europe.

Specification C.16/46 to which the Apollo was designed, called for a turboprop-powered airliner to carry between 24 and 30 passengers over a range of 1609 km (1000 miles) at 483 km/h (300 mph). The engine selected was the axial-flow Armstrong Siddeley Mamba, which had the advantage of commendably low frontal area compared with contemporary centrifugal-flow turboprops. However, it was of a basic type still in its design infancy, and so prone to severe teething problems. A clear example of this is seen in the case of the Mamba: in the form first used on the Apollo, the engine should have developed 1010 shp plus 139-kg (307-lb) thrust, whereas it developed only 800 shp.

Right from the beginning of the design, the AW.55 (first named Achilles and Avon before finally becoming Apollo) had a span of 28.04 m (92 ft), but length was increased from 19.66 m (64 ft 6 in) to 20.73 m (68 ft) and at the production stage to 21.79 m (71 ft 6 in), providing accommodation for between 26 and 31 passengers seated two-abreast on each side of a central aisle.

Construction began in 1948 of two flying prototypes and a fuselage for static testing. The first prototype was given the Ministry of Supply serial VX220, and made its initial flight on April 10, 1949. Right from the beginning there were severe problems with the Mamba engines' power output and reliability, and the aircraft itself lacked longitudinal and directional stability. The control problems were remedied without undue difficulty, and the first prototype, re-registered G-AIYN, was available from October 30, 1950 for proving flights, starting with a successful flight to Paris on March 12, 1951. Finally, in July 1951, Mamba Mk 504 engines became available, but even these had severe limitations and problems. This proved the last straw, and in June 1952 further development was halted. The second prototype was subsequently completed, and both aircraft were used for a variety of experimental work for the Ministry of Supply, which had funded them. Both aircraft ended their flying lives in December 1954 when they became structural-test airframes.

196

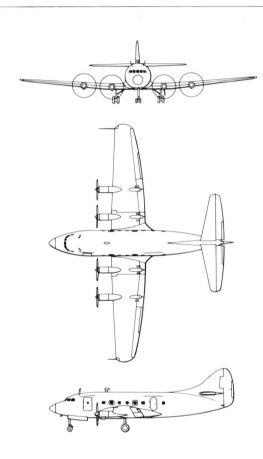

AW.55 Apollo

Type: medium-range transport
Maker: Armstrong Whitworth Aircraft
Span: 28.04 m (92 ft)
Length: 21.79 m (71 ft 6 in)
Height: 7.92 m (26 ft)
Wing area: 91.6 m^2 (986 sq ft)
Weight: maximum 20 412 kg (45 000 lb); empty 13 791 kg (30 800 lb)
Powerplant: four 1010-shp Armstrong Siddeley Mamba Mk 504 turboprops
Performance: cruising speed 444 km/h (276 mph) at 6096 m (20 000 ft); range 1513 km (940 miles)
Payload: 3402 kg (7500 lb); seats for up to 31 passengers
Crew: 3
Production: 2

Left: The prototype Apollo in the early months of 1950 when it suffered problems with its engines and stability
Top: The same prototype in new livery with four-bladed propellers on the inboard engines and an increased tailplane span and fin area to compensate for its earlier stability problems

Princess, Saro

FIRST FLIGHT 1952

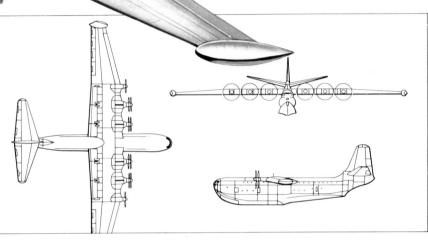

THE ultimate expression of the large civil flying boat concept, the Saunders-Roe SR.45 Princess marks a vital stage in the development of turboprop-powered airliners, combined with an obsolescent notion of the air travel requirements of the world in the aftermath of World War II. The origins of this huge aircraft lie in the days leading up to World War II, when Saunders-Roe built the A.37, a scaled-down flying model of a projected maritime-reconnaissance flying boat with an anticipated all-up weight of 83462 kg (184000 lb). The design ultimately bore fruit in the Short/Saunders-Roe Shetland reconnaissance flying boat, with a gross weight of 56700 kg (125000 lb).

At the end of World War II, however, the possibility of using high-power turboprop engines led Saunders-Roe to revive its interest in giant flying boats, this time as long-range passenger transports. This coincided with renewed official interest in the type, and in July 1945 Saunders-Roe was asked to tender for such an aircraft, which so suited the needs of the British Overseas Airways Corporation that in January 1946 the airline asked the Ministry of Supply to order three examples.

The order was placed in May 1946, and subject to final revision with Bristol Proteus turboprops after the cancellation of the Rolls-Royce Tweed programme, was named Princess, after the name Dollar Princess had been considered and rejected.

Of relatively conventional flying boat layout, the Princess was powered by ten Bristol Proteus turboprops, each rated at 3200 shp with 363-kg (800-lb) thrust. Eight of the engines were mounted in pairs

driving contra-rotating propellers 5.64 m (18 ft 6 in) in diameter, and the last two units were mounted singly in the outboard of the three nacelles in each wing. Some 65916 litres (14500 Imp gal) of fuel would give the Princess a range of 8851 km (5500 miles), it was hoped. The fuselage was of the 'double-bubble' type, the upper lobe being pressurized to ensure the comfort of the passengers, who were provided with a bar, bunks, and several lavatories and powder rooms.

The building programme was slow, and it was not until August 20, 1952 that the first Princess was launched, taking to the air two days later. Flight trials revealed serious problems with the gearboxes for the contra-rotating propellers, however, and BOAC cancelled its order.

SR.45 Princess

Type: long-range transport flying boat
Maker: Saunders-Roe Ltd
Span: 66.9 m (219 ft 6 in)
Length: 45.11 m (148 ft)
Height: 17.38 m (57 ft)
Wing area: 466.28 m² (5019 sq ft)
Weight: maximum 149687 kg (330000 lb); empty not available
Powerplant: ten 3200-shp Bristol Proteus 600 turboprops
Performance: maximum cruising speed 612 km/h (380 mph) at 11278 m (37000 ft); range 8851 km (5500 miles)
Payload: generally seats for up to 105 passengers
Production: 3

Top and left: G-ALUN, the only SR.45 Princess to fly. It was powered by ten Proteus 600 series turboprops, eight paired in the inner four nacelles, with two single engines in the outers

Viscount, Vickers-Armstrongs

FIRST FLIGHT 1948

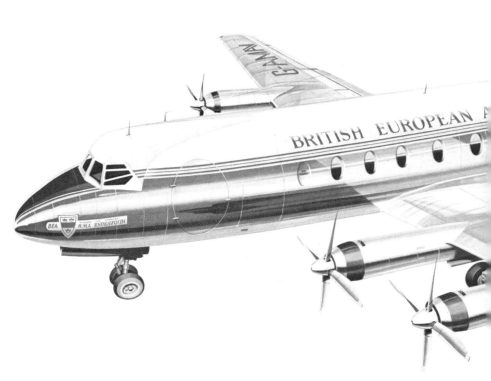

THE origin of the Viscount lay in the 1944 discussions between the members of the Brabazon Committee and the designers of Vickers-Armstrongs on the possibility of developing a turboprop transport for European operations.

Vickers was already working on the VC1 Viking, a civil transport derived in part from the Wellington bomber, but was more than interested in a possible successor to the type, powered by turboprop engines. Resulting from deliberations between the industry and the committee, therefore, requirements were drawn up for two high-speed transports intended for European routes. The Brabazon IIA resulted in the piston-engined Airspeed Ambassador, while the Brabazon IIB led to the turboprop Vickers VC2 Viscount.

Three concepts for a Brabazon IIB were presented to the committee and the Ministry of Aircraft Production, the choice finally being made in April 1945 of a pressurized model capable of carrying 24 passengers or a payload of 3402 kg (7500 lb) at a speed of 478 km/h (297 mph) at 6096 m (20 000 ft) over a range of 1674 km (1040 miles) on the power of four Rolls-Royce Dart turboprops each rated at 1130 ehp. Designated Type 453 by the company, the aircraft was the design of Rex Pierson assisted by George Edwards. Two prototypes, detailed in specification C.8/46 of April 17, 1946, were ordered on March 9, 1946. This specification reduced the required range to 1127 km (700 miles) and the speed to 444 km/h (276 mph). The name envisaged for what was now the Type 609 was Viceroy. This was changed to

Viscount after the partition of India in 1947.

Production of the two prototypes for the Ministry of Supply began in December 1946, as did work on a third prototype, funded by Vickers. By this time the ministry called for Armstrong Siddeley Mamba engines and a fuselage stretch of 2.74 m (9 ft) to raise passenger capacity to 32, a figure specified by the newly formed British European Airways. The Dart engine, temporarily superseded in official favour by the promising Mamba, was reinstated on August 27, 1947 and it was four RDa.1 engines which powered the prototype when it first flew on July 16, 1948 as the Type 630.

Already, though, official and airline interest in the Viscount had waned in favour of the Airspeed Ambassador. The situation was remedied by the

Top left: Close-up of the nose of the prototype Vickers Viscount 630 showing the last two letters of its designation G-AHRF. It was assembled at Foxwarren and flew at Wisley in July 1948
Above: The Viscount became one of the mainstays of medium-range airlines in the 1950s and 1960s
Below: The Dart 506 or 510 series engines were installed in beautifully engineered powerplants with four cowl panels arranged in two hinged groups. Rotol supplied the propellers

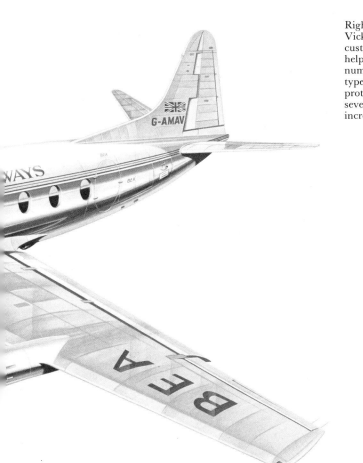

Right: The willingness of Vickers-Armstrongs to custom-build for an airline helps to explain the large number of Viscount sub-types. Starting with the V.630 prototype it was 'stretched' several times, with steadily increasing gross weight

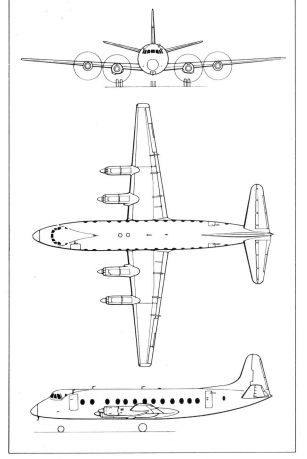

Viscount, Type 810

Type: short- and medium-range transport
Maker: Vickers-Armstrongs Aircraft Ltd
Span: 28.56 m (93 ft 8½ in)
Length: 26.11 m (85 ft 8 in)
Height: 8.15 m (26 ft 9 in)
Wing area: 89.47 m² (963 sq ft)
Weight: maximum 32 886 kg (72 500 lb); empty 19 731 kg (43 500 lb)
Powerplant: four 1990-ehp Rolls-Royce Dart RDa. 7/1 Mk 525 turboprops
Performance: maximum cruising speed 575 km/h (357 mph) at 6096 m (20 000 ft); range with maximum payload 2554 km (1587 miles)
Payload: 6350 kg (14 000 lb); seats for up to 65 passengers
Crew: 5
Production: 445 (all types)

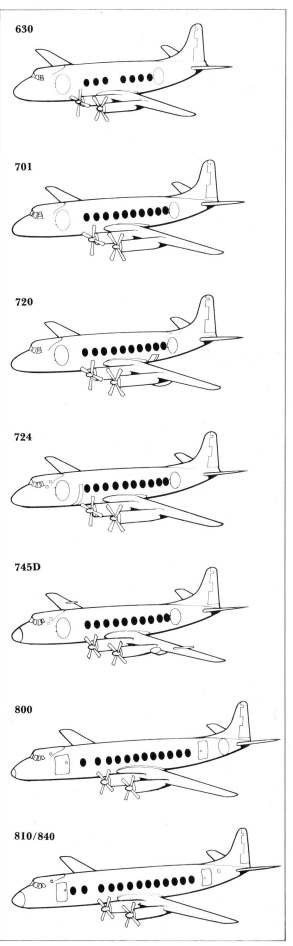

630

701

720

724

745D

800

810/840

appearance of the RDa. 3: with 40% more power available, Vickers could increase span by 1.52 m (5 ft) and length by 2.24 m (7 ft 4 in) to produce the 53-passenger Type 700, which could cruise at 536 km/h (333 mph) on its four 1550-ehp RDa. 3s. The Ministry of Supply ordered the prototype of such a model on February 24, 1949, this machine first flying on August 28, 1950. The performance of the Type 700, capable of cruising with 53 passengers at 499 km/h (310 mph), considerably impressed BEA, which had already flown fare-paying services between London and Paris with the Vickers-owned Type 630. On August 3, 1950, therefore, BEA ordered 20 Type 701s, improved Type 700s for which the order was later raised to 26.

The first of these aircraft was delivered on January 3, 1953 and after receiving its certificate of airworthiness on April 17, 1953, began the world's first turboprop-powered scheduled service on the next day, some eight years after the Brabazon Committee's requirement had been formulated.

The success of the new type was confirmed by a number of important orders, notably from Trans-Canada Air Lines for 15 Type 724s in November 1952, and from Capital Airlines for 40 Type 745s in August 1954.

Major design variants were the Types 724 (new fuel system, two-pilot cockpit and increased weight), 745 (RDa. 6 Mk 510 engines and increased weight), 800 (fuselage stretched by 1.17 m [3 ft 10 in] to accommodate 71 passengers) and 810 (RDa. 7/1 engines, structural strengthening and increased weight)

Above: G-AOHL *Charles Sturt*, a Vickers V.802 Viscount which first flew in 1957
Left: The left-hand side panel of the cockpit
Below: The right-hand side panel of the cockpit

Tu-114, Tupolev

FIRST FLIGHT 1956

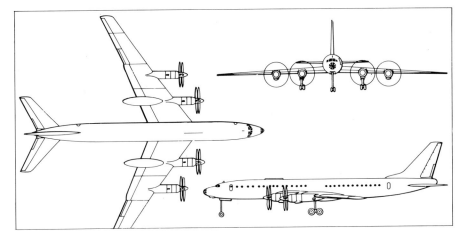

THE Tupolev Tu-114 long-range airliner was developed in parallel with the Tu-95 (Tu-20) heavy bomber. Among the many distinctions of the Tu-114 is the fact that it was the world's fastest propeller-driven transport, and with the Tu-95 the world's only all-swept propeller-driven aircraft.

Early details of the Tu-114 are sparse, but it seems that the prototype completed its flight test programme in 1956, the powerplant at this time comprising four 12 000-ehp Kuznetsov NK-12M turboprops developed by a team under N D Kuznetsov from an unsuccessful unit produced by 'liberated' German engineers at Kuybyshev on the basis of the wartime Junkers Jumo 012. On production aircraft the engines were fully developed NK-12MVs, each with a higher rating and driving four-blade contrarotating propellers.

Accommodation options were wide, thanks to the provision of three main cabins and four smaller cabins. For continental operations the seating was normally for 170 passengers basically six-abreast; for intercontinental operations normal accommodation was between 100 and 120; and for shorter-range flights up to 220 passengers could be carried in seven- or eight-abreast seating. The cabins, were furnished in a somewhat old-fashioned way, with brass lamps and luggage racks.

The Tu-114, called *Rossiya*, was intended as a replacement for the Ilyushin Il-14 twin-engined medium-range airliner on Aeroflot's longer routes, and the new aircraft's capabilities were well demonstrated by a number of records set up in 1960 and 1961 with NK-12M engines. Considerable trouble was experienced with engine overheating and fires, however, and the Tu-114 did not enter scheduled service until April 1961, autumn 1959 having been the target.

Aeroflot's routes and the emergence of pure jet airliners had by this time reduced the need for the Tu-114, hence restricting the numbers built. The only variant of the type was the Tu-114D, probably a demilitarized Tu-95 with a few windows and intended for urgent flights over very long ranges.

Retired from airline service in October 1976, the Tu-114 has since been given a new lease of life by transformation into the Tu-126 'Moss' airborne warning and control system (AWACS) aircraft, with a large radar scanner in a rotodome above the fuselage.

Tu-114

Type: long-range transport
Maker: Tupolev Design Bureau
Span: 51.1 m (167 ft 8 in)
Length: 54.1 m (177 ft 6 in)
Height: 13.1 m (43 ft)
Wing area: 311.1 m² (3349 sq ft)
Weight: maximum 175 000 kg (385 802 lb); empty 93 000 kg (205 026 lb)
Powerplant: four 15 000-ehp Kuznetsov NK-12MV turboprops
Performance: cruising speed 770 km/h (478 mph) at 9000 m (29 528 ft); range with a payload of 15 000 kg (33 069 lb) and reserves 8950 km (5561 miles)
Payload: 30 000 lb (66 138 lb); seats for up to 220 passengers
Crew: 6
Production: approx 30

Left and below: The Tu-114 is the only major propeller-driven transport with a marked swept-back wing. Each four-blade unit of its vast contraprops could be pushed round independently by hand

Britannia, Bristol

FIRST FLIGHT 1952

THE Britannia resulted from requirement C.2/47, issued by the Ministry of Supply on behalf of the British Overseas Airways Corporation, for a Medium-Range Empire airliner. Bristol had at first responded to a BOAC requirement of 1946 by proposing the Lockheed L.749 Constellation re-engined with Bristol Centaurus 660 radials, but Treasury refusal of such expenditure of US dollars led to the C.2/47 requirement. Eight designs proposed by five firms resulted, but only the Bristol Type 175 came anywhere near meeting the exacting specifications.

Consultations during October 1947 resulted in the design being fixed at a span of 39.62 m (130 ft); a payload of 48 passengers, luggage and 1529 kg (3370 lb) of freight; a gross weight of 46 857 kg (103 300 lb); and a speed of 499 km/h (310 mph) on the power of four Centaurus 662 radials. It was also considered whether or not Bristol Proteus turboprops or Napier Nomad compound engines might be fitted, but Bristol would not guarantee the type's performance with the alternative engines. Financial wranglings between the Ministry and the airline followed, but on July 5, 1948 the Ministry of Supply ordered three prototypes. All were to have the Centaurus radial, though the second and third were to be convertible to Proteus turboprops, and the third was to be fitted out to full airline standards.

An entry-into-service date of 1954 was anticipated, but the project was thrown back into the melting pot in October 1948 when BOAC decided that the model engined with Proteus turboprops

merited more attention. The result was a design suitable for African and Far Eastern routes, to be engined with either Proteus or Centaurus engines. BOAC agreed to buy 25, to operate initially with Centaurus but later with Proteus engines, the contract being signed only on July 28, 1949.

The delay before signature gave Bristol yet more time for reflection, this time centred on the possibility of upgrading the basic design for transatlantic operations with extra fuel, a maximum weight of 58 968 kg (130 000 lb), a payload of 10 660 kg (23 500 lb) including 83 passengers, and four-wheel main bogies instead of two-wheel units. Either Centaurus or Proteus engines were possible, though the success of the Proteus 3 in 1950 led to the abandonment of the Centaurus concept even in

Above: A Britannia Series 101 comes in to land at Filton, Bristol. This aircraft was damaged beyond repair at Littleton-upon-Severn in 1954 Below: A Britannia Series 312 *County of Argyll* of Caledonian. It was withdrawn from service at Luton in 1972

BOAC's strategy. Structural testing of a specimen wing and attached fuselage was so impressive that maximum take-off weights up to 63504 kg (140000 lb) became possible, with a consequent increase in fuel capacity.

The first prototype of what had by now become the 90-seat Britannia took to the air on August 16, 1952 under the power of four Proteus 625 engines in place of the proposed Proteus 705s. This engine was specified for the 15 Series 100 aircraft now to be bought by BOAC, but the first scheduled service flown by this original operator was delayed until February 1, 1957 as a result of a harrowing number of teething troubles with the Proteus turboprops, centred mostly on icing problems.

The Series 100 aircraft was followed by the project-only Series 200 all-cargo model with longer fuselage; the Series 250 long-fuselage mixed cargo/freight model for the Royal Air Force (23 aircraft); and finally, in May 1955, by the definitive long-range Series 300, whose fuselage was 3.12 m (10 ft 3 in) longer than that of the Series 100. All three long-fuselage models were cleared for take-off at 70308 kg (155000 lb), though this figure was increased as more powerful engines and outer-wing tankage were incorporated in the 310 series.

Total production of the Series 300 reached 45 aircraft, all of which proved highly successful in service. The early delays had caught up with the design, however, and the availability of the Series 300 was overshadowed by the appearance of the considerably faster long-range turbojet airliners.

Above left: The first Laker Britannia, G-ANBM, on overhaul at Prestwick. The aircraft was passed to an Indonesian operator in 1969 – 12 years after receiving a certificate of airworthiness
Above: The flight-deck of a Britannia 102 G-ANBF, which operated with BOAC and Britannia Airways

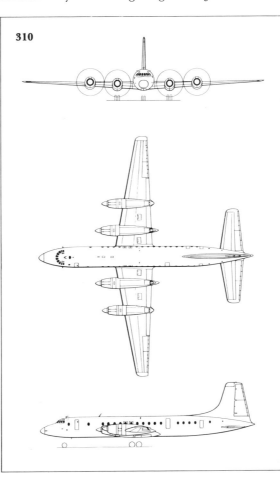

310

Britannia 311-319 Series

Type: long-range transport
Maker: Bristol Aircraft Ltd
Span: 43.36 m (142 ft 3 in)
Length: 37.87 m (124 ft 3 in)
Height: 11.43 m (37 ft 6 in)
Wing area: 192.77 m²
(2075 sq ft)
Weight: maximum 83915 kg
(185000 lb); empty 37439 kg
(82537 lb)
Powerplant: four 4450-ehp
Bristol Proteus 761
turboprops
Performance: cruising speed
575 km/h (357 mph) at
7925 m (26000 ft); range with
maximum payload 6868 km
(4268 miles)
Payload: 15831 kg
(34900 lb); seats for up to 139
passengers
Crew: 7
Production: 85 (all types)

F27 Friendship, Fokker

FIRST FLIGHT 1955

GIVEN the company's long association with the production of twin-engined medium-range airliners, it is hardly surprising that the first major civil aircraft developed by Fokker after World War II was such a type. While the British were developing their first turboprop-powered airliners against a relatively sated market, Fokker was building up a comprehensive picture of what most operators would like in the way of a DC-3/C-47 replacement from the mid 1950s onwards.

From this bank of information the Fokker designers came up with their P.275 concept during the late summer of 1950. The aircraft was to be a shoulder-wing machine with accommodation for up to 32 passengers and powered by a pair of Rolls-Royce Dart turboprops. From this idea emerged the F27, able to carry up to 40 passengers in pressurized comfort over a range 500 km (311 miles), and capable of operating from small airfields thanks to the provision of double-slotted flaps. Confident that the type was a potential best-seller, the Dutch government in 1953 funded the production of two flying and two test aircraft.

While construction of the prototypes was underway, the company launched an intensive sales effort, and this soon began to yield orders. The first prototype flew on November 24, 1955 and was immediately involved in an intensive flight trials programme. The second prototype, which flew on January 29, 1957, was typical of the production standard aircraft, with Dart 511 engines in place of the first prototype's Dart 507s, and the fuselage stretched by 0.91 m (3 ft) to seat 36 passengers in

place of 32. In this guise maximum take-off weight was 16 193 kg (35 700 lb). Tests revealed that the double-slotted flaps were unnecessary for an adequate short-field performance, so less complex and costly single-slotted flaps were decided upon.

The local-operator interest generated by the F27, now named the Friendship, is indicated by the fact that Fairchild secured a licence-production agreement for the type in the United States. The first Fokker-built F27 flew on March 23, 1958, entering service with Aer Lingus in December of that year. The Dutch-built F27 was beaten into service, however, by the Fairchild F-27, which had a longer nose for weather radar, extra fuel tankage, American instrumentation and seating for up to 40 passengers. The first two American F-27s flew on

Above right: The F27 featured a very long-legged Dowty main landing gear which was, unusually, pneumatically operated. The twin-wheel main units retract backward into the engine nacelles

Above: An F27 of Wien Air Alaska; like many operators in the USA Wien Air Alaska was formed through amalgamations of smaller firms. Among these airlines was Alaska's oldest, Wien Alaska Airlines founded by Noel Wien in 1924

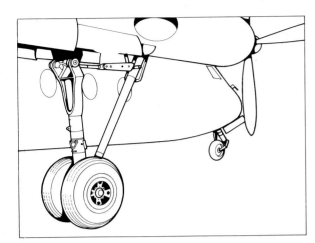

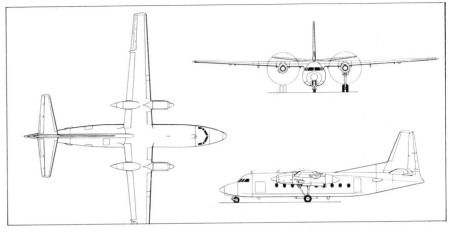

April 12 and May 23, 1958, and the aircraft received its Federal Aviation Administration Type Approval on July 16.

The F27 and F-27 were produced largely in parallel for some time, and the type is still in Dutch production as the world's best-selling turboprop airliner. The initial model was the F27 Mk 100/F-27, soon followed by the F27 Mk 200/F-27A with uprated Dart Mk 528s for higher speeds and better airfield performance, especially in 'hot and high' conditions, and take-off weights up to 20 412 kg (45 000 lb).

To meet airline requirements for a model able to operate as a freighter if necessary, there appeared in 1958 the F27 Mk 300/F-27B with a strengthened floor and large freight-loading door in the left side

of the forward fuselage. The F27 Mk 400, and closely similar F27M Troopship, had Dart Mk 528 engines, and being intended mainly for military operators, had no Fairchild equivalent. There followed the F27 Mk 600, derived from the convertible Mk 300 and 400, but with improved RDa. 7 turboprops in place of the earlier RDa. 6s, and a simplified fuselage floor. The F27 Mk 700 was similar, but powered by RDa. 6 engines.

All the models described above were of the same basic type. The first model to deviate from the norm is the F27 Mk 500, which was proposed in 1961 but only ordered initially in 1966. This has a fuselage stretch of 1.5 m (4 ft 11 in), and was partnered by the Fairchild FH-227, which has a fuselage extension of 1.83 m (6 ft).

F27 Mk 500

Type: medium-range transport
Maker: Fokker-VFW BV
Span: 29 m (95 ft 2 in)
Length: 25.06 m (82 ft 2½ in)
Height: 8.71 m (28 ft 7¼ in)
Wing area: 70 m² (753 sq ft)
Weight: maximum 20 412 kg (45 000 lb); empty 11 950 kg (26 345 lb)
Powerplant: two 2140-hp Rolls-Royce Dart 532-7R turboprops
Performance: cruising speed 480 km/h (298 mph) at 6096 m (20 000 ft); range with 52 passengers and reserves 1740 km (1082 miles)
Payload: 5967 kg (13 155 lb); seats for up to 60 passengers
Crew: 2 to 3
Production: 500 (Fokker orders) and 207 (Fairchild-built) by 1980

Far left: An F27-400 operated by Gulf Aviation, which has been called Gulf Air since 1973
Left: A Fokker Friendship at Austin, Texas. The special long-nosed version, built by Fairchild, was designed to incorporate an all-weather radar

Il-18, Ilyushin

FIRST FLIGHT 1957

THE Ilyushin Il-18 was the second turbine-powered Russian airliner, but the first to be specifically designed as such, the turbojet-engined Tupolev Tu-104 being a civil derivative of the Tu-16 bomber. The Il-18, at first called *Moskva*, was produced in response to an Aeroflot requirement for a turboprop-powered medium-range airliner.

The aircraft designed to meet this fairly exacting specification was a clean-looking four-engined machine similar in most respects to the contemporary British and US turboprop airliners, the Vickers Vanguard and Lockheed L-188 Electra. Powered by 4000-ehp Kuznetsov NK-4 turboprops, the first prototype took to the air on July 4, 1957 and soon proved itself to have admirable performance and handling. This aircraft was followed by four other

prototypes, and then by 20 pre-production aircraft powered alternately by NK-4 and 4000-ehp Ivchenko AI-20 turboprops for comparative purposes. (The AI-20 and NK-4 were parallel developments of the same corpus of German research and development in World War II.) The AI-20 proved itself generally superior to the NK-4, and it was this engine which was selected for the initial production model, the Il-18V.

Trials of the Il-18 were completed by March 1958 after a highly satisfactory series of flights had been made, the most notable, perhaps, being that from Moscow via Irkutsk to Petropavlovsk in Kamchatka. The distance of 9000 km (5592 miles) was flown at an average speed of 600 km/h (373 mph) at an altitude of 8000 m (26 246 ft).

Above: An Il-18D operated by Cubana, the nationalized airline of Cuba, which was formed in 1929 and taken over by Castro in 1959
Below: The Il-18 has been used by CSA, Interflug, Malev. LOT and by non-Soviet bloc operators like Air Guinée, Air Mali and United Arab Airlines/Egyptair

Production of the Il-18 began in 1957 at Factory No 30 outside Moscow, ending in 1968. Early operations were in the form of extended route-proving trials with loads of freight and mail in the Ukraine. Passenger-carrying services were inaugurated on April 20, 1959 on the route from Moscow to Adler and to Alma Ata, with the first international service being flown from Moscow to London in October 1959. These operations, flown with Il-18s and Il-18Bs (derived from the Il-18 but with take-off weight increased by 2000 kg [4409 lb] and with accommodation for 84 instead of 75 passengers), proved the general efficiency of the type, which was marred by some serious crashes resulting from problems with the AI-20 engines.

With these difficulties resolved, production was switched to the Il-18V in 1961. This model could seat up to 111 passengers, and is distinguishable by its repositioned windows and forward door, and by the smoother contours of the nose. More efficient AI-20Ks were at first fitted, but these have generally been replaced by AI-20Ms of higher rating.

Next to appear was the single long-range Il-18I, with more fuel tankage in the wings to increase range from 4700 km (2921 miles) to 6500 km (4039 miles), and the ability to carry an additional 500 kg (1102 lb) of payload in the form of an increase in passenger capacity to 125 by extending the pressurized cabin back into the previous rear baggage compartment. The Il-18I did not enter service, but many of its improvements were incorporated in the long-range Il-18D, which entered service in 1966, powered by 4250-ehp AI-20Ms.

The final production variant was the Il-18E or Il-18Ye, with the fuselage of the Il-18D but the wings of the Il-18V with their 32% lower fuel capacity. The Il-18E was designed for rapid conversion into any of four seating layouts: six-abreast 122-seat summer, five-abreast 100-seat summer, six-abreast 110-seat winter and five-abreast 90-seat winter. This model entered service with Aeroflot during 1966 and it appears likely that earlier models have been brought up to Il-18E standard.

The most successful Russian airliner to date, the Il-18 was also supplied to non-Soviet bloc countries: Air Guinée (4), Air Mali (3), Ghana Airways (8, all returned), Royal Afghan Airlines (1), and United Arab Airlines/Egyptair (4). The latest development of the Il-18 has been into the Il-38 'May' maritime-reconnaissance aircraft.

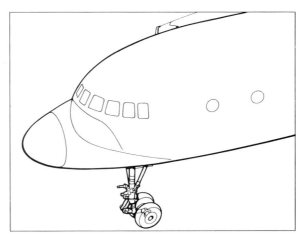

Left: The long-nosed front fuselage of the Il-18 was unusual in having a pressure bulkhead immediately ahead of the cockpit and a long way from the tip of the nose.

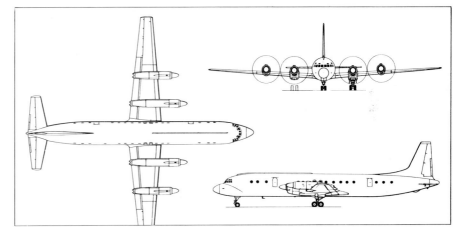

Il-18E

Type: medium-range transport
Maker: Ilyushin Design Bureau
Span: 37.4 m (122 ft 8 in)
Length: 35.9 m (117 ft 9 in)
Height: 10.3 m (33 ft 9½ in)
Wing area: 140 m² (1507 sq ft)
Weight: maximum 61 200 kg (134 920 lb); empty 34 630 kg (76 345 lb)
Powerplant: four 4250-ehp Ivchenko AI-20M turboprops
Performance: cruising speed up to 650 km/h (404 mph) at 8000 m (26 246 ft); range with maximum payload and reserves 2500 km (1553 miles)
Payload: 13 500 kg (29 762 lb); seats for up to 122 passengers
Crew: 4 to 5
Production: minimum 800

CU-T900

L-188 Electra, Lockheed

FIRST FLIGHT 1957

THE Lockheed L-188 Electra has the distinction of being the only large American airliner to have been developed with turboprop engines. Potentially an excellent aircraft, the Electra was unfortunately beset by severe structural problems and then surpassed in performance and operating economics by pure jet aircraft just as its fortunes were beginning to improve once again. To a great extent the L-188 was the result of the Capital Airlines' order for the Vickers Viscount. Though the 'big four' US operators did not follow suit, neither did they ignore the possibilities of turboprop power, and this foresight resulted in an American Airlines' requirement for a high-capacity short-haul airliner suitable for US inter-city routes.

Lockheed's L-188 was designed to meet this need, and the promise of the type was reflected in American Airlines' order of June 10, 1955 for 35 L-188s, and in Eastern Air Lines' order of September 27, 1955 for 40 similar aircraft.

The Lockheed concept was for an aircraft with considerably greater capacity (86 passengers) than the Viscount, but with comparable field performance thanks to the use of Allison 501 turboprops and an efficient wing design. The L-188 seemed ideal for its designed task, and Lockheed received a total of 144 orders by the time the first Electra flew on December 6, 1957, some 16½ months before the rival Vickers Vanguard. By the time of this first flight, the Electra had been fixed at a capacity of 100 passengers to be carried over a range of 3701 km (2300 miles) after take-off at a weight of

Above: The Electra operated with a number of major airlines in the early 1960s but accidents led to a fall off in orders

Below: A Jet Set Travel Club L-188C Electra at Long Beach International Airport, California

51 257 kg (113 000 lb). Three further development aircraft followed in 1958, and American Airlines received the first production Electra on December 5, 1958. The airline could not begin scheduled services with its new aircraft, however, as a result of a pilots' strike, leaving Eastern Air Lines this honour on January 12, 1959 with a service between New York and Miami.

Thereafter the Electra quickly established itself as an extremely popular inter-city airliner in North America. The success of the Electra seemed assured, with orders from several US airlines, the Dutch flag carrier KLM, and several operators in South-east Asia and Australia. But only a week after American Airlines finally began Electra services on January 23, 1959, one of its Electras crashed, as did a Braniff Electra on September 28, 1959 and a Northwest Airlines Electra on March 17, 1960.

After evidence that the aircraft had broken up in the air, there was considerable pressure on the Federal Aviation Administration for the grounding of all Electras while the cause was investigated. The FAA merely imposed a 'speed limit' on the surviving 52 Electras: from March 25, 1960 they were restricted to 510 km/h (317 mph), reduced a few days later to 417 km/h (259 mph). During the following investigation, it was discovered that the Electra had a major design defect in the engine mountings. If such a mounting were only slightly damaged (in a heavy landing, for example), it was then possible for a structurally disastrous engine/propeller oscillation to ensue, resulting in

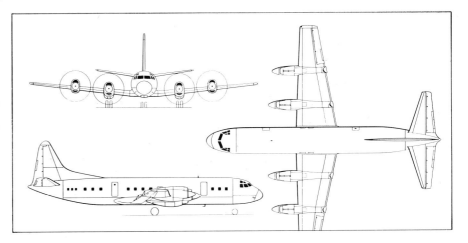

wing failure. Lockheed immediately set about 'beefing up' Electras already built, type approval for the revised aircraft being secured on January 5, 1961. Modified aircraft, designated Electra IIs, returned to operations on February 24, 1961.

Lockheed had already developed the L-188C Electra for overwater operations, with additional fuel increasing range from the 4023 km (2500 miles) of the L-188A to 4860 km (3020 miles) with maximum fuel. The last 55 Electras built were to this standard, but it is interesting to note that the earlier crashes had so curtailed Electra orders that only 26 more were later sold. The manifest virtues of the Electra have been recognized by the type's development into the most widely sold maritime-reconnaissance aircraft, the Lockheed P-3 Orion.

L-188C Electra

Type: medium-range transport
Maker: Lockheed Aircraft Corporation
Span: 30.18 m (99 ft)
Length: 31.9 m (104 ft 8 in)
Height: 10.04 m (32 ft 11¼ in)
Wing area: 120.8 m² (1300 sq ft)
Weight: maximum 52 617 kg (116 000 lb); empty 25 855 kg (57 000 lb)
Powerplant: four 3750-ehp Allison 501-D13 turboprops
Performance: maximum cruising speed 652 km/h (405 mph) at 6706 m (22 000 ft); range with a payload of 9979 kg (22 000 lb) 4023 km (2500 miles)
Payload: 11 975 kg (26 400 lb); seats for up to 99 passengers
Crew: 3 to 4
Production: 170

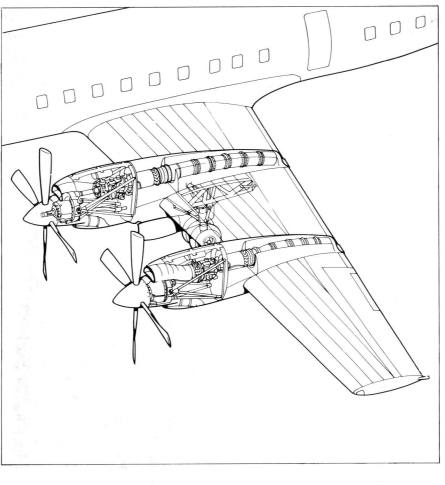

Left: The Electra was notable for its Allison 501-D13 turboprop with its separately mounted reduction gearbox. In 1959 serious defects in the engine mountings were discovered, and the engine nacelle and surrounding wing structure had to be strengthened

BAe 748, British Aerospace

FRIST FLIGHT 1960

THE origins of the BAe 748 can be traced back to the now infamous government white paper foretelling the demise of the manned military aircraft, on which Avro had devoted its exclusive efforts for more than ten years. The company therefore turned its attentions to a feederliner replacement for the Douglas DC-3.

From the Avro point of view, the difficulty was that Fokker was already well along the way to production with the F27 Friendship, and had secured considerable orders. The Avro competitor, the company felt, should therefore be able to attract customers with superior performance allied to cheaper purchasing and operating costs. After initial studies for a machine resembling a scaled-down F27, Avro finally opted for a 748 design centred on two Rolls-Royce Dart turboprops and a low-wing configuration. Detail design of the Hawker Siddeley 748, as it had by then become, was started in January 1959: maximum weight was to be 14 969 kg (33 000 lb) and accommodation for 36 passengers four-abreast was to be provided.

Two prototypes for flight trials were begun in parallel with two static test airframes, the first aircraft flying on June 24, 1960 and the second on April 10, 1961. Flight trials soon proved that structural weight-saving by the use of fail-safe rather than safe-life structures had benefited the type, and that the provision of slotted Fowler flaps gave the 748 good short-field performance.

The two prototypes, powered by Rolls-Royce Dart RDa. 610 Mk 514 engines, were followed by 18 generally similar Series 1 aircraft, the main buyer being Aerolineas Argentinas with 12, but the first purchaser was Skyways Coach-Air (now Dan-Air) with three for cross-Channel flights early in 1962.

The next model was the 748 Series 2, which entered production in 1961. This model features more powerful Dart RDa. 7 Mk 531 engines and a maximum take-off weight of 20 183 kg (44 495 lb), some 2266 kg (4995 lb) greater than the maximum take-off weight of the Series 1 aircraft. A Series 1 aircraft converted to Series 2 standard first flew on November 6, 1961 and deliveries began in October 1962. A total of 198 were built before production was switched to the Series 2A.

This model was introduced to improve the performance of the Series 2 by the provision of more powerful engines, the Dart RDa. 7 Mk 532-2L or -2S (later redesignated Mk 534-2 and 535-2 respectively), each rated at 2280 ehp. Orders for the type total 71, with another 25 of a sub-model unofficially designated Series 2C. This model, intended primarily for military users, is fitted with a large freight door, measuring 1.72 m (5 ft 7¾ in) in height and 2.67 m (8 ft 9 in) in width, in the left side of the rear fuselage. A strengthened floor is fitted, and an air-portable freight hoist is optional. This model first flew on December 31, 1971, in the form of a converted Series 2A aircraft.

Hawker Siddeley was eventually absorbed into British Aerospace, and it was this concern which introduced from early 1979 the Series 2B aircraft. This is intended for operations in 'hot and high' conditions, admirably suited for the increasing numbers of airlines in West Africa and the Caribbean. Power is provided by a pair of 2280-ehp Dart

Series 2B

748 Series 2A

Type: short-range transport
Maker: British Aerospace Aircraft Group
Span: 30.02 m (98 ft 6 in)
Length: 20.42 m (67 ft)
Height: 7.57 m (24 ft 10 in)
Wing area: 75.3 m² (811 sq ft)
Weight: maximum 21 092 kg (46 500 lb); empty 12 159 kg (26 806 lb)
Powerplant: two 2280-ehp Rolls-Royce Dart 534-2 or 535-2 turboprops
Performance: cruising speed 452 km/h (281 mph); range with maximum payload and reserves 1360 km (846 miles)
Payload: 5304 kg (11 694 lb); seats for up to 58 passengers
Crew: 3
Production: 352 ordered by 1980

Left: Checking the right-hand engine of a BAe 748. The twin Rolls-Royce Dart RDa.7 Mk 536-2s each drive a Dowty Rotol four-blade constant-speed fully-feathering propeller

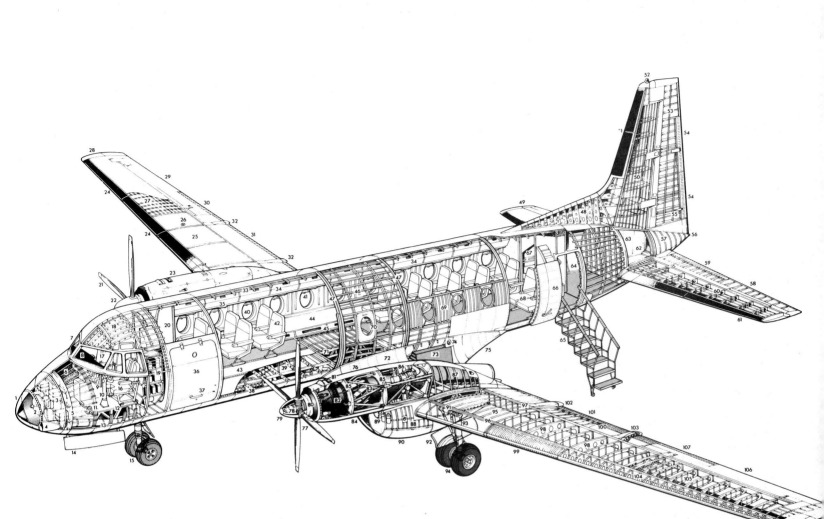

BAe 748

1 Radome
2 Radar scanner
3 Electrical equipment
4 Air intake
5 Front bulkhead
6 Nose structure
7 Windscreens
8 Instrument panel shroud
9 Instrument panel
10 Control column
11 Rudder pedals
12 Nosewheel bay structure
13 Air ducting
14 Nosewheel door
15 Twin nosewheels
16 Pilot's seat
17 Co-pilot's seat
18 Cabin roof structure
19 Radio rack
20 Forward baggage hold
21 Dowty Rotol four-blade propeller
22 Spinner
23 Right engine cowlings
24 Leading edge de-icing sections

25 Right wing fuel tank
26 Fuel filler
27 Wing stringers
28 Right wingtip
29 Right aileron
30 Aileron tab
31 Right flap
32 Flap fairings
33 Fuselage frames
34 Overhead baggage lockers
35 Passenger service units
36 Door handle
37 Door handle
38 Air conditioning heat exchangers
39 Cabin floor structure
40 Cabin windows
41 Window blind
42 Passenger seats
43 Floor fixing rails
44 Cabin trim panels
45 Air louvres
46 Centre fuselage construction
47 Wing beam carrying frames
48 Fin root fairing
49 Right tailplane

50 Fin construction
51 Fin leading edge de-icing
52 Anti-collision light
53 Rudder construction
54 Rudder tabs
55 Tab control rod
56 Navigation light
57 Tailcone
58 Left elevator
59 Elevator tab
60 Left tailplane construction
61 Tailplane leading edge de-icing
62 Fin-tailplane joint
63 Aft fuselage bulkhead
64 Aft baggage hold
65 Folding airstairs
66 Passenger door
67 Toilet compartment
68 Rear cabin seating
69 Window frame panel construction
70 Escape hatch
71 Centre wing construction
72 Wing root fillet
73 Water methanol boost tank
74 Filler cap

75 Trailing edge fairing
76 Left engine top cowling
77 Dowty Rotol four-blade propeller
78 Propeller pitch change mechanism
79 Spinner
80 Engine air intake
81 Oil cooler duct
82 Rolls-Royce Dart 535-2 turboprop
83 Engine mounting frame
84 Engine bottom cowlings
85 Fireproof bulkheads
86 Engine accessory equipment
87 Jet pipe
88 Undercarriage bay
89 Hydraulic equipment
90 Mainwheel doors
91 Mainwheel leg pivot
92 Leg fairing doors
93 Shock absorber strut
94 Twin mainwheels
95 Left wing fuel tank
96 Front spar
97 Rear spar
98 Fuel tank bulkheads
99 Leading edge de-icing

100 Flap profile structure
101 Trailing edge flap
102 Flap fairing
103 Flap tracking
104 Leading edge construction
105 Outer wing construction
106 Left aileron
107 Aileron tab

Far left: The spacious cockpit of a 748
Left: Normal accommodation in the 748 civil transport is for 40 to 58. The main passenger door is on the left at the rear

Above: HK-1409, a BAe 748 of the Colombian airline Avianca

Far left: A brightly coloured twin-engined Bahamasair BAe 748. Founded in 1973, this airline is the only one providing scheduled services throughout the Bahamas

Left: making adjustments to the Bendix solid-state radar

Below left: Loading baggage; this door can also serve as an emergency exit

RDa 7 Mk 536-2 turboprops, and the wings have been increased in span by 1.22 m (4 ft) but reduced in drag, with the tail modified.

Apart from these models, the aircraft has also appeared as the Andover for the Royal Air Force (31 Andover C.1/Series 2A and six Andover CC.2/Series 1), and is also being built under licence in India by Hindustan Aeronautics Limited. HAL is producing a total of 79 aircraft, 62 of them for the Indian air force and the rest for Indian Airlines.

The Series 2B is currently offered by British Aerospace in the form of the 748 Civil Transport, the 748 Military Transport, and the 748 Coast-guarder maritime-reconnaissance aircraft with search radar under the forward fuselage.

Herald, Handley Page
FIRST FLIGHT 1955

THE development of the HPR.3 Herald began in 1954, and the first of two prototypes flew on August 25, 1955, orders by this time totalling 29 from one Colombian and two Australian operators. The second prototype flew a year later, but although an initial batch of 25 aircraft was proposed, it soon became clear that in its current form the Herald fell far short of the performance that operators would like, and which turboprop-powered aircraft such as the Vickers Viscount could offer.

Handley Page had already begun to consider a turboprop-powered variant, the HPR.4 with a pair of Napier Eland engines. Then in July 1955 the company made a serious study of the basic Herald powered by two Rolls-Royce Dart turboprops, and in July 1957 Handley Page made the sensible decision to abandon further development of the HPR.3 in favour of the HPR.7 Herald. The two HPR.3 prototypes were re-engined, flying on March 11, and December 17, 1958 respectively, with the initial name Dart-Herald, later changed to Herald.

The first production type was the Series 100, the initial example of which (a company-owned aircraft) flew on October 30, 1959. The only other Series 100 Heralds were three aircraft for British European Airways, for use on the airline's routes in the highlands and islands of Scotland. Apart from the use of two Dart 527s in place of four radial engines, the Series 100's main distinguishing feature compared with the HPR.3 was a 50.8-cm (20-in) lengthening of the forward fuselage to bring the door clear of the propellers.

The next model was the Series 200, produced to meet a requirement of Jersey Airlines. This had a number of detail improvements, but was most notable for a fuselage stretch of 1.09 m (3 ft 7 in) to make possible the accommodation of up to 56 passengers instead of 47. The second prototype HPR.3/HPR.7 was converted to the new standard, first flying on April 8, 1961 with an increase in maximum take-off weight of 907 kg (2000 lb). The first production Series 200 aircraft flew on December 13, 1961, deliveries to the airline beginning in January 1962. Production of the Series 200 totalled only 36 before the financial collapse of Handley Page in August 1969.

The only other Heralds were eight Series 400 aircraft for the Malaysian air force. Today, the largest operator is Air UK, with 20.

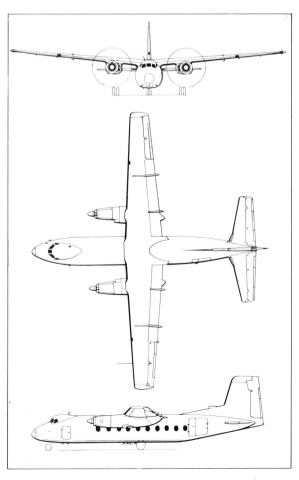

Above left: A Handley Page Herald of Air UK
Above right: Captain J North and Flight Officer I Reed at the controls of a BEA Herald
Above: Fitting long-range fuel tanks for a South American tour

HPR.7 Herald

Type: short-range transport
Maker: Handley Page Ltd
Span: 28.89 m (94 ft 9½ in)
Length: 23.01 m (75 ft 6 in)
Height: 7.11 m (23 ft 4 in)
Wing area: 82.3 m² (886 sq ft)
Weight: maximum 19 505 kg (43 000 lb); empty 11 322 kg (24 960 lb)
Powerplant: two 2105-ehp Rolls-Royce Dart 527 turboprops
Performance: cruising speed 435 km/h (270 mph) at 4572 m (15 000 ft); range with maximum payload and reserves 1127 km (700 miles)
Payload: 5307 kg (11 700 lb); seats for up to 56 passengers
Crew: 2
Production: 48

Vanguard, Vickers-Armstrongs

FIRST FLIGHT 1959

THE Vickers Vanguard, designed basically as a replacement for the highly successful Vickers Viscount, was in essence an excellent design. Resulting from a British European Airways requirement for an airliner somewhat larger than the Viscount, with superior operating economics and performance, to enter service in 1959, the Vanguard fitted the BEA requirement well.

Entirely by coincidence, it was on April 15, 1953 that BEA and Trans-Canada Air Lines issued requirements for similar aircraft, that of Trans-Canada specifying a load of 60 passengers to be carried over transcontinental ranges at a maximum take-off weight of 32 659 kg (72 000 lb). BEA at first held out for a high-set wing, to afford passengers the best possible view, but eventually came into line with Trans-Canada when the advantages of loading freight into the large lower-lobe of the 'double-bubble' fuselage were taken into account.

Some 60 preliminary designs were considered, including several with swept wings, but the combination of a cruising speed of 644 km/h (400 mph) and the specified low landing speed finally decided the Vickers design team on a straight wing set at the low mid-wing position, and a powerplant comprising four Rolls-Royce RB.109 turboprops. The engine later became the Tyne RTy. 1. After a prolonged interim period as the Type 870, the Vickers aircraft was finally designated the Type 900. Up to 100 passengers or a payload of 9526 kg (21 000 lb) were to be carried, and gross weight was to be 61 236 kg (135 000 lb) in the ultimate design, the Type 950 named Vanguard by BEA. During

1955 and 1956 BEA negotiated for the purchase of 20 Vanguards, the contract being signed on July 20, 1956 and calling for the type to be in service during 1960.

Trans-Canada had meanwhile been biding their time, as the basic Vanguard (BEA's Type 951) did not meet their stringent requirements. Vickers therefore evolved the Type 952 for Trans-Canada, with maximum seating for 139 passengers six-abreast, a maximum payload of 10 886 kg (24 000 lb) and a gross weight of 63 958 kg (141 000 lb). The different ranges specified by BEA and Trans-Canada (1609 km [1000 miles] and transcontinental) had been catered for in the original design by the incorporation of high fuel tankage. In January 1957 Trans-Canada ordered

Top: An Air Canada Vanguard CF-TKK in August 1970. It was subsequently transferred to Europe Aéro Service, Perpignan, in 1972 as F-BTYB
Above: G-APEB which first flew in 1959 and was delivered to BEA in 1961
Above right: The seating and baggage accommodation
Above far right: Preparing to unload a Vanguard Merchantman

214

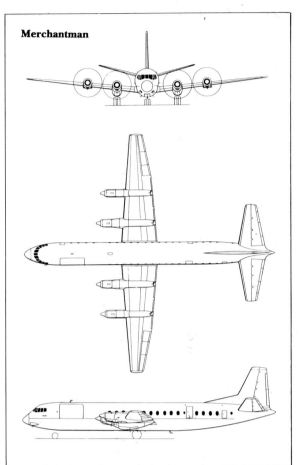

Merchantman

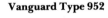

Vanguard Type 952

Type: medium-range transport
Maker: Vickers-Armstrongs Aircraft Ltd
Span: 35.97 m (118 ft)
Length: 37.45 m (122 ft 10½ in)
Height: 10.64 m (34 ft 11 in)
Wing area: 141.9 m² (1527 sq ft)
Weight: maximum 63 958 kg (141 000 lb); empty 38 556 kg (85 000 lb)
Powerplant: four 5545-ehp Rolls-Royce Tyne RTy. 11 Mk 512 turboprops
Performance: maximum cruising speed 684 km/h (425 mph) at 6096 m (20 000 ft); range with maximum payload 2945 km (1830 miles)
Payload: 16 783 kg (37 000 lb); seats for up to 139 passengers
Crew: 3
Production: 44

20 Type 952s, and later ordered another three.

With construction of the prototype Type 950 underway, BEA in 1958 realized that where maximum-fuel range was not required, the weight thus saved could be traded for extra payload at the same gross weight of 63 958 kg (141 000 lb). The result was the Type 953, announced by Vickers in July 1958, with a payload of 13 154 kg (29 000 lb). The BEA order was thus altered to six Type 951 and 14 Type 953 Vanguards.

The first Vanguard flew on January 20, 1959 and performance in general was all that could be asked for in an aircraft with turboprop engines and conservative structural design. Although Vickers tried hard to secure further orders, none were forthcoming as at that time the airlines had a

fixation on buying the latest pure jet airliners.

The first Vanguard Type 951, with 4985-ehp Tyne 506s, was delivered to BEA on December 2, 1960, and the type entered scheduled service on March 1, 1961. The first Vanguard Type 952 for Trans-Canada, with 5545-ehp Tyne 512 engines, had meanwhile flown its first service on February 1, 1961. The first Vanguard Type 953 entered service late in May 1961.

By October 1968 the limited success of the Vanguard for passenger operations persuaded BEA to start converting its aircraft to an all-freight configuration, with the name Merchantman. The conversion was carried out by Aviation Traders, and nine Vanguards were converted with large freight doors in the left side of the forward fuselage.

An-10, Antonov

FIRST FLIGHT 1957

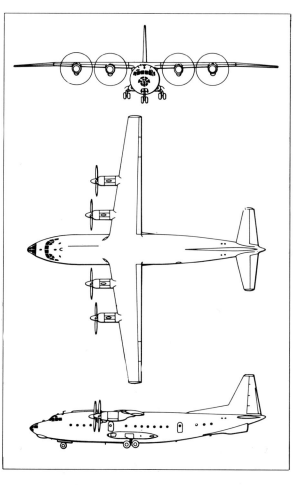

Above; An Aeroflot An-10; in 1966 An-10s and 10As were operating on more than 90 routes and carried 4 200 000 passengers
Left: An An-10 comes in to land. The retractable landing gear was designed for soft-field operations and the endplate fins were intended to rectify instability

THE Antonov An-10 was derived from the An-8, which had itself been produced to meet a joint military and civil requirement, in the light of Aeroflot's revised needs in 1955, shortly after the An-8 had first flown. The new Aeroflot requirement called for four instead of two engines, increased passenger capacity, and full pressurization. The design of the An-10, as the new aircraft was designated, began in November 1955: the plan of the wings, tail unit and undercarriage (the last specifically designed for rough-field operations, with its main units retracting into fuselage blisters) remained substantially unaltered, while the new fuselage was circular in section not slab-sided.

The first prototype flew on March 7, 1957 and because of the similarity of the design to that of the An-8, it was expected that production An-10s would rapidly be in service. The engines used in the first two prototypes were 4000-ehp Kuznetsov NK-4 turboprops, but all other An-10s were fitted with 4000-ehp Ivchenko AI-20s, which offered a usefully lower specific fuel consumption. All was not well with the design, however, and instead of the projected nine months, it took some 30 months to get the An-10 into Aeroflot service.

The exact nature of the problem is not certain, but probably included lateral and directional instability. The interval between the first flight and the service introduction of the type was marked by a number of modifications, including the provision of anhedral on the outer wing panels and a number of auxiliary vertical tail surfaces. Apart from an extension forward of the dorsal fillet, these com-

An-10A

Type: medium-range transport
Maker: Antonov Design Bureau
Span: 38 m (124 ft 8 in)
Length: 34 m (111 ft 6 in)
Height: 9.38 m (30 ft 9 in)
Wing area: 121.73 m² (1310 sq ft)
Weight: maximum 54 000 kg (119 048 lb); empty not available
Powerplant: four 4000-ehp Ivchenko AI-20 turboprops
Performance: cruising speed up to 680 km/h (423 mph) at 8000 m (26 247 ft); range with maximum payload and reserves 1220 km (758 miles)
Payload: 14 500 kg (31 966 lb); seats for up to 110 passengers
Crew: 5
Production: approx 200

prised a fairly large ventral fin, later supplemented by relatively small endplate fins.

With its stability problems apparently solved, the An-10 began freight operations in the Ukraine during May 1959, and the type flew its first scheduled passenger service on July 22, 1959, with a flight from Moscow to Simferopol in the Crimea. Passenger accommodation of the An-10 was 90. Though the first prototype had featured a small playroom for children, at the rear of the main cabin, this was replaced on production aircraft by a cabin for six passengers.

In 1958 the Russians announced the An-10A stretched version of the An-10, which had been named Ukraine. This improved model was lengthened by 2 m (6 ft 6¾ in), and could seat up to 100 passengers five- and six-abreast for normal operations, or up to 110 passengers for high-density routes. The An-10A also had reversible-pitch propellers to reduce landing run, and late-production An-10As also had twin ventral fins replacing the previous arrangement of one ventral and two endplate fins.

The performance of the An-10A was recognized by the establishment of two records: in May 1960 an An-10A covered 2000 km (1243 miles) with a payload of 15 000 kg (33 069 lb) at an average speed of 723 km/h (449 mph); and on April 29, 1961 another An-10A covered a 500-km (311-mile) closed circuit at 731 km/h (454 mph).

At the same time that the An-10A was announced, it was also reported that there was to be an An-10B (otherwise reported as the An-16),

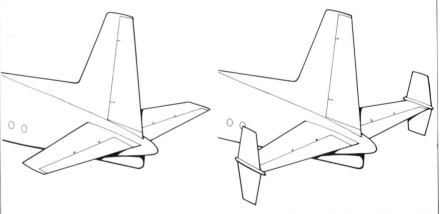

with a fuselage stretch of 3 m (9 ft 10 in) to increase the freight volume and also passenger capacity to 130. This model was apparently not built. One An-10 derivative was built, however, in the form of the An-12 logistic transport. This featured a totally revised, upswept rear fuselage, and though designed principally with the needs of the Soviet air force in mind, has been used by a number of civil operators, often with rear turret fitted.

All An-10s and An-10As were withdrawn from service after one of the type crashed near Kharkov on May 18, 1972, killing all 108 passengers and crew.

By mid 1967 the two versions, about 300 in total by this time, had among them managed to transport the respectable total of 12 million passengers.

Top: An Aeroflot An-10A at Moscow Domodedovo Airport on July 9, 1967, to mark the 50th anniversary of the Soviet October Revolution. Note the large twin ventral fins which replaced the auxiliary rear fins
Above: The prototype An-10 had early directional stability problems which were remedied on the An-10A by adding, initially, an under-fin, and later still endplate fins on the tailplane

An-24, Antonov

FIRST FLIGHT 1959

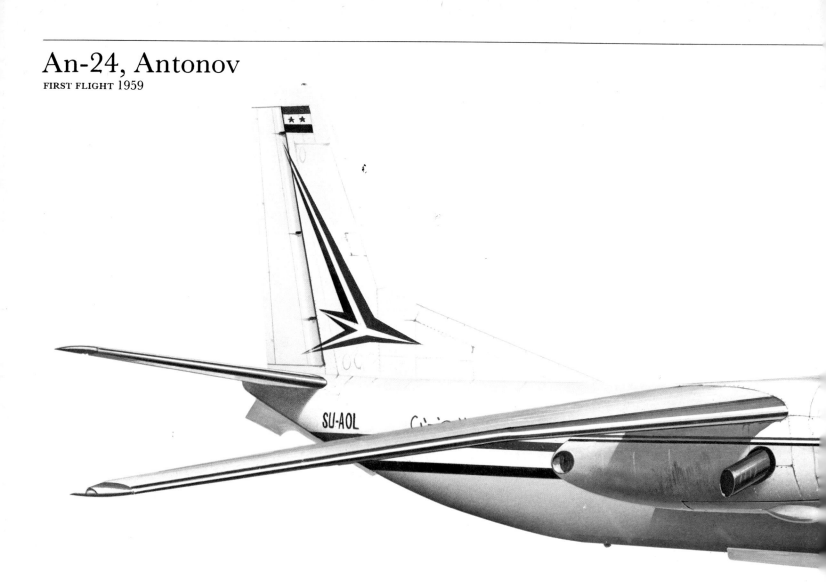

SU-AOL

THE Antonov An-24 marks yet another effort by the world's aircraft manufacturers and users to find a twin-turboprop replacement for the Douglas DC-3, in this instance the licence-built Russian version, the Lisunov Li-2. The origins of the An-24 lie in a 1957 Aeroflot requirement for a 40-seat turboprop airliner able to replace the Ilyushin Il-14 and Li-2 over stages of up to 1000 km (621 miles), and able to operate from airfields that possessed only short, unpaved runways. It was this last factor, together with the desirability of easy loading, which led the Antonov design team to choose a high-wing for their An-24.

Design began in 1958, and the first prototype flew on December 20, 1959, having been built in only 14 months despite a change in the Aeroflot requirement which entailed a fuselage stretch to allow the aircraft to carry up to 50 passengers in a high-density internal layout, or up to 44 in normal circumstances. All necessary trials were completed by September 1962.

Only a few An-24s, with seating for 40 passengers, were built. These were distinguishable from the prototypes by their longer engine nacelles, and by the standardization of the ventral fin tested on the second prototype. The first scheduled service by the type was flown with an An-24 in October 1962 between Kiev and Kherson. This 40-seater was soon supplanted in production by a 44-seat model, which was distinguishable by having nine windows instead of eight on each side.

Still fairly early in the type's production career the An-24 was replaced by the An-24V Series I,

powered by a pair of 2550-ehp Ivchenko AI-24As. Essentially a scaled-down version of the powerful AI-20, the AI-24 was developed specially for the An-24, and in its AI-24A form can be boosted to 2800 ehp by water injection at the compressor inlet. This modification considerably improved the An-24V Series I's 'hot and high' performance, complementing the revised wing, enlarged from 72.46 m² (780 sq ft) to 75 m² (807 sq ft) by a centre section of wider chord and enlarged flaps.

From 1967 production was of a further improved model, the An-24V Series II, presumably introduced to better still more the 'hot and high' performance of the An-24V Series I. This model is fitted with 2820-ehp AI-24T turboprops and, most interestingly, a 900-kg (1984-lb) st Tumansky RU

Top: An Antonov 24 of Misrair, a charter subsidiary of Egyptair which connects Cairo with Luxor, Aswan and Abu Simbel
Above: SP-LTI, and An-24 of LOT, Polskie Linie Lotnicze, the Polish airline which operates 18 passenger-carrying An-24s and one cargo-carrier

19-300 auxiliary turbojet in the rear of the right nacelle in place of the TG-16 auxiliary power unit. The RU 19-300 is optional, and aircraft fitted with it are designated An-24RV. Passenger accommodation on the An-24V Series II aircraft is for a maximum of 52 seated four-abreast. The An-24V Series II is nearing the end of its production run, but is still available in convertible or mixed passenger/ freight configurations.

Antonov have also produced two versions of the An-24V Series II for freight operations. These are the An-24T and An-24RT, basically similar to the An-24V Series II and An-24RV respectively. Like their passenger counterparts, these can take off at altitudes up to 3000 m (9843 ft). Maximum payload is 4612 kg (10 168 lb) for the An-24T, and 5700 kg (12 566 lb) for the An-24RT, and these loads can be handled by means of a large ventral door with an electric winch.

The An-24P is a special model intended for forest fire-fighting, first tested in the autumn of 1971. It is fitted with provision for the dropping of parachutists and fire-fighting equipment.

Other An-24 derivatives are the An-26 freighter, fitted with an enlarged ventral hatch in a new beaver-type tail, and two 2820-ehp AI-24Ts with an RU 19-300 turbojet; the An-30 aerial-survey model derived from the An-24RT/An-26, with four camera ports in the fuselage floor and a glazed nose; and the An-32 'hot and high' transport, fitted with two 5180-ehp Ivchenko AI-20M turboprops enabling the type to operate from airfields up to an altitude of 4500 m (14 764 ft).

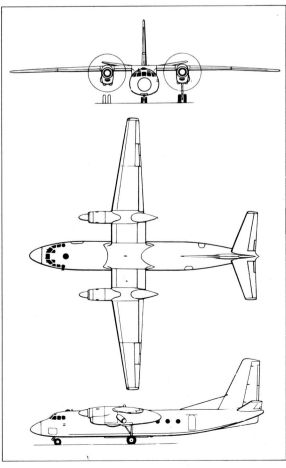

An-24V Series II

Type: short-range transport
Maker: Antonov Design Bureau
Span: 29.2 m (95 ft 10 in)
Length: 23.53 m (77 ft 2 in)
Height: 8.32 m (27 ft 4 in)
Wing area: 75 m² (807 sq ft)
Weight: maximum 21 000 kg (46 296 lb); empty 13 300 kg (29 321 lb)
Powerplant: two 2550-ehp Ivchenko AI-24A turboprops
Performance: cruising speed 450 km/h (280 mph) at 6000 m (19 685 ft); range with maximum payload and reserves 550 km (342 miles)
Payload: 5500 kg (12 125 lb); seats for up to 52 passengers
Crew: 3 to 5
Production: 729 ordered by 1980 (An-24, An-26 and An-30)

CV-580, Convair

FIRST FLIGHT 1960

THE Convair 240, 340 and 440 short-range airliners were built between 1947 and 1957 as pressurized replacements for the Douglas DC-3. All three models were built to the same basic design, and were powered by a pair of Pratt & Whitney R-2800 Double Wasp radials. But in the early 1950s Convair came to appreciate the importance of the turboprop, and saw that in its 240, 340 and 440 designs it had an admirable starting point for a simple conversion of existing aircraft to turboprop power.

Convair produced an experimental conversion of a 240 with Allison 501-A2 (T56) turboprops as early as 1950, and though the concept was entirely validated, it was not until 1954 that commercial conversion was considered, in this case by the British engine manufacturer Napier. Re-engined with two 3060-ehp Napier Eland NE. 1 turboprops, the first 340 conversion flew on February 9, 1955 as the Convair 540. This and six other conversions were operated by Allegheny Airlines, while the Royal Canadian Air Force used ten as CL-66Bs, built as such by Canadair, who also produced three conversions.

Though successful, no further Eland conversions were possible as a result of the cancellation of the Eland programme in 1962. Thus the next model was the definitive Convair 580, 130 of which were produced by the installation of 3750-ehp Allison 501-D13 turboprops on Convair 340s and 440s. The conversion was undertaken by Pacific Airmotive, the first re-engined aircraft flying on January 19, 1960. The 580 received its Federal Aviation Administration certification on April 21, and the first delivery was made in May of the same year.

The other major turboprop conversion of the Convair-Liner series was with the Rolls-Royce Dart RDa. 10 Mk 542, rated at 3025 ehp. The conversion of all three members of the family was undertaken by Convair itself, and the revised aircraft were at first designated 240D, 340D and 440D, these subsequently being altered to 600 and 640, the latter covering both the 340D and 440D.

The impetus for the programme came from Central Airlines, who ordered ten Convair 240Ds. The first of these flew on May 20, 1965 and the type entered service on November 30 of the same year; the Convair 340D and 440D programme was contemporary, and the first Convair 640 entered service on December 22, 1965.

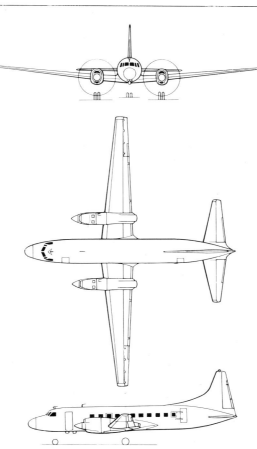

Top: The Convair CV-580 as operated by Aspen Airways of Colorado
Above: A CV-580 of the Cleveland, Ohio-based Wright Air Lines at Atlanta, Georgia in December 1977

CV-580

Type: local service transport
Maker: Convair division of General Dynamics Corporation; Pacific Airmotive Inc
Span: 32.12 m (105 ft 4 in)
Length: 24.84 m (81 ft 6 in)
Height: 8.89 m (29 ft 2 in)
Wing area: 85.47 m² (920 sq ft)
Weight: maximum 26 372 kg (58 140 lb); empty approx 13 835 kg (30 500 lb)
Powerplant: two 3750-ehp Allison 501-D13H turboprops
Performance: cruising speed 550 km/h (342 mph); maximum range 4611 km (2865 miles)
Payload: 4023 kg (8870 lb); seats for up to 56 passengers
Crew: 3 to 4
Production: 20 (CV-540), 130 (CV-580), 39 (CV-600) and 28 (CV-640)

CL-44, Canadair

FIRST FLIGHT 1960

DERIVED from the Bristol Type 175 Britannia, the Canadair CL-44 resulted from a Royal Canadian Air Force requirement for a heavy freighter and maritime-reconnaissance aircraft based on the same airframe, and manufactured largely in Canada. As a result, in 1954 Canadair signed a licence agreement with Bristol. The CL-28 Argus reconnaissance aircraft was built between 1957 and 1960, and was followed on Canadair's production line by 12 of the CC-106 Yukon freighters for the RCAF.

Derived from the Britannia 253 but with a lengthened fuselage, the Yukons had large freight doors on the left side, forward and aft of the wing. Although it was at first planned to engine these aircraft, which had the company designation CL-44D, with Bristol Orion turboprops, the cancellation of the Orion programme in 1958 led to a redesign with Rolls-Royce Tyne turboprops.

With this military commitment running smoothly, Canadair in 1960 turned to the production of a civil counterpart of the Yukon. Designated CL-44D-4, this had the unusual feature of a hinged rear fuselage and tail surfaces. These could be swung to the right, allowing bulky loads and pallets to be loaded straight into the fuselage. The first such aircraft flew on November 16, 1960 and was followed by an initial batch of 17 production examples for Seaboard World Airlines, the Flying Tiger Line and Slick Airways. These same three cargo operators and Loftleidir of Iceland subsequently bought another ten CL-44D-4s, the Loftleidir aircraft being used for low-fare transatlantic flights with up to 178 passengers. Wishing to carry yet more passengers, Loftleidir approached Canadair with a view to a stretched version.

This resulted in the last of Loftleidir's four CL-44D-4s being modified on the production line to Canadair 400 (CL-44J) standard, with its already lengthened fuselage stretched further and seating for 214. Loftleidir's other CL-44D-4s were later converted to the same standard.

The only other CL-44 variant was the CL-440, produced by Conroy Aircraft. This was an ex-Flying Tiger Line CL-44D-4 modified with a bulged upper portion of the fuselage to accommodate loads up to 4.24 m (13 ft 11 in) in height.

The CC-106 Yukons were sold from military service in 1973, and several of them have been bought by civil operators.

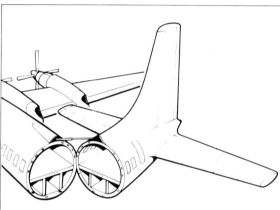

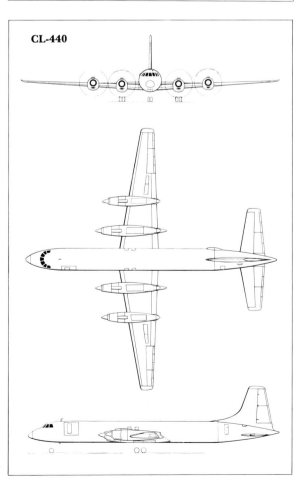

CL-440

Above: HB-IEO, formerly G-AWOV, one of two Canadair CL-44s operated by Transvalair, a Swiss charter firm carrying cargo to Europe, the Middle East, Far East and Africa
Left: The CL-44D-4, the freighter version which had a hinged rear fuselage and tail surfaces for loading bulky cargo and pallet loads

CL-44D-4

Type: long-range freighter
Maker: Canadair Ltd
Span: 43.37 m (142 ft 3½ in)
Length: 41.73 m (136 ft 10¾ in)
Height: 11.79 m (38 ft 8 in)
Wing area: 193 m² (2075 sq ft)
Weight: maximum 95 256 kg (210 000 lb); empty 40 348 kg (88 950 lb)
Powerplant: four 5730-ehp Rolls-Royce Tyne Mk 515/10 turboprops
Performance: maximum cruising speed 620 km/h (385 mph) at 6096 km (20 000 ft); range with maximum payload 5246 km (3260 miles)
Payload: 29 995 kg (66 128 lb); seats for up to 178 passengers
Crew: 3
Production: 12 (CL-44D), 27 (CL-44D-4 and CL-44J)

Guppy, Aero Spacelines

FIRST FLIGHT 1962

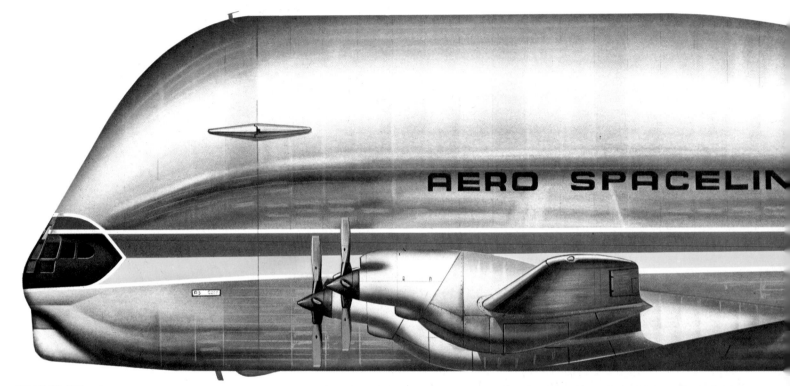

FORMED in 1961, Aero Spacelines existed specifically to produce conversions of the Boeing 377 Stratocruiser and C-97 freighter into high-capacity freighters capable of transporting high-volume hardware, such as boosters, for the US space effort.

The first aircraft to be produced by the company was the Pregnant Guppy, which made its initial flight on September 19, 1962. Formally designated B-377PG, the Pregnant Guppy retained the flying surfaces and 3500-hp Pratt & Whitney R-4360 Wasp Major piston engines of the C-97, but had a highly bulged upper lobe fitted to the fuselage, which was also stretched by 5.08 m (16 ft 8 in). The whole of the rear fuselage and empennage could be detached for the straight-loading of booster stages.

Next appeared the B-377SG Super Guppy, which first flew on August 31, 1965. This was based on a Boeing C-97J, but was more extensively modified than the Pregnant Guppy. The radial engines were replaced by 7000-ehp Pratt & Whitney T34-P-7WA turboprops, wing span was increased by 4.57 m (15 ft) and the fuselage by 9.4 m (30 ft 10 in). The yet larger upper lobe could accommodate loads up to 7.62 m (25 ft) in diameter.

Although both the Pregnant and Super Guppies had been produced entirely as commercial enterprises, both aircraft were contracted for the exclusive use of the National Aeronautics and Space Administration (NASA) and US Department of Defense, and so Aero Spacelines turned to further conversions to meet the needs for a commercial bulky freight transport.

The B-377MG Mini Guppy 'reverted' to piston engines, in this instance four 3800-hp Pratt & Whitney R-4360-B6 Wasp Majors. Derived from a Stratocruiser, but fitted with a wider and longer fuselage and a hinged tail section, the Mini Guppy first flew on May 24, 1967. The B-377MG was lost in a crash on May 12, 1970.

Next to appear, on March 13, 1970, was the Guppy-101, derived from a Stratocruiser, but powered by four 4912-shp Allison 501-D22C turboprops. The Guppy-101 also introduced a new feature to the family: a hinged nose in place of the earlier detachable or hinged rear fuselage and tail unit.

Finally there appeared the Guppy-201, or B-377SGT. Design of this aircraft (intended for the

Top: The Super Guppy which was built by Aero Spacelines to carry cargo such as launchers in the US space programme
Above: The Pregnant Guppy which can carry a complete Saturn S-IV second stage of the Apollo moon rocket
Right: A dramatic view of a Super Guppy at Bergstrom Air Force Base, Austin, Texas. The Stratocruiser cockpit can be seen clearly in this view
Far right: Side elevations showing the development of the Guppy

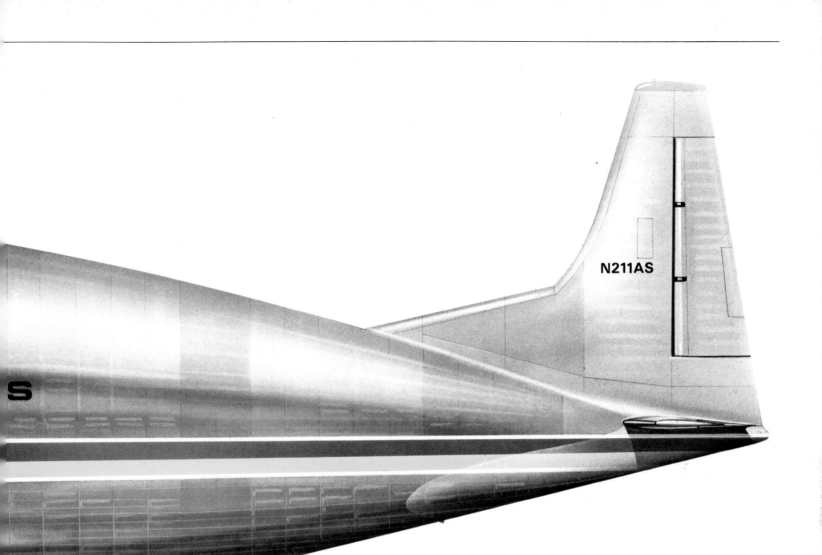

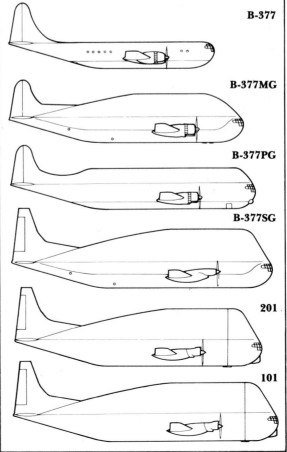

B-377

B-377MG

B-377PG

B-377SG

201

101

carriage of major airframe components of machines such as the Airbus A300, BAe/Aérospatiale Concorde, Lockheed TriStar and McDonnell Douglas DC-10) was begun in January 1968. Construction of the first Guppy-201 began in September 1969, using standard portions of the B-377/C-97 family such as the wings, tail unit, cockpit and lower fuselage. (Parts of several lower fuselages had to be joined to produce the necessary length.)

In essence the Guppy-201 is a Super Guppy re-engined with Allison 501-D22C turboprop engines. Two examples were planned originally, these first flying on August 24, 1970 and August 24, 1972 respectively. US Federal Aviation Administration Type Approval was granted on August 26, 1971. Both Guppy-201s were quickly bought by Aérospatiale for operation by Aéromaritime to ferry major sub-components of the A300B and Concorde from local assembly factories to the final assembly locations at Toulouse.

The cargo hold of the Guppy-201 has a floor width of 3.96 m (13 ft), bulging out to a maximum width of 7.65 m (25 ft 1 in) before curving in once again prior to reaching the compartment's ceiling 7.77 m (25 ft 6 in) above the floor. The hold's length is 33.99 m (111 ft 6 in), though only 9.75 m (32 ft) of this has a constant section. Access to this volume of 1104 m³ (39 000 cu ft) is through the hinged nose section, which swings back through 110° to ensure unimpeded loading and unloading.

There currently appears to be every likelihood of further Guppy-201 production meet Airbus Industries' need for increased output.

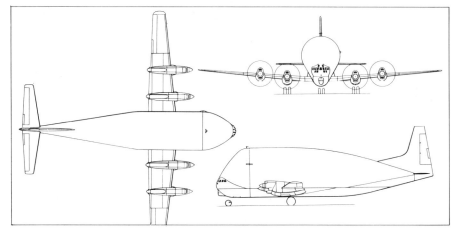

Guppy-201

Type: bulky freight transport
Maker: Aero Spacelines Inc; Airbus Industrie
Span: 47.62 m (156 ft 3 in)
Length: 43.84 m (143 ft 10 in)
Height: 14.78 m (48 ft 6 in)
Wing area: 182.55 m² (1965 sq ft)
Weight: maximum 77 111 kg (170 000 lb); empty 45 360 kg (100 000 lb)
Powerplant: four 4912-ehp Allison 501-D22C turboprops
Performance: maximum cruising speed 463 km/h 288 mph) at 6096 m (20 000 ft); range with maximum payload 813 km (505 miles)
Payload: 24 494 kg (54 000 lb)
Crew: 3 to 4
Production: 1 (Pregnant Guppy), 1 (Super Guppy), 1 (Guppy-101), 4 (Guppy-201) by 1980, 1 (Mini Guppy)

Above left: An Aero Spacelines Guppy in service with Aéromaritime serving the Airbus Industrie consortium. By 1984 Airbus hopes to have built two more of these outsize freighters Left: An Airbus Guppy at Reykjavik in 1978. In 1980 two were used to ferry Airbus parts from partner factories to Toulouse for assembly

Br.941, Breguet

FIRST FLIGHT 1961

DESIGNED as a rugged STOL (short take-off and landing) transport for both civil and military operators, the Breguet 941 was a relatively unsophisticated aircraft in structure and capabilities. It was, however, provided with an extensive deflected-slipstream STOL system. In this, the slipstream of four large-diameter propellers driven by engines located evenly along the leading edges of the wing blew over the entire span of the wings before being turned downwards by the double-slotted full-span trailing-edge flaps, the rear member of which was fitted with a fixed leading-edge slat. To ensure a smooth and consistent airflow in the event of engine failure, the four engines were mechanically linked by a high-speed transmission shaft through the wings.

The prototype Breguet 941 first flew on June 1, 1961, this aircraft having been produced in response to a French air force order of February 22, 1960. At this time, Breguet's thoughts were turned to two basic models, the Br.941C civil model with a retractable airstair in place of the ventral ramp for the boarding of passengers, and the Br.941M military freight model. Extensive flight trials followed, and in November 1965 the French government ordered four pre-production aircraft, designated Br.941S, together with the tooling and jigging needed for large-scale production. These four aircraft were powered by 1500-shp Turboméca Turmo IIID$_3$ (later IIID$_6$) turboprops in place of the 1250-shp Turmo IIIDs of the prototype, and also differed from the prototype in having larger nose radomes, a wider cargo hold and a revised rear ramp configuration. The first Br.941S flew on April 19, 1967 and was soon joined by the three other pre-production. The original Br.941 was also re-engined to take part in the trials programme.

US interest in the type was evinced by an offer from McDonnell Aircraft to co-operate in the project. To this end the prototype was tested in the United States during 1964 and 1965. Neither of the two US airlines to test the type, Eastern Air Lines and American Airlines, ordered the McDonnell aircraft, designated Model 188, effectively halting the McDonnell initiative.

Changing requirements, coupled with the availability of the Nord Noratlas and Transall C-160 for military use, finally led to the end of the Br.941 programme in France during the early 1970s.

Above: The prototype Br.941 in French air force insignia. It was envisaged as a civil or military transport
Left: The McDonnell Model 188 demonstrates its STOL (short take-off and landing) performance during trials at American cities in the mid 1960s

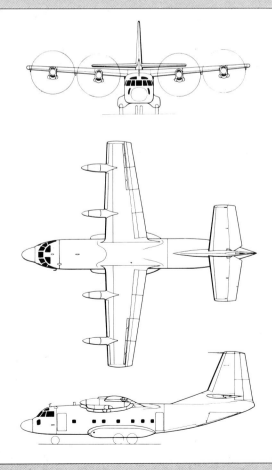

Br.941S

Type: STOL utility transport
Maker: Breguet Aviation
Span: 23.4 m (76 ft 8½ in)
Length: 23.75 m (77 ft 11 in)
Height: 9.65 m (31 ft 8 in)
Wing area: 83.78 m² (902 sq ft)
Weight: maximum 24 500 kg (58 422 lb); empty 14 700 kg (32 408 lb)
Powerplant: four 1500-shp Turboméca Turmo IIID$_6$ turboprops
Performance: maximum cruising speed 417 km/h (259 mph) at 3050 m (10 000 ft); range with maximum payload 1000 km (621 miles)
Payload: 10 000 kg (22 046 lb); seats for up to 57 passengers
Crew: 3
Production: 5

YS-11, NAMC

FIRST FLIGHT 1962

DESPITE the fact that it was built only in relatively small numbers, the Nihon Kokuki Seizo Kabushiki Kaisha (Nihon Aeroplane Manufacturing Company) YS-11 twin-turboprop airliner has the unique distinction of being the first, and so far the only, Japanese civil transport to have been produced in substantial numbers, apart from types of foreign origin dating from before and during World War II.

Work on the concept which was to appear as the YS-11 began in 1956, when the Ministry of International Trade and Industry called for a short- and medium-range airliner. With the aid of a government subsidy, design work under the leadership of Dr Hidemasa Kimura was started, overall control of the project being vested in the Transport Aircraft Development Association, superseded in 1959 by the NAMC.

This controlling body, 54% government owned, was responsible for design, sales and production control, while production itself was vested in a consortium of six companies: Fuji Heavy Industries for the tail, Japan Aircraft Manufacturing for the ailerons and flaps, Kawasaki Aircraft for the main wings and engine nacelles, Mitsubishi Heavy Industries for the main fuselage and final assembly, Shin Meiwa Industry for the rear fuselage, and Showa Aircraft Industry for the honeycomb components such as doors. The proportion of the total aircraft produced by each company reflected its percentage holding in the 46% of the NAMC left in private hands.

Though substantial foreign sales were hoped for,

the design parameters most closely applied during the design phase were the needs of Japan's growing domestic air routes. This meant that although the YS-11 was yet another contender in the Douglas DC-3 replacement field, it was intended to carry a substantially larger payload than aircraft such as the Fokker F27, the Handley Page Herald and the Hawker Siddeley 748.

For ease of loading a low-wing layout was selected, accommodation for a basic payload of 60 passengers was provided, and the powerplant selected was a pair of Rolls-Royce Dart RDa. 10/1 turboprops, the model being specially developed for the YS-11 and preferred to the Allison 501 and Napier Eland.

Construction of two flying and two static-test

Above: A YS-11 under evaluation by Japanese airlines during a visit to a British airport
Right: A YS-11 of Hawaiian at Honolulu International Airport
Below: The YS-11 in TOA livery; the type is used by All-Nippon Airways, Southwest Air Lines and TOA Domestic Airlines, which link the cities and islands of Japan

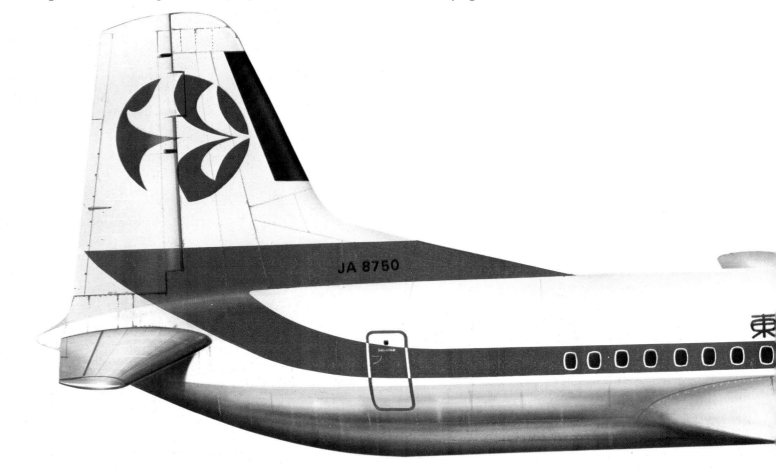

prototypes began in May 1957 with the formation of the Transport Aircraft Development Association. The first prototype flew on August 30, 1962, with the second following on December 28 of the same year. Intensive flight trials yielded the YS-11 its Japanese Civil Aviation Bureau type certificate on August 25, 1964, and its US Federal Aviation Administration Type Approval on September 7, 1965.

Production had meanwhile started, and the first production aircraft flew on October 23, 1964. It was delivered to the Japanese Civil Aviation Bureau in March 1965. The first airline user was Toa Airways, operating the first YS-11 scheduled service in April 1965, followed by Japan Domestic in May and by All Nippon in July 1965.

Perhaps reflecting the strong domestic elements in the design, sales of the YS-11 to foreign operators were initially slow, Filipinas Orient buying two YS-11s in September 1965, Hawaiian Airlines three in 1966, and LANSA (Peru) three in 1967. There foreign sales faltered, and NAMC thus felt it essential to try for a breakthrough into the lucrative US market. The Charlotte Aircraft Corporation were appointed sole agents in the United States, and largely as a result of the agency's recommendations there appeared the YS-11A stretched model, available in three sub-types.

All three models have the same basic dimensions as the YS-11, as well as the water-methanol-injected hot high Dart Mk 542 engines. The most successful of the whole YS-11 family, the YS-11A-

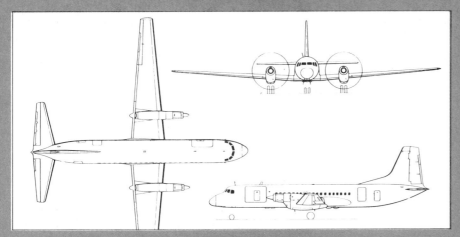

YS-11A

Type: short- and medium-range transport
Maker: Nihon Aeroplane Manufacturing Co
Span: 32 m (105 ft)
Length: 26.3 m (86 ft 3½ in)
Height: 8.99 m (29 ft 6 in)
Wing area: 94.8 m² (1020 sq ft)
Weight: maximum 24 500 kg (54 013 lb); empty 15 050 kg (33 179 lb)
Powerplant: two 3060-ehp Rolls-Royce Dart Mk 542 turboprops
Performance: cruising speed 472 km/h (293 mph) at 4572 m (15 000 ft); range with maximum payload and reserves 346 km (215 miles)
Payload: 6949 kg (15 320 lb); seats for up to 64 passengers
Crew: 4
Production: 182

200 reached a production total of more than 90. With seating for 60 passengers in normal operations, the YS-11A-200 had higher operating weights, and the payload was increased by some 1270 kg (2800 lb) to 6949 kg (15 320 lb). As in the basic YS-11, seating was five-abreast. Ordered initially by Piedmont Airlines, which as Piedmont Aviation finally operated some 17 of the type, the YS-11A-200 first flew on November 27, 1967, with initial deliveries beginning during 1968. Subsequently the model entered service with eight other airlines.

The next model was the YS-11A-300CP, a mixed-traffic derivative of the YS-11A-200. This had a large freight door (2.5 m [8 ft 2 in] by 1.83 m [6 ft]) in the left side of the forward fuselage, leading into a forward freight hold with a volume of 10 m³ (360 cu ft). Behind this is accommodation for 46 passengers, together with another 5 m³ (176 cu ft) of cargo space. Production of the YS-11A-300CP totalled 16.

Subsequent production was of the YS-11A-400 freight model, with a storage volume of 79 m³ (2790 cu ft) and a large loading door, measuring 3.05 m (10 ft) by 1.83 m (6 ft) aft of the wing trailing edge.

The YS-11A-400 was intended for military use, and the first of the type flew on September 17, 1969. Final production was of the YS-11A-500, -600 and -700, basically similar to the YS-11A-200, -300 and -400 but with maximum take-off weight raised by 500 kg (1102 lb).

Above: JA-8733, a YS-11 of All-Nippon, comes in to land at Fukuoka, Japan in March 1978. In 1980 All-Nippon were operating 30 examples of this short-haul turboprop

Beech 99 Airliner

FIRST FLIGHT 1965

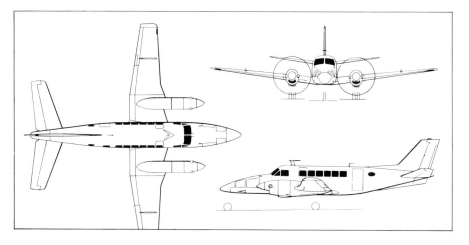

THE Beechcraft B99 Airliner was in its day the largest aircraft produced by Beech, perhaps the world's best known manufacturer of twin-engined light aircraft. Derived closely from the Beechcraft Queen Air B80 and Queen Airliner B80, the unpressurized B99 Airliner was designed to meet the specific requirements of third-level commuter service operators and air-taxi concerns by lengthening the fuselage to provide more accommodation, and by fitting two turboprops in place of the B80's twin Lycoming piston engines.

To provide the passenger accommodation needed for the new type's role, the basic fuselage of the B80 was lengthened by 3.07 m (10 ft 0¾ in) from 10.82 m (35 ft 6 in), thus increasing seating from the nine of the Queen Airliner B80 to the 15 of the 99 Airliner series, with a longitudinal row of eight seats on the right side of the fuselage, and seven seats on the left side. An airstair door is located in the left side of the rear fuselage. Also available as an option is a cargo door just forward of the passenger door, to provide operators with the capability of using their aircraft as mixed freight-passenger carriers. Another option is a ventral freight and baggage pod, with a capacity of 1.01 m³ (35½ cu ft) and up to a weight of 363 kg (800 lb).

The aerodynamic prototype of the 99 series was a converted Queen Air, which was first flown in December 1965. Fitted with 550-ehp Pratt & Whitney Aircraft of Canada PT6A-20 turboprops, this aircraft became the definitive 99 Airliner prototype in July 1966. Progress of the type towards US Federal Aviation Administration Type

Approval was leisurely, this not being granted until May 2, 1968. On the same day Beech delivered the first production aircraft.

First deliveries were of the 99 Airliner model, powered by 550-ehp PT6A-20 turboprops. The next production variant was the 99A Airliner, with a pair of PT6A-27 turboprops, normally rated at 680-ehp each, but in this instance derated to 550 ehp. The same powerplant was used in the A99A Airliner, which introduced a number of detail modifications. Finally in the definitive B99 Airliner, fully rated PT6A-27s were introduced.

The same basic aircraft was also produced as the B99 Executive, with a variety of internal layouts suiting the aircraft for the carriage of between 8 and 17 corporate officers.

B99 Airliner

Type: short- and medium-range light transport
Maker: Beech Aircraft Corporation
Span: 14 m (45 ft 10½ in)
Length: 13.89 m (45 ft 6¾ in)
Height: 4.38 m (14 ft 4¼ in)
Wing area: 26 m² (280 sq ft)
Weight: maximum 4944 kg (10 900 lb); empty 2620 kg (5777 lb)
Powerplant: two 680-ehp Pratt & Whitney Aircraft of Canada PT6A-27 turboprops
Performance: maximum cruising speed 451 km/h (280 mph) at 2438 m (8000 ft); range with maximum payload and reserves 853 km (530 miles)
Payload: seats for up to 15 passengers
Crew: 2
Production: 164

Left: A Beech 99 in its manufacturers livery
Below left: The accommodation for 15 passengers
Below: The airstair and under-fuselage baggage pod open. These facilities are useful in a third-level airliner

Nord 262, Nord-Aviation

FIRST FLIGHT 1962

THE origins of the Nord-Aviation 262 lie with the Holste MH.260 Super Broussard, itself evolved from the MH.250 prototype. The latter, designed as a small utility aircraft, was powered by a pair of Pratt & Whitney Wasp radial piston engines, replaced in the MH.260 by two 960-shp Turboméca Bastan turboprops.

Design of the N 262 began in earnest in the first quarter of 1961, the object being to produce a small but comfortable airliner suitable for regional operators flying routes up to 1000 km (621 miles) and able to operate from poor airfields. In this latter respect, the simple tricycle undercarriage of the Super Broussard, with its main units retracting into fuselage blisters, was well suited, as was the high-wing layout.

The prototype N262 first flew on December 24, 1962, and was supplemented in the trials programme by three pre-production aircraft. The N 262's French certificate of airworthiness was granted on July 16, 1964. The first production aircraft had flown some eight days earlier, and this was soon in service with the type's first scheduled operator, Air Inter.

Paradoxically, the first four aircraft (all for Air Inter) were N 262 Series B machines and it was one of these four which flew the first service on July 24, 1964. Subsequent N 262s of the early production types were Series A aircraft, with minor improvements but the same 1080-ehp Turboméca Bastan VIC turboprops. Production of the N 262 Series A totalled 72 aircraft, the first flying early in 1965. This received its US Federal Aviation Adminis-

tration Type Approval on March 15, 1965, and the initial production N 262 Series A entered service with Lake Central Airlines during late August 1965 after delivery on August 17.

Lake Central Airlines bought 12 N 262As, which continued in service after the company was bought by Allegheny Airlines. In 1974 Allegheny initiated a programme whereby the company's Mohawk Air Services subsidiary contracted with Frakes Aviation for the installation in the nine surviving N 262As of 1180-shp Pratt & Whitney Aircraft of Canada PT6A-45 turboprops, thus making the aircraft Mohawk 298s. The first conversion flew on January 7, 1975 and the type entered service with Allegheny early in 1977. The Mohawk 298 also has new wingtips to improve low-level performance

Above: A Nord 262A of Altair Airlines of Philadelphia, Pennsylvania. This aircraft was previously operated in Denmark

Below left: The Nord 262 uses the simple tricycle landing gear of the Super Broussard, housed in fuselage blisters, but introduced a pressurized fuselage of circular section. Bulkheads had to be cut away above and below to provide headroom

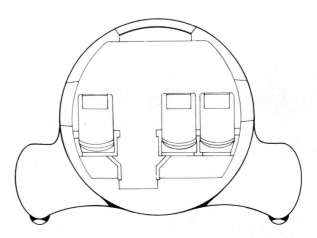

and handling, and it certificated with up to 30 passengers, or a payload of 3402 kg (7500 lb).

On January 1, 1970 Nord-Aviation and Sud-Aviation merged to become the Société Nationale Industrielle Aérospatiale, and subsequent development of the N 262 was undertaken by this new company. Two new variants, the N 262 Series C and Series D, were produced, both models later being given the common name Frégate. The main difference between these two models and their predecessors was the installation of 1145-ehp Bastan VII turboprops in place of the lower-powered Bastan VICs, and an increase in span of 0.7 m (2 ft 3½ in) with new wingtips designed to improve low-speed handling. The two new features were test flown on a converted N 262A from July 1968, and production began in 1970, the types being certificated on December 24, 1970. The two Frégate types are basically similar, the former Series C aircraft being intended for civil operators, and the Series D for military users. Of the 33 Frégates built, 24 went to the French air force.

The effect of the more powerful engines has been a general increase in the Frégate's performance and capabilities compared with the N 262, though payload has been reduced by 195 kg (430 lb). Speed is increased by 33 km/h (20½ mph), rate of climb is better, and maximum fuel range is 270 km (168 miles) greater.

Production of the N 262 and Frégate ended in 1976, despite Aérospatiale's proposal of a revised version, the N 262A-II, with improved performance and capabilities.

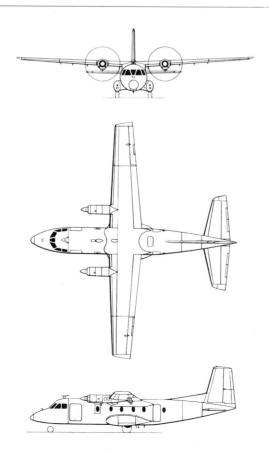

Above: A Nord 262 in the livery of Allegheny Airlines of Washington, DC
Right: An N262B of Touraine Air Transport; it was previously registered as F-WLHS. TAT has two N262s on its books, and operates an inter-city service within north and eastern France

Nord 262A

Type: short-range light transport
Maker: Nord-Aviation; Société Nationale Industrielle Aérospatiale
Span: 21.9 m (71 ft 10 in)
Length: 19.28 m (63 ft 3 in)
Height: 6.2 m (20 ft 4 in)
Wing area: 55 m² (592 sq ft)
Weight: maximum 10 600 kg (23 369 lb); empty 6763 kg (14 910 lb)
Powerplant: two 1080-ehp Turboméca Bastan VIC turboprops
Performance: maximum cruising speed 375 km/h (233 mph); range with 26 passengers and reserves 975 km (606 miles)
Payload: 3270 kg (7209 lb); seats for up to 29 passengers
Crew: 2
Production: 77 (N 262) and 33 (Frégate)

DHC-6 Twin Otter, de Havilland Canada

FIRST FLIGHT 1965

THE DHC-6 Twin Otter, constructed by the de Havilland Aircraft Company of Canada, was first announced in 1964. It is a logical progression from the company's other STOL (short take-off and landing) utility and light transport aircraft, starting with the 1947 DHC-2 Beaver and progressing with the DHC-3 Otter of 1951. De Havilland Canada's next two aircraft, the DHC-4 Caribou and DHC-5 Buffalo, are twin-engined STOL utility transports intended mainly for military users, but with the DHC-6 Twin Otter the company made a determined and highly successful attempt to capture a large portion of the twin-turboprop commuter airliner market.

Design of the Twin Otter began in January 1964, and the aircraft has many points of similarity with the Otter. The fuselage is based on that of the Otter, but lengthened and provided with new nose and tail sections. The wing is also based on that of the Otter, but is of greater span. In addition, as with other STOL types produced by de Havilland Canada, the STOL performance is achieved by a large wing of high aspect ratio, provided in the case of the Twin Otter with double-slotted wide-span trailing-edge flaps. Power is provided by a pair of Pratt & Whitney Aircraft of Canada PT6A turboprops and the Twin Otter is fitted with a fixed tricycle undercarriage for the sake of simplicity and reduced cost, despite the small penalty that must be paid in terms of drag.

Construction of the first five Twin Otters began in November 1964, and the initial aircraft took to the air on May 20, 1965 powered by two 579-ehp

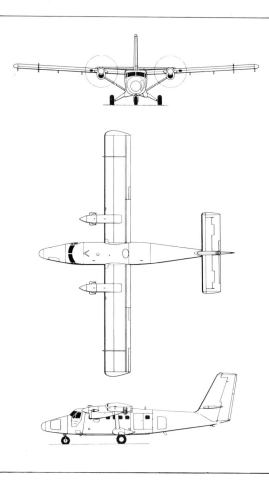

DHC-6 Series 300

Type: short-range STOL light transport
Maker: de Havilland Aircraft of Canada Ltd
Span: 19.81 m (65 ft)
Length: 15.77 m (51 ft 9 in)
Height: 5.66 m (18 ft 7 in)
Wing area: 39 m² (420 sq ft)
Weight: maximum 5670 kg (12 500 lb); empty 3320 kg (7320 lb)
Powerplant: two 652-ehp Pratt & Whitney Aircraft of Canada PT6A-27 turboprops
Performance: maximum cruising speed 338 km/h (210 mph) at 3048 m (10 000 ft); range with an 1157-kg (2550-lb) payload 1278 km (794 miles)
Payload: 2005 kg (4420 lb); seats for up to 20 passengers
Crew: 1 to 2
Production: minimum 700

PT6A-6 turboprops. The next two aircraft had the same powerplant, but subsequent machines had the PT6A-20, also of 579-ehp rating.

The first production model was the Series 100, of which 115 in all were built. US Federal Aviation Administration Type Approval of the Twin Otter was secured in May 1966, and the first production aircraft was delivered to the Ontario Department of Land and Forests in July 1966.

The first Twin Otter Series 200 was delivered in April 1968, and total production of this model was also 115. The Series 200 aircraft was in nearly every respect similar to the Series 100, the one major difference being the provision of a larger nose with increased baggage stowage on the Series 200.

From the spring of 1969 the standard production model became the Series 300, fitted with 652-ehp PT6A-27 turboprops enabling maximum take-off weight to be increased by about 454 kg (1000 lb). As with the two earlier models, the Series 300 can be used on float and ski undercarriages. All float-equipped Twin Otters are fitted with the short nose characteristic of the Series 100 aircraft. Also an unusual feature of the Twin Otter is the provision for the fitting of an optional freight pack in the ventral position under the fuselage. This can carry a load up to 272 kg (600 lb) in weight.

Although the Twin Otter was designed for relatively spartan commuter services, the type's good STOL performance in 1973 persuaded the Canadian government to order six special models, designated Series 300S, to test the feasibility of STOL commuter services on an inter-city basis.

Passenger accommodation on the six Series 300S aircraft was for 11, all provided with full airline seating, and the aircraft were modified to increase their safety in operations from small paved runways in urban areas.

These improvements include the provision of upper-wing spoilers, high-capacity brakes, emergency brakes, an anti-skid braking system, improved protection in the event of an engine fire, other systems modifications, and the installation of full airline-standard avionics.

The six aircraft were used from July 24, 1974 by Airtransit Canada, a subsidiary of Air Canada, on the route between Montreal and Ottawa, fully vindicating the inter-city commuter concept for STOL aircraft.

Left: A Twin Otter of the Norwegian airline Widerøe's Flyveselskap
Below left: A Twin Otter at the Canadian National Air Show in 1973
Below: Air Wisconsin operated the DHC-6 in the mid 1960s when they were established
Bottom: A DHC-6 of Rio Airways at San Angelo, Texas, in May 1979

L-100 Hercules, Lockheed

FIRST FLIGHT 1964

THE Lockheed-Georgia company's Hercules, designed in 1951 to a US Air Force tactical airlift requirement, has enjoyed unparalleled success as a military freighter, more than 1500 having been delivered by 1979. However, preliminary attempts to market a commercial version were unsuccessful.

On April 21, 1964, however, Lockheed flew the first example of a civil Hercules, designated Model 382-44K-20 and derived from the military C-130E. This model received its US Federal Aviation Administration Type Approval on February 16, 1965, with deliveries of the initial Model 382B and L-100 aircraft beginning later in the year, notably to Alaska Airlines, Continental Air Services and Zambia Air Cargoes. These were supplemented in 1966 and 1967 by Airlift International, Delta Airlines, Interior Air Service, and Pacific Western Airlines. Not one of the following model, the L-100-10, was built: this was a proposed variant with 4500-shp Allison 501-D22A turboprops in place of the L-100's 4050-shp Allison 501-D22 engines.

The next model was thus the Model 382E, later redesignated L-100-20. Lockheed-Georgia began work on this variant in 1967, stretching the fuselage, with a view to producing a civil Hercules with better operating economics. The resulting Model 382E is some 2.54 m (8 ft 4 in) longer than its predecessor thanks to the insertion of plugs of 1.52 m (5 ft) in the forward fuselage, and of 1.02 m (3 ft 4 in) in the aft fuselage. The powerplant comprised four 4500-shp Allison 501-D22As, and though maximum weight remained unaltered at 70 308 kg (155 000 lb) the performance and capa-

bilities of the L-100-20 were considerably improved when compared with those of the L-100.

The original Model 382 company demonstration aircraft was converted to L-100-20 standard and first flew in its new form on April 19, 1968. With FAA Type Approval being secured on October 4, 1968, the L-100-20 was soon in service, and so successful did the new type prove that many of the original L-100/Model 382B aircraft were modified to L-100-20 standard. Two basically similar Model 382Fs were produced, the powerplant being four 4050-shp Allison 501-D22s.

Next to appear was the Model 382G, or L-100-30, with yet another fuselage stretch, this time of 2.03 m (6 ft 8 in). The origins of this sub-type lie with Saturn Airways, which had a requirement for an aircraft to carry the entire powerplant sets for the Lockheed-California L-1011 TriStar airliner, consisting of three Rolls-Royce RB.211 turbofan engines, from England to California. Lockheed-Georgia took the opportunity presented by the development of this model to eliminate some purely military features from the aircraft, these including JATO (jet-assisted take-off – strictly speaking this should be rocket-assisted take-off) capability, paratroop doors and the rear cargo windows. The first L-100-30 flew on August 14, 1970 and with FAA Type Approval following on October 7, Saturn was able to begin operating L-100-30s in December 1970.

Lockheed-Georgia is currently seeking customers for its proposed L-100-50, intended as a prime freighter in the resources-support field. The key to

Right: The interior of an Indonesian L-100-30. The rear cargo windows and paratroop doors are eliminated on this model, and the seats can be removed to carry freight

the L-100-50, which the company hope to launch in 1980, is a further stretch of the fuselage. Two plugs (one forward of the wing measuring 6.1 m [20 ft] and one aft of the wing measuring 4.57 m [15 ft]) would increase length by 10.67 m (35 ft) overall. To improve the freight hold, Lockheed-Georgia propose to redesign the main undercarriage units to eliminate the L-100-30's 'bulges'.

Among other L-100 proposals, Lockheed-Georgia have suggested a corporate passenger-carrier, with palletized seating and other facilities for 105 passengers, this accommodation being loaded straight through the rear doors when needed. There is also the L-400 proposal: a cut-down L-100 with a shorter wing and two 4591-shp Allison 501-D22D turboprops.

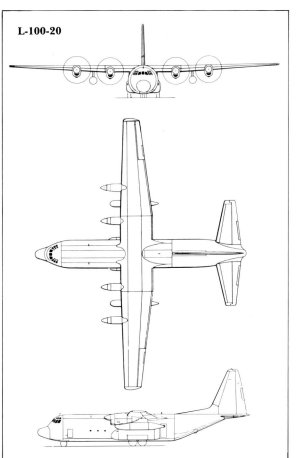

L-100-20

L-100-30

Type: medium- and long-range transport
Maker: Lockheed-Georgia Co
Span: 40.41 m (132 ft 7 in)
Length: 34.37 m (112 ft 9 in)
Height: 11.73 m (38 ft 6 in)
Wing area: 162 m² (1745 sq ft)
Weight: maximum 70 308 kg (155 000 lb); empty 33 563 kg (73 993 lb)
Powerplant: four 4508-ehp Allison 501-D22A turboprops
Performance: maximum cruising speed 581 km/h (361 mph) at 6096 km (20 000 ft); range with maximum payload and reserves 3363 km (2090 miles)
Payload: 23 137 kg (51 007 lb); seats for up to 105 passengers
Crew: 4 to 5
Production: 65 ordered by 1980

Far left: A Saturn Airways L-100-30, the first airline to operate the type in December 1970
Above: A colourful Angola Airlines L-100-30 in flight, with extended nose and slightly stretched body. The HF rail aerial along the top of the fuselage was seldom fitted to other L-100 versions
Left: The twin Hercules L-400 flying over Stone Mountain, Atlanta. Lockheed-Georgia have retained all the transport features of the standard Hercules, including the large cargo compartment

Carstedt Jet Liner

FIRST FLIGHT 1966

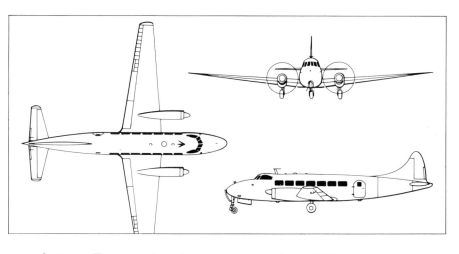

THE basic soundness of the concept which led de Havilland to produce its classic DH.104 Dove and DH.114 Heron light transports is attested in a number of ways, but none of these is more cogent than the variety of turboprop conversions made of the two types. Typical of Dove conversions is the Jet Liner 600 produced by Carstedt of Long Beach, California. The object of the exercise was to produce a low-cost turboprop light transport with seating for 18 passengers, and a high performance guaranteed by the installation of two relatively powerful turboprops, the chosen type being the 605-ehp Garrett-AiResearch TPE331. The type of customer whom Carstedt sought to attract is indicated by the fact that no provision was made for cabin heating, and adequate cooling was ensured by the provision of an AiResearch refrigeration system.

Intended for third-level and commuter operators, the Jet Liner 600 was first flown on December 18, 1966 and soon showed its paces and advantageous operating economics. Basic seating for 18 passengers was standard, the extra accommodation compared with the Dove coming from a plug of 2.21 m (7 ft 3 in) inserted in the rear fuselage. At the same time, improved performance was aided by lowering the height of the cockpit. This necessitated lowering the crew's seats and shifting forward the instrument panel by 20.3 cm (8 in), to give the crew adequate headroom.

The two TPE331 engines were fitted in long nacelles, and drove constant-speed, fully feathering and reversible three-blade propellers of Hartzell manufacture. To provide adequate range, the prototype Jet Liner 600 was fitted with additional fuel tankage of 850 litres (187 Imp gal) in the wings outboard of the engines. The feature was optional on production Jet Liner 600s.

A similar conversion was undertaken by Channel Airways at Southend, but the attempt was given up before much work had been done. Other American efforts towards the modernization of the Dove have not been notably successful, a typical example being the Riley Turbo Executive 400, with two 400-hp Lycoming piston engines.

Final marketing of the Jet Liner 600 was undertaken by the Texas Airplane Manufacturing Company and the aircraft had uprated engines and was designated CJ600.

CJ600

Type: light transport
Maker: Texas Airplane Manufacturing Co Inc
Span: 17.37 m (57 ft)
Length: 14.17 m (46 ft 6 in)
Height: 4.06 m (13 ft 4 in)
Wing area: 31.12 m² (335 sq ft)
Weight: maximum 4762 kg (10 500 lb); empty approx 2721 kg (6000 lb)
Powerplant: two 705-ehp Garrett-AiResearch TPE331-101E turboprops
Performance: maximum cruising speed 463 km/h (288 mph) at 3048 m (10 000 ft); range with maximum payload 805 km (500 miles)
Payload: seats for up to 18 passengers
Crew: 2
Production: not available

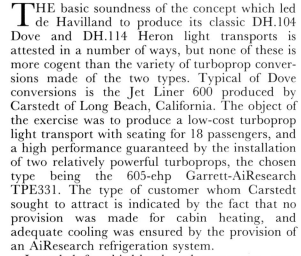

Top: The Carstedt Jet Liner in manufacturer's livery
Left: A Jet Liner at Love Field, Dallas, Texas in September 1972. The aircraft is intended for third-level commuter operators, and can carry 18 passengers

ST-27, Saunders

FIRST FLIGHT 1969

THE Saunders Aircraft Corporation was formed in 1968, with the specific intention of manufacturing turboprop conversions of the successful de Havilland DH.114 Heron. Powered by four rather than two piston engines, the Heron was designed for economical operations over short- and medium-range routes, using the most primitive of airfields. However the DH.114 Series 1 had a fixed undercarriage, whereas the definitive Series 2 had a simple retractable undercarriage.

Saunders rightly appreciated that the Heron Series 2's capabilities and field performance were admirably suited for the requirements of small operators, and that performance could be brought up to a higher level by the installation of two turboprop engines in place of the four 250-hp de Havilland Gipsy Queen 30 piston engines. The engine selected was the 715-ehp Pratt & Whitney Aircraft of Canada PT6A-27, and the first such conversion flew on May 18, 1969. Apart from a measure of structural strengthening and modification associated with the new powerplant, the most notable difference between the Heron and the ST-27, as the new type was designated, was the lengthening of the fuselage from 14.78 m (48 ft 6 in) to 17.93 m (58 ft 10 in) to increase seating from 17 to 23. In all, 13 ST-27 conversions were produced before a shortage of Herons suitable for conversion led Saunders to explore a new type design.

This was the ST-27B, pioneered in fact by the thirteenth ST-27 under the designation ST-27A. This aircraft first flew on July 18, 1974 and its success fully vindicated the concept of building the

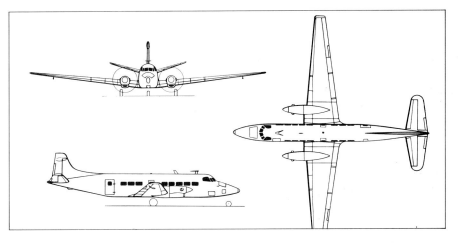

new aircraft from scratch, which also allowed the structure and systems to be revised to meet updated requirements. At the same time the vertical tail surfaces were redesigned, the interior modified, more powerful engines fitted, and fuel tankage increased. The ST-27B was redesignated ST-28 on February 1, 1975, and some seven of the type had been ordered by the end of the month.

Saunders initiated the production of a first batch of 15 ST-28s, but early in 1976 the company was forced into liquidation by the withdrawal of financial support by the provincial government of Manitoba, just after the sole ST-28 had taken to the air on December 12, 1974. At the time of this flight, the company had secured orders for 34 ST-28s, which indicated that it had a useful future.

ST-27

Type: short-range light transport
Maker: Saunders Aircraft Corporation Ltd
Span: 21.79 m (71 ft 6 in)
Length: 17.98 m (59 ft)
Height: 4.75 m (15 ft 7 in)
Wing area: 46.36 m² (499 sq ft)
Weight: maximum 6124 kg (13 500 lb); empty 3175 kg (7000 lb)
Powerplant: two 715-ehp United Aircraft of Canada PT6A-27 turboprops
Performance: maximum cruising speed 370 km/h (230 mph); maximum range 1315 km (817 miles)
Payload: 435 kg (960 lb) baggage; seats for up to 23 passengers
Crew: 2
Production: 13

Top: An ST-27 in Saunders Aircraft Corporation colours
Left: The ST-27 was judged ideal for firms like Tropic Air which operates an inter-island service in Barbados

239

Metro, Swearingen

FIRST FLIGHT 1970

THE Metro pressurized third-level airliner was designed by E J Swearingen before the absorption of his company, Swearingen Aviation Corporation, by Fairchild Industries in 1971.

Planned for third-level commuter airlines, the Metro has basic seating for 20 in single seats on each side of the central aisle, and all the comforts of a full-size airliner. With considerable foresight and ingenuity, however, Swearingen also made the basic design capable of accepting alternative interiors suiting the aircraft to executive use, as a flying ambulance, as a flying hospital, as a photographic-survey aircraft, and as a cargo aircraft.

The Metro first flew on June 11, 1970, and after receiving its US Federal Aviation Administration Type Approval, entered service in the first part of 1971. The type found ready acceptance, and the order book grew satisfactorily. Matters were further improved in 1974 with the introduction of the Metro II. This introduced a number of improvements to the flight deck and aircraft systems, larger windows, and provision for a JATO (jet-assisted take-off) unit. This last is most unusual in civil aircraft, and consists of an optional 159-kg (350-lb) st rocket in the tail to improve the Metro II's performance in 'hot and high' conditions. For the same purpose there is also provision for water/alcohol injection to the Garrett-AiResearch turboprops.

Separated from the passenger cabin by an optional bulkhead is a freight compartment. This is pressurized, and has a volume of $3.85 \, m^3$ (136 cu ft). Loading is effected through a large door

in the left side of the rear fuselage. The Metro is also offered in an all-freight configuration without windows. The elimination of passenger seating and facilities allows the payload to be increased slightly, from 1778 kg (3920 lb) to 2064 kg (4550 lb). Baggage is carried, in the passenger version, in an unpressurized compartment in the nose, and this has a volume of $1.27 \, m^3$ (45 cu ft).

The main variant of the Metro is the Merlin IV, the Merlin IVA being similarly derived from the Metro II. These aircraft have no link with earlier Merlin models, except for the fact that they are intended as executive transports. The Merlin IV and IVA are at first glance externally similar to their 'parent' aircraft, with the exception of a reduced number of fuselage windows reflecting

Above: A Swearingen Metro, a popular commuter aircraft in the USA, taxies off the main landing strip of a US domestic airport

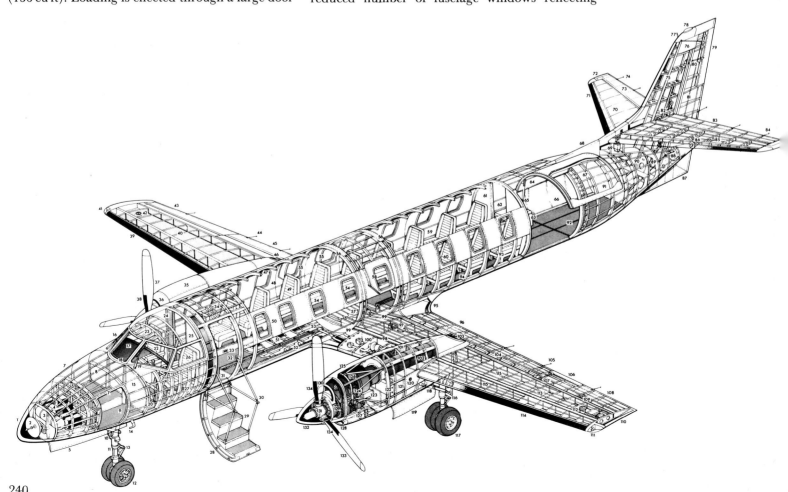

Left: A Metro of Air
Wisconsin Inc at Purdue
University Airport. Air
Wisconsin operates 13 Metros
and connects with towns
around Chicago and
Minneapolis/St Paul

the smaller passenger capacity of the Merlins.

Designed as comfortable transports for corporate officers, the Merlin IV and IVA have seating for 12 to 15 passengers, together with a lavatory and increased baggage stowage. This latter has a volume of 4.05 m³ (143 cu ft). Another difference is that the fuel capacity of the Merlin IV and IVA is reduced from the 2452 litres (539 Imp gal) of the Metro II to 2096 litres (461 Imp gal). The Merlin IVA cruises at a speed some 26 km/h (16 mph) faster than that of the Metro II, and also at an altitude of 4877 m (16 000 ft) rather than 3048 m (10 000 ft). The reduction in fuel capacity is reflected in the Merlin IVA's ferry range of 3371 km (2095 miles) compared with the Metro II's 3952 km (2456 miles).

The pressurization and full airline-standard instrumentation of the Metro II prepares the aircraft well for its other intended missions. In the air ambulance role the aircraft can carry up to 10 litter patients, while in the flying hospital role the aircraft can be fitted out as an emergency operating theatre. For aerial survey work the Metro II can accommodate one or two cameras.

It is the type's ease of conversion to these other roles which has made it popular with the armed forces of smaller countries such as the Royal Oman Police Air Wing, which has two, and the Chilean Police Department, which has four. Other major users are Air Wisconsin and Southern Airways, the former with 12 aircraft and the latter with eight. By 1980 Metros were in worldwide use.

SA-226TC Metro II

Type: short-range transport
Maker: Swearingen Aviation Corporation, Fairchild Industries
Span: 14.1 m (46 ft 3 in)
Length: 18.1 m (59 ft 4¾ in)
Height: 5.12 m (16 ft 9¾ in)
Wing area: 25.78 m² (278 sq ft)
Weight: maximum 5670 kg (12 500 lb); empty 3379 kg (7450 lb)
Powerplant: two 940-shp Garrett-AiResearch TPE331-3UW-303G turboprops
Performance: maximum cruising speed 473 km/h (294 mph) at 3048 m (10 000 ft); range with maximum payload and reserves 346 km (215 miles)
Payload: 1778 kg (3920 lb); seats for up to 20 passengers
Crew: 2
Production: minimum 86 by January 1979

Swearingen Metro II

1 Radome
2 Weather radar scanner
3 Oxygen bottle
4 Radio and electronics equipment
5 Nosewheel door
6 Baggage restraint net
7 Baggage doors, forward opening
8 Fuselage nose construction
9 Nose baggage hold
10 Landing and taxi lamp
11 Nosewheel leg
12 Twin nosewheels
13 Torque scissors
14 Pitot tube
15 Cockpit pressure bulkhead
16 Windscreen panels
17 Instrument panel shroud
18 Curved centre panel
19 Windscreen wipers
20 Rudder pedals
21 Control column
22 Co-pilot's seat
23 Cockpit roof construction
24 Cockpit bulkhead
25 Electrical panels
26 Pilot's seat
27 Pilot's side control panel
28 Passenger door
29 Airstairs
30 Handrails
31 Entry doorway
32 Cabin centre aisle floor
33 Air conditioning duct louvre
34 Forward fuselage frame construction
35 Right engine cowlings
36 Engine intake
37 Hartzell three-blade constant-speed reversing and feathering propeller
38 Propeller de-icing boot
39 Leading edge de-icing
40 Right wing fuel tank
41 Right navigation light
42 Fuel filler tank
43 Right aileron
44 Static dischargers
45 Right flap
46 Tailpipe exhaust duct
47 Fuselage frames
48 Cabin interior trim panels
49 Passenger seats
50 Window side panel
51 Cabin floor construction
52 Seat rails
53 Air trunking
54 Cabin windows
55 Right emergency escape hatches
56 Main fuselage frames
57 Centre box construction
58 Left emergency escape hatch
59 Right seating, ten passengers
60 Left seating, nine passengers
61 Cabin rear bulkhead
62 Toilet compartment door
63 Toilet
64 Rear cargo door
65 Door actuator
66 Rear cargo and baggage compartment
67 Fuselage frame and stringer compartment
68 Fin root fillet
69 Tailplane electric trim jacks
70 Right tailplane
71 Leading edge de-icing
72 Elevator horn balance
73 Right elevator
74 Static dischargers
75 Fin construction
76 Rudder balance
77 Antenna
78 Anti-collision light
79 Rudder trim tab
80 Trim tab control jack
81 Rudder construction
82 Elevator hinge control
83 Left elevator
84 Static dischargers
85 Tailplane construction
86 Tail navigation light
87 Ventral fin
88 Rudder hinge control
89 Tailplane control cables
90 Fin attachment frame
91 Cargo hold rear bulkhead
92 Baggage/cargo hold floor
93 Rear fuselage frames
94 Seat fixing rails
95 Trailing edge root fillet
96 Left flap
97 Fuel pumps
98 Wing main spar
99 Wing spar attachment
100 Air conditioning plant
101 Engine cowling construction
102 Tailpipe
103 Engine exhaust duct
104 Double slotted flap construction
105 Static dischargers
106 Aileron trim tab
107 Trim tab hinge control
108 Left aileron
109 Aileron hinge control
110 Left wing-tip
111 Left navigation light
112 Fuel tank filler cap
113 Wing rib construction
114 Leading edge de-icing
115 Left wing fuel tank
116 Main undercarriage leg
117 Twin mainwheels
118 Retractable strut
119 Mainwheel door
120 Leading edge ice inspection light
121 Main undercarriage wheel bay
122 Hydraulic system reservoir
123 Engine oil tank
124 Engine bearers
125 Detachable engine cowlings
126 Garrett AiResearch TPE 331-3UW-303G turboprop
127 Oil cooler
128 Oil-cooler intake
129 Propeller gearbox
130 Engine intake
131 Propeller reversing and feathering hub mechanism
132 Spinner
133 Hartzell three-blade propeller
134 Propeller blade de-icing boots

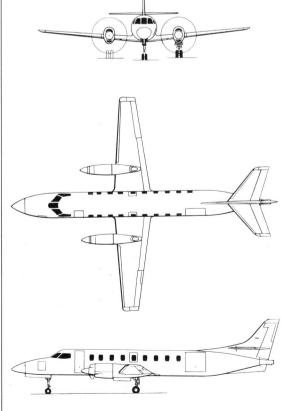

Shorts 330

FIRST FLIGHT 1974

THE Shorts 330 is essentially a refined and enlarged version of the Skyvan utility transport, intended mainly for third-level and commuter operators requiring a slightly larger and higher-powered aircraft to replace the first-generation of such aircraft. Developed as the SD3-30, the 330 uses outer-wing panels based on those of the Skyvan, and a fuselage with the same rectangular section as that of the Skyvan, but lengthened by some 3.78 m (12 ft 5 in).

The basic accommodation is for 30 passengers seated three-abreast (2+1) with an offset aisle. The seats are mounted on rails, however, for the easy conversion of the type to other seating configurations. Maximum use is made of the rectangular-section of the fuselage for the carriage of baggage and freight.

The 330 can also be used for mixed freight/passenger operations, with a bulkhead separating the rear passenger cabin for about 18 people from the forward freight compartment.

The mainwheel units retract neatly into sponsons projecting from the fuselage sides and forming the lower attachment points for the wing bracing struts. The wheels are carried on short pivoted levers rather than legs, and this keeps the fuselage of the 330 close to the ground, thus facilitating loading and unloading.

A natural evolution from the dumpier Skyvan, the 330 was an immediately attractive prospect. One of the major design objectives was to produce quickly an aircraft with a selling price of less than US $1 million, and this was made feasible by the use of Skyvan components.

The first prototype, powered by Pratt & Whitney Aircraft of Canada PT6A-45 turboprops, flew on August 22, 1974, with the second prototype following on July 8, 1975. American orders for the 330 had started to come in some eight days before the first prototype flew.

The first production aircraft flew on December 15, 1975 and was delivered to Time Air of Canada. Time Air flew the first 330 service on August 24, 1976.

Since then the growth of orders has been satisfactory, and should eventually reach 300. Shorts have also planned the military SD3-M version seating 32 troops and a multi-sensor maritime patrol variant, the SD3-MR Seeker which looks superior to most of its competitors.

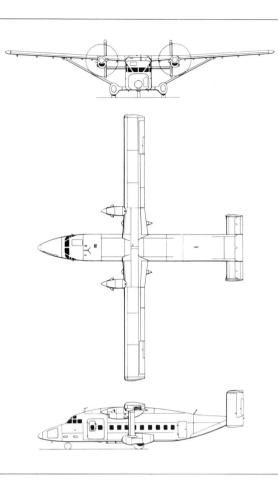

Shorts 330

Type: short- and medium-range transport
Maker: Short Brothers Ltd
Span: 22.76 m (74 ft 8 in)
Length: 17.69 m (58 ft 0½ in)
Height: 4.95 m (16 ft 3 in)
Wing area: 42.1 m² (453 sq ft)
Weight: maximum 10 161 kg (22 400 lb); empty 6536 kg (14 410 lb)
Powerplant: two 1156-shp Pratt & Whitney Aircraft of Canada PT6A-45A turboprops
Performance: maximum cruising speed 365 km/h (227 mph) at 3048 m (10 000 ft); range with maximum payload 804 km (506 miles)
Payload: 3402 kg (7500 lb); seats for up to 30 passengers
Crew: 3
Production: 58 orders by March 1980

Below: N-331GW Shorts 330 (formerly G-BEWT), of Golden West Airlines at Orange County Airport, California
Bottom: A Shorts 330 of Time Air, a Canadian internal airline operating from Lethbridge, Alberta

Jetstream, British Aerospace

FIRST FLIGHT 1967

THE design of the BAe Jetstream started life as the Handley Page HP.137, was taken over by Jetstream Aircraft on the failure of Handley Page, was then bought by Scottish Aviation, and is now the responsibility of the British Aerospace Aircraft Group, Scottish Division.

The decision was made in August 1965 to develop the type for initial single-pilot operation with a maximum take-off weight of up to 5670 kg (12 500 lb), full pressurization, 1.83-m (6-ft) cabin height, a long fatigue life, and provision for the type to be used as a 20-seat commuter aircraft or as an eight-seat executive aircraft.

Considerable interest in the project was immediately shown in the United States, Riley Aeronautics Corporation ordering 20 Jetstreams 'off the drawing board' – even before the decision was made in January 1966 to press ahead with the construction of four prototypes with company funding. Soon after this, the government also decided to invest in the project in the form of a loan. Continued American interest is attested by the conversion of Riley Aeronautics into the Riley Jetstream Corporation, and its subsequent take-over by the International Jetstream Corporation, which had by September 1965 received 65 orders for the as yet unflown aircraft.

The key to the Jetstream's design was an extreme refinement of conventional design, based on a well streamlined fuselage of considerable diameter, straight wings and tailplane, and a swept fin and rudder. One of the main reasons for the selection of the Turboméca Astazou XIV as the

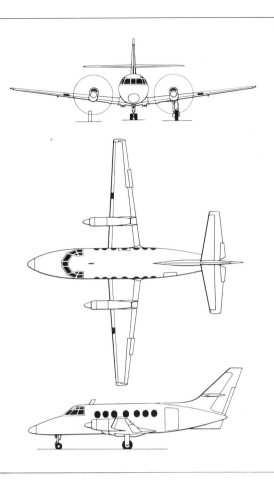

Jetstream Series 200

Type: short- and medium-range light transport
Maker: British Aerospace Aircraft Group, Scottish Division
Span: 15.85 m (52 ft)
Length: 14.37 m (47 ft 1½ in)
Height: 5.32 m (17 ft 5½ in)
Wing area: 25.08 m² (270 sq ft)
Weight: maximum 5700 kg (12 566 lb); empty 3485 kg (7683 lb)
Powerplant: two 996-ehp Turboméca Astazou XVIC2 turboprops
Performance: maximum cruising speed 454 km/h (282 mph) at 3048 m (10 000 ft); range with reserves 2244 km (1380 miles)
Payload: 1730 kg (3814 lb); seats for up to 16 passengers
Crew: 2
Production: 36

Below: A Handley Page Jetstream of Apollo Airways, which provides a commuter link for towns in California

basic powerplant was its small diameter, which confirmed with Handley Page's strenuous efforts to reduce drag to a minimum.

The first prototype flew on August 18, 1967, by which time production of the Jetstream Mk 1 had already started. Although the remaining three prototypes first called for were also engined with Astazou turboprops, the American preference for their own engines was reflected in the provision of Garrett-AiResearch TPE331 turboprops on a fifth prototype.

The TPE331s were largely the result of strong interest in the type shown by the US military. Although the Beechcraft 99 had at first been selected as the US Air Force's new 'mission support' transport, the Secretary of Defense overruled the USAF and called for an initial batch of 11 Jetstreams for trials under the company designation Jetstream 3M. In October 1969 the USAF cancelled their order on the grounds of late delivery, thus placing the whole Jetstream Mk 3 programme for military and civilian users in jeopardy.

Meanwhile the first production Jetstream Mk 1 had flown on December 6, 1968, and was soon ferried to the United States, where Federal Aviation Administration Type Approval was secured in April 1969. Demand for the new aircraft was brisk in the United States, but Handley Page's severe financial problems were badly hampering production, and only 38 aircraft had been delivered by the time of the company's collapse in 1970. Another ten Jetstreams were subsequently built from components already produced, five by Jetstream Aircraft and five by Scottish Aviation.

Scottish Aviation also took up development of the Astazou XVI-powered Jetstream Mk 2 (Series 200), 26 of which were produced for the Royal Air Force as Jetstream T.1, some of them subsequently becoming Royal Navy T.2s.

Current hopes for a renaissance of the Jetstream in production rest with the Mk 31, proposed by the Scottish Division during 1978 with a pair of Garrett-AiResearch TPE331-10 turboprops flat-rated to 840 shp each. The Astazous have been unpopular in the United States (one Jetstream has been re-engined with PT6A-34s by Riley, while Century Aircraft and Volpar have produced the Century Jetstream III with TPE331-3U-303s), so the proposal clearly has merit for this otherwise first-rate aircraft.

Be-30, Beriev

FIRST FLIGHT 1967

THE Beriev Be-30 feederliner has the distinction of being the only landplane known to have been produced by the Beriev design bureau, which has since 1932 concentrated on the development of flying boats. Design of the Be-30 began in 1965 in response to an Aeroflot requirement for a replacement for the Antonov An-2, Ilyushin Il-14 and Lisunov Li-2 as a feederliner able to operate from the most primitive airfields over routes up to 300 km (186 miles) in length. The primitive-field requirement is clearly recognized in the Be-30's adoption of a high-wing layout to keep the engines and propellers clear of runway debris, though this entailed the provision of main undercarriage legs of considerable 'stalkiness'.

The first Be-30 prototype flew on March 3, 1967 on the power of a pair of 740-hp Shvetsov ASh-21 radial piston engines. It seems that at this stage the Russians were contemplating the installation on production Be-30s of 922-shp Turboméca Astazou XIV turboprops. This scheme came to nothing, however, and while an experimental installation of a pair of turboprops appears to have been made in 1967, the Russians maintain that a turboprop-powered Be-30 did not take to the air until July 14, 1968.

The powerplant in this instance was a pair of 950-ehp Glushenkov TVD-10 turboprops in slim nacelles projecting to the rear of the trailing edge to provide a housing for the long legs of the rearward-retracting main undercarriage legs. To facilitate operations from rough fields, the tyres fitted were of the low-pressure type.

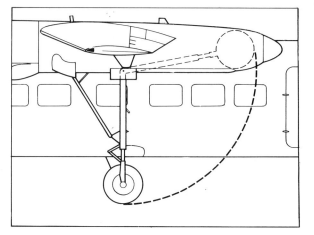

An unusual feature of this STOL (short take-off and landing) type was the mechanical linkage of the two engines by means of a drive shaft through the wings. This provided for both propellers to be driven from one engine in the event of the other engine failing. Such a feature was thought desirable for the type of operations to be undertaken by the Be-30, extra low-speed handling and lift capacity being provided by the double-slotted ailerons and flaps.

Intended for limited services only, the Be-30 was designed for single-crew operation. This meant that an extra passenger could sit in the cockpit alongside the pilot, raising passenger capacity in the standard layout to 15. The other 14 passengers sat in the unpressurized main cabin in single seats

located on each side of the central aisle. To the rear of the passenger cabin were the lavatory and baggage compartment, the latter having a volume of 1.6 m³ (57 cu ft).

An additional quantity of baggage can be stowed in a compartment between the cockpit and passenger cabin. The payload of the Be-30 was supplemented by a main compartment in the nose of the aircraft. Entry and exit from the aircraft were effected by means of an inbuilt folding airstair. The Be-30 was also to have been offered in a high-density configuration with seating for 20 passengers in the main cabin at the expense of baggage.

Figures released by Aviaexport, the Russian aircraft export agency, revealed the Be-30 as having impressively low operating costs over a stage length of 600 km (373 miles) with a payload of 1285 kg (2833 lb), but the type was not seen in the West after its appearance at the Paris air show of 1969. Any further mention of the aircraft in the Russian media ended in 1971. It is now clear, however, that despite earlier assessments that the Be-30 had been abandoned because of development problems, the real reason for the type's failure to enter production is different.

The Be-30 was evaluated against a Czech competitor, the Let L-410 Turbolet, and rejected in favour of the Czech aircraft. This led to the termination of the Be-30 programme, which had also envisaged other versions of the aircraft: as an executive aircraft, an aerial survey aircraft and an ambulance aircraft with accommodation for nine litters, six sitting casualties and an attendant.

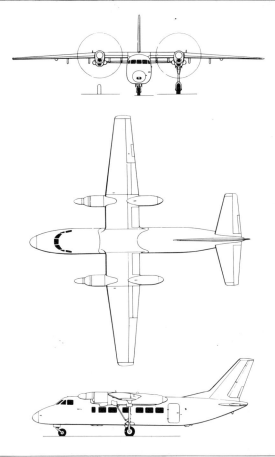

Be-30

Type: short- and medium-range STOL transport
Maker: Beriev Design Bureau
Span: 17 m (55 ft 9½ in)
Length: 15.7 m (51 ft 6 in)
Height: not available
Wing area: 32 m² (344½ sq ft)
Weight: maximum 5860 kg (12 919 lb); empty not available
Powerplant: two 950-ehp Glushenkov TVD-10 turboprops
Performance: cruising speed up to 480 km/h (298 mph); range with 1250-kg (2756-lb) payload and reserves 600 km (373 miles)
Payload: 1500 kg (3307 lb); seats for up to 15 passengers
Crew: 1
Production: not available

Turbo-Islander, Britten-Norman

FIRST FLIGHT 1977

THE Britten-Norman Turbo-Islander, essentially a turboprop-powered derivative of the best-selling Islander utility transport and feeder-liner, was announced by the manufacturer on October 29, 1975. The substitution of two 400-shp turboprops for the Islander's 260- or 300-hp Lycoming piston engines can be achieved with minimal structural alteration, which increases performance and payload without a commensurate increase in specific fuel consumption.

Design of the Turbo-Islander began in August 1975, the engine envisaged being the 600-shp Avco Lycoming LTP101, flat-rated to 400 shp. To cater for the increased power of this unit the wings have been strengthened structurally, as has the fuselage. The maximum take-off weight of the Turbo-Islander being 318 kg (700 lb) greater than that of the standard Islander, the undercarriage has also been beefed up. The fuselage is basically that of the Islander provided with the optional nose extension of 1.15 m (3 ft 9¼ in) for baggage stowage.

The Turbo-Islander can be fitted with either of the wings developed for the Islander: the BN-2B-40 set with a span of 14.94 m (49 ft), or the BN-2B-41 set with the extended-tip span of 16.15 m (53 ft). These sharply raked-back tip extensions house additional fuel (111.5 litres [24½ Imp gal] in each), providing the Turbo-Islander with a maximum fuel weight of 849 kg (1872 lb). As with the Islander, the Turbo-Islander can also carry additional fuel tanks on pylons under the wings, each of the two tanks carrying 227 litres (50 Imp gal).

The first Turbo-Islander, with BN-2A-41 wings

from an initial production Islander (rather than from the later Islander II which forms the basis of the Turbo Islander), flew on April 6, 1977. The basic Islander was placed in production in 1966 and by 1974 had become the most successful British multi-engined airliner, orders exceeding the figure of 540 achieved by the de Havilland Dove. This is all the more impressive when it is remembered that the Islander was designed and produced by a small company. Britten-Norman designed the Islander to meet the requirements of Cameroon Air Transport, in which it had a 25% holding, for a twin-engined short-range airliner able to seat at least six passengers, with good take-off performance and minimal maintenance requirements.

The BN-2 Islander first flew on June 13, 1965,

Top left: F-OCRG, one of four Islanders in service with the New Hebrides-based firm of Air Melanesiae at Port Villa in July 1977
Above left: An Islander of Munz Northern Airlines of Alaska, which was previously registered G-BDZL
Above: A pre-delivery flight for a Trislander for Inter-Island Airways of the Seychelles

Left: A Pilatus Britten-Norman Turbo-Islander over Southampton water

and in this prototype form was powered by two 210-hp Rolls-Royce Continental IO-360 piston engines. Performance was adequate but the designers felt that more power and increased wing area would be beneficial, and so the prototype was revised with 260-hp Lycoming O-540-E inlines and span increased from 13.72 m (45 ft) to 14.94 m (49 ft). The first production Islander flew on April 24, 1967, and deliveries began on August 13, 1967 to Glos-Air following the receipt of British certification on August 10. Type approval by the US Federal Aviation Administration followed on December 19, 1967.

The standard aircraft has proved highly successful and Britten-Norman has developed other variants to meet specific requirements: longer ranges made possible by the use of extra tanks in extended span wings of 16.15 m (53 ft); better hot and high performances bestowed by the installation of 300-hp Lycoming IO-540-K1B5 engines; other performance benefits are available with the use of supercharged TIO-540-K engines or standard engines fitted with Riley-Rajay superchargers; and extra capabilities can be bestowed by crop spraying and dusting equipment, a water-bombing installation, float or ski undercarriages, and a number of other detailed improvements.

The Trislander, evolved in 1968, is basically an Islander with a stretched fuselage capable of accommodating 17 passengers, and a third 260-hp Lycoming O-540-E4C5 engine mounted in a bullet, in a cell, half-way up the fin to ensure adequate performance at increased weight.

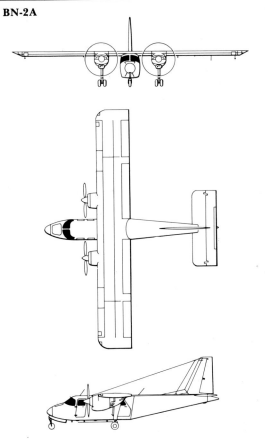

BN-2A

BN-2B-40 Turbo-Islander

Type: short-range transport
Maker: Pilatus Britten-Norman (Bembridge) Ltd
Span: 14.94 m (49 ft)
Length: 12.02 m (39 ft 5¼ in)
Height: 4.18 m (13 ft 8¾ in)
Wing area: 30.19 m² (325 sq ft)
Weight: maximum 3311 kg (7300 lb); empty not available
Powerplant: two 600-shp (flat-rated to 400-shp) Lycoming LTP101 turboprops
Performance: maximum cruising speed 354 km/h (220 mph) at 3048 m (10000 ft); range with maximum fuel and reserves 1260 km (783 miles)
Payload: seats for up to 9 passengers
Crew: 1
Production: still under development

L-410, Let

FIRST FLIGHT 1969

THE L-410 Turbolet produced by the Let Narodni Podnik (Let National Corporation) is an interesting Czech competitor in the world market for a twin-turboprop third-level and commuter airliner, and is the first major type to be designed by the company. In common with most of its contemporary equivalents, the L-410 is a high-wing design, and it is capable of mixed freight/passenger operations.

The L-410 was from the beginning planned with a view to the same basic airframe being suitable for passenger, freight, aerial survey, flying ambulance, training and executive operations. Serious design work began in 1966 on the basic passenger version with seating for between 15 and 19 three-abreast (2+1) with the aisle offset to the left. At the same time the Motorlet company began full-scale development of the chosen engine, the Walter M 601 turboprop, rated at 740 ehp.

Essential features of the L-410 include a somewhat dumpy fuselage, a high-set straight wing with an aspect ratio of 9.3:1, a straight tailplane, a slightly swept fin and rudder assembly, and a retractable tricycle undercarriage. The main units of the undercarriage fold into large blisters on each side of the fuselage, thus keeping the fuselage as close to the ground as possible. This means that loading and unloading the L-410 is very simple (the door sills are only 0.8 m [2 ft 7½ in] from the ground). The seats can be stripped out of the aircraft quickly, and as the fuselage floor is at truck-bed height, freight transfer is singularly easy.

Provision was also made for the use of the L-410

for paratrooping, by the removal of both halves of the door in the left side of the rear fuselage; for de luxe transport, with individual seating for 12 passengers; for executive use with eight individual seats and four desks; and for flying ambulance work with provision for an attendant, five seated casualties and six litters. There are baggage compartments, in the nose and behind the passenger cabin, and a lavatory is standard.

Design and construction proceeded smoothly, but somewhat in advance of engine development. This meant that when the first prototype flew on April 16, 1969, it was powered by a pair of 715-ehp Pratt & Whitney Aircraft of Canada PT6A-27 turboprops. Despite the slightly lower power of the PT6A-27s compared with the M 601s planned, the

Above: A Let L-410AF (aerial photography and survey version). This example was the only one built of this sub-type, and was exported to Hungary in 1974. The nose compartment was larger, wider and more extensively glazed than that of the L-410A passenger version
Below: An L-410 of Slov-Air; the first aircraft was delivered in 1971. During trials it proved superior to the Soviet Beriev Be-30

performance and handling of the four prototypes was more than adequate, the only problem being with airframe vibration and cabin noise, cured by the installation of Hartzell propellers.

Production of the L-410A, as the initial production model was designated, began in 1970 and the first aircraft was delivered to Slov-Air during 1971. Scheduled services began towards the end of the year. It was this model, which had slight increases in wing span and overall length compared with the prototypes, that proved superior to the Beriev Be-30 in comparative evaluation of the two types.

The next model was the L-410AF aerial-survey aircraft. This is derived from the L-410A, but has a larger, glazed nose for the navigator, two cameras in the lower fuselage, and a darkroom in the previous passenger accommodation. The nose modification, it should be noted, prevents the nosewheel from being retracted.

The M 601 turboprop finally made its appearance in the form of the 730-ehp M 601A on the L-410M. This model has seating for 17 passengers, and was first flown in 1973. Whereas the L-410A with Canadian engines is intended principally for the western market, the M 610A-engined L-410M is designed for the simpler needs of the Communist bloc airlines operating the type since 1976.

The latest version, whose designation is not yet known, is a stretched model currently under development. This has a fuselage some 0.6 m (1 ft 11⅔ in) longer than the L-410A and L-410M, presumably to accommodate an extra row of seats.

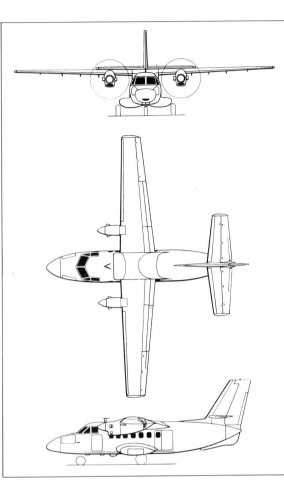

L-410A Turbolet

Type: short-range light transport
Maker: Let Národní Podnik
Span: 17.48 m (57 ft 4¼ in)
Length: 13.61 m (44 ft 7¾ in)
Height: 5.65 m (18 ft 6½ in)
Wing area: 32.86 m² (353⅔ sq ft)
Weight: maximum 5700 kg (12 566 lb); empty 3400 kg (7495 lb)
Powerplant: two 715-ehp Pratt & Whitney Aircraft of Canada PT6A-27 turboprops
Performance: maximum cruising speed 370 km/h (230 mph) at 3000 m (9842 ft); range with maximum payload 300 km (186 miles)
Payload: 1850 kg (4708 lb); seats for up to 19 passengers
Crew: 1 to 2
Production: minimum 95

DHC-7 Dash 7, deHavilland Canada

FIRST FLIGHT 1975

THE DHC-7 Dash 7 is perhaps one of the most important airliners developed in recent years, whose full impact on short-haul air transport will only become clear when the operating and 'environmental' aspects of its career are assessed in future years. The Dash 7 is the largest of the aircraft yet developed by de Havilland Canada, but is essentially the latest reflection of the company's continuing concern with STOL (short take-off and landing) aircraft.

The Dash 7 originated in 1972 after the manufacturer had examined carefully the market requirements for such an aircraft. What was needed, de Havilland Canada concluded, was an aircraft capable of offering 50 passengers all the comforts of 'full-size' airliners, yet able to operate from runways only 610 m (2000 ft) long in built-up urban areas where the aircraft's noise signature should be less than 95 EPNdBs (effective perceived noise decibels) 152 m (500 ft) from take-off or landing. In short, the Dash 7 was to offer airline comfort with highly competitive operating economics and 'quiet STOL' performance.

The building of two prototypes began in 1972 with funding supplied by the government of Canada. The key to the design was a high-wing, T-tail configuration powered by four 1120-shp Pratt & Whitney Aircraft of Canada PT6A-50 turboprops driving five-blade propellers, and fitted with a number of high-lift devices. The engine, derived from the PT6A-41 and designed with quietness in mind, is fitted with a special reduction gear to allow the use of a slow-turning five-blade propeller.

As usual with DHC aircraft, the high-lift features are aerodynamic, consisting of double-slotted flaps over some 80% of the trailing edges. Also provided on each wing are two inboard lift dumpers/ground spoilers and two outboard air spoilers, the latter being capable of symmetrical or differential action. The flap system is made the more effective for being located in the slipstream of the four large-diameter propellers.

The first prototype flew on March 27, 1975, the second joining it on June 26 of the same year. There followed a period of intensive trials to assess the performance of the aircraft in differing air and ground régimes. In general performance in all respects was found to be first class, noise levels being below those laid down, and field perform-

Above: A Greenlandair Dash 7 on the apron at Reykjavik airport. In 1980 the two examples operated by this airline were being used on Arctic communications

Below: The first prototype DHC-7 demonstrating the STOL (short take-off and landing) characteristic which is a feature of this aircraft

ance only slightly worse than hoped for (take-off run is 686 m [2250 ft] at sea level.

This convinced the Canadian government, which had bought de Havilland Canada in June 1974, to authorize the production of an initial batch of 50 Dash 7s, starting in 1976. The first such aircraft flew on May 30, 1977, and joined the two prototypes in the programme leading to Canadian certification on May 2, 1977. The problem now facing the manufacturer was that of sales, for although the type had quickly attracted interest, firm orders had been few. The first aircraft to enter service was the second production machine, which was delivered to Rocky Mountain Airways early in 1978 and entered service on February 3, 1978. During that year production ran at only one aircraft per month.

During 1979 the position altered radically in favour of the Dash 7, the aircraft's excellent operating record having convinced many sceptics. Production has been increased to three aircraft per month, and the factory is being expanded to make possible the production of four aircraft per month. Most importantly, the type has now been ordered by five US operators; deregulation in the USA has allowed many small operators to consider larger aircraft, and here the Dash 7 is a front runner.

Future developments may include a Dash 7 Series 200 with the uprated PT6A-55, and a Dash 7 Series 300 with a fuselage stretch to accommodate 60 passengers. Two variants in production are the DHC-7 Dash 7C freight model, and the DHC-7R Ranger maritime-reconnaissance model.

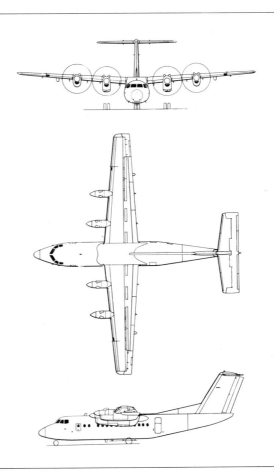

DHC-7 Dash 7

Type: short- and medium-range STOL transport
Maker: de Havilland Aircraft of Canada Ltd
Span: 28.35 m (93 ft)
Length: 24.58 m (80 ft 7¾ in)
Height: 7.98 m (26 ft 2 in)
Wing area: 79.9 m² (860 sq ft)
Weight: maximum 19 731 kg (43 500 lb); empty 12 178 kg (26 850 lb)
Powerplant: four 1120-shp Pratt & Whitney Aircraft of Canada PT6A-50 turboprops
Performance: maximum cruising speed 426 km/h (265 mph) at 4572 m (15 000 ft); range with maximum payload and reserves 1303 km (810 miles)
Payload: 5511 kg (12 150 lb); seats for up to 50 passengers
Crew: 3 to 4
Production: 20 orders, 20 options by 1980

AR 404, Ahrens

FIRST FLIGHT 1976

THE Ahrens AR 404 is conceived as a low-cost DC-3 replacement: a simple, sturdy utility aircraft capable of undertaking a number of functions with only minimal alterations. To this end the aircraft has been planned on the modular principle, with items such as engines replaceable in only 20 min. To simplify design, construction and maintenance, as well as the loading of pallets and containers, a square-section fuselage has been adopted. To the front of this is attached the cockpit section together with the nose, while to the rear is fixed the tail section carrying the empennage and loading door.

The parallel-cord wing with its underslung engine pods, is a single structure attached to the upper surface of the fuselage to avoid encroachment into the payload volume. The retractable tricycle undercarriage has short legs to keep the fuselage close to the ground and the main units retract in sponsons on the lower fuselage sides.

Design of this interesting 'minimum aircraft' began in January 1975, construction of the prototype, which had a fixed undercarriage, being started in August 1975. This prototype flew on December 1, 1976. At this stage work was carried on by the Ahrens Aircraft Corporation in California, but the project was later transferred to Puerto Rico, whose government offered to finance the project and then help launch an initial batch of 18 production aircraft. In Puerto Rico, therefore, Ahrens Aircraft maintain the progress of the aircraft towards certification, with the parent company doing sub-assembly work. US Federal Aviation Administration Type Approval was secured in the closing stages of 1978, and by 1980 production was well underway.

The key to the aircraft's internal simplicity is the provision of a five-track restraint system in the fuselage floor. This can be used for the anchoring of seating for 30 (2+1) with an offset aisle for the commuter role, or alternatively for the lashing down of freight (12 D-3 containers) or the installation of rollers for the handling of pallets.

Passengers board the aircraft by means of doors on each side of the fuselage aft of the wing, while freight can be loaded straight into the fuselage, the undersurface of the rear fuselage being a two-part door, the lower half of which forms a loading ramp. This can be left open in flight for the carriage of large loads, or for the dispatch of paratroops.

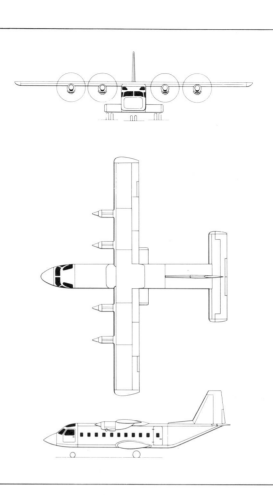

AR 404

Type: short- and medium-range utility transport
Maker: Ahrens Aircraft Inc
Span: 20.12 m (66 ft)
Length: 16.08 m (52 ft 9 in)
Height: 5.33 m (17 ft 6 in)
Wing area: 39.2 m^2 (422 sq ft)
Weight: maximum 7711 kg (17 000 lb); empty 3719 kg (8200 lb)
Powerplant: four 420-shp Allison 250-B17B turboprops
Performance: maximum cruising speed 314 km/h (195 mph) at 1524 m (5000 ft); range with standard fuel but no reserves 1575 km (978 miles)
Payload: seats for up to 30 passengers
Crew: 2
Production: 18 by 1980

Left and below: The AR 404, which was conceived as a 'minimum aircraft', with an emphasis on simplicity and versatility. It can be used in a cargo or passenger-carrying role. Up to 30 seats can be attached to the strong cargo floor of the fuselage. The type is intended to appeal to operators in undeveloped areas

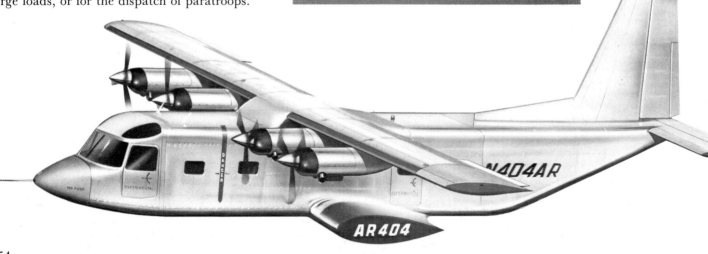

LTA, Dornier

ESTIMATED FIRST FLIGHT 1982

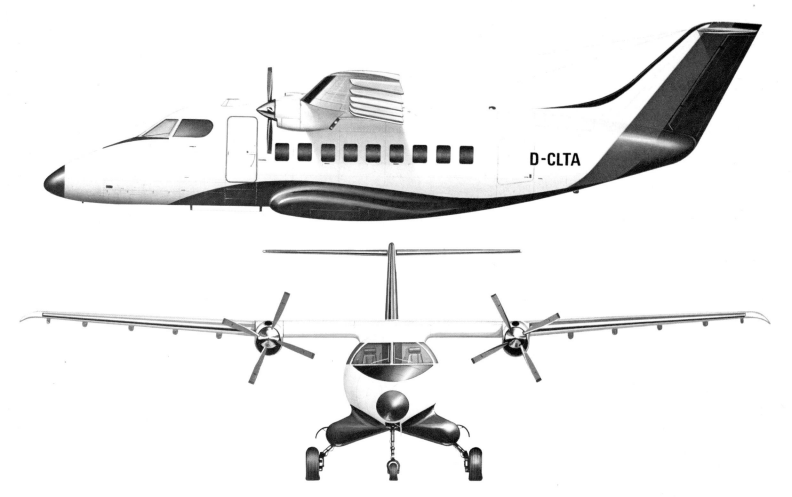

THE Dornier LTA is planned as an advanced-technology Light Transport Aircraft for service in the mid 1980s. Of basically conventional configuration (high-wing and T-tail layout, with a circular-section fuselage and tricycle undercarriage whose main units retract into fuselage blisters), the unusual features of the LTA lie in its use of the latest structural techniques, using advanced materials, and supercritical aerodynamics. The supercritical-section wing, on which the success of the LTA will ultimately depend, was due for flight testing during 1979 on a converted Dornier Do 28D-2 Skyservant.

The LTA's wing is to be of a Dornier-developed supercritical section, made of a combination of advanced-technology and conventional materials, and incorporating positive gust-absorption capacity with active controls, derived from the ZKP programme run jointly by Dornier and DFVLR. The wing leading edges, together with the raked and highly cambered wingtips, are to be made of a Kevlar/glassfibre composite, the slotted Fowler flaps and ailerons are to be made of carbon-fibre composites, and the rest of the wing is to be of conventional light-alloy construction. The ailerons are to be capable of differential action in their capacity as roll controllers, and of symmetrical action to supplement the flaps in providing nearly full-span trailing-edge high-lift devices for take-off and landing.

Kevlar/glassfibre will also be used for the nose, tailcone and main gear blisters, and for the leading edges of the fin and tailplane. The rudder and elevator will be of carbon-fibre composite. The rest of the fuselage and empennage will be of light-alloy construction, but the use of the advanced materials is expected to make significant contributions to the reduction of structure weight.

Two models of the LTA are envisaged. The Basic LTA is to have a crew of two, and accommodation for 19 passengers in an unpressurized cabin. A wardrobe and lavatory will be standard. The other model, which is to be known as the Commuter, is to seat 24 passengers, the extra capacity being obtained by sacrificing the wardrobe and lavatory. Seating will comprise seven pairs of seats on the right side of the cabin, separated by an aisle from six single seats along the left side, with four seats abreast occupying the rear of the cabin.

Above: The Dornier LTA, Light Transport Aircraft, uses a mix of advanced design features and modern materials. The wing, with its downward-curving tips and slotted Fowler flaps, is designed to give high-lift and positive gust-absorption

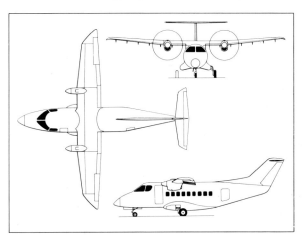

Commuter

Type: short-range light transport
Maker: Dornier GmbH
Span: 17.81 m (58 ft 5¼ in)
Length: 16.6 m (54 ft 5½ in)
Height: 5.55 m (18 ft 2½ in)
Wing area: 33.93 m² (365¼ sq ft)
Weight: maximum 6850 kg (15 102 lb); empty 3544 kg (7813 lb)
Powerplant: two 725-shp Garrett-AiResearch TPE 331-8 turboprops
Performance: (estimated) maximum cruising speed 410 km/h (255 mph) at 3000 m (9842 ft); range with 24 passengers 400 km (249 miles)
Payload: seats for up to 24 passengers
Crew: 2 to 3
Production: still under development

Tri Turbo-3, Specialized Aircraft

FIRST FLIGHT 1977

SINCE the introduction of turboprop engines, many ambitious small companies have considered the attractive prospect of producing a DC-3 replacement not in the form of a new aircraft, but rather in the form of a turboprop-powered DC-3.

The most ambitious such project has been the Tri Turbo-3, produced by the Aircraft Technical Services Corporation on behalf of the Specialized Aircraft company. Taking as a starting point the Conroy Super Turbo-Three, previously engined with a pair of Rolls-Royce Dart turboprops, ATSC during 1977 developed the Tri Turbo-3 powered by three 1174-ehp Pratt & Whitney Aircraft of Canada PT6A-45 turboprops, one in each of the wing positions, and the third in the fuselage nose.

Despite the increase in the number of engines, the inherently lower weight of the turboprops has helped to reduce basic aircraft weight considerably, and it is this factor which has helped raise the type's payload to 5443 kg (12 000 lb) from the DC-3's 2994 kg (6600 lb), and also enabled the type to undertake operations in 'hot and high' conditions which would defeat the DC-3.

The Tri Turbo-3 first flew on November 2, 1977, and the type's certification in 1978 was purely for transport operations. Specialized Aircraft's plans are now to offer the type in several forms, the customer being given the option of having his own DC-3 converted by the company to the new standard, or alternatively to undertake the conversion himself in some 3000 man-hours with the aid of a kit; a third option is to buy a converted aircraft from Specialized Aircraft. There is also the option of two basic powerplants: the 1174-ehp PT6A-45 driving a three-blade propeller, or the 903-ehp PT6A-41 driving a four-blade propeller.

Key to the Tri Turbo-3's performance is the nose-mounted engine. This is used mainly for take-off and high-speed cruise, being shut down and propeller feathered for economical cruise. For example, the maximum cruising speed of 370 km/h (230 mph) at 3048 m (10 000 ft) on three engines is reduced to 290 km/h (180 mph) at optimum altitude on two engines; conversely, range with optional outboard wing tanks is 4345 km (2700 miles) on three engines, but 5150 km (3200 miles) on two engines.

The utility of the type is further increased by the provision, tested during 1979, of a swing-tail to facilitate the loading of bulky items.

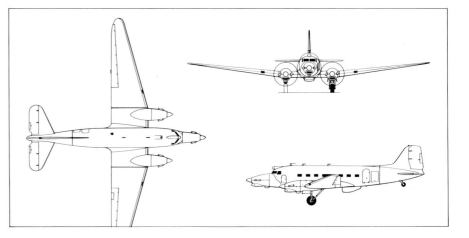

Tri Turbo-3

Type: short- and medium-range transport
Maker: Specialized Aircraft Co
Span: 28.96 m (95 ft)
Length: not available
Height: 5.56 m (18 ft 3 in)
Wing area: 91.7 m² (987 sq ft)
Weight: not available
Powerplant: three 1174-ehp Pratt & Whitney Aircraft of Canada PT6A-45 turboprops
Performance: cruising speed 370 km/h (230 mph); range 4345 km (2700 miles)
Payload: 5443 kg (12 000 lb)
Crew: 3
Production: 1 (prototype) by 1980

Top: The DC-3 airframe is clearly recognizable in this Polair Tri Turbo-3
Above left: The *Spirit of Hope*; the central engine is used for take-off and high-speed cruise
Left: The flight-deck of a Tri Turbo-3. Converting the airframe takes 3000 man-hours

Index

Page numbers in bold refer to the main entry of the aircraft

Right: A Boeing CL-4S
Bottom left: A Short Scylla
Bottom right: A Sikorsky S-42

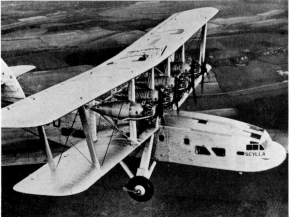

Top right: The Bristol Proteus turboprop engines of a Britannia
Centre right: Handley Page Dart Herald
Bottom left: Specialized Aircraft Tri Turbo-3
Bottom right: An Aero Spacelines Super Guppy

Picture Credits